THE SEA, IDENTITY AND HISTORY

THE SEA, IDENTITY AND HISTORY

From the Bay of Bengal to the South China Sea

Edited by

SATISH CHANDRA AND HIMANSHU PRABHA RAY

MANOHAR
2013

First published 2013

ISBN 978-81-7304-986-6

Published by
Ajay Kumar Jain *for*
Manohar Publishers & Distributors
4753/23 Ansari Road, Daryaganj,
New Delhi 110 002

Printed at
Salasar Imaging Systems
Delhi 110 035

Contents

Preface

The papers in this volume are based substantially on the International seminar on 'Maritime Cultures and Traditions of the Bay of Bengal' organized by the Society for Indian Ocean Studies at Nehru Memorial Museum & Library – Teen Murti House, New Delhi, on 22-3 April 2011. The purpose of the seminar was to examine the maritime traditions of the countries around the Bay of Bengal as also a discussion on cultural links across the Bay of Bengal to the South China Sea. The littoral comprising of the present Indian states of Bengal, Orissa, Andhra, Tamil Nadu as well as the nation states of Bangladesh, Sri Lanka, Sumatra, Malaysia, Thailand and Myanmar share several historical connections, such as participation in trading systems and the colonial legacy. The Society for Indian Ocean Studies has been engaged in the study of the cultural, economic and strategic links between India and these countries, and has already brought out two publications: *Indonesia: A New Beginning* (2002) and *India and South East Asia: Cultural, Economic and Strategic Linkages* (2011). We hope to continue this work.

The seminar also visualized how maritime traditions were reflected in sculptures, architectural complexes, oral traditions, social life dealing with food, lives of fisher-folk, festivals and rituals dedicated to the sea. This implied a close convergence between historians largely engaged in the study of the ocean, and historians mainly concerned with domestic developments. Attempts to bring together these two groups of historians who have so far remained as virtually separate tribes was only partly successful. A reason for this was the current approaches in the universities in the country, which we hope would gradually broaden.

I am deeply grateful to Professor Himanshu Prabha Ray of Jawaharlal Nehru University and Associate Director of the seminar, for her efforts to expand and deepen the seminar by bringing together scholars from different parts of the world. In a scholarly Introduction, she has focussed on the main themes of the seminar in the present volume. She has been successful in inducing a number of scholars who had not presented papers at the seminar to contribute to the present volume which has been renamed as *The Sea, Identity and History: From the Bay of Bengal to the South China Sea.* In the process, a number of papers which did not focus on the main themes have been excluded.

At the end I would like to thank Shri Ramesh Jain of Manohar Publishers & Distributors for undertaking this publication. I would also like to thank Professor Mridula Mukherjee, then Director, Nehru Memorial Museum & Library, and her associates for extended help to the seminar. I would also like to acknowledge the financial grant from the Ministry of Culture for the seminar and for the preparation of this volume. Thanks are also due to all others who made the seminar a success, including Ms. Annamma Abraham of the Society for Indian Ocean Studies for typing and re-typing the various texts, and digitizing them in the electronic form for publication.

SATISH CHANDRA
Vice-Chairman

Contributors

Cynthia Chou is at the Department of Cross-Cultural and Regional Studies, University of Copenhagen. She has published extensively on Indonesian Sea Nomads starting with a 2002 book (jointly with G. Benjamin) on the *Tribal Communities in the Malay World* to her most recent 2010 study of *The Orang Suku Laut of Riau, Indonesia* (Routledge).

Charlotte Minh-Hà Pham is currently conducting her PhD research at the Asia Research Center, Murdoch University, Western Australia, in conjunction with the West Australia Maritime Museum. She is supported by a Murdoch University/MCRI Scholarship linked to the Indian Ocean World Centre project, 'The Indian Ocean World: The Making of the First Global Economy in the Context of Human-Environment Interaction', anchored at McGill University. The present paper, however, was prepared while she resided in Vietnam on a bursary from the Ecole Française d'Extrême Orient (2009-10). Her time in Hanoi enabled her to establish the groundwork for the doctoral research she is currently conducting, which is attempting to reconstruct aspects of the maritime history of Champa through the study of boat-building traditions. This approach, encompassing the disciplines of history, ethnography and archaeology, ensures a continuity between her background as a restorer and maritime archaeologist and her Vietnamese origins, as this project will marry maritime material culture with archival documents and ethno-historical research to provide an innovative approach and methodology towards understanding classical central Vietnam.

Farish A. Noor is presently a Senior Fellow at the S. Rajaratnam School of International Studies; where he is part of the research cluster 'Transnational Religion in Contemporary Southeast Asia' that is part of the RSIS Contemporary Islam Programme. He is the author of *The Madrasa in Asia: Political Activism and Transnational Linkages*, edited with Martin van Bruinessen and Yoginder Sikand, (University of Amsterdam Press, Amsterdam, 2008); *Islam Embedded: The Historical Development of the Pan-Malaysian Islamic Party PAS: 1951-2003* (Malaysian Sociological Research Institute (MSRI), Kuala Lumpur, 2004); *Writings on the 'War on Terror'* (Globalmedia Press, India, 2006); *Islam Progresif: Peluang, Tentangan dan Masa Depannya di Asia Tenggara* (SAMHA, Jogjakarta, 2005), and *New Voices of Islam* (ISIM, Leiden, Netherlands, 2002).

Geoff Wade is Senior Research Fellow with the Nalanda Sriwijaya Centre of the Institute of Southeast Asian Studies, Singapore. His research interests include Sino-Southeast Asian historical interactions and comparative historiography. He has worked on a range of other related issues including early Islam in Southeast Asia, Chinese expansions, Asian commercial networks, Chinese textual references to Southeast Asia and the Cold War in Southeast Asia. His online database, *Southeast Asia in the Ming Shi-lu: An Open Access Resource* (http://epress.nus.edu.sg/msl/), provides in English translation over 3,000 references to Southeast Asia as extracted from the Ming imperial annals, while his most recent edited work *China and Southeast Asia* (Routledge, 2009) comprises a six-volume survey of seminal works on Southeast Asia-China interactions.

Himanshu Prabha Ray is Professor at the Centre for Historical Studies, Jawaharlal Nehru University, New Delhi. Her research interests include maritime history and archaeology of the Indian Ocean, the history of archaeology in South and Southeast Asia and the archaeology of religion in Asia. Her recent books on maritime contacts include *The Archaeology of Seafaring in Ancient South Asia* (Cambridge University Press, Cambridge, 2003), as also edited volumes titled *Memory as History: The Legacy of Alexander in Asia*, edited with Daniel T. Potts (Aryan Books International, New Delhi, 2007); *Sacred Landscapes in Asia: Shared Traditions, Multiple Histories*, (India International Centre-Asia Project, Manohar Publishers,

New Delhi, 2007); and *Cross Currents and Community Networks: Encapsulating the History of the Indian Ocean World*, edited with E.A. Alpers (Oxford University Press, New Delhi, 2007).

Murari Jha studied history at Jawaharlal Nehru University (JNU), New Delhi, where his research mainly focused on the economic and social history of Gujarat in the early modern period. While doing research at JNU, he also did some anthropological work to document the oral traditions of Gangetic Bihar. At Leiden University, he did his second MA/MPhil and wrote a dissertation on 'The World of the Ganges River: The Political Economy of the mid-Gangetic Basin, Bihar; *c.* 1600-1800'. Presently he is working towards his PhD dissertation to be completed in 2012.

Pius Malekandathil teaches at the Centre for Historical Studies, Jawaharlal Nehru University and has written extensively on maritime history. His books include: *The Germans, the Portuguese and India.* (LIT Verlag: Münster (Germany), 1999); *Portuguese Cochin and the Maritime Trade of India, 1500-1663*, a Volume in the South Asian Study Series of Heidelberg University, No. 39, Germany (Manohar, New Delhi, 2001); *Jornada of D. Alexis Menezes: A Portuguese Account of the Sixteenth Century Malabar* (LRC Publications, Cochin, 2003); *Maritime India: Trade, Religion and Polity in the Indian Ocean* (Primus Books, New Delhi, 2010); *The Portuguese, Indian Ocean and European Bridgehead: Festschrift in Honour of Prof. K.S. Mathew*, jointly edited with T. Jamal Mohammad, Fundação Oriente (Lisbon/IRISH, Tellicherry, 2001); *The Portuguese and the Socio-Cultural Changes in India:1500-1800*, jointly edited with K.S. Mathew and Teotonio R. de Souza, Fundação Oriente (Lisbon/IRISH, Tellicherry, 2001); *The Kerala Economy and European Trade*, jointly edited with K.S. Mathew (Muvattupuzha, 2003); *Goa in the Twentieth Century: History and Culture*, jointly edited with Remy Dias (Institute Menezes Braganza, Panaji, 2008).

Prapassorn Posrithong studied Art History at Silpakorn University, Bangkok and Museology at MS University, Vadodara. She has worked as Cultural Researcher and Curator for the Thai Fine Arts

Department. She was Director of Thalang National Museum, Phuket and has also lectured on Museology in the Post-Graduate Program in Cultural Studies, Institute of Language and Culture for Rural Development, Mahidol University at Salaya. She has written extensively on Indian textiles for the Thai market, the most recent being on 'Persian Cultural Influence in the Thai Royal Court of Ayutthaya', *Islamic Journal*, Embassy of Iran, Bangkok, 2002 (in Thai); and 'Role of Muslim Merchants in Indian textile trade with Thailand,' *Aksornsat Journal*, Chulalongkorn University, Bangkok 2007 (in Thai).

Somasiri Devendra commissioned as an Instructor Officer in the Sri Lankan Navy, retiring as Commandant, Naval & Maritime Academy, Trincomalee. A second career in mercantile service followed as Company Director; Chairman, Colombo Brokers' Association and a Founder Director of the Colombo Stock Exchange. After a short spell in Sharjah, UAE, he joined the Centre for Studies in Human Rights (CSHR), Faculty of Law, Colombo University teaching Human Rights to Military and Police Personnel. His major research and fieldwork began during retirement, introducing maritime archaeology to Sri Lanka and participating in Indian initiatives in the same field. A founder member of the ICOMOS Scientific Committee, he remains a Member of the International Committee on the Underwater Cultural Heritage (ICUCH). He has conducted Heritage Impact Assessments on several proposed port sites (Galle, South Colombo and Hambantota) and is presently researching the naval architectural aspects of Sri Lankan ships and boats. He has authored/co-authored/edited books and published many papers in several languages on biography, naval history, archaeology, ethnology, maritime archaeology and the maritime heritage.

Tom Hoogervorst grew up in the small town of Alkmaar, the Netherlands. From 2003 to 2006 he took an undergraduate degree in Languages and Cultures of Southeast Asia and Oceania at the University of Leiden. He pursued his MPhil programme in Asian Studies from 2006 to 2008 at the same university, focusing on Asian history and linguistics. Since 2008 he has been a member of the

Oxford-based Sealinks Project, supervised by Dr. Nicole Boivin. His current DPhil research at the University of Oxford aims to offer new perspectives on early maritime trade and inter-ethnic contact in the Indian Ocean through a combination of archaeology and historical linguistics. His further interests include Asian philology, descriptive linguistics, maritime archaeology and archaeo-botanics.

CHAPTER 1

Introduction: Beyond National Boundaries

HIMANSHU PRABHA RAY

The Bay of Bengal forms the north-eastern part of the Indian Ocean. It resembles a cone in shape, and is bordered on the east by Myanmar and the Malay peninsula and on the west by India. The southern extremes reach the island of Sri Lanka, and the Andaman and Nicobar Islands. It is beyond these islands that the waters of the Bay of Bengal merge with those of the South China Sea that extends from the Malacca Straits to the Strait of Taiwan encompassing the coasts of Thailand, Vietnam and south China. Though the seas have been important for the five millennia of human history, they are also the most glossed over in historical discourse, which has tended to focus on predominantly land-based national histories.

In recent decades the sea appears to be emerging from this indifference, with scholars adopting varied perspectives in the study of the ocean, extending from the Bay of Bengal to the South China Sea. Trade and commerce and European interventions have been two persistent themes and secondary literature on these is both extensive and rich (Ray, 2011: 27-54). By the ninth century the major states on the islands of Java and Bali, especially the central Javanese state of Mataram had developed complex economic infrastructures and had integrated diversifying agricultural systems into a web of regional and long-distance trade networks. Sanskrit inscriptions from Buddhist sites refer to religious teachers travelling to the region from Gujarat, Sri Lanka and Gaur in Bengal. Mataram also produced maritime Southeast Asia's first standardized indigenous coinage based on gold and billon (silver-copper alloy) divided into weight-value units integrating local and Indian systems. By the tenth-century coins based on the same system of weights and values were beginning to be minted across the maritime region from Sumatra to Bali and to the Philippine island of Luzon (Christie, 1999: 222-3).

From the ninth to the mid-fourteenth centuries several merchant associations dominated economic transactions in peninsular India, such as the Ainurruvar, Manigramam, Nanadesi and the Anjuvannam. Associated with these merchant associations were communities of craftsmen such as weavers, basket-makers, potters, leather-workers and so on. The topographical distribution of the inscriptions is significant and they are clustered in the Dharwad–Bijapur and Mysore localities of Karnataka, while in Tamil Nadu larger numbers are found in the Thanjavur, Tiruchirapalli and Madurai districts. Not only did these merchant associations develop powerful economic networks, but they also employed private armies. They donated regularly to temples, which were at times named after them and also contributed to the construction of tanks (Abraham, 1988; Karashima, 2002; Kulke, Kesavapany and Sakhuja, 2009). The range of their operations extended well beyond the boundaries of the Indian subcontinent into Southeast Asia.

Several clusters of Tamil inscriptions have been found on the eastern fringes of the Indian Ocean from Burma (Myanmar) to Sumatra. Of the seven mid-ninth to late-thirteenth century Tamil or part-Tamil language inscriptions found so far in Southeast Asia, one has been discovered near Bagan in Burma, two just south of the Isthmus of Kra in the Malay peninsula and four in north and west Java. Perhaps the easternmost record is the bilingual Tamil and Chinese language inscription found associated with remains of one of the two Siva temples at Quanzhou in south China. These inscriptions connect merchants associations operating out of south India with the founding or the endowing of temples or other structures for the use of the resident Indian merchant community.

In the tenth century, local versions of these merchant guilds, termed the *banigrāma*, appeared in the north coast ports of both Java and Bali, especially at Julah on the Balinese coast. There are seven Javanese inscriptions dating from CE 902 to 1053 that refer to merchant associations called *banigrāma* and to the various tax concessions granted to them. While some foreign merchants may have been included in these groups, these appear largely as indigenous organizations associated with the local economic networks as tax-farmers (Christie, 1999: 242-5).

Chinese records of the 1060s and 1070s report that the Imperial Court received missions from the Chola kingdom of south India as well as from the ruler of Srivijaya located on the island of Sumatra, but by the last decades of the eleventh century the Chinese court had begun to encourage Chinese traders to venture out to the sea. Perhaps the most relevant example for this paper is the Buddhist monastery at Nagapattinam, which was a major landmark on the Tamil coast from the seventh to the nineteenth centuries CE. A Buddhist temple was erected at Nagapattinam specifically for Chinese Buddhists at the instance of a Chinese ruler during the reign of the Pallava king Narasimhavarman II (*c.* CE 695-722). One of the later Srivijayan king, Maravijayottungavarman, is known to have provided for its construction and the Chola king Rajaraja I granted revenues of a large village, Anaimangalam, for its upkeep in CE 1006.

Scholars such as Haraprasad Ray (2004) and Tansen Sen (2004) have documented commercial exchanges between India and China on the basis of references in Chinese literature and have postulated direct links between the two countries, bilateral relations, as also the fact that these exchanges had a tremendous impact on intermediary states. In place of the earlier Buddhist networking, the Tang and Song governments took greater interest in commercial rather than religious exchanges with the regions to China's south and trade networks proliferated. Recent writings, especially by Kenneth Hall, have, however, questioned the notion of bilateral Indo-China trade in which 'Southeast Asian societies are portrayed as bystanders, contented agriculturalists who were members of communal agricultural and tribal societies, who were hosts and/or marginal participants in the international trade' (Hall, 2004: 213-60). Hall underscores the participatory nature of Indian Ocean networks in the ancient period and their reliance on economic and cultural dialogue rather than hegemony and dominance.

Undoubtedly, Chinese ceramics have a wide distribution in the Indian Ocean region (Rougelle, 1996) and two of the most popular wares are the Yue ware dated from the eighth to twelfth centuries CE and the Longquan ware present at sites of the thirteenth and fourteenth century CE, although scholars continue to debate unities of time and space as encompassed by the use of these two terms. A search for Chinese ceramics along the Indian coasts has yielded mainly post-eleventh century-ceramics, a majority belonging to the thirteenth and fourteenth centuries along the Tamil and Malabar coasts (Karashima, 2004).

Relevant to this discussion are the voyages of Zheng He, who is regarded within the Chinese tradition as a Ming envoy sent abroad at the head of naval armadas by the Yong-le emperor (1403-25) on seven occasions to develop relations of peace and friendship with rulers in the Indian Ocean region. During these voyages Zheng He engaged in trade and brought many of the foreign rulers back to China to offer tribute to the imperial court. It should not, however, be forgotten that the primary motivation of these voyages was military expansion. The voyages sent by the Yong-le emperor were different from earlier ones in that they were commanded by eunuchs. 'It is obvious that these fleets were crewed by a wide range of peoples. Many of the eunuch commanders were Muslims, the navigators were often non-Chinese, and it is possible that descendants of Fu-jian Arabs were also included in the crew' (Wade, 2004). The primary motivation was, however, clear: that of establishing staging posts at centres such as Malacca in the Malay peninsula and of subduing the local rulers by their might and strength. Accounts of these voyages are replete with descriptions of violence and attacks on the local forces of Java, Burma, Sri Lanka and Sumatra and can at best be termed 'gun-boat diplomacy'. It would nevertheless seem that these increased contacts between China, Southeast and South Asia provided an impetus to trade networks.

Reid has characterized the period from the fifteenth to the seventeenth century as the Age of Commerce, with increased commercialization and the growth of cosmopolitan urban centres along the coasts of the South China Sea (Reid, 1988-93). He attributes this expansion to intensified Chinese maritime activity from the beginning of the fifteenth century onwards, which impacted parts of Southeast Asia as well. Although small quantities of pepper had been exported from Java in an earlier period, the fifteenth-century demand from China led to the cultivation of Indian pepper in Sumatra and, henceforth, Indonesian pepper and Siamese sappan wood used for dye became items of mass consumption in East Asia (Reid, 2007: 120). Several cultivated crops, such as cloves, cotton, sugar and benzoin (the resin of the tree *Styrax benzoin* used for incense) were grown for export and whole communities in island Southeast Asia depended on trade for their livelihood. Chinese maritime networks were by no means limited to the South China Sea but are known to have extended into South Asia and the Arabian Sea.

Trading networks from the east coast of India to the South China Sea are thus well-represented in secondary writings. More recently other perspectives have emerged. As World History acquires centrality and the focus shifts from national histories to globalization, islands are often seen as a middle plane of analysis between the globe and the region. Increasingly the history of the sea is discussed as 'connected history' across porous borders, linked through boat-building traditions, community networks and cultural practices (Vink, 2007: 41-62).

In his overview of the history of the Indian Ocean, Pearson (2003: 249-88) wrote of movements of people and goods across the waters, as also the spread of religious ideas and migrations of labour, and of traditional groups with trading and banking skills. His emphasis was on tracing transformations both spatially and temporally, with the final push being provided in the late nineteenth and early twentieth century that saw radical changes in the ideologies of Empire, colonization, the introduction of new technologies in shipping and the establishment of ports at Madras, Calcutta and Bombay by the English East India Company almost from scratch. Equations in the Indian Ocean changed from the mid-eighteenth century when the British began to acquire land in eastern India and steamship navigation altered the balance of power in the region (Pearson, 2003: 148).

This collection of papers attempts a study of this large expanse of water flowing past the coasts of Bengal and Sri Lanka to the coast of Vietnam through three broad issues which provide unity to this volume. The first relates to an emphasis on boat-building traditions and the communities who traversed the region (Cynthia Chou, Tom

Hoogervorst, Geoff Wade, Charlotte Minh Hà Pham and Somasiri Devendra in this volume). The challenge is to use the ethnographic 'present' and mobility for an understanding of the history of the sea. Linked to this movement across the waters are the narratives of trans-locality inherent in memories of communities in the region (paper by Farish A. Noor). The third issue relates to European intervention, starting with the Portuguese and the Dutch (Murari Jha, Pius Malekandathil, Himanshu Prabha Ray and Prapassorn Posrithong in this volume). In the sixteenth century, the Portuguese did not designate a space that was well-defined, but a complex of enclaves subordinate to the Portuguese crown, all of which were linked together as a maritime network. The Portuguese system was a vast protection racket—protection from violence that they themselves had created. By the middle of the seventeenth century most of the Portuguese major forts had been lost mainly to the Dutch (Subrahmanyam and Thomaz, 1991: 304).

The engagement of the English East India Company with the countries of the Bay of Bengal was of a different order from that of its predecessors. The establishment of colonies in South and Southeast Asia resulted in the introduction of new disciplines such as archaeology, which had far-reaching implications for the cultural identity of the sea and the communities who navigated it. The eighteenth century thus, raised a different set of issues with the colonization of large parts of the region. How did notions of a maritime empire impact the study of the region's past? It is these themes that we address in the volume thereby shifting the focus from chronological markers and national histories to communities who traversed the waters and the changes that these underwent in time. A brief overview of the themes is presented in the next five sections, starting with a discussion of maritime communities.

Maritime Communities

Anthropological studies have shown the close interaction that maritime communities maintain with the sea and the extent to which their knowledge of the waters and seafaring knowledge are vital to their identity construction.

The history and culture of the mobile boat-dwelling people [of Southeast Asia], often known as sea nomads, dates back many centuries. Today, they continue to traverse the waters of the archipelago and to challenge the classical idea of citizenship that is defined within bounded territories and guaranteed by a sovereign state. Their continued widespread distribution throughout the area bears testament to a very different indigenous perception and mapping of the region (Chou, 2006).

How are histories of these mobile communities to be factored into an understanding of the history of the sea? Historically these communities, variously termed sea-gypsies or boat-people have travelled unhampered across the waters and claimed sovereignty through kinship ties. They have facilitated movement of commodities and have forged links with littoral states. These communities are by no means homogeneous and instead consist of at least three major ethno-linguistic groups, each with their own histories, culture, and speech patterns. They are: (a) the Moken and related Moklen of the Mergui Archipelago of Burma with extensions southward into the islands of south-west Thailand; (b) the Orang Suku Laut, of the Riau-Lingga Archipelago and the coastal waters of eastern Sumatra and southern Johor and, until recently, Singapore; and (c) the Bajau Laut, the largest and most widely dispersed of these groups living in the Sulu Archipelago of the Philippines, eastern Borneo, Sulawesi, and the islands of eastern Indonesia. The data for the study of these groups either comes from scattered references in European accounts of the region or from anthropological studies and raises issues of historicity.

Fishing as a subsistence strategy dates from at least 10,000 BCE in coastal areas of the Bay of Bengal and the South China Sea (Ray, 2003: Chapter II; McPherson, 2007: 34-49). A few coastal shell middens, and open and cave sites with marine shell deposits dating from 8,000 years ago have been identified in northern Sumatra, western peninsular Malaysia and north Vietnam. At present, many of these sites are found inland, e.g. in Sumatra on an old shoreline 10-15 km away from the coast, thereby reflecting higher sea levels during the middle Holocene (Bellwood, 1992: 87).

One of the groups that has been studied ethno-archaeologically is the 'Chaw Lay' based in the Phuket group of islands in south Thailand, Phuket being the meeting point and ceremonial centre of the widely dispersed network of maritime hunter-gatherers. Of the 4,500 Chaw Lay living along the south-west coast of Thailand in 1981, a third were resident on Phuket island itself—the groups ranging in size from two to more than eight hundred people. The specialized subsistence strategy of these groups is based on an exploitation of marine resources, especially fish. As a result of dependence on a mobile resource such as fish, these communities inevitably maintain a peripatetic way of life,

> with a compact and easily transportable material culture and social attitudes which encourage the spirit of adventure, group co-operation and an outgoing hospitable attitude to other nomadic groups they may meet on the foraging expeditions and upon whom they may have to depend for food and shelter. (Engelhardt and Rogers, 1997: 179)

One of the problems associated with this subsistence strategy is that it is difficult to isolate it in the archaeological record, especially in the sandy beach matrix of the coast. These habitation areas are generally occupied in short stretches and in keeping with a complex spatial patterning. While a site or a portion of a site is being used as a base camp by one Chaw Lay group, other smaller and transient groups could occupy portions of the site, sometimes temporarily. At the same time the site could also be exploited by other Chaw Lay groups for water and vegetable collection. The use pattern is further complicated by the fact that while some of the sites indicate seasonal occupation, others are left fallow to allow regeneration (Engelhardt and Rogers, 1997: 182). Nevertheless, by adopting this ethno-archaeological approach, the authors have provided insights into the symbiosis between mobile sea-people and coastal groups.

These small-scale fishing and sailing communities were also probably the agency for the spread of crops across the waters. A number of cultivars found in south India have their wild origins in Southeast Asia, such as the arecanut palm. Sandalwood probably originated in the wild in the driest parts of Indonesia, such as eastern Java and the Lesser Sundas. Wood charcoal from the latest Neolithic levels of sites on the Sannarachamma hill, north of the village of Sanganakallu in the Bellary district of Karnataka in south India, identified as *Santalum,* however, places it in the southern Deccan by *c.* 1300 BCE. The banana is another crop-plant that travelled westward to the Indian subcontinent around 2000 BCE, as evident from banana phytoliths from the Harappan site of Kot Diji in southern Pakistan (Fuller et al., 2011: 548-9). Thus histories of these mobile communities are crucial to an understanding of cultural networks and the spread of plants and crops. Another area that is known for its varied traditions of boat-building and complex of channels is deltaic Bengal that participated in both riverine as well as trans-oceanic networks.

Inland Navigation and the Region of Bengal

Writing in 1792, Rennell was struck by the unique inland navigation network of Bengal and remarked on the brisk trade carried out throughout the region in boats. Salt, fish and rice have been the major resources of the region that were transported through the inland network and traded in the historical period. To these must be added 'the transport of commercial exports and imports, probably to the amount of two million sterling per annum; the interchange of manufactures and products throughout the whole country' (Deloche 1994: 25). At present, in Bangladesh, the expression country-boat, synonymous with the Bengali term *nouka* 'denotes any wooden non-mechanised craft used on inland waters, along the coast or in the Bay of Bengal'. The sea-going boats found in the Chittagong area ply as far as Myanmar, while a variety of watercraft carry goods and agricultural products to inland ports (Jansen et al., 1989: 72-3). This fluvial network not only provided a distinctive environment throughout the early history of Bengal but it also linked Bengal to the larger Ganga and Brahmaputra Valley networks, on the one hand, and the east coast and Bay of Bengal systems that extended to the South China Sea, on the other.

By the sixth century Bengal is described as a region bordering the eastern sea (*prāksamudra*) in the Faridpur copper plates of Dharmaditya and by the eighth century Dharmapala Deva announced his control of the oceans 'forming the encircling ditches of the earth'. The Khalimpur charters of the king were issued from Pataliputra 'where a variety of boats had formed a bridge on the Bhagirathi' (Kielhorn, 1896-7: 243-54). By the tenth century CE the Bay of Bengal had acquired a territorial identity as indicated by the use of the term Vangasagara or sea of Bengal in the Madanpur copper plate charter of Srichandra (Sircar, 1949: 337-9).

Another region that continued to play a crucial role in the early history of Bengal was Pundravardhana with Mahasthangarh as a major centre until the thirteenth century when the political focus shifted somewhat south to the Gaur-Pandua area. In the twelfth and thirteenth centuries at least three of the Pala kings adopted the title of Gaudesvara or lord of Gaur. This area formed a part of a larger trading network with routes traversing the Brahmaputra Valley of Assam to Tibet, upper Burma and China. In addition, it was linked via the lower Bengal coast to the Bay of Bengal coastal system, viz., Arakan and the Irrawaddy Valley on the east and the Andhra, Tamil and Sri Lankan coasts to the south. Its strategic location at one end of the Ganga River system provided Pundravardhana access to the ancient historical network of the Ganga plains.

Attention should also be drawn to the overlapping frontiers between Bengal and the kingdom of Arakan lying on its eastern edge, which saw cultural and religious interaction between them, on the one hand, and Burma and mainland Southeast Asia on the other. It is significant that stone and copper plate inscriptions of the Chandra dynasty that ruled Arakan from *c.* CE 454 to 600 were found from the ruins of stupas and indicate that at this time Arakan was looking to Bengal for models of kingship and administration. In addition to adopting the format of the copper plate grants prevalent in Bengal, Bhuticandra's inscription (496-520) also incorporates several riparian terms known from Bengal such as *jola* (channel) and *khalla* (canal) (Sircar, 1957: 109; 1967: 61-6).

In contrast to the copper plate charters of the Chandras, their coinage struck in silver was closely related to that of Southeast Asia (Wicks, 1992: 86). In addition to the silver coinage of the Chandras, a coinage commenced around Chattagrama (Chittagong) with the legend 'Harikela' and circulated widely in south-east Bengal. At the same time gold coins were minted in the kingdom of Samatata and also circulated in the region. These two were further supplemented by the use of cowries not only for small transactions, but also for land revenue and other high-value transactions. It would seem that cowries were obtained from the Maldives against the export of rice, while silver came from the Shan states and from Yunnan. Thus Bengal participated both in the riverine and the maritime networks of the region and this is what made it an exceptional trading node in the Bay of Bengal (Deyell, 2011: 279-314).

It is necessary to draw attention to another distinguishing feature of the region—the brick temples with terracotta decoration (Mitra, 2000-3; Gill, 2010). What is particularly relevant for this volume is the depiction of boats on these brick temples, a distinctive feature in the history of temple building in the subcontinent. These boat representations date to the eighteenth and nineteenth centuries and depict sixty-two panels showing riverboats and fifty-three panels with sailing vessels. The former category included houseboats, passenger and pleasure boats as also war boats, while the latter included European vessels (Deloche, 1991). How are these boat depictions to be explained?

A corresponding development was the enormous popularity of the mythological story of Kamale-Kamini glorifying the power of the Goddess Chandi. The story appeared in literature in the Chandi *Maṅgala Kāvyas* as early as the thirteenth-century version of the poet Manik Datta and came to be known through several versions from sixteenth to eighteenth centuries. Story-tellers recited the *Maṅgala Kāvyas* at village gatherings and this undoubtedly influenced terracotta artists and *paṭa* scroll painters. In some *Maṅgala Kāvyas* there are elaborate references to the wealth and fortune of merchants like Chand Saudagar and Dhanapati. This prosperity is also reflected in representations on temples, especially the temple of Sridharpur, the Lakshmi-Janardan temple at Dubrajpur and at Karkai, where merchants are shown in large boats accompanied by assistants and carrying cargoes, including animals (Haque, 1980: 30-1).

There was a spurt in temple construction in Bengal from the thirteenth century onwards with a marked increase in the eighteenth and nineteenth centuries. Most of the temples were erected in areas closely linked to riverine trade and relate to the rise of a new middle class, as the shrines were located in or adjacent to the houses from which landholders governed their estates (Michell, 1983: 8). An analysis of inscriptions found on the temples indicate donations made by several local zamindars or landlords, the raja family of Burdwan, the Mallas at Bisnupur, queens, merchants and several private individuals. Thus it is evident that the brick temples not only provided connectivity between agrarian space and the inland navigation network in Bengal, but also provided cultural and religious identity to the emerging local elite.

These temples have been studied for their architectural styles and terracotta decorations (McCutchion, 1972; Michell, 1983), but not as indicators of the cultural identity of newly emerging elite groups. The assumption is that these were later interventions in the medieval landscape of Bengal and owed their origin to religious movements, such as the Gaudiya Vaisnava movement led by Chaitanyadeva (1486-1533). This contention may be debated on the basis of archaeological data, which indicates a continuous temple-building tradition in Bengal from the fifth and sixth centuries to the fourteenth and fifteenth centuries CE as evident from archaeological sources (Sengupta and Chakraborty, 2002: 395-413). Nevertheless the unique identity of the region is evident.

Ethnographic Studies of the Boat

The boat or the ship, the vehicle essential for mobility on the waters, can itself be interpreted as a complex cultural artefact, one which is traded, modified, renamed, and accepted or rejected for a variety of reasons. Historically the data on boats is sparse and fragmentary in nature. The actual find of a log-boat in Europe dates to the eighth millennium BCE, and that of the earliest plank boat to the third millennium BCE, though there is indirect evidence for the use of water transport as early as 40,000 BCE. In the absence of actual boat remains from India, ethnographic accounts provided by early Europeans are valuable for an understanding of the boat-building traditions of the region. The earliest reference to Indian sewn-plank boats occurs in the sixteenth-century writings of Duarte Barbosa, a Portuguese who worked on the Malabar coast from 1500 to 1515.

Those on the east coast were described by the Dutchman, Peter Floris who worked at Masulipatnam on the Coromandel coast in CE 1611 (McGrail, 2004: 270).

The Indian Ocean presented a unique environment to the sailor in antiquity, different both from that in Egypt or the Mediterranean. To sail in this region, the ships had to be 'good weatherly sailers, fast, good carriers, deep-drafted and able to go to windward as well. In short they had to be *real* sailing ships' (Villiers, 1952: 56-7). At the same time, the region also presents special problems for the historian and the archaeologist. On the one hand, it provides a profusion of ethnographic data on local traditions of fishing and boat-building while on the other, actual remains of wrecks are rare.

Thomas Bowrey (1650-1713) may be credited with the introduction of new classifications such as the *masula*—a term that continues to be used for the frameless stitched boats of India's east coast. This is not a term used by local boat-builders and users who adopt the generic term for the boat such as *padagu*, *padava* and *padhua*. Nor does the term incorporate any typical boat type, as there are significant variations in the size, shape and method of construction among the vessels that are said to form a part of the *masula* family (Kentley, 1996: 250).

Admiral Paris (1806-93) formulated the hypothesis that indigenous watercraft were as much expressions of a culture as were palaces, religious buildings or fortresses. As a trained French navigator he circumnavigated the Indian Ocean aboard the *Astrolabe*, the *Favorite* and the *Artemis* and catalogued the 'extra-European' craft (Reith, 1993). This trend continued in the writings of Hornell who argued that a distinctive climate and coast formation dominated or influenced by distinct ethnic stocks resulted in the evolution of characteristic boat-types (Hornell, 1946: 195). In accordance with this correlation, boat-types were seen as 'co-extensive in range with the limits of race and language or the influence of foreign sea-trade' (Hornell, 1946: 195). The influence of Portuguese sea-trade, he stated, was particularly noticeable in the larger vessels of the far south:

> Until the arrival in the Indian Ocean of the Portuguese at the end of the fifteenth century little improvement or change appears to have taken place. It was the intrusion of the Europeans into the trade of the Indian Ocean

which brought about a revolution in the designing of the larger craft operating there. (1970: 236)

Attempts at correlating boat-types with race and language do not explain the presence of different boat-types in the same cultural milieu or similar boat construction methods which independently evolved in different environments. Several examples could be quoted but a typical one is that of the clinker-built *patia* in the estuary of the Panchapara in north Orissa together with flush-laid boats, both types of boats being built by the same group of carpenters. While this tradition survives in a few pockets today, it was earlier common on the upper Ganga. Similarly, foreign influences cannot be identified by isolating a few traits and linking their incorporation to European contacts. Instead the crucial issue is to discuss the nature of interaction between different boat-building traditions and the reasons why one dominated and prevailed.

It is significant that before the construction of coastal facilities, such as docks and ports, sailing ships anchored at some distance from the coast and small boats were used to ferry passengers and cargo to the shore:

From the southern point of the coast of Coromandel to the Bay of Balasore it is impossible to make a good landing in European boats. An European boat attempting this passage would run the risk of touching on the bank and being swallowed up by the waves. To prevent this, flat-bottomed boats called *chelinques* are constructed without beams and which have the planks sewed together instead of being nailed. This formation gives them more elasticity; they are so flat that they do not draw when loaded above six inches water, and some not even so much . . . they are in less danger of being filled. They are generally manned with nine Blacks, and when the sea runs high with eleven. . . . When the sea runs so high that they are apprehensive of an accident, they take extra precaution by providing a *catimaron*. . . . On vessels of this frail description the natives of India and particularly the islanders of the Andamans and the Straits undertake long voyages by putting up a sail. (Grandpre, 1803: 85-90)

In addition to the range and variety of ethnographic data on ship-building available in the Indian Ocean, it is significant that a text codifying this information was produced in Sanskrit, i.e. the *Yuktikalpataru*, a treatise on ship-building attributed to King Bhoja and dated to the eleventh century. The work refers to a variety of woods used in ship-building and classifies water-craft into two main categories: ordinary and sea-going; providing detailed measurements for these. But perhaps the characteristic feature of water-craft that it emphasizes is the stitched tradition and the absence of iron in holding or joining the planks together. This feature of Indian Ocean vessels seems to have persisted almost into the present as evident from notices by travellers to the region.

R.K. Mookerji's compilation of this text has been reworked by subsequent scholars. While Chaudhuri (1976) based her paper on the *Yuktikalpataru*, Schlingloff (1982) elaborated on the textual sources and compared these with representations in art. It is evident that none of the textual sources on ship-building are adequately detailed to allow for the reconstruction of water-craft based on these. It is nevertheless significant that in the eleventh century, these instructions should have been incorporated in a work on state-craft and attributed to the authorship of a king. In the wider context of South and Southeast Asian maritime history, it is from the ninth-tenth centuries onwards that there are increasing references in inscriptions to fishing rights, duties levied on commodities brought through the water-routes, and to revenue obtained from taxes on fishing. This is also a period of expanding maritime networks in the Indian Ocean, as discussed above.

Narratives of Trans-Locality

It is often suggested that the Arabs dominated the trade networks in the Indian Ocean after the introduction of Islam in the eighth century, which saw the formation of an 'Islamic world-economy' (Chaudhuri, 1985; Wink, 1990). Dionisius Agius, on the other hand, shows that with the spread of Islam, Arabic was enriched by borrowings from Aramaic, Persian, Greek, Sanskrit and other Indian languages (2008: 10-11). He also cautions against equating religious with ethnic identity as Arabic sources do not make this distinction and label all non-Arab foreigners who converted to Islam as Muslim, irrespective of their ethnic background. There are nevertheless exceptions. For example, the historian and geographer al-Mas'ūdī (d.

345/956-7), writing in the tenth century states that the Sirafis and Omanis were the leading seafarers of the time, thereby highlighting regional coastal identities.

It is generally agreed that local conversions in Southeast Asia began largely in the thirteenth and fourteenth centuries, as indicated by the presence of early Islamic cemeteries in Sumatra and on the north Javanese coast. Recent research indicates that marble carvings for Muslim patrons across the Indian Ocean from East Africa to Java were produced in the workshops at Khambat in Gujarat between the late thirteenth and fifteenth centuries. This marble carving expertise grew out of a pre-existing tradition involving the production of sculptures for Hindu and Jain patrons and continued to be practised well into the nineteenth century. From the thirteenth to the fifteenth century, however, the main demand was for Muslim grave memorials followed by foundation inscriptions and architectural elements (Lambourn, 2004: 99-133; 2008: 252-86).

Islam is said to have reached Southeast Asia through the Sufi orders (Arabic *tariqa*, Malay *tarekat*) and to have flourished from the fourteenth to the seventeenth century. Muslim gravestone inscriptions from east Java date to the fifteenth century and belong to locals. Around the beginning of this century, Melaka on the west coast of the Malay peninsula grew from a fishing village into a trading entrepôt. According to a well-known Malay epic, Melaka's hero was taught to recite the Quran by a trader from the Coromandel coast of India (Andaya and Ishii, 2007: 172). Trading contacts with Persia and Central Asia led to the development of Sino-Muslim communities along the south-east coast of China, especially Canton, and many of the Chinese Muslim groups were actively involved in maritime commerce with South-east Asia. We have earlier referred to the voyages of the Chinese admiral Zeng He, which were commanded by Muslims.

Bayly has argued that trans-locality and long-distance pilgrimage and devotional networks have been enduring features of cultural life in South and Southeast Asia for many centuries. The Sufi *pir* (saint) Shahul Hamid of Nagaur in south India, for example, was known among his devotees for travels across time and space. Earth from his shrine at Nagaur was taken for setting up replica shrines at Penang and Singapore (Bayly, 2004: 703-4). Sufism contains inherently trans-regional, transnational, and trans-ethnic dimensions. In any particular locality there is a wide range of Sufi saints, from major shrines of great antiquity to minor saints with a highly localized clientele (Werbner, 2003), nor is Sufism the only devotional network in South and Southeast Asia.

An important text for the study of pilgrimage in early Buddhism is the *Gaṇḍavyūha* which dates back in all probability to the early centuries CE and describes the travels of Sudhana who is inspired to travel by the Bodhisattva Manjusri and advised to visit fifty-three 'spiritual friends' in order to learn *bodhicarya* (the Bodhisattva practice). It is not known when and by whom the *Avataṁsakasūtra*, one of the most influential Mahayana *sūtras* was first composed, but is thought to have issued from different hands in the Indic cultural sphere. Comprehensive renditions of the latter text were made in China in the early fifth and late seventh centuries CE from versions of the text obtained from Khotan (Cleary, 1993: 2). It was propagated in at least three different versions all over the Far East and in the third and last translation, the *Gaṇḍavyūha* occurs as an individual text and not as a part of the *Avataṁsakasūtra*. An autographed manuscript of the *Gaṇḍavyūha* is said to have been presented to the Chinese emperor in CE 795 by an Orissan king, generally accepted to be a member of the Bhaumakara dynasty. This text and a letter were entrusted to the monk Prajna who was asked to provide a translation into Chinese (Levi, 1919-20: 363-4).

The *Gaṇḍavyūha* describes the attainment of enlightenment through tales of pilgrimage, the primary aim of the scripture being to stress that constraints placed by fixed systems need to be overcome to attain full consciousness:

> It suggests that all views that are conditioned by cultural and personal history are by definition limiting, and there is a potential awareness that cuts through the boundaries imposed by conventional description based on accumulated mental habit. According to the scripture, it is the perennial task of certain people, by virtue of their own development, to assist others in overcoming arbitrary restrictions of consciousness so as to awaken to the full potential of mind. (Cleary, 1993: 47)

These enlightened people, according to the scripture, could belong to all walks of life and to all regions because 'the wisdom and virtues of Buddha are in all people, but people are unaware of it because of their preoccupations' (Cleary, 1993: 47). Historicity is of little account in this Buddhist scripture as the discourse is presented by trans-historical symbolic beings representing various aspects of universal enlightenment.

The starting point of Sudhana's journey was Dhanyakara, often identified with Dhanyakataka in Andhra, and the littoral played a significant part in his travels (Fontein, 1967: 3). One of the *bhikshus* he visits is Sagaramegha in Sagaramukha, followed by the monk Supratisthita of Sagaratira on his way to Sri Lanka. For twelve years, Sudhana travels through peninsular India; passes through 110 cities and visits the grammarian Megha at Vajrapura; the merchant Muktaka of Vanavasi; the monk Saradhvaja at the tip of the continent and the seer Bhishmottaranirghosha in the land of Nalayur on the coast. This is followed by visits to centres such as Samudrapratisthana where he meets the lay devotee Prabhuta; Bharukaccha or Broach at the mouth of the Narmada on the west coast of India to visit the treasurer Muktasara; Magadha, an ancient kingdom in north India; Kalingavana in the land of Shronaparanta; Dvaravati to see the celestial Mahadeva, and Kapilavastu where the Buddha was born. The text, however, does not contain any details of the centres visited, but is instead full of repetitions and descriptions of miracles, as also standard phrases and lengthy discourses. These narratives of travel and pilgrimage across the seas lost their centrality with the development of the so-called 'scientific' disciplines such as archaeology and the search for national histories.

The Beginnings of Archaeology and the Search for Origins

> The exuberant diversity of Southeast Asian life was chopped up by European colonialism into a dozen colonial states with fixed borders. Colonialism and nationalism made common cause in establishing unified institutions and identities within these borders. (Reid, 1999: 39)

The larger issue that concerns this book is the process through which the ancient past of the region came to be configured in the colonial period, as a result of control over the newly emerging discipline of archaeology. The history of archaeology in India is closely linked to that of the colonial state. The Archaeological Survey of India (ASI) was founded in 1861 and Alexander Cunningham (1814-93) appointed its first head, barely three years after imperial rule had been established. The idea of government-sponsored archaeology was largely the result of Cunningham's bold initiatives and was in marked contrast to the policies of the Asiatic Society. The Cunningham era marked a break from the earlier notion of history of the pre-Muslim period instituted by Sir William Jones (1746-94) and his colleagues working under the aegis of the Asiatic Society. Jones and others had largely concentrated on the Purāṇas, the epics and the law books to work out a history of the Hindus. In contrast, research by James Prinsep and Cunningham clearly brought Buddhism to the forefront and established its study as a legitimate branch in the second quarter of the nineteenth century.

Prior to the founding of the Asiatic Society of Bengal in 1784, Dutch officials founded a learned body known as the Batavian Society of Arts and Sciences in Java on 24 April 1778 for the promotion of oriental learning and there seems to have been a close collaboration between the two. Valuable Burmese books mainly on religious and mythological subjects collected by Capt. J. Canning during his stay in the kingdom of Ava were presented to the Asiatic Society of Bengal. On 25 November 1811, William Hunter presented to Horace Hayman Wilson 'the facsimile of an inscription engraved on seven copper plates in the possession of the Batavian Society of Science with the hope that some persons in Bengal may be able to read it'. The Society also received 'two images from the interiors of Java as specimen of ancient sculpture of that country' (De, 2003: 6).

It should also be remembered that during the British occupation of Java (1811-17) several British administrators who had served in India were now posted to Indonesia, a good example being John Crawfurd (1783-1868) who was in the medical service in India. After serving in north-west India, he was transferred to Penang and acquired extensive knowledge of Java and Bali. In 1816, he presented a paper on 'The Existence of Hindu Religion in the Island of Bali' at the meeting of the Asiatic Society of Bengal and subsequently published the three-volume *History of the Indian Archipelago*. Crawfurd stated that the first Indian colony was set up in Java in the second century CE and that the Javanese considered Kalinga 'as the country from which the civility, laws and religion of India were introduced among them' (Crawfurd, 1820: 337; Kejariwal, 1988: 19-21). Tytler had accompanied Crawfurd on one of his visits to Prambanan and had collected 'sundry Hindu statues and vessels discovered on the Island of Java', which he presented to the Asiatic Society of Bengal, while on 6 August 1817, Captain Barker presented a 'Memorandum of Antiquities from Java', which remained unpublished and is now lost (Kejariwal, 1988: 121).

The eighteenth to the twentieth century also saw the establishment of museums in Europe and the proud display of collections from the colonies in Asia. A common concern of the European states was to publicize information about their newly-acquired territories and to add to scientific writings on recent 'discovery' based on first-hand knowledge.

The first museum collection in India dates to 1796 when the Asiatic Society proposed the idea of establishing a suitable building to house the archaeological, ethnological, geological and zoological specimens that had been collected by its members. Donations were invited for the purpose and in May 1799, the Asiatic Society received some of the books and manuscripts looted by the British from Tipu Sultan's personal library in Seringapatam. It was not, however, until 1808 that the Society was able to occupy a building erected at the corner of Park Street on land granted by the government (Mookerji, 1914: 1-2).

The museum itself was established in 1814 and Nathaniel Wallich offered his honorary services as the curator of the geology and zoology section. The other section dealing with archaeology, ethnology and technology was placed in the charge of the librarian of the Society. This Asiatic Society Museum provided the nucleus of the Indian Museum, which was founded under Act XVII of 1866, though it moved into its present premises in Chowringhee in 1875. John Anderson and James Wood-Mason were in-charge of the organization of the archaeological and zoological galleries, which opened to the public in 1878 (Mookerji, 1914: 8).

Of interest to this volume are the sculptures and other antiquities from Southeast Asia that were brought to the museum at Kolkata at this time. Colonel Low discovered stone inscriptions at Kedah on the west coast of the Malay peninsula along with a Buddhist stupa carved in relief—a feature that does not occur among records from the Indian subcontinent. The most interesting inscription is that of Buddhagupta, which refers to the setting up of the stone by the master mariner Buddhagupta, resident of Raktamrttika, on the successful completion of his voyage. Texts very similar to these inscriptions have been found on the island of Borneo and on the coast of Brunei. The precise details of the transfer of these inscriptions to India are not known, but the Buddhagupta record is now in the Indian Museum, Kolkata (Low, 1848: 62-6; 1849: 247-9).

The emphasis on conservation in the late nineteenth century and the change in status of the ASI in 1895 resulted in the division of the organization into five regionwise circles, with Burma, which the British had annexed in 1852, being provided for separately 'by the continuance of the existing Imperial grant to the local government of Rupees ten thousand a year' (*Archaeological Survey of India—Annual Report 1902-03*: 7, henceforth *ASIAR*). The archaeology of Burma continued to receive the attention of the British government, and by 1913-14, the local government instituted an archaeological scholarship (*ASIAR 1913-14*: 33). In 1905-6 the local archaeological office was transferred from Rangoon to Mandalay to facilitate revising the lists of antiquities and for supervising conservation work at Mandalay (*ASIAR 1905-06*: 5). The Burmese archaeologist, Taw Sein Ko (1864-1930) carried out archaeological explorations at Hmawza and Pagan in Burma and announced spectacular results regarding the early history of the country, such as the finds of Pyu inscriptions on urns and fifth- and sixth-century Pali epigraphs, which provided data on the early introduction of Buddhism in that country (*ASIAR 1911-12*: 19-20). Architectural fellowships were constituted for training Burmese scholars, though they worked under the supervision of the Consulting Architect to the Government of Bombay (*ASIAR 1922-23*: 196). Following the constitutional changes brought about by the Government of India Act of 1935, the Burma Circle was detached from the ASI and reorganized on an independent basis (Roy, 1961: 116).

How were these discoveries received by scholars involved in the study of the past ? The response to this question draws in the work of James Fergusson (1808-86), an indigo merchant who travelled around India from 1836 to 1841. In Fergusson's frame of reference, Indian architecture provided an important missing link in the development of architecture in the world, especially the twelfth-thirteenth century flowering of architecture in Europe. Besides, even though India could never reach 'the intellectual supremacy of Greece, or the moral greatness of Rome' architecture in India was still a living art, which could inform in a variety of ways about developments in Europe (Fergusson, 1910: 4-5). This was significant, as argued by Fergusson, since there was a lack of historical texts in India and post-fifth-century Indian history could only be studied through monuments and inscriptions.

Fergusson's interest in architecture coincided with technological developments, such as the use of the camera in archaeological work and the development of a photo archive was crucial to his study of Indian architecture from 1842 onwards after he left India and settled in London. In 1876 Fergusson published the *History of Indian and Eastern Architecture* and it is significant that he used the writings of Crawfurd, Forchammer and several others who had travelled to Southeast Asia for his own work. Fergusson argued that Burma and Cambodia received their religion through proselytising missions from India.

Thus it is evident that already in the nineteenth century British political interests in Burma, Indonesia and other regions of Southeast Asia had resulted in the concept of 'Further India', as John Marshall termed Southeast Asia in 1902 (*ASIAR 1902-03*: 2). The academic discourse then included discussions on language, architecture and religious structures in Southeast Asia, in addition to the more direct ASI intervention in conservation policies in Burma.

The complex dynamics of the survival of ancient relics, monuments and religious architecture, their recovery and resuscitation through the discipline of archaeology in the nineteenth and twentieth century, and the process of imbuing them with new meanings has generally been neglected in historical discourse or has often been subsumed under the overarching category of nationalism. It is these complexities of the creation of novel methodologies and transnational interests that mark the beginnings of archaeology in the past 200 years. Histories written over the last five decades in different countries of Asia have primarily dealt with the ancient period of the present nation states and the discussion has largely centred on present national boundaries and local identities *versus* external influences. Perhaps it is time to move beyond the paradigm of the nation state in researching the history of Asia as these frontiers had little meaning in the earlier period.

REFERENCES

Abraham, Meera, 1988, *Two Medieval Merchant Guilds of South India*, New Delhi: Manohar.

Agius, Dionisius A., 2008, *Classic Ships of Islam: From Mesopotamia to the Indian Ocean*, London/Boston: Brill.

Andaya, Barbara Watson and Yoneo Ishii, 2007, 'Religious Developments in Southeast Asia, *c.* 1500-1800', in N. Tarling (ed.), *The Cambridge History of Southeast Asia*, Cambridge: Cambridge University Press: 164-227.

Anderson, Benedict Richard O'Gorman, 2006, *Imagined Communities: Reflections on the Origin and Spread of Nationalism*, London: Verso.

Bayly, Susan, 2004, 'Imagining "Greater India": French and Indian Visions of Colonialism in the Indic Mode', *Modern Asian Studies*, 38, 3: 703-44.

Bellwood, Peter, 1992, 'Southeast Asia before History', in N. Tarling (ed.), *The Cambridge History of Southeast Asia*, Cambridge: Cambridge University Press: 56-136.

Christie, Jan Wisseman, 1999, 'Asian Sea Trade between the Tenth and Thirteenth Centuries and its Impact on the States of Java and Bali', in Himanshu Prabha Ray (ed.), *Archaeology of Seafaring: The Indian Ocean in the Ancient Period*, ICHR Monograph I, New Delhi: Pragati Publications: 221-70.

Chaudhuri, Kirti Narayan, 1985, *Trade and Civilisation in the Indian Ocean: An Economic History from the Rise of Islam to 1750*, Cambridge: Cambridge University Press.

Chaudhuri, Mamta, 1976, 'Ship-building in the *Yuktikalpataru* and *Samarāṅga Sūtradhāra*', *Indian Journal of History of Science*, 11: 137-47.

Chou, Cynthia, 2003, *Indonesian Sea Nomads; Money, Magic, and Fear of the Orang Suku Laut*, London: Routledge Curzon.

———, 2006, 'Recent Trends on Southeast Asian Sea Nomads', *Kyoto Reviews*, http://kyotoreviewsea.org/images/images/pdffiles/Chou_final.pdf accessed on 3 December 2011.

Crawfurd, John, 1820, 'The Ruins of Prambanan in Java', *Journal of the Asiatic Society of Bengal*, 13: 337.

Cunningham, Alexander, 1854, *The Bhilsa Topes*, London: Smith Elder & Co.

De, Amalendu, 2003, *Introduction to the Early Correspondence of the Asiatic Society*, Kolkata: The Asiatic Society.

Deloche, Jean, 1991, 'Boats and Ships in Bengal Terracotta Art', *Bulletin de l'École Française d'Extrême-Orient*, LXXVIII: 1-23.

———, 1994, *Transport and Communications in India*, New Delhi: Oxford University Press.

Deyell, John, 2011, 'Monetary and Financial Webs: The Regional and International Influence of pre-Modern Bengali Coinage', in R. Mukherjee (ed.), *Pelagic Passageways: The Northern Bay of Bengal Before Colonialism*, Delhi: Primus Books: 279-314.

Engelhardt, Richard A. and Pamela R. Rogers, 1997, 'Maritime adaptive strategies in post-Pleistocene Southeast Asia', in P. Bellwood and D. Tillotson (eds.), *Indo-Pacific Prehistory: The Chiang Mai Papers*, Canberra: Australian National University.

Fergusson, James, 1876, *History of Indian and Eastern Architecture*, London: Murray.

———, 1910, *History of Indian and Eastern Architecture*, vols. I & II, revised and ed. James Burgess (Indian Architecture) & R. Phene Spiers (Eastern Architecture), London: John Murray.

Fuller, Dorian Q. et al., 2011, 'Across the Indian Ocean: The Prehistoric Movement of Plants and Animals', *Antiquity*, 85: 544-58.

Gill, Sandrine, 2010, 'The Kāntānagar Temple: Hindu Temples in East Bengal under the Mughals', in Himanshu Prabha Ray (ed.), *Archaeology and Text: The Temple in South Asia*, New Delhi: Oxford University Press: 124-46.

Grandpre, Louis De, 1803, *A Voyage in the Indian Ocean and to Bengal*, 1, London: G. and J. Robinson.

Greenhill, Basil 1995, *The Archaeology of Boats and Ships*, London: Conway Maritime Press.

Hall, Kenneth R., 2004, 'Local and International Trade and Traders in the Straits of Melaka Region 600-1500', *Journal of the Economic and Social History of the Orient*, vol. 47 (2): 213-60.

Haque, Zulekha, 1980, *Terracotta Decorations of Late Medieval Bengal: Portrayal of a Society*, Dacca: Asiatic Society of Bangladesh.

Hornell, James, 1946, 'The Sailing Craft of Western India', *The Mariner's Mirror*, 32: 195-217.

———, 1970, *Water Transport*, Newton Abbott: David & Charles.

Jansen, Eirik G. et al., 1989, *The Country Boats of Bangladesh: Social and Economic Development and Decision-Making in Inland Water Transport*, Dhaka: University Press Limited.

Karashima, Noboru (ed.), 2002, *Ancient and Medieval Commercial Activities in the Indian Ocean: Testimony of Inscriptions and Ceramic Sherds*, Tokyo: Taisho University Press.

———, 2004, *In Search of Chinese Ceramic-sherds in South India and Sri Lanka*, Tokyo: Taisho University Press.

Kejariwal, Om Prakash, 1988, *The Asiatic Society of Bengal and the Discovery of India's Past*, New Delhi: Oxford University Press.

Kentley, Eric, 1996, 'The Sewn Boats of India's East Coast', in Himanshu Prabha Ray and J.-F. Salles (eds.), *Tradition and Archaeology*, New Delhi: Manohar.

Kielhorn, F., 1896-7, 'Khalimpur Plate of Dharmapaladeva', *Epigraphia Indica*, IV: 243-54.

Kulke, Hermann, K. Kesavapany and V. Sakhuja, 2009, *Nagapattinam to Suvarnadwipa: Reflections on the Chola Naval Expeditions to Southeast Asia*, Singapore: Institute of Southeast Asian Studies.

Lambourn, Elizabeth, 2004, 'Marble Carving for Muslim Patrons at Khambāt and around the Indian Ocean Rim, Late Thirteenth-mid-Fifteenth Century', *Ars Orientalis*: 99-133.

———, 2008, 'Tombstones, Texts and Typologies: Seeing Sources for the Early history of Islam in Southeast Asia', *Journal of the Economic and Social History of the Orient*, vol. 51, Issue 2: 252-86.

Low, James, 1848, 'An Account of Several Inscriptions found in Province Wellesley on the peninsula of Malacca', *Journal of the Asiatic Society of Bengal* 17 (2): 62-6.

———, 1849, 'On an Inscription from Kedah', *Journal of the Asiatic Society of Bengal* 18 (1): 247-9.

McCutchion, David J., 1972, *Late Medieval Temples of Bengal*, Calcutta: The Asiatic Society.

McGrail, Sean, 2004, *Boats of the World: From the Stone Age to Medieval Times*, Oxford/New York: Oxford University Press.

McPherson, Kenneth, 2007, 'Maritime Communities: An Overview', in Himanshu Prabha Ray and Edward A. Alpers (eds.), *Cross Currents and Community Networks: The History of the Indian Ocean World*, New Delhi: Oxford University Press: 34-49.

Michell, George (ed.), 1983, *Brick Temples of Bengal from the Archives of David McCutchion*, Princeton: Princeton University Press.

Mitra, Shambhunath, 2000-3, 'Brick Monuments of West Bengal', *Pratna Samiksa*, vols. 9-12, Kolkata: Directorate of Archaeology and Museums.

Mookerjee, Asutosh, 1914, *The Indian Museum 1814–1914*, Centenary Volume, Calcutta: Indian Museum.

Pearson, Michael N., 2003, *The Indian Ocean*, London/New York: Routledge.

Ray, Harprasad, 2004, *Chinese Sources of South Asian History in Translation: Data for Study of India-China Relations through History*, Kolkata: Asiatic Society.

Ray, Himanshu Prabha, 2011, 'Writings on the Maritime History of Ancient India', in Sabyasachi Bhattacharya (ed.), *Approaches to History: Essays in Indian Historiography*, New Delhi: Primus Books: 27-54.

———, 2003, *Archaeology of Seafaring in Ancient South Asia*, Cambridge: Cambridge University Press.

———, 2007, 'Economic and Social Change', *c.* 1400-1800', in N. Tarling (ed.), *The Cambridge History of Southeast Asia*, Cambridge: Cambridge University Press: 116-63.

———, 1999, *Charting the Shape of Early Modern Southeast Asia*, Bangkok: Silkworm Books.

———, 1988-93, *Southeast Asia in the Age of Commerce*, New Haven: Yale University Press.

Reith, Eric, 1993, *Voiliers et Pirogues du monde au début du xixe siècle*, Paris: Du May.

Rougelle, Axelle, 1996, 'Medieval Trade Networks in the Western Indian Ocean', in Himanshu Prabha Ray and J.-F. Salles (eds.), *Tradition and Archaeology: Early Maritime Contacts in the Indian Ocean*, New Delhi: Manohar: 159-80.

Roy, Sourindranath, 1961, *The Story of Indian Archaeology*, New Delhi: Archaeological Survey of India.

Schlingloff, Dieter, 1982, 'Indische Seefahrt in römischer Zeit', *Zur geschichtlichen Bedeutung der frühen Seefahrt*, München: Verlag C.H. Beck.

Sen, Tansen, 2004, *Buddhism, Diplomacy and Trade: The Realignment of Sino-Indian Relations 600-1400*, New Delhi: Manohar.

Sengupta, Gautam and Shambu Chakraborty, 2002, 'Local Material and Monuments: Begunia Group of Temples, Barakar, West Bengal', in Gautam Sengupta and Sheena Panja (ed.), *Archaeology of Eastern India: New Perspectives*, Kolkata: Centre for Archaeological Studies and Training, Eastern India: 395-413.

Sircar, Dinesh Chandra, 1949, 'Madanpur Plates of Sricandra year 46', *Epigraphia Indica*, XXVIII: 337-9.

———, 1957, 'Inscriptions of Candras of Arakan', *Epigraphia Indica*, XXXII: 109.

———, 1967, 'Fragmentary Copper-plate Grant from Arakan', *Epigraphia Indica*, XXXVII: 1-66.

Stark, Miriam T., 2004, 'Pre-Angkorian and Angkorian Cambodia', in Ian Glover, and Peter Bellwood (eds.), *Southeast Asia: From Prehistory to History*, London and New York: Routledge Curzon: 89-119.

Subrahmanyam Sanjay and L.F. Thomaz, 1991, 'Evolution of Empire: The Portuguese in the Indian Ocean in the Sixteenth Century', in James Tracy (ed.), *The Political Economy of Merchant Empires: State, Power and World Trade 1350–1750*, Cambridge/New York: Cambridge University Press: 298-331.

Travers, Robert, 2007, *Ideology and Empire in Eighteenth Century India: The British in Bengal*, Cambridge: Cambridge University Press.

Villiers, Alan, 1952, *Monsoon Seas: The Story of the Indian Ocean*, New York: McGraw Hill Book Co.

Vink, Markus, 2007, 'Indian Ocean Studies and the new "thalassology"', *Journal of Global History*, 2: 41-62.

Wade, Geoff, 2004, *The Zheng He Voyages: A Reassessment*, Asia Research Institute Working Paper Series, 31.

Werbner, Richard P., 2003, *Pilgrims of Love: The Anthropology of a Global Sufi Cult*, Bloomington: Hurst Publishers and the University of Indiana Press.

Wicks, Robert S., 1992, *Money, Markets and Trade in Early Southeast Asia*, New York: Cornell University Press.

Wink, Andre, 1990, *Al-Hind: The Making of the Indo-Islamic World*, vol. I, New Delhi: Oxford University Press.

CHAPTER 2

Space, Movement and Place: The Sea Nomads

CYNTHIA CHOU

Introduction

The maps of modern-day cartographers divide the maritime space of the Bay of Bengal into two distinct regions, namely, South and Southeast Asia. Moreover, the chain of islands along the littoral is further divided as belonging to and under the sovereignty of the nation states of India, Bangladesh, Sri Lanka, Indonesia, Malaysia, Thailand and Myanmar/Burma respectively. Yet, in the study of the history of this considerable gulf of the Indian Ocean, there has been no doubt about the fluvial unity of this maritime space. From early records about navigational routes and trading networks to more contemporary works about the uses of this maritime cultural landscape as life and living spaces, they all clearly show the interactions of its inhabitants that manifest the unity of this largest bay in the world (cf. Rennell, 1792; Prakash and Lombard, 1999).

In the study of maritime cultures though, little is known about the various groups of sea nomads who have regarded the ocean and coastal areas as their life and living spaces for centuries and for whom modern-day political borders and boundaries are but artificial temporary constructions. This paper will discuss their spatial imaginings of the maritime cultural landscape. As skilled mariners who have gained mastery of the ocean, they have sailed to various places to appropriate resources and open new settlements. Barriers between land and sea peoples have been significantly bridged by their seafaring activities. In due course, this has led to the development of a mosaic of cultures occupying different environments and to the emergence of an intricate network of interrelated territories around the Bay of Bengal.

In discussing the ethnography of the sea nomads, I intend to re-ignite the debate concerning the artificiality of the partitioned maritime landscape of the cadastral maps of modern-day cartographers and administrators. To further our understanding of the unity of the maritime cultures and traditions of the Bay of Bengal, I intend to probe the most fundamental level of our understandings of space and spatial relations. First, and foremost, this paper explores another way of conceptualizing the sea. That is, rather than perceiving it merely as a boundary that delineates one group of land inhabitants from another, a conceptual shift is called for to see the sea as important socio-cultural spaces through the lenses of the sea nomads. By doing so, our conceptualization of maritime spaces takes on new meanings. The intention is to raise questions pertaining to the diverse yet equally compelling ways in which people feel, experience and think about space and how they form territories.

The challenge in developing a new perspective to understand forms of ownership of maritime territory or maritoriality with regard to the sea nomadic community inevitably entails the need to rethink the theory of the politics of mapping. When staking claims to the ownership of territory, there emerge different imagined spatial ideas which underpin official and community mapping. Much of the politics of mapping theory has so far not adequately encapsulated the intricacies of contemporaneous mapping politics between sea and land-based ideologies. Hence, this article will look into issues concerning indigenous narratives, histories and geographies and cartographic silencing as well as other forms of knowledge with a view towards widening our inquiry into the different means, and perhaps less understood ways, of communicating spatial imaginings.

Background

The Bay of Bengal, covering an area of over 2 million sq km that includes the Andaman, Nicobar and Mergui islands, is an area of long-established maritime traditions. The bay houses one of the world's largest marine ecosystems and with its wealth of coral reefs, estuaries and mangroves, it is a haven for fish-spawning grounds and sea-animal sanctuaries. Maritime food resources and oceanic minerals abound in this area. Hence, the bay has been an important channel for international trading routes that span across the regions of South and Southeast Asia. For centuries, groups of sea nomads with conceptual understandings of maritoriality that are not constrained by political borders and boundaries have sailed across this vast expanse of maritime space and set-up intricate networks of communities that have been crucial for bringing about the fluvial unity of the bay.

In the ethnography of sea nomads in this region, there are at least three known groups: the Moken, the Orang Suku Laut and the Bajau Laut. These groups of boat-dwelling mariners are widely dispersed throughout the Bay of Bengal. The Moken inhabit the Mergui Archipelago of Burma, the south-western coast of Thailand and the waters bordering Malaysia (Court, 1971; Hogan, 1972; Ivanoff, 1985). The Orang Suku Laut (literally, People of the Sea) consist of variously named groups located in the northern and southern gateways to the Straits of Melaka and the southern tip of the Malay Peninsula extending all the way into Batam and the Riau Lingga archipelago of Indonesia. They are also to be found in the estuaries of major rivers in eastern Sumatra and in the coastal and maritime waters stretching across thousands of islands all the way into the South China Sea. The Bajau Laut is the biggest and most widely spread out group of sea nomads. They are located on the north-eastern coast of Borneo and the Sulu Archipelago of the Philippines, and stretch all the way into Sulawesi, Maluku and the Lesser Sundas in Indonesia (Sather, 1997).

Today, the sea nomads are looked upon with great disdain by many land-based communities as a marginalized, backward and un-progressive people. State authorities are imposing great pressure to quell their mobility and are systematically re-orientating them towards becoming citizens of the state with the obligation to observe new concepts of borders and boundaries that presently demarcate the region into numerous nation states. Thai authorities, for instance, refuse to issue identity papers to the Moken because they do not see them as having an address (Ivanoff, 1997: 3). The current marginal status of the mariners, though, is one that has been culturally and politically constructed through shifts in political rule in the region. Until the middle of this century, their mobile seafaring lifestyles were highly valued by the power-holders of the early Malay states of the western Malay region and by the various sultanates that arose in coastal Borneo, the southern Philippines and eastern Indonesia. They were in fact the key players and the building blocks for the sustenance of sedentary communities that developed around the Bay of Bengal. Their mastery of the seas enabled them to move about easily to exploit a range of island and sea resources for their own needs as well as for the purposes of trade and exchange. Simultaneously, they discovered new areas thus paving the way for the establishment of a multitude of settlements. Vital sea lanes were also secured and defended by the sea nomads to generate trading wealth for the sustenance of these land-based communities. The mariners were indispensable integrating information-carriers who linked together a wide and complex network of micro-polities that constituted the power base for the land-based rulers. All of this contributed significantly towards enabling the large-scale integration of the increasingly centralized polities that shaped and developed the political and cultural maritime landscape of the Bay of Bengal (Benjamin, 1986: 16).

Indeed, the seafaring activities of the sea nomads gave them the ability to dominate the region (Urry, 1981: 7). As an example, the Orang Suku Laut were so respected by the Malay rulers for their indispensable services that they were duly granted possession of 'the seas and what floated on them by hereditary feudal right from the Sultan of Johor' (Trocki, 1979: 56). It was only until the middle part of this century that the sea nomads knew no other home than their boats. Pressures to curb their seafaring lifestyle began with the dominance of European colonialists in the region who categorized them negatively as pirates and criminals. The colonial administrators saw it as their 'sacred obligation to ameliorate the moral condition' (Logan, 1849: 466) of the mariners. The legacy of the European colonialists in cultivating a negative view of the sea nomads is lasting. Pressures to transform the boat-dwelling mariners into sedentary land-based communities continue to this time by present day state administrators. While some have moved ashore, others persist in maintaining their seafaring lifestyle (Figure 2.1).

In spite of the unceasing pressures that are inducing the sea nomads to transform their way of life, they continue to distinguish themselves by identification with the sea itself. They speak of themselves as *a'a dilaut* (sea people) or Orang Laut (sea people) as opposed to *a'a déa* (land people) or *orang darat* (land people). The sea is regarded as an inalienable gift from their ancestors, and as such their occupancy of it cannot be separated, removed or alienated from them. Based upon this understanding, they claim ownership of and sovereignty over this entire space. They deem the region to have been founded upon networks of genealogical and kinship ties that prevail over present-day political borders and boundaries which they see as

Figure 2.1: House Boat.

temporary and artificial. The sea nomads thus possess an identity that is capable of being carried anywhere in the vast maritime world and the region is mapped according to wherever and, however, far their navigational skills take them to. Other local inhabitants of the region acknowledge the mariners as the indigenous peoples of the region. Expressions acknowledging this recognition include *orang asli* (indigenous peoples), 'true', 'genuine', or 'real' inhabitants. The homeland of the sea peoples lies in what cartographers now call 'South' or 'Southeast Asia' but their own perception of the space they occupy is very different.

It is pertinent, at this point of our discussion, to examine the dynamics of juxtaposing the issue of the sea nomads' understanding of belonging with the question that is central to our discussion of how to understand and make sense of the maritime landscape of the Bay of Bengal: 'What is space?'.

Space

The study of space has captured the attention of many a researcher. Spatial relations is an issue that has long inspired works on political organization in the region of South and Southeast Asia. Most notably, the thought-provoking works of Stanley Tambiah's (1976) galactic polity, Benedict Anderson's (1991) imagined communities, Thongchai Winichakul's (1994) geo-body to James C. Scott's (2009) Zomia have opened many paths in discussions and debates to refine our understanding of space and spatial relations in these regions. As Scott (2009: xiv) observes, the numerous seas in the region 'conjure up a whole watery Zomia that deserves a place [of study] here . . . [t]he sea is bigger, emptier than the mountains and the forest.'

'Space' is a concept of an intricate matrix of ideas. People of different socio-economic and political backgrounds and persuasions differ in how they delineate their world, designate values to its parts and appraise them. Ways of perceiving space vary greatly in complexity and sophistication, as do methods of assessing measurements. Yet certain similar cross-cultural traits prevail: people are the actors who measure all things (Tuan, 1977: 34).

The conception of space manifests the quality of human senses, the modes and sophistication of thinking and the complexity of social relations (Tuan, 1977: 16). The sea can be perceived as an infinite mass or there can be numerous conjectures of the imagination that give meaning to the massive seascape to see it as a complex whole. The question is, 'How do people affix meaning to as well as configure space?' Space is a conceptual schema that centres on the power of our mental faculties to extend far beyond the sense data (Tuan, 1977: 17).

Administrators measure and map space, classify resources and implement spatial laws to define 'space'. In their conception, 'space' is an undifferentiated, pragmatic and abstract area around which to construct borders and boundaries. This pragmatic space is often mapped and demarcated by specific political or economic agendas (Tuan, 1977: 17). Hence, professional planners need to simplify the sea to create space for maritime use. Yet once this maritime world is established, it becomes an ordered world of meaning—boundlessness means going off course, being disorientated, going adrift or going astray. Professional administrators, with their urgent, if not well-meaning, need to implement action, move towards designing paradigms and producing inventories. This is arguably a valid approach, but it assumes universality and connotes human passivity in understanding space. It overlooks cultural particularities and diversities that co-exist to constitute human culture. The problem is the glossing over of 'experiential data' (Tuan, 1977: 5) to understand how people feel about space. It disregards the different modes of experience and feelings to interpret space as images of complex feelings. The ability to take the pragmatic level one step further like the sea nomads, and to also describe space in terms of signs, symbols and signals, would be a move towards a more sophisticated conceptual mode of understanding space and spatial relations—and in this case to develop a more comprehensive understanding of the Bay of Bengal as a region.

The sea nomads' sense of space differs markedly from that of cadastral map makers. A study of their conception of space reminds us that we need to return to our rudimentary thoughts of 'space as that which allows movement; that place is pause; and that each pause in movement makes it possible for location to be transformed into place' (Tuan, 1977: 6). Space is: (i) a range of knowledge and experience that can be direct and intimate, or indirect and conceptual mediated by symbols (Tuan, 1977: 6); and (ii) a 'condition for biological survival' (Tuan, 1977: 57).

The sea nomads draw our attention to other human insights and conceptual frames. My aim here is to present a study of them and to traverse unknown spaces for further deliberation. The study of movement and space is important. Today, there is much interest in the study of movement, space and identity. This has come about due to what is believed to be the complex movement of transnational migrants, tourists, refugees and exiles. It is argued that movement plays a part in our modern imagination and that 'modern culture is practiced through, and the work of, wandering' (Rapport and Overing, 2000: 265). The study of these groups of people in movement will hence lead to a conceptual shift in the study of space. This is because it challenges cultural fixity and opens our understandings to a cosmopolitan global framework of socio-cultural interaction, which sees human society as fluid and inclusive (Rapport and Overing, 2000: 263). In fact, this is no new phenomenon of any kind if one does a careful examination of, for example, the sea nomads who have inhabited the Bay of Bengal. Movement and the conceptualization of space have always been practised by nomadic groups; yet they have always been relegated to the time capsule of pre-modern groups and are not taken seriously by modern-day cadastral map makers.

Movement and the ability to move around constitute the basics to the awareness of space. Space is experienced as having the scope to move. Space is discerned in all its aspects via the way people feel and think. Space presupposes a rough coordinate frame pivoted on the axis of mobility (Tuan, 1977: 12). Therefore, 'space can be variously experienced as the relative location of objects or places, as the distances and expanses that separate or link places, and—more abstractly—as the area defined by a network of places' (Tuan, 1977: 12). Together with the spatializing faculties of sight, sound and touch, these senses all evoke spatial cognizances and deepen our understanding of the world's multi-dimensional character. Perception of forms connotes an awareness of one's bearings. Spatial organization and spatial relations are exclusively dependent on these sensory spatializing faculties (Tuan, 1977: 12). As Anderson (1991: 173) cautions us, cadastral maps by present-day cartographers situate space in a global geometrical grid based upon calculations of longitudes and latitudes. On the basis of a totalizing classification, it squares off seas, land and all things in it into measured boxes for surveillance. Administrative maps and mapping thus represent only certain forms of knowledge. Paying heed to this caution, we must note that the ability of the sea nomads to sail across the sea many times over and to develop navigational skills in reading the stars and the waves reflect the triumphant accomplishments of a people of a very advanced culture whose knowledge of mapping areas seems to elude modern-day cartographers in understanding the reality of the region.

Borderless Seascape (Figure 2.2)

South and Southeast Asia or for that matter, the nation states of India, Bangladesh, Sri Lanka, Indonesia, Malaysia, Thailand and Myanmar/Burma are not regarded by the sea nomads as fixed place names for an unchanging geographical reality. These are not terms of reference used by the boat-dwelling mariners for their spatial imaginings of the expanse of the Bay of Bengal. Instead, they map this maritime

Figure 2.2: Borderless World.

expanse in terms of their permanent mobility across spaces to engage in and maintain social relationships with sites, navigational routes and coastal areas so as to gather maritime resources or to rotate their maritime harvests in order to ensure the sustainability of resources. Their social relationships of maritoriality ownership and rights are firmly anchored in the seascape via movement rather than that based upon permanent settlements delineated by borders and boundaries. The seascape is perceived as life- and living-spaces not hampered by state-defined borders and boundaries.

The boat-dwelling mariners are aware that this vast maritime space is presently divided into numerous nation states with different political powers claiming sovereignty over different demarcated areas. Nonetheless, they consider these borders and boundaries as artificial and recent impositions that reflect the ascent and collapse of different political powers that are constantly changing. In contrast to nation state narratives about the history and making of the region, the sea nomads regard their oral histories as offering a richer discourse of the past that leads to the present. Their oral histories reflect their political ideologies. Moreover, they demonstrate the amalgamation between social and rhetorical space, which form the way in which they perceive spaces and mentally map the region. Their mental maps demonstrate how they experience space as lived social relationships and the histories of their interactions with the surrounding strand and maritime spaces. Narrations of oral histories by the Moken, Orang Laut and Bajau Laut have much to tell of the fluvial unity of the Bay of Bengal.

During the sixteenth and seventeenth centuries, the Mergui, homeland to the Moken, became a coveted region for traders and explorers from China, India and the Persian Gulf because of its strategic navigational route through Asia. It was also the shortest route between the China Sea and the Indian Ocean. For that reason, Siam and Burma were often at war with each other to gain control of this area. By 1760, the Burmese took control of the Mergui province. They were, however, incompetent seamen and lost possession of the islands belonging to their territory. Inhabitants along the coast and in the lowlands abandoned their homes and merchant ships stopped calling en route to the rest of Asia. During this time though, the

Moken were the most independent people of the provinces (Helfer, 1839: 987).

By 1826, the Mergui archipelago came under British control. Except for a few prospectors who occasionally ventured into the area to exploit precious resources such as timber and mother-of-pearl shells, the area remained seemingly uninhabited (Ivanoff, 1997: 51). Travellers' accounts though record the sighting of a strange people roaming the archipelago (Hamilton, 1828). During this period, the British attempted to evangelize and send the Moken to school. However, any rule enforced on the Moken was futile (Ivanoff, 1997: 3). After independence and under Burmese rule, other rules were applied on the Moken to integrate them within a federal ethnic system. An invitation was issued for them to travel to Rangoon to participate in a festival for ethnic groups. However, the criterion to gain formal recognition as an ethnic group was based upon the donning of a group's traditional costume. Unable to fulfil this requirement, the case of the Moken was swiftly dismissed. During the Second World War, the Japanese became the overlords of the archipelago. The Moken recall this period as one of intense torture, suffering, hunger and captivity. They were taken as slaves to look for gold, silver and tin (Ivanoff, 1997: 19-21).

The Moken have clear recollections of these different periods of varying political domination and frequently stress the transient nature of these political phases. A favourite narration concerns the adventures of six Moken who escaped Japanese captivity in St. Matthew's island. One dark night, the six Moken decided to flee in their boats. However, as soon as they made their way out of Japanese captivity, a British submarine sank their boats and caught them. Soon they found themselves in the British submarine. Through sign language and an interpreter who spoke to them in Malay, the British discovered very quickly that the Moken possessed superior navigational skills that were an asset for war against the Japanese. The British contacted their headquarters and then set out for India with the Moken. Undoubtedly, the latter were fully aware that the British represented a rival form of political domination to the Japanese. In exchange for their assistance, the British promised that after the victory, the Moken would be able to administer their island territory.

Thus, the Moken described all the movements of the Japanese boats to the British and navigated them through all the possible routes, channels and canals to India. In contrast to the Japanese, the Moken speak of the British as kinder political power-holders (Ivanoff, 1997: 21-2).

In the few written accounts about the Moken, they have been described and oversimplified as an unreliable people who have no respect for any kind of schedule (cf. Anderson, 1890: 1; Bernatzik, 1939 and White, 1922: 63-4). It is said that there is no assurance that they would appear for appointments. Neither is there any kind of certainty in their schedules. They are deemed as a people with no concept of time who would constantly and instantaneously alter their plans, as well as move around without giving prior notice to anyone. They seem intent on keeping others ignorant of their movements and completely disregard rules and regulations that might restrict their movement in any way. Hence, they often illicitly enter restricted zones and get arrested for violating border laws. Their constant movement has also been interpreted as a lack of structure and organization in Moken society. All of these assumptions though show the failure to understand that these are the ways in which the Moken assert their choice of a lifestyle of independence and freedom. It is also a way of protecting themselves and managing against all kinds of unforeseen circumstances in the maritime world. Fixed schedules are impractical as it would for example only be rational to alter one's navigational course according to weather conditions.

Contrary to common belief, the Moken do know about contemporary political boundaries and borders. Nonetheless, they possess several conceptual levels of reality that orientate them towards perceiving these boundaries as temporary intrusions. For the Moken, 'on land and during the rainy season, time is a historical and ritual phenomenon; at sea, and during the dry season, time is mythical ... the idea that . . . different epochs develop within the same unique temporal axis, and can be surpassed, is to be found in their traditional oral narratives' (Ivanoff et al., 1997: 12). Below is a Moken narration concerning the creation of a borderless seascape:

Long ago, there was only the earth. . . . One day some evil serpents threw enormous rocks into the sea which flooded all the land. The tops of the mountains escaped the catastrophe and became islands. Only our ancestors who found refuge and hastily constructed flat boats and agile monkeys escaped death. (Iu, a Moken in Ivanoff et al., 1997: 45)

The Moken epic of Gaman further reflects their spatial imaginings of the region. Gaman was a Malay whose arrival epitomized the infiltration of the rice-growing world into Moken social space. For the Moken, rice represented civilization. It was regarded as a cultural force threatening to dominate and change their lifestyle. They had to decide between two ways of life, that is, either to adopt farming and expand their territory or to pursue demographic stabilization and gathering. They chose not to grow the crop but to carry it in their boats. This meant that they saw themselves as carrying civilization. It was also a decision to protect their freedom of movement and to retain their distinctive identity (Ivanoff et al., 1997: 113).

In ways similar to the Moken, the Orang Laut are aware of the various eras of political domination that have come and gone and that numerous political borders and boundaries currently divide the region into various nation-states (Chou, 2006a; 2006b). They have a clear recollection of living in a region that has been re-mapped many times over by different political eras. As explained by Awang Ketah and his two sons Sman and Bego, who are Orang Laut men from Dapur Enam, which lies within what is currently the Republic of Indonesia, each new political era has also meant the need to negotiate new orders of political, economic and social relations.

AWANG KETAH: I have lived through the period of the Japanese, British and the Dutch. [Each of these periods was] very different. Things [were] cheap. Although the price of fish was low, everything else was very cheap.
SMAN: Now, the value of our currency is small. Formerly, we could buy lots of things with just five cents.
BEGO: Things were also very cheap during the time of the Dutch. One box of match-sticks cost only 50 *perak*. Now, we cannot get anything for so little.
AWANG KETAH: Do you know how much things cost during the time of the British? Five kilos of rice cost only sixty cents. One big loaf of bread cost one cent. Now, with one thousand rupiah, we can hardly get anything. I know everything about the time of the British, Japanese and Dutch.

BEGO: [During the Japanese Occupation], we continued fishing. However, we could not go very far and we did not take our women along either. The Japanese would harm our women.
SMAN: [The Japanese considered] our women [as] their women [too].
AWANG KETAH: [It was peaceful during the period of the Dutch and British], not the period of the Japanese Occupation. It was difficult.

The Orang Laut understand that money is a symbol of an overarching political authority or the state that is issuing it (Hart, 1986). In these terms, they thus explain that a change in the type of currency that is used often indicates a change in the central political body that is issuing it. They clearly understand that the imposition of borders and boundaries signals various changing political powers and everyday practices in the region. Nevertheless, through their oral histories, they offer another perspective with regard to their spatial imaginings of the maritime world and what the imposition of borders has meant to them. In an extended conversation with the Orang Laut men from Dapur Enam cited above, they explained the formation of the borderless seascape:

SMAN: The *Raja Laut* (King or Queen of the Sea) . . . is even more powerful [than all other rulers]. . . . The *Raja Laut* is ruler of all the islands. . . . When a Malay ruler meets the *Raja Laut*, [the former] is unable to lift his hands and legs against the latter. . . . If the Malay ruler meets the *Raja Laut*, [the former will shuffle around as though he is] treading on dried grass. The Malay ruler will [have to] praise our *Raja Laut*.
BEGO: The *Raja Laut* can be a man or a woman. . . . Our grandfather told us our history. . . .

Formerly, we all lived in boats out at sea. We had no houses. If it had not been for us the indigenes, how could there be islands now? We say that we own all the islands. In our history, the *Raja Laut* had fifteen children. He gave each of them rings and islands. This is how the islands came into being.

The Orang Laut, like the Moken, consider all political borders and boundaries imposed on the region as temporary intrusions and recently constructed phenomena. They too regard the region as a borderless social space and maintain that it was through their mobility that this space was discovered, formed and expanded. They call this social space the Alam Melayu or Malay World, a social space unified by their history and the network of genealogical and kinship ties that continue to prevail today in spite of the interference of modern-day political boundaries. It is an era of unbroken historical tradition that overrides all borders and the ultimate sovereignty lies with the rule of the *Raja Laut*.

The Bajau Laut, too, maintain that it was their mobility that led to the founding and shaping of the region. In the narration of their origin, there existed only eternal beings, namely *Tuhan* (God) the Supreme Being and the *saitan* (spirit) in the beginning. *Tuhan* created the first *mbo'* (human ancestors) who lived in Arabia. The first ancestors, lived in house-boats and carried out subsistence fishing. One evening, the leader of a cluster of boat-living families who were anchoring together accidentally thrust his mooring pole into the gills of a giant ray that was asleep at the bottom of the sea. As the families slept soundly through the night, the ray awoke and swam off, hauling their boats which had been strung together, out into the open sea. When they awoke, they discovered that they were in an unknown area encircled by unfamiliar islands. They were not able to retrace their journey and so they remained there. Through time, they scattered and divided into a network of anchorage groups throughout this vast maritime expanse (Sather, 1997: 18). This was how the region stretching across what modern maps mark as South and Southeast Asia came into being.

Bajau crews are geographically dispersed and highly fissiparous. Prior to the imposition of contemporary political boundaries that interferes with their movement, they navigated freely between the waters of present-day Sabah, Philippines, Kalimantan and Sulawesi. Via their seafaring activities, they retain links with a network of Bajau Laut, while simultaneously distinguishing themselves into smaller groups through their identification with certain islands and places of origin (Owen, 1922: 73; Sather 1997: 4). New settlements are continually founded and connected to the wider network of communities that form the region, and the chief internal dynamic of the Bajau Laut society appears to be one of social geographic proliferation (Owen, 1922: 36).

A Network of Interrelated Territories and Ancestral Estates

The sea nomads organize their space within a network of interrelated and collectively owned territories that are based on kinship ties (Chou, 1997). Although they have highly transnational lifestyles, they do not speak of themselves as South or Southeast Asians but in more precise toponymic references that signify their place of origin and principal area of settlement. They revere their life and living spaces and regard them as inalienable gifts of ancestral estates received from their ancestors (Chou, 2010). As such, these spaces are indestructible and cannot be given away, exchanged or sold and likewise, their occupancy of these spaces cannot be separated, removed or alienated from them. These inalienable possessions define who they are in the historical sense bringing the past into the present, so that the histories of their ancestors and mythological events become part of their present personal identity. This inalienable gift of territory is therefore not just an economic resource but more of an affirmation of social relations (Weiner, 1985: 210). The oral histories of the sea nomads reveal how places are linked together via kinship ties to form a region with a time dimension represented by ancestral estates. The origins, rights and linkages of these ancestral estates are contingent upon the exclusive stories that reflect and confirm which specific boat-dwelling group was the first to discover the potential of a place, and function as indigenous collective title deeds. The process is much the same in all three major groups.

The Moken comprise several dialect groups. Each group identifies itself with an island or cluster of islands where they moor to seek shelter during the monsoons. Ivanoff (1985: 173-5) has identified five distinct dialect groups in the Mergui Archipelago who are scattered along a north-south axis. They are, from north to south, the Dung (Ross islands), Jait (Owen island), Lebi (Sullivan and Lampi islands), Niawi (St. James island), and Chadiak (St. Matthew island). Groups of Moken have also extended into the island of Phra Thong in what is known today as the Phang Nga province of the south-west coast of Thailand. Sopher (1977: 70-1) presents a more comprehensive list of the geographic subdivisions of the Moken in the Mergui archipelago: the Tavoy Island group, the Doung group which includes rights to the islands of Elphinstone, Ross, King and Maingyi, the Bentinck group which also lays claim to the Domel and Kisseraing islands, the Owen-Malcolm islands group, the Loughborough group, the Sullivan-Clara island group, and the St. Matthew-St. Luke islands group. Both Ivanoff and Sopher, however, agree that the Moken refer to themselves in toponymic terms and conceptualize the region as a network of places connected by kinship ties.

All through the year, the Moken chart a migratory round of their network of kin-related islands (Sopher, 1977: 61). In accordance with the seasons, groups move back and forth from west to east along parallel seaward and landward routes. Each territorial group consists of approximately forty boats and everyone reunites for an annual celebration of feasting and ritual activity (Sopher, 1977: 77) (Figures 2.3 and 2.4).

In ways similar to the Moken, the Orang Laut speak of their region as *tempat saya* (my area or place) or *tanah saya* (my territory or my region) and identify themselves in toponymic terms (Chou, 2005: 241). Their region is conceptualized as constituting a network of interrelated territories owned by different Orang Laut groups. Their

Figure 2.3: Repairing a boat.

Figure 2.4: Building a boat.

tenure of territoriality is based upon their oral traditions, which have been passed down through generations, concerning which particular group first discovered a *tempat* (area or place) as moorage and settlement zones, and how a network of these places constitute their *tanah* (territory or region) (Figures 2.5 and 2.6).

Below is an explanation by Meen, an Orang Laut man of the Teluk Nipah island explaining how his family claim ownership of the place:

My mother's name was Nenah and my father's name was Gebak. Their ancestry is Daik. We were facing difficulties there, so we rowed over here to fish. We were boat-dwelling. We set up a small cultivation plot and built a house on Teluk Nipah. There [was] already [another group of Orang Laut] on [the opposite] Pulau Nanga. Apong had settled there, but our origin is different. Although there were Orang Laut on Pulau Nanga, we did not want to settle there. We are different. We were the first Orang Laut to settle on Teluk Nipah. This is our territory.

The following is another story exclusive to the Orang Laut of the Dapur Enam island as told by Joya, an Orang Laut woman. This story has been transmitted orally through generations that enables them to stake their collective claims of territorial ownership.

Figure 2.5: Setting up a new settlement.

Figure 2.6: A child's house boat.

JOYA: Our ancestry is from Dapur Enam. My grandfather Umur lived in a boat. He was the first to move into Dapur Enam. He would return to live in his boat whenever he needed to fish for food. My father, Awang

Ketah, was the first to settle in Dapur Enam. When the weather is bad and when the sea is choppy, one can feel very dizzy in a boat. Hence, my father decided to move to land. . . . All the houses in Dapur Enam belong to my father's children. My father feels that it would be a pity if he should ever have to leave our territory. . . . We have many family graves in Dapur Enam. Although my father has moved to land. . . . From time to time, he returns to live in his boat.

Through stories such as those narrated by Meen and Joya, respective Orang Laut groups speak of *punya* (possessing) a network of kin-based territories that form the region. These stories are an assertion and certification of their collective title deeds to a particular place. These stories must also be understood as revelatory myths whereby local spirits showed particular Orang Laut groups the areas' potential. Other groups of Orang Laut and non-Orang Laut neighbours acknowledge these stories as a group's right to a place or a network of territories. A space or a number of spaces together can constitute a territory in which they are dispersed. In no way are territories demarcated by borders or boundaries. The Orang Laut allow free access to sea and land space to anyone who seeks the permission of the head of the group that holds the area. As custodians of sea and coastal spaces, the Orang Laut are responsible for guarding, preserving and looking after their territories, including maintaining and reproducing resources in their areas to ensure the sustainability of their community as well as that of others. Regular rituals are performed to affirm their custodianship of the region (Chou, 2010).

The Bajau Laut are part of a larger group of Sama-Bajau-speaking people that is widely dispersed through the region. A majority of the Sama-Bajau speakers identify themselves as Sama (or *a'a Sama*, the Sama people) (Sather, 1997: 5). The term Sama is often also used in combination with a toponymic reference to an island, a cluster of islands or to a strand area which denotes the speaker's geographical or linguistic affiliation. As an example, Sama Sibuat would mean Sama speakers who originate from or who live on Sibaut island in the cluster of Tapul islands in Sulu. Toponymic names are also sometimes used together with the term *a'a* which means 'people'. People could thus speak of themselves as, for instance, the *a'a Sibaut* or the 'Sibaut people', particularly if they are conversing with other Sama speakers. Those who are still nomadic refer to themselves as *Sama Dilaut* or *Sama Mandelaut*, which literally mean the Sea (*laut*) or Maritime Bajau, *Sama to'ongan* which means the 'real' or 'true' Bajau or simply as *a'a dilaut* or sea people (Sather, 1997: 5-6).

A Network of Cultural Economic Units

A network of interrelated kinship territories of the boat-dwelling people that make up what are now known as the regions of South and Southeast Asia comprises a matrix of interrelated and kin-infused cultural-economic units (Andaya, 1993). This region stretching across the ocean and littoral areas of the Bay of Bengal is about family too. This network of kinship-infused cultural-economic units translates into spheres of resource sites that spawn sustenance. Mariners can select areas where it would be best to eke out a living among kin-related territories. This arrangement parcels out resources to each group to enable them to get the best harvest for each and every season in addition to conserving and preventing over-exploitation of resources. This network of kin-related territories also links the sea nomads in space and time. The migratory round of resource use charted according to the seasons reunites groups of sea nomads. These movements from place to place also mean that the mariners are never concentrated in any one place, which might lead to an over-utilization of the area's resources. This arrangement serves the purpose of population dispersal and evenly spreads out resource consumption over a wide area, consequently generating the fluvial unity of a very vast expanse of maritime space.

The Moken are divided into flotillas. Each flotilla generally consists of about 10 boats. Its nucleus comprises an extended family of the same Moken sub-group. Formerly, the flotillas were described as *kabang*. However, the term now only refers to the boat. Today, the word *an*, with strong connotations to the Thai word for 'house', (ban) is now used to refer to a flotilla (Ivanoff, 1985: 3). A Moken man from the St. Matthew cluster of islands will identify himself as *bonem ban salaman alang Chadiak* or Bonem of the Salamah flotilla, a man from St. Matthew. Such self-references though do not conform to present-day bureaucratic categories which require people to have fixed addresses.

The flotillas engage in annual migrations. They move from island to island within their respective networks of kin-related islands and strand areas. Some make charcoal while others harvest shellfish. During the dry season, nomadism means the division of territory known and respected by all. Each territory group consists of about 40 boats, and members reunite annually at the conclusion of the dry season for a period of feasting and rituals (Ivanoff, 1985: 6).

In ways similar to the Moken, the Orang Laut have organized their maritime space around a web of interrelated and collectively owned cultural-economic territories based on kinship ties. It is common practice, for Orang Laut families from Pulau Nanga for example, to go to Tiang Wang Kang during the season to obtain *comek* (a variety of cuttlefish) and for those in Tiang Wang Kang to move to Pulau Nanga when they want to harvest sea cucumbers. Likewise the Orang Laut from Teluk Nipah would head for Bertam and Pulau Cakang and vice versa.

Among the Bajau Laut, a married couple is referred to by the term *mataan*. The root word for this term is *mata*, which would normally mean eye. However, *mata* when used in this context implies the mesh or individual openings of a fishing net. The *mataan* is therefore a part that is linked to a bigger whole comprising a web of similar parts. Just like an eye within the meshwork of a fish net, a married couple is a part of a wider network of interrelated couples and families. The Bajau Laut consider themselves as part of a *damataan*, literally those of one mesh and speak of themselves as *kami damataan*, 'we of one mesh'. The term *mataan* in general usage can also mean the larger mesh itself. What this advocates is that those of one 'eye' are linked to others in relational and generational terms. Therefore, when the term is used in a wider sense, one's *mataan* includes not only people related within the same 'mesh' but a more extended kin-related network of related couples and families, all linked via marriage and filiation (Sather, 1997: 134-5).

Those of one house do not have to (and are not expected to) live together throughout the year. Rather, each family identifies itself with a 'band' or local moorage community. Each band is linked to a permanent anchorage site whereby members of that group would usually return after their fishing voyages. Closely-related families usually moor together as a group and secure their boats to one or several common moorage posts. Such groups are known as *pagmunda* and normally comprise at least two sets of siblings related by marriage (Sather, 1997: 56).

Bands from a region usually fish in the same areas. Families from neighbouring bands may sometimes fish together. Fishing grounds are regarded as an 'unowned resource' by the Bajau Laut. However, families tend to fish most intensively in places closest to their anchorage sites. Hence, anchorage sites provide a sense of territorial definition for respective groups of band members. As there is open access to fishing grounds, there is often an overlap of areas that are used by different groups. When meetings happen at a fishing site, families usually pool their resources together to form short-term fleets. Families inhabiting the same region usually know each other and wider social networks of cooperation are sustained across band boundaries (Sather, 1997: 56-7). The Bajau Laut trace *turunan* (descent line, genealogies) in order to preserve their *dampo'onan* (an individual's close cognatic kin) and to chart their genealogical connections. Such links establish *kampong* (village or community) ties (Sather, 1997: 219) (Figure 2.7).

Figure 2.7: The sea and strand as life and living spaces.

Conclusion

Boat-dwelling mariners see themselves as part of a region, but the words 'South' and 'Southeast Asia' as terms of reference for that region or its various nation state borders have no meaning for them. The most crucial point is that space has always been conceptualized as a continuous expanse for them that is defined by movement, perception and behaviour or activity.

In their collective spatial imaginings and social experience, the region is a borderless space defined according to their permanent mobility, conceptions of unbounded spaces and group identification with a network of places. An intricate web of social relations unifies the expanse of this space. These include networks of resource utilization, trading and seafaring activities as well as living spaces. New centres of settlements are continually set-up and connected to the existing network of interrelated communities, which means that their life and living space is continually expanding.

The Bay of Bengal is shaped by a historical experience that links places through genealogy to constitute a region with a time dimension that is represented by ancestral estates. The phenomenon of sea nomadism confronts the rifts brought about by the surge of territorially-grounded boundary delineations that have long hindered a more comprehensive academic inquiry into spatial orientations and the appropriation of space by human groups. I have attempted to place this maritime-cum-nomadic-oriented world in a larger framework, a conduit by which new cultural orders are instituted. This merits attention in widening our spatial imaginings for advancing our understanding of the unity of the Bay of Bengal, and even more so, our theory of space and spatial relations.

REFERENCES

Andaya, Barbara, 1993, *To Live as Brothers: Southeast Sumatra in the Seventeeth and Eighteenth Centuries*, Honolulu: University of Hawaii Press.

Anderson, John, 1890, *The Selungs of the Mergui Archipelago*, London: Trubner and Company.

Anderson, Benedict, 1991, *Imagined Communities*, London: Verso.

Benjamin, Geoffrey, 1986, 'Between Isthmus and Islands: Reflections on Malayan Palaeo-Sociology', Working Paper, 71, Singapore: Department of Sociology, National University of Singapore.

Bernatzik, Hugo Adolf, 1939, 'The Colonization of Primitive Peoples with Special Consideration of the Problem of the Selung', *The Journal of the Siam Society* 31 (March): 17-28.

Chou, Cynthia, 1997, 'Contesting the Tenure of Territoriality: The Orang Suku Laut', in Cynthia Chou and Will Derks (eds.), *Riau in Transition, Bijdragen Tot de Taal-, Land- en Volkenkunde*, 153 (4e): 605-29.

———, 2005, 'Southeast Asia through an Inverted Telescope: Maritime Perspectives on a Borderless Region', in Paul H. Kratoska et al. (eds.), *Locating Southeast Asia: Geographies of Knowledge and Politics of Space*, Singapore and Athens: Singapore University Press and Ohio University Press: 234-49.

———, 2006a, 'Borders and Multiple Realities: The Orang Suku Laut of Riau, Indonesia', in Alexander Horstmann and Reed L. Wadley (eds.), *Centering the Margin: Agency and Narrative in Southeast Asian Borderlands*, New York and Oxford: Berghahn Books: 111-34.

———, 2006b, 'Multiple Realities of the Growth Triangle: Mapping Knowledge and the Politics of Mapping', *Asia Pacific Viewpoint*, 47 (2): 241-56.

———, 2010, *The Orang Suku Laut of Riau, Indonesia: The Inalienable Gift of Territory*, London and New York: Routledge.

Court, Christopher, 1971, 'A Fleeting Encounter with the Moken (The Sea Gypsies in Southern Thailand)', *Journal of Siam Society*, 59 (1): 83-97.

Hamilton, Walter, 1826, *East India Gazetteer*, London: Wm. H. Allen and Co., III.

Hart, Keith, 1986, 'Heads or Tails? Two Sides of the Coin', *MAN*, 21 (4): 637-56.

Hefler, John William, 1839, 'Third Report on Tenasserim—the Surrounding Nations—Inhabitants, Natives and Foreigners—Character Morals and Religion', *Journal of the Asiatic Society*, 96: 973-1005.

Hogan, David, 1972, 'Men of the Sea: Coastal Tribes of South Thailand West Coast', *Journal of the Siam Society*, 60: 205-17.

Ivanoff, Jacques, 1985, 'L'épopée de Gaman: Histoire et Conséquences des relations Moken/Malais et Moken/Birmans', *Asie de Sud-Est et Monde Insulindien*, XVI (1-4): 173-94.

Ivanoff, Jacques et al., 1997, *Moken: Sea-Gypsies of the Andaman Sea Post-war Chronicles*, Bangkok: White Lotus Press.

Logan, James R., 1849, 'Malay Amoks and Piracies. What Can We do to Abolish them?', *Journal of the Indian Archipelago and Eastern Asia*, 3: 463-67.

Owen, Rutter, 1922, *British North Borneo: An Account of Its History, Resources and Native Tribes*, London: Constable.

Om Prakash and Denys Lombard, 1999, *Commerce and Culture in the Bay of Bengal, 1500–1800*, New Delhi: Manohar and Indian Council of Historical Research.

Rapport, Nigel and Joanna Overing, 2000, *Social and Cultural Anthropology: The Key Concepts*, London and New York: Routledge.

Rennell, James, 1792, *The Peninsula of India, from the Kistnah River to Cape Comorun; From the Latest Authorities: Exhibiting its Political Division, According to the Partition Treaty Made at Seringapatam*, London: J. Rennell.

Sather, Clifford, 1997, *The Bajau Laut: Adaptation, History, and Fate in a Maritime Fishing Society of South-eastern Sabah*, Kuala Lumpur: Oxford University Press.

Scott, James, 2009, *The Art of Not Being Governed: An Anarchist History of Upland Southeast Asia*, Yale: Yale University Press.

Sopher, David, 1977, *The Sea Nomads: A Study of the Maritime Boat People of Southeast Asia*, Singapore: National Museum Publication.

Tambiah, Stanley Jeyaraja, 1976, *World Conqueror and World Renouncer*, Cambridge and New York: Cambridge University Press.

Thongchai, Winichakul, 1994, *Siam Mapped: A History of the Geo-body of a Nation*, Honolulu: University of Hawaii Press.

Trocki, Carl A., 1979, *Prince of Pirates: The Temenggongs and the Development of Johore and Singapore, 1784-1885*, Singapore: Singapore University Press.

Tuan, Yi-Fu, 1977, *Space and Place: The Perspective of Experience*, Minneapolis and London: University of Minnesota Press.

Urry, James, 1981, 'A View from the West: Inland, Lowland and Islands in Indonesian Prehistory', Paper presented at the 51st ANZAAS Congress, Brisbane.

White, Walter G., 1922, *The Sea Gypsies of Malaya. An Account of the Nomadic Mawken People of the Mergui Archipelago, With a Description of Their Ways of Living, Customs, Habits, Boats, Occupations*, London: Seeley Service and Company.

CHAPTER 3

If Only Plants Could Talk . . . : Reconstructing Pre-Modern Biological Translocations in the Indian Ocean*

TOM HOOGERVORST

Introduction

The human impact on landscapes reveals itself in various ways. Human populations affect their environment, but also adjust to it. The plants they cultivate shape their agricultural systems, village structures, culinary and medicinal traditions, rituals and art. Therefore, the study of plant remains from archaeological sites (archaeobotany) provides us with valuable insights into the early agriculture and cultural contact of a region. The names given to plants tell a different story, highlighting the actors featuring on the prehistoric stage of inter-ethnic contact. The Indian Ocean, with its favourable sea currents and monsoon winds, has facilitated maritime trade since time immemorial. Along with the exchange of religions and religious ideas (cf. Noor, this volume), material culture and technology, several cultigens diffused widely and across ethno-linguistic boundaries as a result of the interconnectedness of the

* I would like to express my gratitude to the organizers and participants of the International Seminar on Maritime Cultures and Traditions of the Bay of Bengal (22 and 23 April 2011) for their hospitality and stimulating academic environment. I am also indebted to Nicole Boivin, Waruno Mahdi and Alexander Adelaar for their useful comments on an earlier version of this paper and to the European Research Council for financially supporting my research.

regions around this ocean. This is often reflected by the adoption of loan-words from the people who introduced certain plants into a geographically contiguous society. In other words, lexical data can tell us who gave what to whom. Hence, this study focuses on the anthropogenic dispersal of a set of Southeast Asian plants and their distribution across the Bay of Bengal and beyond, using a combination of archaeobotanical and linguistic evidence.

Although bringing together linguistic and archaeobotanical data is a rather novel approach, previous scholars have established the benefits of such an interdisciplinary enterprise in gaining new perspectives on an otherwise poorly documented part of history (e.g. Mahdi, 1998; Blench, 2003; Beaujard, 2010). This study does not claim to present a complete picture of plant translocations from Southeast Asia into the wider Indian Ocean. The dispersal of spices and aromatics will be dealt with elsewhere (Hoogervorst, 2012) and plants that travelled in the opposite direction will also not be addressed here (but cf. Gonda, 1973: 322-9). Instead, this paper focuses on the origins and transoceanic dispersal of sandalwood, the coconut palm, lime cultivars, ginger and galangal. These plants originated in Southeast Asia, although the coconut palm may have been domesticated independently. After their translocation across the Bay of Bengal, the cultigens travelled further westward to the Middle East and East Africa. Archaeobotanical data tell us very little about the agents in these transoceanic dispersals. Therefore, this study will examine lexical data, both attested and reconstructed, to cast new light on this insufficiently explored aspect of the Indian Ocean's pre- and proto-history. In the light of Southeast Asia's sophisticated ship types and its people's renowned seafaring skills (cf. Pham, this volume), this paper especially aims to provide new perspectives on the role of Malay and other Southeast Asian speech communities in the trans-regional setting of the Indian Ocean.

Recent archaeobotanical research has shed new light on agricultural developments in this region. To understand the time-depth and distances travelled by the early navigators of the Indian Ocean, it is of special significance to look at the introduction of East African crops into South Asia and, to a lesser extent, South Asian domesticates travelling in the opposite direction. This series of agricultural exchanges probably started around 2000 BCE (Blench, 2003; Fuller, 2003; Boivin et al., 2009). They were followed by the translocation of Southeast Asian cultigens, which are the focus of this study. Upon examining these biological translocations, one should keep in mind that discontinuous distributions of phylogenetically related species, if not caused by climate change, are strong indicators of anthropogenic dispersal (Asouti and Fuller, 2008: 71-4). Such human-mediated distribution patterns are found throughout the Indian Ocean. A better known instance of long-distance travelling foodstuffs is the prehistoric introduction of several insular Southeast Asian agricultural items into Africa, including yam varieties (*Dioscorea alata* and *D. esculenta*), taro (*Colocasia esculenta*), banana/ plantain (*Musa* spp.), sugar cane (*Saccharum* spp.) and possibly Asian rice (*Oryza sativa*) (Murdock, 1959: 222ff.; Mitchell, 2005: 106-8). In addition, recent mitochondrial DNA analysis reveals a Southeast Asian contribution in the gene pool of East African chicken populations (Bjørnstad et al., 2009; Mwacharo et al., 2011). Chami (2001) reports the finding of chicken bones in Zanzibar dated to the last millennium BCE, but it is uncertain as to which part of Asia these domestic chickens originated from. In any case, most of these agricultural items seem to have transgressed the Indian Ocean through a trajectory not yet fully understood, in the form of a package, which has been called the 'Malaysian complex' (Murdock, 1959: 223-4) or the 'Tropical Food Kit' (Blench, 2009: 364). While African bananas/plantains have received a fair deal of scholarly attention (cf. Blench, 2009: 365-7; Neuman and Hildebrand, 2009: 353-4), our general understanding of biological translocations across the Indian Ocean is still in its infancy.

Sandalwood

The sandalwood tree (*Santalum album*) is a 4 to 9 m high species of the *Santalaceae* family. This parasitic tree grows best in semi-arid areas and partly draws its nourishment from the roots of other trees. Although the sandalwood tree is easily cultivated, its bark is very delicate and suffers considerably from accidental injuries. The tree is therefore often found in protected areas, such as forests or stony soils (Watt, 1889-96/vi.ii: 462; Burkill, 1966/2: 1987). Sandalwood is famous for its fragrance, which develops after its dead wood dries (Heyne, 1927/1: 590). In some textual sources, the wood is called 'white sandalwood' to distinguish it from the inferior 'red sandalwood' (*Pterocarpus santalinus*), a tree native to south India. In Indic cultures, sandalwood powder was initially used as a cosmetic and subsequently acquired a ceremonial function with the emergence of Hinduism and Buddhism (Burkill, 1966/2: 1989). In insular Southeast Asia, sandalwood is traditionally made into a porridge known for its aromatic and medicinal properties (Heyne, 1927/1: 591). The presence of sandalwood in South Asia seems to be of considerable antiquity and its use is deeply rooted in Indic culture. Sandalwood occurs in various Sanskrit texts, such as the late 1st millennium BCE *Rāmāyaṇa* and the fourth-fifth century CE works of Kālidāsa. The identification of sandalwood in the charcoal records at Sanganakallu in southern India suggests that it was used in South Asia by at least 1400-1300 BCE (Asouti and Fuller, 2008: 117; Fuller and Madella, 2009: 345).

In the light of the antiquity of sandalwood in South Asia, it is difficult to imagine that this tree might be of foreign origin. Nevertheless, this has been claimed by some early twentieth-century scholars (Sprague and Summerhayes, 1927; Fischer, 1927, 1938) and more recent archaeobotanical work points towards the same conclusion (Harbaugh and Baldwin, 2007). These studies provide several arguments for the non-indigenous origin of the sandalwood tree in South Asia. First, the geographical distribution of species in the genus *Santalum* shows remarkable discontinuity between southern India on the one hand and the entire area between Nusa Tenggara, northern Australia and most of the Pacific region on the other, which, if not caused by massive extirpation in the intervening area, can only be the result of human-mediated introduction. Second, there is an absence of entirely wild populations in the South Asian subcontinent, even though the tree is known for its ability to reproduce quite easily without human intervention. Third, early European sources uniformly identify Nusa Tenggara (also known as the Lesser Sunda islands) as an important export centre, whereas they do not mention any South Asian agency in the sandalwood trade.

In addition, the Chinese seem to have obtained their sandalwood directly from Southeast Asia, not from India (Laufer, 1919: 318).

Despite the insular Southeast Asian origin of the tree, the nomenclature for 'sandalwood' is almost entirely of Indic derivation. Only in Nusa Tenggara and adjacent regions, where the tree is found in wild populations, are several local names used (Heyne, 1927/1: 589). Although Sanskrit has many synonyms to refer to the tree (cf. Donkin, 2003: 22), the most widespread term is *candana*, itself a borrowing from a Dravidian source (Burrow and Emenau, 1984 #2448; Zvelebil, 1990: 80). This Sanskrit form yielded various reflexes across South Asia (cf. Turner 1966 #4658), spread westward as Farsi *čandan* ~ *čandal*; Aramaic *sˤ-n-d-r* (Löw, 1881: 107); Arabic *ṣandal*, Swahili †*sandali* and eastward as Late Middle Chinese **tşian-tán* (旃檀) ~ **thian-tán* (填檀) (Hirth and Rockhill, 1912: 209; Burkill, 1966/1: 1988), Tibetan *tsan dan*, Khmer *can*, Malay *cəndana* and Cham *candal*. This word has also been identified as the attested form *santálina* found in the *Periplus* (Schrader, 1917-23/2: 279). In addition, it occurs in sixth century CE Hellenistic texts as *sándanon* (*Sixteen Books on Medicine*) or *tzandánē* (*Topographia Christiana*), although these words were later replaced by *sántalon* (Quaritch, 1893: xxxii; Yule & Burnell, 1903: 790; Dalby, 2000: 31). Thus, throughout the Indian Ocean littoral and beyond, the adopted word for 'sandalwood' was Sanskrit *candana*. The fact that even the insular Southeast Asian speech communities adopted this word may have been partly trade related: the Indians made the world aware of the high economic and religious value of the tree. Its important function in Hindu and, later, Buddhist rituals made the use of a Sanskrit name for 'sandalwood' even more likely.

Coconut Palm

The coconut palm (*Cocos nucifera*) is a large, pinnate-leaved palm with a straight or slightly curved stem. The tree is currently found throughout the tropics, where it is mainly cultivated for its nuts. In addition, practically every other part of the coconut palm can be used, making the tree of high economical value and cultural significance. Its leaves are used for roof-thatching, and making mats or baskets, while the leaf-veins can be bound together to make brooms. In Indonesia, the young pale coconut leaves (*janur*) are made into ceremonial decorations. The roots of the coconut palm are used medicinally for various illnesses, including dysentery (Heyne, 1927/1: 400). Its wood, known as 'porcupine wood', can be used for house construction and boat-building in the absence of more suitable timbers. The juice of the inflorescence (toddy) is known for its sweet taste and can be boiled down to make palm sugar (jaggery) or distilled to make a strong spirit (arrack) or vinegar, although sugar cane and palm species in the *Borassus* and *Arenga* genera are preferred for this purpose. Finally, the haustorial organ or 'coconut apple' of a germinating embryonic nut can be eaten as cabbage or pickled (Watt, 1889-96/ii: 448; Heyne, 1927/1: 401).

The coconut is characterized by various stages of development. After flowering, a green fruit bud develops. In the Malay world, these young fruits (*mumbang*) are used medicinally. As the nut ripens, a shell develops within (endocarp), whereas the outer skin (exocarp) and the husk (mesocarp) become harder and darker. An air cavity develops on the inside, allowing the formation of kernel liquid. This substance, commonly known as coconut water, is enjoyed as a refreshing beverage throughout the tropics. At a later stage, the husk dries and the kernel meat (endosperm) develops, at first thin, creamy and transparent and later succulent, firm and white. The coconut meat, also known as desiccated coconut, is used to make coconut milk and other culinary condiments. At the next growing stage, the exocarp becomes brown, the kernel liquid turns bitter and the endosperm becomes harder and thicker, after which the dry nut falls from the tree and sprouts. As is the case with parts of the coconut palm in general, almost all parts of the nut can be used. Coconut shells are used as drinking beakers, bailers, resonators for musical instruments and coals for goldsmiths (Heyne, 1927/1: 402; Burkill, 1966/1: 617; Kapil and Bhatnagar, 1976: 451), whereas the coarse fibre from the husks of matured fruits (coir) is manufactured into ropes, mats or mattresses by a process of manual removal (de-husking), beating, soaking and re-drying. Coir ropes play a key role in the boat-building traditions of South Asia (Varadarajan, 1998: 50-

81). The sundried kernel meat (copra), in addition to its nutritional value, can be grated and boiled to produce coconut oil. In India, this oil is traditionally used for lamps, to make soap and to adorn the body (Watt, 1889-96/ii: 441). The de-oiled residue (poonac) is rich in proteins and can be used as fodder for domestic animals.

The coconut palm has a large number of different cultivars, reflecting mankind's continuous attempts to improve its quality, productivity and shape (Foale, 2003: 21). Recent research on coconut phylogeography points out that there were at least two separate domestication events of the tree, resulting into two highly differentiated genetic sub-populations corresponding to the Pacific and Indian Ocean basins, the latter probably from a south Indian or Sri Lankan centre of domestication, with an admixture between the two populations occurring in East Africa (Lebrun, 1998; Gunn et al., 2011). This dual origin sheds new light on earlier theories of coconut dispersal. Hornell (1920: 221ff.), for example, correlated the introduction of the coconut, purportedly from Indonesia to Sri Lanka and thence to the mainland, with the migration of certain Sri Lankan palm tree cultivator and toddy-tapper castes known as *Tīvāṉ*, *Īḻavaṉ* or *Cāṇār* to coastal south India (Caldwell, 1875: 110; Iyer, 1909: 277; Thurston, 1909: 37-8). This hypothesis, which has found its way into the wider literature, is based on a number of assumptions. The Tamil word for 'coconut', it is argued, is *tēṅkāy*, which can be explained as 'fruit from the south', alluding to its presumed insular origins. This etymology, however, is not watertight, as *tēṅkāy* can equally well mean 'sweet fruit'. Its connection to the south, if any, could be the result of folk etymology. In further support of an insular origin of the coconut palm, scholars have noted that coconut cultivation plays an extremely marginal role in the large corpus of Indic literature prior to the beginning of the Common Era (Kosambi, 1965: 189; Mahdi, 1998: 396ff.), strongly suggesting that is was carried out by peripheral, coastal populations but not (yet) by the early Brahmins. Hornell (1920: 232ff.) believes these coastal populations were of partly 'Malayo-Polynesian' ancestry and cites the results of cranial measurements conducted among several communities to support this claim. Regardless of whether this excursus contains any element of truth or not, a Sri Lankan origin of the coconut palm in South Asia is the most plausible scenario. In Sri Lanka, the tree may have been domesticated independently.

In accordance with the dual domestication of the coconut tree, the Indian Ocean features two major protoforms (i.e. forms that can be reconstructed to an earlier stage of a language family based on regular sound correspondences) for 'coconut palm': proto Malayo-Polynesian **niuR*, which is regularly reflected in insular Southeast Asia and the Pacific (but not in Taiwan), and Old Indo-Aryan **nārikēla*. Although the somewhat unsettled character of the Old Indo-Aryan form (cf. Turner, 1966 #7075) suggests borrowing, I do not agree with the view that the Old Indo-Aryan form is connected to or derived from the Malayo-Polynesian form, as has been suggested by several authors (Chatterji and Bagchi, 1929: xxii; Merrill, 1939: 123-4; Blench, 2008: 122). Instead, a Dravidian etymology from **nari* 'fibre, rope' and **keṭ-i-a-u* 'tree, bush', as first suggested by Bloch (1930: 740) and later reaffirmed by Southworth (2005: 82), seems to be more in line with the linguistic data. Either way, the Indo-Aryan form spread throughout South Asia (e.g. Turner, 1966 #7075), from which it was adopted as Farsi *nārgīl* 'coconut palm', Arabic *nārǧīl* and Swahili *nazi id.* We may also compare the Hellenistic textual attestations *argellia* (*Topographia Christiana*) and *naúplios* (*Periplus*). The latter is usually emended to *nargílios*, which resembles its tentative Indic precursor even more. In addition, the traditional coconut growing regions of the world display a large amount of specific vocabulary, including terms for different cultivars, various parts of the tree, growing stages of the nut and items manufactured from the tree. Although many of these terms are of descriptive nature and vary from one language to another, a small set of terms have been borrowed cross-linguistically. The Malay word *kəlapa*, referring predominantly to what Burkill (1966/1: 607) describes as 'the dry nut which the trader stocks and carries about', seems to be a borrowing from Sanskrit *kalāpa* 'bundle', alluding to the way in which the nuts were sold (Uri Tadmor, http://wold.livingsources.org/s.v.). Another instance of lexical borrowing is Swahili *ki-tamli* 'k.o. coconut', which appears to go back to Sinhala *tǟmbili* 'king coconut (*Cocos nucifera* var. *aurantiaca*)' (Krain et al., 2002), a variety bearing yellow, ovoid nuts famous for their sweet juice.

Two specific palm-related terms from Malay seem to have found their way into Tamil. The first is the Malay *kajang* 'mat-awning'. In the Malay world, thatching is done with the leaves of several palm species, especially the mangrove palm (*Nypa fruticans*). This word appears to have been borrowed twice into Tamil: (1) *kacaṅku* 'wild date-palm; stalk, as of the date-leaf used in making plaited baskets' and (2) *karicaṅku* 'temporary roof of coconut leaves put up in an Indian raft for protection against inclemencies of weather'. However, it has been argued that palm thatching was a European introduction into south India (Yule & Burnell, 1903: 139-40), so the intermediate form might have been Indian-English 'cadjan'. Of more interest, therefore, is the word for 'palm wine'. The Malay word *tuak* 'fermented palm sap' has travelled across the Indian Ocean. It occurs as *ṭuwāq* in an account by the eighth-century CE Arabic author Abū Ḥanīfa (Ferrand, 1913-14/1: 295). It also found its way into the Tamil language, which generally displays *kaḷ* 'toddy'. However, we also find the forms *tuvacar* 'toddy-sellers, dealers in spirituous liquors' and *tuvaca-maṅkaiyar* 'women selling toddy'. The insular Southeast Asian provenance of these Tamil words seems beyond doubt, although the exact route by which they spread to southern India remains obscure. It is tempting to speculate that these toddy-sellers were of Southeast Asian origin. In that regard, we may also note that the Malay *nira* 'fresh palm-sap' is borrowed from the Sanskrit or Tamil *nīra* 'water; juice, liquor'. The adoption of this South Asian word by Malay is additional evidence suggesting that Malay toddy-sellers once operated in the subcontinent, adopting local terms such as *nira* and *kəlapa*. In addition, Beaujard (2010: 370) argues that Swahili *tembo* 'toddy' is derived from Malay *təbu* 'sugar cane', which suggests that Malay-speaking toddy-tappers played a similar role in East Africa. As mentioned before, both sugar cane and palm species are used in the Malay world to produce alcoholic spirits.

Lime cultivars

Citrus trees are small evergreens known for their acidic fruits. The genus *Citrus* is believed to have originated in Southeast Asia, north-east India and southern China. At present, citrus fruits are predominantly cultivated for their culinary properties, in particular the sweet orange (*C. sinensis*), mandarin (*C. reticulata*) and grapefruit (*C. paradisi*). Nevertheless, human consumption might be a relatively late addition to the wide range of functions that people have attributed to citrus fruits. Citric acid has traditionally been used as a sanitizer, disinfectant, insecticide, fungicide and medicine for various diseases. Indeed, the first citrus variety introduced into Europe and the Middle East from India was the inedible citron (*C. medica*), which was used medicinally and in (Jewish) religious ceremonies. Sweet varieties from China and Southeast Asia arrived on the scene much later (Burkill, 1966/1: 569; Zohary and Hopf, 1994: 173). Our understanding of citrus taxonomy is still quite rudimentary. Citrus fruits hybridize easily, accounting for an unclear number of species and difficulties in reconstructing their early phylogeographic dispersal. For this reason, the history of citrus cultivars cannot be seen in isolation from related species. The lemon (*C. limon*), for example, is probably a citron-based cultivar (*C. medica*) with phylogenetic contributions of the pummelo (*C. maxima*) and mandarin (*C. reticulata*) subspecies (Gulsen and Roose, 2001). Conventional thinking has it that citron cultivation commenced in the area of present-day north-eastern India and northern Myanmar. More recently, Gmitter and Hu (1990) have made a convincing case for its origins in Yunnan, south China, where uncultivated citron populations are found in the wild. Other citrus cultivars, such as the mandarin (*C. reticulata*) and the bitter orange (*C. aurantium*), probably originate from the same region. The round, green citrus varieties known as 'limes' are native to Southeast Asia. The best known limes are the key lime (*C. aurantiifolia*) and kaffir lime (*C. hystrix*).

The global dispersal of lime cultivars is of particular interest to linguists. The words used for 'lime'—together with an (ultimately) related set of words denoting 'lemon'—are among the world's most widespread borrowings, equalled only by the word 'tobacco' (Laufer, 1934: 143). European languages obtained their words for both 'lemon' and 'lime' through distinct lines of borrowing from Farsi through Arabic. Arabic medieval accounts lead us to believe that the fruits were imported into the Middle East from India, perhaps by Persian merchants (Glidden, 1937: 381ff.). Although the linguistic data support this scenario, the word used by early authors may have denoted either 'lemon', 'citron' or 'lime' (Johnson, 1934: 50). The apparently related Indo-Aryan form (**nimbū*) is not attested in any literature prior to the 1235-50 dated *Rājanighaṇṭu* (Glidden, 1937: 386), a neo-Sanskrit lexicon on herbs, suggesting that the denoted fruit was an introduced species in the South Asian subcontinent as well. A century prior to its earliest attestation in the Indic literary record, we encounter the word in a Chinese botanical account by Fan Chengda as Late Middle Chinese **liaj-məwŋ* (黎朦; hence the Vietnamese *nịnh mông* 'lemon'), after which it re-occurs in various contexts and renderings throughout Chinese literature (Laufer, 1934: 145ff.). Again, it is impossible to determine which variety was meant in these literary sources. The great variation of Chinese transcriptions strongly suggests that the word is borrowed. From the south of China, the word was probably propagated westwards by Persian merchants as a word meaning 'lemon', e.g. the Farsi *līmūn* 'lemon, citron', Arabic *laymūn* 'lemon' and eventually the European words for both 'lime' and 'lemon' (cf. Mahdi, 1998: 408).

It has been pointed out that many Indo-Aryan forms display fluctuation between /n/ ~ /l/ in the word-initial consonant and between /e/ ~ /i/ in the initial vowel (Mahdi, 1998: 408; Southworth, 2005: 215). The level of irregularity in the vernacular attestations and the late occurrence of the literary Sanskrit form put into questio the hypothetical reconstruction of the Old Indo-Aryan **nimbū*. Instead, we may consider the possibility of a back-formation from a vernacular term, e.g. the Hindi *līmū* 'lime'. Uhlenbeck (1898-9: 148) suggests that the hyper-corrected form *nimbū* may have been influenced by *nimba* 'neem' (*Azadirachta indica*), another tree used in traditional Indian medicine. In any case, a foreign introduction is the most plausible scenario to account for its late occurrence in the literature. Early scholars have suggested various Austro-Asiatic precursors of the word **nimbū* in Indo-Aryan languages. However, upon closer inspection the Muṇḍā attestations appear to be derived from the Indo-Aryan forms, rather than the other way around (Osada, 2009: 136), while Mon-Khmer languages display unrelated reflexes of **kruəc* ~ **kruuc* 'citrus' (Shorto, 2006 s.v.). A Dravidian etymology is equally unlikely, since the phonological system of Dravidian languages does not permit a word-initial /l/

(Burrow, 1945: 614-15). Having discarded the Austro-Asiatic and Dravidian etymologies, let us now explore the terms for citrus fruits in Austronesian languages. Several scholars consider the possibility of an insular Southeast Asian, in particular Malayic, etymology for this word (Bonavia, 1890: 237-44; Kern, 1897: 272-3; Uhlenbeck, 1898-9: 148; Mahdi, 1998: 407ff., 2008: 322). Indeed, many Malayo-Polynesian languages display reflexes of **limaw*, apparently a generic name for citrus fruits (Kern, 1897: 273; Clercq, 1927: 57; Mahdi, 1998: 408), e.g. the Malay *limau* 'citrus fruit' and the Old Javanese *limo* 'a citrus fruit, the lime'. The presence of endemic limes in insular Southeast Asia might hint at the antiquity of this form, which appears to have been borrowed as Sinhala *līma-dehi* '*C. medica* (*dehi* = 'citrus fruit')'; the Arabic *līm(aẗ)* 'lime' (Glidden 1937: 385); the Farsi *līmū* 'lemon, citron' and the Swahili *ndimu* 'lime'.

To substantiate the possibility of a Malayo-Polynesian origin of the word for 'lime' in South Asia, we may also call attention to the more recent trade in citrus fruits from Java to India. As first argued by Bonavia (1890: 30-1), several Indic trade names for citrus fruits are derived from the toponyms 'Jakatra (~ Jakarta)' and 'Batavia', both names for the most important harbour of western Java since the mid-second millennium CE. The following forms are derived from the toponym 'Jakatra': Hindi *chakotara* 'a fruit of the lime kind, a citron; pompelmoose, shaddock', Marāṭhī *cakōtrā* ~ *cakōtra* 'a fruit, pompelmoose or shaddock', Pañjābī *chakotrá* 'the name of a large fruit of the citron kind, the shaddock or pummelo'; Nepāli *cakhetro* ~ *saṅkhetro* ~ *saṅkhatra* 'pummelo' and Bengali *cākhantrā* 'orange' (Turner, 1961: 163). From Malay *Bətawi* (< Dutch *Batavia*) have been borrowed: Tamil *vattāyi* ~ *vattāvi* 'Batavian orange', Bengali *bātābi* 'the shaddock, the pompelmoose, the pummelo' and Hindi *māhtābī* 'a sort of muskmelon'. If we accept that citrus cultivars, presumably lime varieties, were exported from insular Southeast Asia to the Indian subcontinent, we need to also re-examine the antiquity of the precursor **limaw*. Many of its reflexes look surprisingly uniform and could be Malay loanwords, while the regional languages of Indonesia display slightly more variation. Austronesianists have registered different opinions on the antiquity of **limaw*, varying from an assignment to proto-Austronesian (Tryon, 1994: 490) or proto-

Malayo-Polynesian (Zorc, 1994: 547) to a relatively late introduction via Portuguese *limão* 'lemon' (Wolff, 1994: 532; Jones, 2007: 183; Blust, 2009: 703). However, the antiquity of **limaw* reflexes in insular Southeast Asia predates the arrival of Portuguese sailors in the Indian Ocean. The form *limo* has several attestations in Old Javanese literature prior to European contact (Zoetmulder, 1982/1: 1030). The earliest of these is found in the Javanese *Rāmāyaṇa* (Kern, 1900: 89 l. viii.10, 178 l. xvi.44), which is dated to mid-ninth century CE (Jiří Jakl, pers.comm.). The word also occurs on the Keboan Pasar copper plate inscriptions dated CE 964 (Krom, 1913: 141 l. lxiii.1b, 2a). Furthermore, it is found in the *Tantri Kāmandaka* (Hooykaas, 1931: 40 l. 24[12]), dated to the mid-fifteenth century CE, and in a later version of that work known as *Tantri Kaḍiri* (Soekatno, 2009: 98). In none of these texts it is clear what kind of citrus variety is denoted by *limo*, making the above textual attestations of less use for the study of citrus phylogenetics.

Next to its occurrence in pre-modern Javanese literature, a closer look at the geographical distribution of **limaw* reflexes across the Malayo-Polynesian languages may help us understand the dispersal of Southeast Asian citrus fruits. To substantiate his claim for an indigenous Southeast Asian origin of **limaw*, Kern (1897: 273) compares the forms *rima*, attributed to an undetermined Formosan language (presumably Siraya), and *moli*, attested in Polynesian languages and purportedly the result of metathesis (a process by which the order of sounds is changed). I have not found Kern's Formosan reflex in the literature; its closest resemblances are Pazeh *ʔarim* 'peach' and Favorlang *aliem* 'all kinds of lemons and citrons' (Tsuchida, 1977: 110). The Polynesian attestations are also slightly problematic. Although the botanical record has it that all edible citrus species were European introductions into the Pacific, there is a regular proto-oceanic reconstruction for 'citrus fruit' (**moliS*), which may have originally denoted inedible or barely edible citrus or citrus-like genera (Ross et al., 2009: 338-9). Species such as the wild orange (*C. macroptera*) and the pummelo (*C. maxima*) were probably present in the Pacific in pre-European times (cf. Bonavia, 1890: 31-2; Thaman and Whistler, 1996; Walter and Sam, 2002). Illustratively, Raluana, a language spoken in New Britain, displays the inherited term *muli* 'the native shaddock or large orange' (*C. maxima*) alongside the borrowing *nimomo* 'lemon or lime'. All things considered, both **limaw* and **moliS* appear to be of considerable antiquity, whether they are related or not (through metathesis or otherwise). The only other Malayo-Polynesian protoform with a comparable geographical distribution is **muntay* 'kind of citrus tree and its fruit' (Clercq, 1927: 57; Pallesen, 1977: 470; Verheijen, 1990: 201; Blust, 1995 s.v.; Sakiyama, 2009: 250; Wolff, 2010/2: 912), which has been attributed to proto-Austronesian (Wolff, 1994: 519) or proto-Malayo-Polynesian (Tryon, 1994: 490; Blust, 2009: 703).

Returning to the discussion on the ultimate etymology of the word for 'lime', it seems that its likeliest source is a Malayo-Polynesian language, in which reflexes of **limaw* tend to denote endemic citrus fruits in general. This form was then adopted into Indic languages, in which it specifically referred to Southeast Asian citrus cultivars. As the Indic languages also display indigenous protoforms for citrus or citrus-like genera, centuries of trade, cross-breeding and hybridization considerably complicated the citrus terminology in this part of the world. From the subcontinent, the word for 'lime' ended up in the Middle East and reached Europe through Middle Eastern merchants. The relation between insular Southeast Asian reflexes of **limaw* 'citrus' and similar-looking Chinese names denoting 'lemon' and possibly other citrus species merits further research. Possibly, both forms go back to a now-extinct language in southern China.

Ginger

The ginger plant (*Zingiber officinale*) is a tuber with spicy rhizomes used widely for human consumption. Ginger is thought to have originated in Southeast Asia, although it is not found in a wild state anywhere today (Purseglove et al., 1981/2: 447). The ginger plant is propagated by replanting pieces of its rhizome, rather than its seeds, so that its dispersal typically requires human intervention. Its introduction into South Asia is presumably anthropogenic (Asouti and Fuller, 2008: 49). From India, the plant was introduced into the Middle East, Africa and Europe. Prior to Ptolemy, Graeco-

Roman authors were unaware of the Asian origin of ginger, as the Middle Eastern traders kept its source a secret (Warmington, 1974: 184). In all these regions, it was (and is) used in cuisine and in medicine, most commonly against the flu, common cold and nausea. Ginger was described by Dioscorides and Pliny and is also mentioned in the Qur'an (Burkill, 1966/2: 2338; Purseglove et al., 1981/2: 448). The most geographically widespread protoform for 'ginger'—reconstructed as Old Indo-Aryan **śṛṅgavēra* (Turner, 1966 #12588)—is indeed reflected across South Asia, the Middle East and Europe, e.g. the Sinhala *iṅguru*, the Dhivehi *iṅguru*, the Farsi *šankalīl*, the Arabic *zanǧabīl*; the Syriac *zangebīl*, the Aramaic *zangebīl* (Ross, 1952: 18; Crone, 1987: 76), the Old Greek *ziggíberi*, the Latin *zingiber* id., hence our 'ginger'. The form was also borrowed by Swahili (*tangawizi*) and several other East African languages, although these reflexes display irregular sound correspondences and their direct origins remain obscure (Ross, 1952: 19).

Interestingly, Malagasy has not inherited a Malayo-Polynesian reflex for 'ginger', suggesting that the plant was not introduced during the initial colonization of the island. Instead, the Malagasy word for 'ginger' is *sakarivo* (Merina dial.) or *sakaviro* (Sakalava dial.), also used for endemic plants in the *Hedychium* genus (Heckel, 1910: 340). Whether or not these Malagasy forms are related to Old Indo-Aryan **śṛṅgavēra* is uncertain. If the forms are of Indic origin, this would seem to be the only instance of an Indic loanword in Malagasy not paralleled in the languages of Indonesia (cf. Tuuk, 1865: 421; Thomas, 1905; Ferrand, 1908: 361-6; Dahl, 1951: 104-7; Simon, 1988: 81; Adelaar, 1989, 1994, 1995, 2009). On the other hand, a reflex of *śṛṅgavēra* may have existed previously in an obsolete variety of Malay. In any case, the Malagasy attestations, especially Sakalava *sakaviro*, represent the Sanskrit form rather faithfully. The Sanskrit form is itself almost certainly a back-formation, regardless of folk-etymologies with *śṛṅga* 'horn'. It probably consists of the Dravidian elements *iñci* 'ginger' and *vēr* 'root' (Burrow & Emenau, 1984 #429, #5535), as suggested by various scholars (Gundert, 1869: 352; Yule and Burnell, 1903: 374; Hultzsch, 1912, 1914; Schrader, 1917-23/1: 541-2; Burrow, 1943: 130 n. 2; Southworth, 2005: 83). The Dravidian forms reflect an earlier **cinki* (Krishnamurti, 2003: 5), which is also attested in various other language families in Asia, such as Tibeto-Burman, Austro-Asiatic and Tai-Kadai (Jolly and Thomas, 1905: 169; Ross, 1952: 15-16; Marrison, 1967/2: 108; Burrow and Emenau, 1984 #429). Therefore, it seems that this protoform for 'ginger' reached South Asia from a north-eastern source through overland trade networks.

In addition, Old Indo-Aryan displays a protoform with possible Malayic origins: **ārdraka* ~ **āllaka* 'fresh ginger' (as opposed to **śuṇṭhī* 'dried ginger'; Turner, 1966 #12515). Burkill (1966/2: 2339) was the first to call attention to the resemblance between the Indic reflexes and the Malay *halia* 'ginger', which goes back to the proto-Malayo-Polynesian **laqeya* through metathesis (Adelaar, 1992: 387). The form **laqeya* is reflected across insular Southeast Asia and the Pacific and is of considerable antiquity (Ross et al., 2009: 414; Wolff, 2010/2: 884). I would reconstruct the dispersal of the above forms as follows. The Malay form *halia* 'ginger' spread to India at an early stage, reflected as MIA **allaya* 'fresh ginger'. This form yielded Marāṭhī *ālẽ* ~ *alẽ* 'fresh ginger, ginger plant' and Kōṅkaṇī *āllẽ* 'ginger' (Turner, 1966 #1341). In addition, we find Kannaḍa *alla* 'ginger', Tamil *allam* id. and Telugu *allamu* 'green ginger'. That the loanword **allaya* was subsequently hyper-corrected, according to regular sound correspondences, to **āllaka* is not an isolated example. Sinhalese also exhibits a back-formation from /y/ to /k/ between vowels, for example *lakāra* 'sail' from *layāra* (another Malay loanword) and *karavika* 'to cause to be made' from *karaviya* (Smith, 1933: 216). Through folk-etymology, some speakers associated the resulting form with **ārdra* 'wet' and hyper-corrected it once more, yielding the late Sanskrit **ārdraka* and forms such as the Nepālī *aduwā* 'dried ginger', the Pañjābī *addā* 'ginger', the Bengali *ādā*, the Hindi *ādā*, the Gujarātī *ādũ* id. (Turner, 1966 #1341) and the Sinhala *adda* 'green ginger'.

Galangal

The *galangal* (*Alpinia galanga*) is a herbaceous plant of the family *Zingiberaceae*, which also encompasses the ginger. Recent molecular phylogenetic analysis of species in the genus *Alpinia* points out that

A. galanga is most closely related to *A. nigra* and *A. conchigera*, both native to Southeast Asia (Rangisiruji et al., 2000). The rhizomes of *galangal* are famed for their culinary and medicinal properties and can be used fresh or in powdered form. Most botanists infer a Southeast Asian origin of the *galangal*, but the plant may have been cultivated in East Bengal and southern India for a long time (Rangisiruji et al., 2000: 11). Early colonial sources mention Java as the greatest exporter of the plant. From India and the Middle East, *galangal* reached Europe in medieval times, where it was valued as a medicine (Dalby, 2000: 78-9). This diffusion is reflected in the linguistic evidence: the late Sanskrit *kulañja(na)* '*galangal*' (*A. galanga*), the Sinhala *kalañjana*, the Hindi *kulījan*, the Dhivehi *kolizān*, the Farsi *ḫalanjān*, the Arabic *kulunǧān* and the late Latin *galangal* id.

Miller (1969: 52) argues that the Indic form probably originates from China, where the plant can be found in the southern regions. A less convincing etymology explains the form as a south Dravidian word in the meaning of 'esculent or bulbous root' (Dalgado, 1919/1: 414; cf. Burrow & Emenau, 1981 #1578). One of its Chinese names is Early Middle Chinese **kaw-liaŋ-kiaŋ* (高良薑) 'superior ginger', which denotes the lesser *galangal* (*A. officinarum*) and other *Alpinia* species. In support of Miller's hypothesis, we may also compare the Old Khmer *raṁtyaṅ* '*galangal* (*A. galanga*)' (hence Khmer *rumdeɛŋ* id.), which resembles the last two elements of **kaw-lɨaŋ-kɨaŋ*. Several insular Southeast Asian attestations look similar and might have been borrowed from Old Khmer or another source on the Southeast Asian mainland, e.g. the Sudanese *laja*, the Makassarese *laja* and the Javanese *laos* (from an older *laja*) id. (Heyne, 1927/1: 480). The attestations in insular Southeast Asia suggest a secondary diffusion of the Javanese term *laos*, cf. the Balinese *ka-lawas-an*, Karo Batak *kə-lawas*, Simelungun Batak *ha-lawas*, Lampung *lawas*, Ternate *galiasa* id. (cf. Heyne, 1927/1: 480). This corresponds to early European observations of Java as the main exporter of *galangal*. The data further suggest that the plant was introduced into Java and other Southeast Asian islands from the mainland—perhaps through interaction with speakers of the Mon-Khmer languages—and ultimately from China. Via an undetermined route, possibly over land, the same Chinese word also ended up in South Asia from which it spread to the Middle East and Europe.

Conclusion

Our understanding of pre-modern inter-ethnic contact and agricultural exchange is the product of various disciplines. In this study, it is demonstrated that several cultigens that are widely in use across the Indian Ocean littoral have their ultimate origins in Southeast Asia. In many cases, the diffusion of these plants from Southeast Asia to the South Asian subcontinent and further westward is supported by linguistic data. Sometimes the linguistic data provide contrasting perspectives, encouraging us to find alternative explanations. The overall picture we get is that South Asia played a key role in the trans-oceanic diffusion of culturally and economically important plants, from where they were eventually dispersed to the Middle East, East Africa and Europe. Many of these cultigens already had a long history in the region prior to their westward dispersal. The agents in these inter-ethnic networks were probably of diverse ethnic origins and included Middle Eastern, South Asian, Chinese and Southeast Asian merchants. In the Bay of Bengal, the linguistic data suggest a significant Malay element.

Some cultigens, such as ginger and *galangal*, might have reached South Asia via overland trade but the introduction of the other plants examined here is in all likelihood the result of maritime trade with insular Southeast Asia. Nevertheless, this study does not claim to present a comprehensive overview of trans-oceanically dispersed Southeast Asian cultigens, highlighting instead only those cases where bringing together data from different disciplines 'works'. Although the exploration of lexical data can tell us who the cultivators and traders of certain plants were in terms of their ethno-linguistic affiliations, it remains inconclusive in other instances. For several plants, such as turmeric (*Curcuma domestica*), sugar cane (*Saccharum officinarum*), mango species (*Mangifera* spp.), jackfruit (*Artocarpus heterophyllus*) and others, the place of first domestication, the possibility of other domestication events and the early diffusion patterns are less known. In the absence of phylogenetic research, I have not found the linguistic data on these plants sufficiently helpful to propose wide-ranging reconstruction hypotheses. New insights from disciplines other than linguistics are likely to increase our understanding of the history of these cultigens in due course. Within historical linguistics, there are caveats as well. We have seen that languages such as Sanskrit can conceal the foreign acquisition of loanwords by 'correcting' them to resemble the indigenous vocabulary. In addition to this, the 'high' status of Sanskrit as a cosmopolitan vehicle of religion and literature *vis-à-vis* the perceived 'low' status of trade vernaculars, such as Malay, accounted for a socio-linguistic situation in which speech communities preferred to borrow Sanskrit terms, even for indigenous concepts, to enrich their parlance, thereby obscuring the geographical origins of certain plants. All these facets make the story of biological translocations in the Indian Ocean an extremely interesting one to unravel.

REFERENCES

Adelaar, Alexander, 1989, 'Malay Influence on Malagasy: Linguistic and Culture-Historical Implications', *Oceanic Linguistics* 28 (1): 1-46.

———, 1992, 'The Relevance of Salako for Proto-Malayic and for Old Malay Epigraphy', *Bijdragen tot de Taal-, Land- en Volkenkunde* 148 (3-4): 381-408.

———, 1994, 'Malay and Javanese Loanwords in Malagasy, Tagalog and Siraya (Formosa)', *Bijdragen tot de Taal-, Land- en Volkenkunde van Nederlandsch-Indië* 150 (1): 50-65.

———, 1995, 'Asian Roots of the Malagasy. A Linguistic Perspective', *Bijdragen tot de Taal-, Land- en Volkenkunde van Nederlandsch-Indië* 151 (3): 325-56.

———, 2009, 'Loanwords in Malagasy', in Martin Haspelmath and Uri Tadmor (eds.), *Loanwords in the World's Languages: A Comparative Handbook*, The Hague: De Gruyter Mouton: 717-46.

Asouti, Eleni and Fuller, Dorian Q., 2008, *Trees and Woodlands in South India: Archaeological Perspectives*, Walnut Creek: Left Coast Press.

Beaujard, Philippe, 2010, 'Les Plantes Cultivées Apportées par les Premiers Migrants Austronésiens à Madagascar', in Chantal Radimilahy and Narivelo Rajaonarimanana (eds.), *Civilisations des Mondes Insulaires (Madagascar, îles de canal de Mozambique, Mascareignes, Polynésie,*

Guyanes). Mélanges en l'Honneur du Professor Claude Allibert, Paris: Karthala: 357-86.

Bjørnstad, Gro et al., 2009, 'Phylogeographic Study of Chicken Mitochondrial DNA Reveals Ancient Old World Maritime and Terrestrial Trading Routes', paper presented at *Ancient Indian Ocean Corridors*, 7-8 November, Oxford, United Kingdom.

Blench, Roger, 2003, 'The Movement of Cultivated Plants between Africa and India in Prehistory', in Katharina Neumann, Ann Butler, and Stefanie Kahlheber (eds.), *Food, Fuel and Fields: Progress in African Archaeobotany*, Köln: Heinrich-Barth-Institut: 273-92.

———, 2008, 'A History of Fruits on the Southeast Asian Mainland', in Toshiki Osada and Akinori Uesugi (eds.), *Occasional Paper 4: Linguistics, Archaeology and the Human Past*, Kyoto: Indus Project, Research Institute for Humanity and Nature: 115-37.

———, 2009, 'Bananas and Plantains in Africa: Re-interpreting the Linguistic Evidence', *Ethnobotany Research & Applications* 7: 363-80.

Bloch, Jules, 1930, 'Some Problems of Indo-Aryan Philology Forlong Lectures for 1929', *Bulletin of the School of Oriental Studies* 5 (4): 719-56.

Blust, Robert, 1995, *Austronesian Comparative Dictionary*, Honolulu: University of Hawai'i. Accessed through http://www.trussel2.com/ACD/

———, 2009, *The Austronesian Languages*, Canberra: Pacific Linguistics Series 602.

Boivin, Nicole, Roger Blench and Dorian Fuller, 2009, 'Archaeological, Linguistic and Historical Sources on Ancient Seafaring: A Multidisciplinary Approach to the Study of Early Maritime Contact and Exchange in the Arabian Peninsula', in M. Petraglia and J. Rose (eds.), *The Evolution of Human Populations in Arabia*, New York: Springer: 1-44.

Bonavia, Emanuel, 1890, *The Cultivated Oranges and Lemons etc. of India and Ceylon with Researches into their Origin and the Derivation of their Names, and Other Useful Information*, London: W.H. Allen.

Burkill, Isaac Henry, 1966, *A Dictionary of the Economic Products of the Malay Peninsula*, Kuala Lumpur: Ministry of Agriculture and Cooperatives, 2nd edn., 2 vols.

Burrow, Thomas, 1943, 'Dravidian Studies III', *Bulletin of the School of Oriental and African Studies* 11 (1): 122-39.

———, 1945, 'Dravidian Studies V', *Bulletin of the School of Oriental and African Studies* 11 (3): 595-616.

Burrow, Thomas and Murray Barnson Emenau, 1984, *Dravidian Etymological Dictionary*, Oxford: Clarendon Press, 2nd edn.

Caldwell, Robert, 1875, *A Comparative Grammar of the Dravidian of South-Indian Family of Languages*, London: Trübner, 2nd edn., revised and enlarged.

Chami, Felix , 2001, 'Chicken Bones from a Neolithic Limestone Cave Site in Zanzibar', in F. Chami, G. Pwiti, and C. Radimilahy (eds.), *People, Contacts and the Environment in the African Past*, Dar-es-Salaam: Dar-es-Salaam University Press: 84-97.

Chatterji, Suniti Kumar and Prabodh Chandra Bagchi, 1929, 'Some More Austric Words in Indo-Aryan', in Sylvain Lévi, Jean Przyluski and Jules Bloch (eds.), *Pre-Aryan and Pre-Dravidian in India*, Calcutta: University of Calcutta, pp. ix-xxix, tr. Prabodh Chandra Bagchi.

Clercq, Frederick Sigismund Alexander de, 1927, *Nieuw Plantkundig Woordenboek voor Nederlandsch-Indië*, ed. A. Pulle. Amsterdam: J.H. de Bussy, 2nd edn.

Crone, Patricia, 1987, *Meccan Trade and the Rise of Islam*, Oxford: Basil Blackwell.

Dahl, Otto Christian, 1951, *Malgache et Maanjan*, Oslo: Egede-Instituttet.

Dalby, Andrew, 2000, *Dangerous Tastes: the Story of Spices*, London: British Museum Press.

Dalgado, Sebastião Rodolfo, 1919, *Glossário Luso-Asiático*, Coimbra: Imprensa da Universidade, 2 vols.

Donkin, Robin Arthur, 2003, *Between East and West: The Moluccas and the Traffic in Spices up to the Arrival of Europeans*, Philadelphia: American Philosophical Society.

Ferrand, Gabriel, 1908, 'l'Origine Africaine des Malgaches, *Journal Asiatique* (10th series) 11: 353-500.

———, 1913-14, *Relations de Voyages et Textes Géographiques Arabes, Persans et Turks Relatifs a l'Extrême-Orient du VIIIe au XVIIIe Siècles*, Paris: Ernest Leroux, 2 vols.

Fischer, C.E.C., 1927, 'Santalum Album in India', *Bulletin of Miscellaneous Information (Royal Gardens, Kew)* 5: 200-2.

———, 1938, 'Where Did the Sandalwood Tree (*Santalum album* Linn.) Evolve?', *Journal of the Bombay Natural History Society* 40: 458-66.

Foale, Mike, 2003, *The Coconut Odyssey. The Bounteous Possibilities of the Tree of Life*, Canberra: Australian Centre for International Agricultural Research.

Fuller, Dorian, 2003, 'African Crops in Prehistoric South Asia: A Critical Review', in Katharina Neumann, Ann Butler and Stefanie Kahlheber (eds.), *Food, Fuel and Fields. Progress in African Archaeobotany*, Köln: Heinrich-Barth Institut: 239-71.

Fuller, Dorian and Marco Madella, 2009, 'Banana Cultivation in South Asia and East Asia: A Review of the Evidence from Archaeology and Linguistics', *Ethnobotany Research & Applications* 7: 333-51.

Glidden, Harold Walter, 1937, 'The Lemon in Asia and Europe', *Journal of the American Oriental Society* 57 (4): 381-96.

Gmitter, Frederick G. and Xulan Hu, 1990, 'The Possible Role of Yunnan, China, in the Origin of Contemporary Citrus Species (Rutaceae)', *Economic Botany* 44 (2): 267-77.

Gonda, Jan, 1973, *Sanskrit in Indonesia*, New Delhi: International Academy of Indian Culture, 2nd edn.

Gulsen, Osman and Mikeal Roose, 2001, 'Lemons: Diversity and Relationships with Selected Citrus Genotypes as Measured with Nuclear Genome Markers', *Journal of the American Society for Horticultural Science* 126: 309-17.

Gundert, Hermann, 1962, *A Malayalam and English Dictionary*, Kottayam: Sahitya Pravarthaka, 2nd edn.

Gunn, Bee, Luc Baudouin and Kenneth Olsen, 2011, 'Independent Origins of Cultivated Coconut (*Cocos nucifera*) in the Old World Tropics', *PLoS ONE* 6 (6), e21143.

Harbaugh, Danica Taylor and Bruce Baldwin, 2007, 'Phylogeny and Biogeography of the Sandalwoods (*Santalum*, Santalaceae): Repeated Dispersals Throughout the Pacific', *Annals of Botany*: 941028-40.

Heckel, Édouard, 1910, 'Les Plantes Utiles de Madagascar', *Annales du Musée Colonial de Marseille* (2nd series) 8: 5-372.

Heyne, Karel, 1927, *De Nuttige Planten van Nederlandsch Indië*, Buitenzorg: Departement van Landbouw, Nijverheid en Handel, 3 vols.

Hirth, Friedrich and William Woodville Rockhill, 1912, *Chau Ju-Kua: his Work on the Chinese and Arab Trade in the Twelfth and Thirteenth Centuries, Entitled Chu-fan-chï*, St. Petersburg: Imperial Academy of Sciences.

Hoogervorst, Tom Gunnar, 2012, 'Southeast Asia in the ancient Indian Ocean World: Combining Historical Linguistic and Archaeological Approaches', Oxford: University of Oxford. Dissertation.

Hooykaas, Christiaan, 1931, *Tantri Kāmandaka. Een Oudjavaansche Pañtjatantra-bewerking in Tekst en Vertaling*, Bandoeng: A.C. NIX & Co.

Hornell, James, 1920, 'The Origins and Ethnological Significance of Indian Boat Designs', *Memoirs of the Asiatic Society of Bengal* 7 (3): 139-256.

Hultzsch, Eugen, 1912, 'Ginger', *Journal of the Royal Asiatic Society of Great Britain and Ireland* (April): 475-6.

———, 1914, 'Ginger', *Journal of the Royal Asiatic Society of Great Britain and Ireland* (January): 93-7.

Iyer, Lakshminarayanapuram Krishna Ananthakrishna, 1909, *The Cochin Tribes and Castes*, vol. I, Madras: Higginbotham's.

Johnson, Helen, 1936, 'The Lemon in India', *Journal of the American Oriental Society* 56 (1): 47-50.

Jolly, Julius and Frederick William Thomas, 1905, 'Ginger', *Journal of the Royal Asiatic Society of Great Britain and Ireland*: 167-70.

Jones, Russell (ed.), 2007, *Loan-words in Indonesian and Malay*, Leiden: KITLV Press. Compiled by the Indonesian Etymological Project.

Kapil, Ravinder Nath and Anil Kumar Bhatnagar, 1976, 'Portuguese Contributions to Indian Botany', *Isis* 67 (3): 449-52.

Kern, Johan Hendrik Caspar, 1897, 'Limoen', *Tijdschrift voor Nederlandsche Taal- en Letterkunde* 16: 271-3.

———, 1900, *Rāmāyaṇa. Oudjavaansch Heldendicht*, 's-Gravenhage: Martinuf Nijhoff.

Kosambi, Damodar Dharmananda, 1965, *The Culture and Civilization of Ancient India in Historical Outline*, London: Routledge and Kegan Paul.

Krain, Eberhard et al., 2002, 'The Natural and Economic History of the Coconut in Zanzibar', *The Palm Enthusiast* 19 (2): 7-20.

Krishnamurti, Bhadriraju, 2003, *The Dravidian Languages*, Cambridge: Cambridge University Press.

Krom, Nicolaas Johannes, 1913, 'Oud-Javaansche Oorkonden. Nagelaten Transcripties van Wijlen Dr. J.L.A. Brandes', *Verhandelingen van het Bataviaasch Genootschap van Kunsten en Wetenschappen* 60.

Laufer, Berthold, 1919, *Sino Iranica, Chinese Contributions to the History of Civilization in Ancient Iran with Special Reference to the History of Cultivated Plants and Products*, Chicago: Field Museum of Natural History.

———, 1934, 'The Lemon in China and Elsewhere', *Journal of the American Oriental Society* 54 (2): 143-60.

Lebrun, P. et al., 1998, 'Genetic Diversity in Coconut (Cocos nucifera L.) Revealed by Restriction Fragment Length Polymorphism (RFLP) Markers', *Euphytica: International Journal of Plant Breeding* 101: 103-8.

Löw, Immanuel, 1881, *Aramæische Pflanzennamen*, Leipzig: Verlag von Wilhelm Engelmann.

Mahdi, Waruno, 1998, 'Linguistic Data on Transmission of Southeast Asian Cultigens to India and Sri Lanka', in Roger Blench and Matthew Spriggs (eds.), *Archaeology and Language II: Archaeological Data and Linguistic Hypotheses*, London & New York: Routledge: 390-415.

———, 2008, 'Review of Jones (2007)', *Archipel* 76: 318-22.

Marrison, Geoffrey Edward, 1967, 'The Classification of the Naga Languages of North-east India', London: School of Oriental and African Studies, Dissertation, 2 vols.

Merrill, Elmer Drew, 1937, 'On the Significance of Certain Oriental Plant Names in Relation to Introduced Species', *Proceedings of the American Philosophical Society* 78 (1): 111-46.

Miller, James Innes, 1969, *The Spice Trade of the Roman Empire*, Oxford: Clarendon Press.

Mitchell, Peter, 2005, *African Connections: An Archaeological Perspective on Africa and the Wider World*, Walnut Creek, etc.: Altamira Press.

Murdock, George Peter, 1959, *Africa: Its Peoples and their Culture History*, New York & Toronto & London: McGraw Hill.

Mwacharo, Joram Mwashigadi et al., 2011, 'Mitochondrial DNA Reveals Multiple Introductions of Domestic Chicken in East Africa', *Molecular Phylogenetics and Evolution* 58: 374-82.

Neumann, Katharina and Elisabeth Hildebrand, 2009, 'Early Bananas in Africa: The State of the Art', *Ethnobotany Research & Applications* 7: 353-62.

Osada, Toshiki, 2009, 'How Many Proto-Munda Words in Sanskrit?: With Special Reference to Agricultural Vocabulary', Toshiki Osada (ed.), *Linguistics, Archaeology and Human Past in South Asia*, New Delhi: Manohar: 127-46.

Pallesen, Alfred Kemp, 1977, *Cultural Contact and Language Convergence*, Berkeley: University of California.

Purseglove, John William et al., 1981, *Spices*, London & New York: Longman, 2 vols.

Quaritch, Bernard, 1893, *The Register of Letters, &c: Of the Governor and Company of Merchants of London Trading into the East Indies, 1600-1619*, London: Bernard Quaritch.

Rangsiruji, A., M.F. Newman and Q.C.B. Cronk, 2000, 'Origin and Relationships of Alpinia galanga (*Zingiberaceae*) Based on Molecular Data', *Edinburgh Journal of Botany*, 57: 9-37.

Ross, Alan S.C., 1952, *Ginger: a Loan-word Study*, Oxford: Basil Blackwell.

Ross, Malcolm, Andrew Pawley and Meredith Osmond, 2009, *The Lexicon of Proto Oceanic. The Culture and Environment of Ancestral Oceanic Society. 3 Plants*, Canberra: Pacific Linguistics 599.

Sakiyama, Osamu (崎山理), 2009, 'マダガスカルにおけるオーストロネシア系言語由来の植物名称の意味変化 (Austronesian etymologies and semantic change of plant names in Madagascar)', 国立民族学博物館研究報告 33 (2): 227-64.

Schrader, Oskar, 1917-23, *Reallexicon des Indogermanischen Altertumskunde: Grundzüge einer Kultur- und Völkergeschichte Alteuropas*, Berlin & Leipzig: Walter de Gruyter, 2nd edn., 2 vols.

Shorto, Harry Leonard, 2006, *A Mon-Khmer Comparative Dictionary*, Canberra: Pacific Linguistics Series 579. Main editor: Paul Sidwell, assisting editors: Doug Cooper & Christian Bauer.

Simon, Pierre, 1988, *Ny Fiteny Fahizany. Reconstitution et Périodisation du Malgache Ancient Jusqu'au XVIe Siècle*, Paris: Institut des langues et civilisations orientales.

Smith, Helmer, 1933, 'Cinghalais *Ruval* <<la Voile>>', *Bulletin de la Société de Linguistique* 34 (2): 216-17.

Soekatno, Revo Arka Giri, 2009, 'Kidung Tantri Kediri. Kajian Filologis Sebuah Naskah Jawa Pertengahan', Leiden: University of Leiden. Dissertation.

Southworth, Franklin, 2005, *Linguistic Archaeology of South Asia*, London & New York: Routledge Curzon.

Sprague, Thomas Archibald and Victor Samuel Summerhayes, 1927, 'Santalum, Eucarya, and Mida', *Bulletin of Miscellaneous Information (Royal Gardens, Kew)* 5: 193-9.

Thaman, Randolph Robert and Wayne Arthur Whistler', 1996, *A Review of Uses and Status of Trees and Forests in Land-use Systems in Samoa, Tonga, Kiribati and Tuvalu with Recommendations for Future Action*, Suva: South Pacific Forestry Development Programme.

Thomas, R.P., 1905, 'l'Origine des Noms de Mois à Madagascar. Notes de Philologie Comparée', *Bulletin de l'Académie Malgache* 4: 17-36.

Thurston, Edgar, 1909, *Castes and Tribes of Southern India. Volume VII–T to Z.*, Madras: Government Press.

Tryon, Darell (ed.), 1995, *Comparative Austronesian Dictionary: An Introduction to Austronesian Studies*, Berlin/New York: Mouton de Gruyter, 4 vols.

Tsuchida, Shigeru, 1977, 'Some Plant Names in Formosan Languages', *Computational Analyses of Asian & African Languages* 7: 79-119.

Turner, Ralph Lilley, 1966, *A Comparative Dictionary of the Indo-Aryan Languages*, London: Oxford University Press.

Tuuk, Herman Neubronner van der, 1865, 'Outlines of a Grammar of the Malagasy Language', *Journal of the Royal Asiatic Society of Great Britain and Ireland* (new series) 1: 419-46.

Uhlenbeck, Christianus Cornelius, 1898-99, *Kurzgefasstes Etymologisches Wörterbuch der Altindischen Sprache*, Amsterdam: Johannes Müller.

Varadarajan, Lotika, 1998, *Sewn Boats of Lakshadweep*, National Institute of Oceanography.

Verheijen, Jilis, 1990, *Dictionary of Plant Names in the Lesser Sunda Islands*, Canberra: Pacific Linguistics Series D–83.

Walter, Annie and Chanel Sam, 2002, *Fruits of Oceania*, Canberra: Australian Centre for International Agricultural Research. ACIAR Monograph 85. Tr. P. Ferrar.

Warmington, Eric Herbert, 1974, *The Commerce Between the Roman Empire and India*, London: Curzon Press/New York: Octagon Books, 2nd edn.

Watt, George, 1889-96, *A Dictionary of the Economic Products of India*, Calcutta: Department of Revenue and Agriculture, 6 vols.

Wolff, John, 1994, 'The Place of Plant Names in Reconstructing Proto Austronesian', in Andrew Kenneth Pawley and Malcolm David Ross (eds.), *Austronesian Terminologies: Continuity and Change*, Canberra: Pacific Linguistics Series C-127: 511-40.

———, 2010, *Proto-Austronesian Phonology with Glossary*, Ithaca, NY: Cornell Southeast Asia Program Publications, 2 vols.

Yule, Henry and Arthur Coke Burnell, 1903, *Hobson-Jobson. A Glossary of Colloquial Anglo-Indian Words and Phrases, and of Kindred Terms, Etymological, Historical, Geographical and Discursive*, London: John Murray. New edition, ed. William Crooke.

Zoetmulder, Petrus Josephus, 1982, *Old Javanese-English Dictionary*, 's-Gravenhage: Martinus Nijhoff, 2 vols.

Zohary, Daniel and Hopf, Maria, 1994, *Domestication of Plants in the Old World: The Origin and Spread of Cultivated Plants in West Asia, Europe, and the Nile Valley*, Oxford: Clarendon Press, 2nd edn.

Zorc, David Paul, 1994, 'Austronesian Cultural History Through Reconstructed Vocabulary (an Overview)', A.K. Pawley, and M.D. Ross (ed.), *Austronesian Terminologies: Continuity and Change*, Canberra: Pacific Linguistics Series C-127: 541-94.

Zvelebil, Kamil Veith, 1990, *Dravidian Linguistics: An Introduction*, Pondicherry: Pondicherry Institute of Linguistics and Culture.

CHAPTER 4

The Pre-Modern East Asian Maritime Realm: An Overview of European-Language Studies[1]

GEOFF WADE

Introduction

The ways in which scholars outside Asia have examined and studied maritime East Asia[2] have differed, in various ways, from the ways in which scholars within Asia have studied the subject. This brief overview intends to introduce the studies of maritime Asia which have been conducted outside Asia (or been published outside Asia or in non-Asian languages) in order to assist those within the region to remain *au fait* with the work of scholars outside the region.

To this end, I will be reviewing the major studies in various spheres relating to pre-modern[3] maritime East Asia conducted over the last fifty years by scholars based beyond East Asia or published in European languages. It is at times difficult to draw a line between the maritime activities of the Bay of Bengal and the Indian Ocean and those of East Asia, so sometimes the discussion below will stray. It must be stressed that the works described are examples of that which exists within the various European-language traditions and make no claim to being exhaustive.

The Austronesians

There is documentary evidence of trade and exchange between island Southeast Asians and people from mainland Asia for about the last two millennia. Yet, for at least 3,000 years before that, extensive trade networks existed in the East Asian maritime realm, extending both eastwards and westwards from the region. Studies conducted on the origin and spread of the 'Austronesians' is essentially based on archaeological and linguistic evidence. Peter Bellwood is one of the key figures on the archaeological side of this research and his individual and joint studies [Bellwood (1978, 1985, 1995); Bellwood and Koon (1989); and Bellwood, Fox and Tryon (1995)] provide much of the evidence upon which the Austronesian thesis is based. He argues (1995) that the Neolithic revolutions in China sparked population growth and that the food supply provided by the new technology allowed a 'continuous generation-by-generation "budding off" of new families into new terrain', which was supported by 'the inherent transportability and reproducibility of the agricultural economy' and 'a developing tradition of sailing-canoe construction and navigation' (Bellwood, 1995: 102-3).

Essentially the thesis is that a people, speakers of a language which was the ancestor of all the Austronesian/Malayo-Polynesian languages,[4] moved out of what is today southern China and into Taiwan approximately 6,000 years ago, and from there over the following 5,000 years, spread to much of Southeast Asia, the Pacific and even to Madagascar.[5] Their technologies were marked by polished stone tools and by agriculture. Jared Diamond notes that they did not settle on islands which could not support their agricultural 'package' (e.g. New Guinea and Australia) because they had no advantage there. These people maintained links with the islands from where they came and thereby created a wide-ranging trade network. Solheim (1975, 1992, 2000) has detailed his ideas on what he calls the Nusantao, the people who carried these technologies and languages across Asia and the Pacific.

Our knowledge of the seafaring activities of the Austronesian people comes mainly from linguistics and archaeology, and the awareness that these peoples crossed large expanses of ocean. Although there are no Austronesian languages currently spoken in China, the fourteen or so remaining indigenous languages of Taiwan are all Austronesian. There are claims that both northern and southern maritime routes out of Taiwan took the Austronesian seafarers to both the Japanese islands and the Philippine islands. Based on linguistic analysis, claims about the early societies have been made. It is suggested that, after the first seafarers moved from Taiwan to the Philippines, major developments in their culture occurred. We are only able to reconstruct a few words relating to sailing technology at the highest levels of the Austronesian family tree. But at the next level down, the level ancestral to all those people who left their Taiwan homeland, we find terms for outriggers, sails, paddles, rudders, and a whole range of new developments in seafaring. New kinds of plants became available, and new species of fauna were encountered.

The claims that the Austronesian maritime expansion moved in a northerly direction as well as southwards derives from both archaeological correlations and linguistic claims of an Austronesian substratum in the Japanese languages. One of the proponents of this idea was Murayama Shichiro (1908-95), who claimed links between Austronesian and Ainu languages. The claim remains contested.

The East Asian Maritime Realm: Nautical Technology

Ships

We know from Austronesian studies that traditional ships made in Southeast Asia were capable of sailing and carrying people across the Indian Ocean to Madagascar and across the Pacific Ocean, eventually as far as Easter Island. Judging from more recent examples of likely similar technologies, we can assume that these ships were made from tropical hardwood, with a pointed bow, outboard rudders on each side, and lateen-rigged sails. In the next few sections, we shall examine what has been written in European languages on the ships of the East Asian maritime realm.

The Dong-so'n Tradition

Among the earliest graphic representations of early East Asia ships are those seen on the Dong-so'n drums from about the first century BCE (Needham, 1971: 446). These warships show a helmsman with a steering oar as well as an after castle, which housed a bronze drum. Such drums thus seem to have been associated with a sea-going or at least ship-going tradition. Given their lack of masts and sails, we must assume that these ships were oar-propelled, like many of the Austronesian ships.

The bronze Dong-so'n drums are found throughout maritime Southeast Asia, as detailed by Bernet-Kempers (1986), Yokokura (1992), Smith (1979) and Sørensen (1986). Examples of the earliest drums—the so-called Heger Type I—have been excavated in the Malay peninsula, Borneo, many of the islands of modern Indonesia, and Thailand, as well as of course in Vietnam and Guang-xi in China. As it appears likely that these drums were all produced in what are today northern Vietnam and the two Chinese provinces of Yun-nan and Guang-xi, their presence throughout Southeast Asia must have derived from trade or other forms of exchange. Whether they were associated with ships as recorded above or had generic ritual purposes, remains a matter of conjecture. Loofs (1991) discusses the drums' possible functions. What we can state is that their presence in these regions does demonstrate a maritime trade dating from at least 2,000 years ago.

Chinese Ships

Much can be gleaned on the early history of Chinese ships from Krause (1915), who brings together, translates and annotates some of the texts on naval warfare in the earliest dynasties. In 219 BCE, when the Qin emperor Qin Shi huang-di sent forces, under Zhao Tuo, to attack the Yue peoples, a large part of the force was marines based on warships with deck castles—the so-called 'castled ships' (*lou-chuan*). The early Han also used their warships to attack Yue and Korea, while the Latter Han rulers sent 2,000 'castled ships' against Jiao-zhi (present-day northern Vietnam) in the first century CE. This term 'lou-chuan' for warships continued through much of Chinese history.

For the most detailed account of Chinese ships over the succeeding 2,000 years, see Needham (1971). He discusses China's nautical history with unsurpassed erudition and unequalled references. Manguin (1984: 199) is of the opinion that the Chinese did not possess large ocean-going vessels before the eighth or ninth century.

Needham suggests the existence of large ships in an earlier period, but does concur that China's shipbuilding tradition saw its most rapid development during the ninth to twelfth centuries. He sees one of the ships portrayed at Borobodur (*c.* CE 800) as being Chinese, and claims that a ship carved on the Bayon at Angkor Thom (*c.* CE 1185) in Cambodia also represents a Chinese merchant ship.[6]

Twelfth-century accounts of Chinese trading ships are given in Chinese texts such as *Ling-wai Dai-da* and Marco Polo also described, in the late thirteenth century, four-masted, four-sailed Chinese merchant ships with up to sixty cabins, a rudder and a bulkhead-built hull. These observations were repeated by Ibn Battuta, half a century later (Needham, 1971: 465-70). In terms of the specific technologies employed in the ships, Needham (1971) examines the historical evolution of sails, rudders, bulkheads, anchors, caulking and other nautical components, while Turnbull and Reynolds (2002) provide a popular account of some Chinese fighting ships and illustrations thereof.

In short, historical evidence and ethnographic records tend to suggest that the ship-building tradition which produced the Chinese trading junk is marked by a number of characteristics. Five technical parameters were selected by Manguin (1984: 197) to describe various shipbuilding traditions and included the general shape of the hull, the type of stem and stern, the method of fastening the planking and frames, the presence or absence of watertight bulkheads and the type of sailing gear. The traditional Chinese designs[7] included the flat bottom hull form and a single layer of carvel planking strengthened by bulkheads and frame timbers and, an approximation to a rectangular cross-section. The vessels found in southeast China, in Guangdong, Hainan and in northern Vietnam also shared the characteristics of strakes and frames fastened with iron nails or clamps; structurally essential bulkheads dividing the hull into watertight components and single axial rudders.

Southeast Asian Ships

Needham (1971), in addition to detailing the history of Chinese ships, also records early Chinese textual references to ships in

Southeast Asia. An account of a Fu-nan boat by Kang Tai in the third century (Needham, 1971: 450) is particularly valuable, as it suggests connections with the dragon boats still seen in the riverine and maritime waters of Asia today. Needham also provides an account of the building of Cambodian ships dating from the thirteenth century.

A Chinese text from *c.* CE 750 also notes that the 'Kun-lun' ships from what is today Southeast Asia carried 1,000 men,[8] and that the ships were built with several thicknesses of side planks, that the parts of the ship were tied together using cord made from coconut fibre, and that the planks were caulked. They were propelled by sail (Needham, 1971: 459). The ships depicted on the walls of Borobodur (*c.* CE 800), with their sewn hulls, prominent stem- and stern-posts, outriggers, bipod or tripod masts, and square sails suggest a long-existing Southeast Asian tradition (Needham, 1971: 458 and Plate CDVII).

Horridge (1982) provides an excellent study of both contemporary and historical Southeast Asian boat-building—specifically 'the lashed lug' boats of the eastern archipelago. These *kora-kora* were fast and were used as warships as evidenced by their attacks on the Fu-jian coast in the twelfth century (Scott, 1981).

It appears that Southeast Asian ships up to the fourteenth century (or at least those documented so far) belong to a range of technical traditions which can be characterized as 'lashed-lug and stitched-plank'. The ships had V-shaped or U-shaped hulls with a keel. The ships were built by raising planks on either side of a keel, the components being held together with a variety of stitches and lashings made from sugar palm fibre. The lashed-lug technique involves carving protruding lugs on the inner side of the planks, with holes in the lugs for the planks to be lashed to ribs and/or thwarts making up a frame. The stitched-plank technique involves passing vegetal fibre through holes drilled at the edges of the planks. The practice of stitching planks gradually gave way to the use of wooden dowels.[9] One of the oldest examples is the *Pontian boat*, discovered in Pahang in modern Malaysia in 1926 and dated to the third to fifth century. This is detailed by Evans (1927) and Carl Gibson-Hill (1952).

It appears that some time in the late thirteenth century (and some say as a result of Kublai Khan's 1000-ship raid on Java in 1293), Southeast Asian ship-builders adopted the Chinese feature of transverse bulkheads. However, excavated vessels show that planking continued to be joined by wooden dowels rather than by iron bolts or nails.[10] This brings us on to the hybrid ships of the region.

The Hybrid 'South China Sea' Shipbuilding Tradition

Needham (1971: 457-8) suggests that even as early as the eighth century, there was mutual influence between Chinese and Southeast Asian shipbuilding traditions, with both being represented on the reliefs which adorn the walls of Borobodur in Java of *c.* CE 800. Poujade (1946) suggests that we can see the intermingling of components from the two traditions in a carving of a ship at the Bayon in Cambodia (*c.* CE 1185), with bulkheads from the Chinese tradition coexisting with a keel and true stem- and stern-posts from the Southeast Asian tradition.

Studies of the ships subsequent to the thirteenth century also suggest a hybrid shipbuilding tradition. Manguin (1984), on the basis of his analysis of a number of shipwrecks saw them as sharing characteristics of both Chinese and Southeast Asian types, a so-called 'South China Sea' tradition. For a probable scenario of this shipping form, see Reid (2000c). These vessels were built from tropical hardwood joined by wooden dowels but with the supplementary use of iron nails to fasten the transverse bulkheads to frames at the hull. This type of vessel, combining hardwood with Chinese construction details, may have been a result of the Ming ban against private overseas trade. Ships of this type have not yet been found prior to 1371 when the Ming ban became effective. It is possible that displaced Chinese merchants who moved to Southeast Asia at that stage may have been the first to order ships built in this manner. The *Nanyang* (*c.* 1380), *Longquan* (*c.* 1400), *Royal Nanhai* (*c.* 1460) and *Singtai* (*c.* 1550), all found in the seas around the Malay peninsula, are of this type, as are a number of shipwrecks found in the Gulf of Thailand. Both the Quanzhou and Shinan ships possess some aspects considered to belong to the hybrid South China Sea tradition. Similarities include the marked (and often hollow) deadrise in the sectional shape of the hull, the use of bulkheads with adjacent frames, the positioning and shape of the main mast step and the use of multi-layered planking. Vessels discovered in the Gulf of Thailand display some characteristics similar to the Quanzhou ship. For example, the Ko Khram shipwreck shows evidence for twelve bulkheads with the main mast step on the forward side of the sixth bulkhead.[11]

Japanese and Korean Shipbuilding

Japanese and Korean ship construction has received little attention in Western-language publications. Purvis (1919) wrote on ship construction in Japan, while Bonar (2000) has discussed more generally the maritime enterprise in Japan. The classic work by Underwood (1934, 1979 rpt) under the title *Korean Ships and Boats*, provides one of the best overviews of Korean ships and their technologies. Much of what Needham (1971) writes on relating to Chinese ship construction also can be shown to have manifestations, to varying degrees, in other north-east Asian shipbuilding traditions. Yang (1990) shows how certain nautical technologies were shared among China, Korea and Japan. Jeon Sang-won (1974), in his study of traditional Korean science and technology, also specifically examines Korean nautical technologies.

Turnbull and Reynolds (2003) suggest that the naval traditions of Japan and Korea have long been closely linked, and discuss and illustrate both Japanese and Korean early ship-types. They describe the manufacture of Korean ships and the existence of double-masted sailing vessels known as *kyongtanson* on which up to 150 persons were sent on missions to China by the kingdoms of Paekche (18 BCE-CE 660) and Silla (57 BCE-CE 935) in the fourth century.

The true Korean military vessels did not see any rapid development until the Koryo period (CE 935-1392), and by the eleventh century the *kwason* (spear vessel) capable of ramming Jurchen vessels was being produced. A Song account of 1123 noted two types of ships—one derived from Song styles and one a Koryo version, being simpler and sturdier. Some of the latter would have been the Korean ships which accompanied the Yuan naval forces in their invasion of Korea in 1281. By the Choson period, the stress was firmly on warships, which were box-like, sturdy, not particularly swift, and carrying crews of eighty, sixty or thirty sailors. By the fifteenth century, new troop-carrying ships were being produced and in the mid-sixteenth century, Korea's first paddle-wheel ship was built.

One of the key developments of the Korean navy in the sixteenth century was the production of *p'anokson* (board-roofed or superstructure ships), which had both sail and oar propulsion, and which had an extra deck so that the oarsmen below could be separated from the fighters above. They carried about 125 persons and it was these ships which formed the majority of the craft in the Korean navy which fought the Japanese in 1592 (Turnbull and Reynolds, 2003). The 'turtle ship' is the most famous of the Korean warships and is always linked with Admiral Yi Sun-sin. Following in the Korean ship tradition, it was wide and solid. Removing the castle from the deck of the *p'anokson*, it roofed over the entire space, providing a 'turtle-like' protection. It was armed with guns.

The Japanese ship-building tradition seems to have been closely connected to that of mainland Asia—China and Korea. Ships were obviously able to carry people to the mainland in the seventh century. However, little is known of the ships of the Heian and Kamakura periods. We do have illustrations of the naval battles of the Gempei War in the twelfth century, showing an imperial flagship with a decorative one-storey superstructure. Others were less decorative and they were accompanied by diverse smaller ships, powered by a single oarsman. The persons termed *wako* who wandered the East Asian maritime realm from the fourteenth century sailed in a range of vessels—some converted merchant junks which were mainly sail-powered, but often had auxiliary oars. Larger ships had two masts and a central deck castle.

The Sengoku period (mid-fifteenth to mid-seventeenth centuries) saw the creation of dedicated fighting ships for the first time. The *ataka bune* were some of the largest such ships, as the battleships of the navies of the various *daimyos*. Similar to the Korean *p'anokson*, it was very square, with the side wall of a single surface. It was both oar- and sail-powered, and the normal complement was eighty oarsmen and sixty fighting men.

East Asian Maritime Activities

The range of activities involving the East Asian maritime realm is huge, but the essential elements have always been transport, trade and warfare. Many of these activities have already been touched upon above, and only a brief overview will be attempted here in order to highlight some of the major Western-language works relating to these spheres.

China

Again Needhams' work (1971) must be invoked as an essential text for any study of maritime activities in the East Asian realm. His study includes nautics, navigation, voyages of discovery, trade and warfare, all centred on the theme of the Chinese maritime realm. The fluctuating fortunes of the Chinese navies have been examined by Lo Jung-pang in his various works (1955, 1958, 1969 and 1976).

In the trade realm, Wang Gungwu (1958) provides an introduction to the so-called 'Nan-hai Trade', examining the diplomatic and trading relations between successive Chinese states and the polities of (mainly maritime) Southeast Asia over the period from the Han until the Five Dynasties, while Wake (1997) examines the ocean-going ships of southern China and their voyages to India from the twelfth to the fifteenth centuries. The developments of Chinese maritime trade in the fifteenth and sixteenth century are included in studies on piracy and smuggling by Wiethoff (1963) and So Kwan-wai (1975).

Deng Gang (2003) has investigated the growth of China's maritime trade activities under the Song, the Ming and the Qing, examining them from the angle of the state *versus* the market as the main agent of economic growth. The Song, he concluded, was the most pro-market by far, but Song growth was unsustainable because of the mismanagement of the country's national defence by the money-hungry state. The Ming had an extremely weak market due to state discrimination and thus a sharp decline in maritime growth was inevitable. He sums up the two periods: the Song pattern was commercially desirable but politically and militarily damaging, while the Ming pattern was politically and militarily motivated but commercially disastrous.

The importance of overseas trade during the Song dynasties is underlined in the various essays in Schottenhammer (2001), which examine the important maritime entrepôt of Quanzhou, as well as the monograph on South Fu-jian by So (2000). This factor is reinforced by Jacq-Hergoualc'h (2002) in his examination of Song interaction with Southeast Asia.

The 'tribute/trade system' which so marked the latter 'Chinese world order' was intimately involved with the maritime realm, as a large percentage of tribute envoys/traders arrived in China by sea. Fairbank (1968) and the contributors to the volume the *Chinese World Order* provide a useful overview of some of the concepts and practices which constituted this tribute/trade system. Hamashita (1988) considers that the Chinese tribute system was the key element in pre-modern relations in East Asia and believes that to understand modern Asia, we need to 'trace how each country and area within Asia attempted to cope with the transformation of the tribute system' (1988: 23).

The Ming dynasty (1368-1644) constituted a key period in Chinese maritime history, both because of the maritime prohibitions that the Ming rulers initially instituted and the fact that the early Ming emperor Yong-le despatched his eunuch admirals on repeated voyages to Southeast Asia and the Indian Ocean. The Ming maritime prohibitions and their effects in terms of the lack of Jingdezhen ceramics reaching Southeast Asia and the response of Southeast Asians to this change have been discussed by Harrisson (1958) and Brown (2002).

The Zheng He voyages have generated a huge literature, and works by Phillips (1885-6), Pelliot (1933, 1935), Duyvendak (1937, 1938), Wang Gungwu (1964, 1968b, 1970), Mills (1974), Ray (1993) and Ptak (1996) stand prominently among the Western-language sources on the voyages. More popular works include those by Levathes and the extremely contentious volume *1421* by Menzies (2002). Needham (1971) characterizes the Zheng He voyages as 'a navy paying friendly visits to foreign ports', echoing the claims by most Peoples' Republic of China historians. The possibility of the Zheng He voyages being much more aggressive and violent than presently represented, as the armadas sought to dominate the trade routes across the East Asian realm and the Indian Ocean has been suggested by Wade (2003), who terms the voyages and their impetus 'proto-colonialism'.

The major studies by Deng Gang (1997, 1999) provide very valuable overviews of China and the maritime realm, and useful summaries of studies originally presented in Chinese. The earlier volume examines the evolution of Chinese maritime technologies and what this meant for the emergence of maritime trade patterns, markets, urbanization of the coastal region and migration overseas. The latter volume also comprises an economic and institutional study of the Chinese maritime realm, but includes more attention to the evolution and decline of China's sea power.

Japan and Korea

Western-language literature relating to Japanese and Korean maritime activities in the pre-modern era is much more limited than that relating to China and Southeast Asia. Ballard (1921) examined the sea as a generic factor in the Japan's history, while the role of naval strategy in Japanese history has been written on by Kiralfy (1944). Sadler (1937) and Turnbull (2002) both studied the sixteenth-century war between Japan and Korea and its maritime elements. Turnbull and Reynolds (2003) examined and illustrated aspects of Japanese and Korean naval warfare. The so-called 'Japanese pirates' in Ming China and their activities during the sixteenth century were studied by So Kwan-wai (1975).

In the trade realm, Mori (1972) has examined the overseas advance of Japanese merchant ships. Ptak (1994) presents a study of Japanese-Chinese maritime trade in about 1550. Links between Japan and Southeast Asia are also studied by Satow (1885), Cho Hungguk (2000), Hasebe (1991), Iioka (2003), Ishii (1971, 1988, 1998).

As for the maritime trade relations of Ryukyu, Kobata and Matsuda (1969) provides important first-hand materials, Ishii (1990) looks at how the islands were tied into Southeast Asian trade, while Ryukyu's trade with China is the subject of Chang Pin-Tsun's thesis (1983). Lee Hyoun-jong (1977) is a study of Ryukyuan links with Korea. Japan's connections with Southeast Asian ports and polities are examined in Satow (1885) and Ishii (1971, 1988, 1992, 1998). Robert Sakai's study (1968) examines Ryukyu as a fief of Satsuma. Momoki Shiro (1999) looks at the rivalry between Ryukyu and Dai Viet as tribute/trade partners of the Ming.

In terms of Korean maritime activities, Needham (1971: 453-4) examines the importance of Korean shipowners and merchants in ninth-century Asian maritime affairs. In the naval realm, Hazard (1973) has examined the rise of the Korean navy, and also written on the Korean response to the Wako (1976). Korean diplomacy with Chinese states is looked at by Chun Hae-jong (1968), Rogers (1991), Shultz (1988), Sung Shee (1995) and Tao Jing-shen (1988).

Maritime linkages between Korean polities and those of Southeast Asia in the pre-modern era include Cho Hungguk (1995) which examines early contacts between Korea and Thailand, while Ch'oe Sang-su (1983) looks at Korea-Indonesia relations in the fifteenth century. Cho Hungguk (2000) also tries to paint an outline of the regional East Asian trading system in the early modern era by examining the trade between China, Japan, Korea and Southeast Asia in the fourteenth to seventeenth centuries.

Southeast Asia

Quite a large corpus of work has been created through Western-language studies of the diverse maritime activities in Southeast Asia. Ferrand's study of 'Le K'ouen-louen' (1919) was a path-breaking work which provided a synthesis of early maritime activities in Southeast Asia. Trade has attracted most attention in the studies of Southeast Asian maritime activities. As mentioned above, Wang Gungwu (1958) has examined trade between Southeast Asia and China in the first millennium CE. Bronson (1977) has created a model to explain the upstream-downstream interactions in the emergence of coastal trading polities in Southeast Asia, while Leong Sau Heng (1990) has also written on collecting centres, feeder points and entrepôts in the Malay Peninsula from 1000 BCE to CE 1400. Kenneth Hall (1985) looks at the interrelationship between trade and statecraft in various periods and across diverse polities in early Southeast Asia. Wolters (1967) engages with early trade in what is today western Indonesia. Van Leur (1955) theorises about the nature of Indonesian trade, while Whitmore (1977) suggests a framework for the study of pre-modern Southeast Asian trade by looking at the patterns of penetration from outside the region. Hall and Whitmore (1976) look at trade as an element in the "isthmian struggles" over the period from CE 1000 to 1200. The various essays in Hutterer (1978) include Bronson's study as well as Hutterer's own study of the role of trade in the emergence of Philippines societies. Other studies which link trade and the emergence of early Southeast Asian polities include Christie (1990), Day (2002), Hall (1985) and the essays in Hall and Whitmore (1976a) and Marr and Milner (1986).

The ninth and tenth centuries were obviously a boom period for trade both between Southeast Asia and China and for ceramics trade between the Middle East and China through Southeast Asian ports. Jacq-Hergoualc'h (2002: 257-300) discusses the ninth century and the role of entrepôt ports in the Malay peninsula, and also sees another commercial boom affecting the peninsula during the twelfth and thirteenth centuries in Tambralinga and Kedah. Christie (1998) looks at Asian sea trade between the tenth and thirteenth centuries and its impact on the states of Java and Bali. Miksic and Yap (1992) examine archipelagic maritime trade over the period twelfth to fourteenth centuries.

The extent to which, and the period during which, maritime commerce played a role in the evolution of the polities of Southeast Asia remains a debated point. Momoki (1998) argues that Đại Việt, the forerunner of modern Vietnam, for example, was no longer a great South China Sea trading centre by the time it gained independence from China in the tenth century. Nevertheless, its subsequent state development continued to depend more on the control of trade networks and export commodities than on peasants and agrarian produce. From the thirteenth to the fifteenth centuries, Đại Việt undertook large-scale hydraulic works on the Red River delta and founded a Chinese-style bureaucracy. Such Sinicization not only increased the area's agricultural potential but also fostered the development of new export commodities, including ceramics. Its strength renewed, Đại Việt crushed the rival polity of Champa and proceeded to seize prosperous ports in modern central Vietnam, thus re-establishing itself as the pre-eminent force in the region's maritime trade.

Moving into later centuries, commerce and trade form the core of Anthony Reid's thesis in *Southeast Asia in the Age of Commerce 1450-1680* (Reid, 1988, 1993a, 1993b). He says that Southeast Asia played a crucial role in the sustained boom of the 'long sixteenth century' which affected Europe and much of Asia, firstly through it being the source of the spices, and secondly because it was through the Southeast Asian port polities—'the leading regional centres of economic life, political power and cultural creativity'—that this trade flowed. He sees this as giving rise to changes in urbanism, commerce, religious organizations and state structures, and ushering in the 'early modern' period in Southeast Asia.

Indic Maritime Links with Southeast Asia

One of the greatest sources of cultural influence on Southeast Asia in the first millennium CE and the first half of the second millennium was the region we generically refer to as South Asia. Influences travelled both overland and via maritime routes, and for island Southeast Asia obviously exclusively by the latter avenue. The major studies by Majumdar (1927, 1933, 1934a, 1934b) on Champa, the Shailendras and the Cholas provided a basis for his later works (1937-8) which examined the overall Indic influences on Southeast Asia, including maritime links. Other Indian scholars who have worked on this area included B.C. Chhabra (1935, 1935a, 1956), and Sarkar (1971, 1986). A number of these studies are seen by some as being excessively Indo-centric, but they were still important bases for later works by George Çoedes (1956, 1957, 1964a, 1964b), Wheatley (1961 and 1975), and Guy (1993-4). The interactions in the art sphere are dealt with by Coomaraswamy (1972). Ramchandran's work (1996) contains an excellent bibliography of works which examine links, including the maritime, between India and Southeast Asia.

The Cholas and their involvement in the maritime and political affairs of Southeast Asian polities has attracted attention from a range of scholars. The classic work is by Nilakanta Sastri (1935-7), and this is supplemented by the earlier Aiyangar and Sewell (1932). Blagden (1920) and Spenser (1988) are also useful in this area.

Indic inscriptions in Malaysia, mainly in Sanskrit, have been well studied over the last 130 years, and the relevant works include Low (1878), Kern (1907), Christie (1988-9) and Weeraprajak (1989). There has also been much work done on the Tamil inscriptions discovered in Southeast and East Asia, and the associated Tamil guilds.[12] The earliest of the associations to have left a record was the Manigramam, which appears to have been actively involved in transit trade bypassing the Malacca Straits during a period of local political turmoil. Most of the thirteenth-century Tamil inscriptions abroad do not appear to mention merchant associations, perhaps reflecting the sharp decline in the economic power of these associations within south India during the course of the thirteenth century. Studies of Tamil links with Southeast Asia include Nilakanta Sastri (1932a, 1932b, 1944, 1949), Hultzsch (1913, 1914), Karashima (1995) and McKinnon (1996).[13]

Maritime Routes and Trade Networks

The routes followed by mariners of diverse origins are necessarily an integral element in studying the East Asia maritime realm, and its historical evolution. Tibbets (1971, 1973, 1979) provides, through his translations of Arabic routiers and other accounts, an inchoate yet useful picture of Asian navigation routes followed by Arab sailors from the ninth to sixteenth centuries.

European-language studies of Chinese navigation routes include those by Mills (1974, 1979), which provide detailed sailing directions for ships travelling between and among Chinese and Southeast Asian ports from the fourteenth to seventeenth centuries. Ptak (1992, 1998d, 2000b) has examined Chinese navigation routes in the region of the Sulu zone and the Moluccas. The Hokkien network which grew around these trade routes from the fifteenth century, and which grew to connect most of the major ports in East Asia, has been detailed in an outstanding new work by James Chin Kong whose thesis on the subject completed in 1998 was undertaken under the supervision of Wang Gungwu.

In terms of more local routes, Pensak Howitz (1977: 2-3) maps what she considers are the three main trade routes out of the Chao Phraya Valley from the fourteenth to sixteenth centuries—the first along the east coast towards Cambodia; the second a sea route directly from the Chao Phraya River to Nakhon Si Thammarat, Songkhla and Phattalung; and the third a coastal route to the west which follows the coast to Prachuap Khiri Khan, Chumpon and Pattani. The shipwrecks found on these various routes had fairly different cargoes. The third route, for example, had smaller ships and inferior cargoes.

There is less literature on the northern East Asian routes and routiers. Yoon Moo-byong (1977) discusses the likely route sailed by the Sinan ship prior to its sinking off Korea.

A few Vietnamese texts relating to maritime Asia have been the subject of studies in Western-language scholarship. One of the more interesting texts which is now being investigated is the *Xiêm-la-Quốc Lồ-trình Tập-lục*, an early nineteenth-century maritime routier, which seems likely to reflect sea routes used for centuries by the Vietnamese. Wade (1998) has translated it into English and annotated the route which extends from the Mekong delta, along the coast of Cambodia and Thailand, down the Malay Peninsula to Singapore and back up to the Phuket island in Thailand.

The Trans-Peninsular Routes (?)

Perhaps one of the most contentious issues relating to Southeast Asian maritime trade routes is whether or not land routes across the Malay Peninsula served as portages between the maritime routes in the South China Sea and those in the Andaman Sea and into the Indian Ocean. In the early sixteenth century, Eredia (1997: facing p. 25) showed the 'Panarican' on his map of the peninsula,[14] a porterage connecting the upper reaches of the Muar and Pahang rivers, providing a trans-peninsular crossing. Wheatley (1961: 163-72) introduces the various references to the Penarikan transpeninsular route, which he considers was used as a route for goods of little bulk but great value such as gold dust. Wheatley (1961: xxvi) also illustrates the major trans-peninsular routes, which may or may not have been used for transportation of cargoes.

Ho Chuimei (1994b) examines the ninth- and tenth-century ceramics found at Kho Khao and Laem Pho-Payang two ports opposite each other across the Isthmus of Kra in the bay of Bandon in southern Thailand. There have been suggestions that these two ports were the ends of a trans-peninsular porterage route, but Ho does not seem to endorse this claim. A decade earlier, Manguin (1983) had stated his opinion on the unlikelihood of trans-peninsular porterages, while Bronson (1996) rejected the idea more openly. Jacq-Hergoualc'h (2002) suggests that the ceramics which were being transported by sea between the Middle East and China or vice versa in the ninth and tenth centuries would not have survived porterage through the land routes, and this leads him to 'doubt even further the reality of these transpeninsular routes'. Reid (1993a) describes the use of these portages in seventeenth-century accounts.

The Coming of Islam to Maritime Asia

One of the great changes that affected maritime Asia over the millennium which extended from the eighth century CE, to the eighteenh century CE was the arrival and gradual adoption of Islam through much of the archipelago. The spread of the religion relied heavily on the maritime links which existed in the region, and thus it can be truly said that the spread of Islam constitutes part of the maritime history of Asia.

In his study of the historiography of the issue, Drewes (1968) considers the gravestones (dating from the eleventh century), local histories and external sources for studying the arrival of Islam in the region. He suggests that the Muslims of the Coromandel coast in India played a major role in introducing Islam to areas which are today in Indonesia. That some Sumatran polities had adopted the religion by the thirteenth century seems to be well-accepted. Not surprisingly, Hugronje (1906) sees the participants in the international maritime trade as having been the carriers of the religion. In 1963, S.Q. Fatimi suggested that the rulers of Pasai derived from Bengal, but other scholars, particularly Marrison, suggest a likely south Indian source for Pasai's Islam. Hall (1977) investigates this issue further, while other ideas are provided by Marrison (1951). Manguin (1985c) and Nakamura (2000) look at the introduction of Islam to Champa, while Islamization in Java has been investigated by Ricklefs (1979). Denys Lombard (1990) places this Islamization in a global perspective.

The contentious *Malay Annals of Semarang and Cirebon* translated by de Graaf, Pigeaud and Ricklefs (1984) offers the possibility of Islamization of much of Nusantara through the efforts of Chinese Muslims during the fifteenth and sixteenth century. This thesis is supported by the work of Tan Yeok Seong (1962). Separately, Alijah Gordon (2001) has usefully brought together a range of Western-language scholarship on Islamization in Southeast Asia into a single volume.

Reid (1995) has discussed how Austronesian societies reacted to the proponents of Islamic beliefs and how they adapted Islamic beliefs and practices into their existing set of beliefs. He has also argued (Reid, 1993c) that Islamization provided the potential for radical changes in these societies by introducing an external set of ideals, changes which he sees as mainly occurring later, in the sixteenth and seventeenth centuries. In his 'The Islamization of Southeast Asia' (Reid, 2000a), he provides an overview of the social and political impacts of the religion on Southeast Asia.

East Asian Maritime Trade Commodities

The ships which traversed the waters of the East Asia maritime realm were, to a large degree, trading vessels, carrying commodities for sale, distribution or on forwarding at other ports. In understanding the economic development of East Asia and its component part, some understanding of the commodities which were traded (and often also produced) in the region is essential. Below, we will discuss the major Western-language studies of maritime trade commodities in East Asia.

Generic Studies of Trade Commodities

In his study of 'The Nan-hai Trade' Wang Gungwu (1958) examined, *inter alia*, the commodities which formed part of this trade during the period from the Qin to the end of the Tang dynasty (second century BCE to tenth century CE). Paul Wheatley (1959) wrote in much detail on the various commodities involved in East Asian trade during the Song dynasties (tenth to thirteenth centuries), including the origins of the products. In his study of the tax rates imposed on various commodities imported into Zhang-zhou during the early seventeenth century, Chang Tseng-hsin (1991) specifically examines those commodities which were being imported into China in the late Ming.

Ceramics

Ceramics are the commodities which have been preserved best in the archaeological record. It is thus that they are sometimes given more prominence than they deserve in our studies of East Asia trade. That said, ceramics were still enormously important in the commercial interactions throughout Asia and one of the key links between the societies of the region.

Chinese and Arab ceramics were being shipped across the South China Sea as early as the ninth century (see Flecker, 2000). By the twelfth century, enormous quantities of Chinese green-glazed ceramics (Celadon) were being exported to the Middle East, India and throughout Southeast Asia. At the beginning of the Ming dynasty (1368-1644), when prohibitions on overseas trade were proclaimed, Chinese potters or at least their technologies appear to have moved to Thailand and resumed production. The earliest Southeast Asian exporters were kilns in what are today Thailand and Vietnam, and these wares were traded frequently with Japan, the Philippines, Borneo and the Indonesian archipelago. Roxanna Brown, in her various publications (1977, 1989), suggests that potters based in Southeast Asian countries made and shipped the largest volumes of ceramics traded on the South China Sea between the fourteenth and sixteenth centuries. Asian markets predominated, despite some trade with the Middle East, until the early seventeenth century when Europeans started to ship large volumes of Chinese blue-and-white porcelain to Europe.

The discussions above suggest the degree to which ceramics have been used in plotting the pre-modern history of East Asia and relations between the societies and polities of the region. There is a large range of Western-language works which discuss the ceramics found in shipwrecks, those imported ceramics excavated on land sites and those imported by waters found in local collections, all of which add to our knowledge of the maritime realm, and which are a huge field of investigation in themselves.[15] An important aspect of Chinese ceramic production for external markets was the degree to which it was ready to adjust to the market demand. Some, for example, incorporated Islamic elements to meet the demand in Southeast Asia and beyond.[16]

Textiles

One of the East Asian trade commodities which is not usually found in archaeological deposits, but which obviously formed a large part of intra-Asian maritime trade goods is textiles. Chinese silks and other textiles were much sought after in places beyond China, while Indian textiles also formed a major cargo item between India and East Asia. The latter trade forms the core of John Guy's recent work *Woven Cargoes* (1998). Haraprasad Ray (1991) has also conducted studies on how Chinese terms can be correlated with types of Indian textiles.[17] Christie (1993) has examined the roles of textiles in medieval Java.

Spices and Aromatics

One of the great impetuses for maritime explorations was the search for spices and aromatics. It was these that motivated the merchants and polities of Southeast Asian trade for ceramics, silks and metals which so obviously constituted the major flow from the north of East Asia to its South.

In respect of pepper and cloves, Bulbeck, Reid, Tan and Wu

(1998) provide an attempt at quantifying the production and trade flows of pepper from the fourteenth century onwards.[18] Ptak (1993b, 1995) looks at the clove trade in Asia in about CE 1500. Other early references to the pepper trade are provided by Tien Ju-kang (1981), who examines the pepper trade *vis-à-vis* the role of the Zheng He voyages, and Ts'ao Yung-ho (1982) who has provided a useful overview of the early pepper trade in East Asia.

Camphor has long been a much sought-after product in East Asia, and it features in many of the early lists of trading goods carried by ships and tribute missions to China. Wheatley (1959) looks at the Song period trade in camphor, while Ptak (2000a) uses Chinese and Portuguese sources to outline the East Asian trade in camphor around CE 1500. His study of Barus (1998a) also relates closely to the topic. Nicholl (1979) examined camphor and its links with Brunei. Bryant (1925) has investigated Chinese camphor and camphor oil, while Donkin (1999) provides possibly the most detailed historical geography of camphor yet available. Ptak (1987) has also examined the trade in sandalwood and the way in which it linked Timor and China. Groom (1981) has investigated the flows of frankincense and myrrh, which were also highly sought after commodities in East Asia.

Conclusion

The studies introduced above are essentially restricted -- by language, to Western language texts and by region, to the East Asian maritime realm. A vast range of other materials is available in Asian and other European languages on these regions, so the materials surveyed herein must be seen as only limited vignettes of the available resources and analyses.

In addition, there is an increasing tendency for historians to not distinguish the Northeast Asian and Southeast Asian maritime spaces from those of the Bay of Bengal and the further Indian Ocean, with scholars now preferring to see these oceans as connected bridges between all of Asia. The importance of such connections is highlighted by a growing literature on inter-Asian interactions through time, and a range of Indian Ocean research programmes which see their scope of research extending from the Indian Ocean into the East

Asian maritime realm.[19] A few works might be cited to assist those interested in further pursuing the most recent studies of Indian Ocean research and its connections with the East Asian maritime realm. These include a number of studies on the general importance of the oceans as connectors, such as those by Lombard and Aubin (1988) and Mukherjee (2012). Overall maritime studies across the Indian Ocean include the works of Hourani (1951) and Chaudhuri (1985); and the research contained in Ray and Salles (1996/2012) and Ray and Alpers (2007). Michael Pearson (2011) has reviewed most recent works in this field. Major Bay of Bengal maritime studies include Prakash and Lombard (1999), Subrahmanyam (1999), Gommans and Leider (2002), and Mukherjee (2011). On the maritime connections between South Asia and Southeast Asia, recent collections include Kulke, Kesavapany and Sakhuja (2009); and Manguin, Mani and Wade (2011), while longer distance maritime links between the South Asian and East Asian seas are examined in Haraprasad Ray (1991) and Sen (2003 and 2006).

Again, these are but suggestions to introduce readers to a much broader range of literature on the Indian Ocean and its connections with the seas of Southeast and Northeast Asia. Like the other contributions to this volume, this chapter is intended to reveal the importance of these seas in terms of trade, human movement and evolving nautical technologies in the lives of those who lived on their shores. The importance of these highways of history is increasingly imposing itself on earlier land-centred conceptions of the human past, and it is hoped that this guide will assist in furthering our understanding of the seas which linked, and indeed today still connect, diverse parts of Asia.

NOTES

1. This is an abridged version of the author's paper that first appeared in the *Asia Research Institute Working Paper Series*, no. 16, December 2003. Due to space constraints, two sections from the 2003 paper, viz., 'Studies of Major Ports and Port Polities' and 'Shipwreck Studies' have not been included here.
2. The term 'East Asia' here is used as a broad shorthand for the West Pacific regions often termed North Asia and Southeast Asia.

3. Roughly, prior to the sixteenth century.
4. Given the name of Proto-Austronesian.
5. There are opponents to this view. See for example, Meacham (1984-5) who argues against a South China origin for the Austronesians.
6. See also Poujade (1946) for a study of this carving.
7. www.mm.wa.gov.au/Museum/march/excavate/Bai_Jiao/ship/bj1_ship.html.
8. Generally this is considered an exaggeration.
9. In South Sulawesi and the Malaysian state of Terengganu, shipbuilders still use dowels, www.maritimeasia.ws/topic/shiptypes.html.
10. www.maritimeasia.ws/topic/shiptypes.html (Brown and Sjostrand, 2000, 2002).
11. www.mm.wa.gov.au/Museum/march/excavate/Bai_Jiao/ship/bj1_ship.html.
12. Of the eight Tamil-language inscriptions only three definitely mention south Indian merchant associations: the ninth-century inscription from Takuapa on the west coast of the peninsula, the inscription dated CE 1088 from Lobo Tua on the west coast of Sumatra, and the thirteenth-century inscription from Pagan in Upper Burma. See: ismaili.net/Source/0104c.html
13. For a general study of the Tamil guilds, see Abraham (1988). Subbarayalu (1998) provides a new interpretation of the Barus inscription. A useful website in this area is that at: http://ismaili.net/Source/0104c.html.
14. In Malay, the term is 'Penarikan'.
15. Some of the more prominent include: Roxanna Brown's publications, Aoyagi (1991, 1999); Brown and Sjostrand (2002); Charoenwongsa and Prishanchit (1990); Diem (1998-2001); Flecker (1999); Goddio (2000); Green and Harper (1987); Gotuaco, Tan and Diem (1997); Guy (1986, 1987); Hadimuljono and Macknight (1983); Ho Chuimei (1994a), Jörg and Flecker (2001); Mikami (1983); Othman bin Mohd Yatim (1984, 1988); Richards (1995); Roxas-Lim (1987); Scott and Guy (1995); Sjostrand (1997); So (1994) and Yun (1998). Chinese and Vietnamese ceramics imported into Japan are detailed in Honda and Shimizu (1993).
16. See the study by Chen Da-sheng (1995) for further details.
17. For a specific study of textiles in Sino-Southeast Asian trade, see Lee Chor Lin (1995).
18. Bulbeck, Reid, Tan and Wu (1998) also examine coffee and sugar exports in Southeast Asia, but these records fall beyond the temporal limits of this paper.

19. These include the Nalanda-Sriwijaya Centre at the Institute of Southeast Asian Studies, Singapore (http://nsc.iseas.edu.sg/), the Indian Ocean World Centre at McGill University, Canada (http://indianoceanworldcentre.com/), the Sealinks Project at the University of Oxford (http://sealinks.arch.ox.ac.uk) and the 'Trade, Migration and Cultural Change in the Indian Ocean' project at the Department of History, University of Bergen, Denmark. A new journal which addresses these maritime connections is *Crossroads*, edited by Angela Schottenhammer.

REFERENCES

Abraham, Meera, 1988, *Two Medieval Merchant Guilds of South India*, New Delhi: Manohar.

Aiyangar S. Krishnaswami and Robert Sewell, 1932, *Historical Inscriptions of Southern India*, Madras: Diocesan Press, Vepery.

Aoyagi, Yoji, 1991, 'Vietnamese Ceramics Discovered on Southeast Asian Islands', The National Committee for the International Symposium on the Ancient Town of Hoi An (ed.), *Ancient Town of Hoi An*, Hanoi: Foreign Languages Publishing House.

———, 1999, 'Production and trade of Champa Ceramics in the 15th Century', Nguyen The Anh, and Ishizawa Yoshiaki (eds.), *Commerce et navigation en Asie du Sud-Est (XIVe-XIXe siecle) = Trade and Navigation in Southeast Asia (14th-19th centuries)*, Paris and Montreal: L'Harmattan.

Ballard, George Alexander, 1921, *The Influence of the Sea on the Political History of Japan*, London: John Murray (Reprinted Greenwood Press London, 1973).

Bellwood, Peter, 1978, *Man's Conquest of the Pacific: The Prehistory of Southeast Asia and Oceania*, Auckland: Collins.

———, 1985, *Prehistory of the Indo-Malaysian Archipelago*, London: Academic Press.

———, 1995, 'Austronesian Prehistory in Southeast Asia: Homeland Expansion and Transformation', in P. Bellwood, J. Fox and D. Tryon, (eds.), *The Austronesians: Historical and Comparative Perspectives*, Canberra: Australian National University: 96-111.

Bellwood, Peter and Peter Koon, 1989, 'Lapita Colonists Leave Boats Unburned! The Question of Lapita Links with Island Southeast Asia', *Antiquity* 63: 613-22.

Bellwood, Peter, James Fox and Darrell Tryon (eds.), 1995, *The Austronesians: Historical and Comparative Perspectives,* Canberra: Australian National University.

Bernet-Kempers, August Johan, 1986, 'The Kettledrums of Southeast Asia', *Modern Quaternary Research in Southeast Asia*, no. 10.

Blagden, Charles Otto, 1920, 'The Empire of the Maharaja, King of the Mountains and Lord of the Isles', *Journal of the Straits Branch, Royal Asiatic Society*, vol. 81: 23-8.

Bonar, H.A.C., 1887, 'On Maritime Enterprise in Japan', *Transactions of the Asiatic Society of Japan*, vol. 15. Reprinted in Stephen Turnbull (ed.), *The Samurai Tradition*, Japan Library, 2000.

Brill Robert H. and J.H. Martin (eds.), 1991, *Scientific Research into Early Chinese Glass*, New York: Corning.

Bronson, Bennet, 1977, 'Exchange at the Upstream and Downstream Ends: Notes Toward a Functional Model of the Coastal State in Southeast Asia', in Karl L. Hutterer (ed.), *Economic Exchange and Social Interaction in Southeast Asia: Perspectives from Prehistory, History, and Ethnography*, Ann Arbor: University of Michigan, Center for South and Southeast Asian Studies: 39-52.

———, 1996, 'Chinese and Middle Eastern Trade in Southern Thailand during the 9th Century A.D.', in Amara Srisuchat (ed.), *Ancient Trades and Cultural Contacts in Southeast Asia,* Bangkok: Office of the National Cultural Commission: 181-200.

Brown, Roxanna, 1975, 'Preliminary Report on the Ko Khram Sunken Ship', *Oriental Art Magazine*, vol. 1/ 4: 356-370.

———, 1977, *The Ceramics of South-East Asia: Their Dating and Identification*, Kuala Lumpur: Oxford University Press.

———, 1989, *Guangdong Ceramics from Butuan and Other Philippine Sites*, Manila: Oriental Cramic Society of the Philippines/Oxford University Press.

———, 2002, 'Sangkhalok and Asia', in Kasetsiri Charnvit (ed.), *Sangkhalok-Sukothai-Ayutthaya and Asia*, Bangkok: Toyota Thailand Foundation: 74-92.

Brown, Roxanna and Sjostrand, Sten, 2000, *Turiang: A Fourteenth Century Shipwreck in Southeast Asian Waters*, Los Angeles: Pacific Asia Museum.

———, 2002, *Maritime Archaeology and Shipwreck Ceramics in Malaysia*, Kuala Lumpur: Department of Museums and Antiquities.

Bryant, P. L., 1925, 'Chinese Camphor and Camphor Oil', *The China Journal of Science and Arts* 3: 228-34.

Bulbeck, David et al. (comp.), 1998, *South East Asian Exports since the 14th Century Cloves, Pepper, Coffee, and Sugar,* Singapore: Institute of South East Asian Studies and The Netherlands: KITV Press.

Chang, Pin-tsun, 1983, 'Chinese Maritime Trade: The Case of Sixteenth century Fu-chien', Princeton University, unpublished PhD dissertation.

Chang, Tseng-hsin, 1991, 'Commodities imported into the Chang-chou Region of Fukien During the Late Ming Dynasty: A Preliminary Analysis of the Tax Lists Found in *Tung-his-yang k'ao*', in Roderich Ptak and Dietmar Rothermund (eds.), *Emporia, Commodities and Entrepreneurs in Asian Maritime Trade, c. 1400-1750,* Stuttgart: Franz Steiner Verlag Wiesbaden GmbH: 231-62.

Charnvit Kasetsiri, 1976, *The Rise of Ayudhya: A History of Siam in the Fourteenth and Fifteenth Centuries,* Kuala Lumpur: Oxford University Press.

Charoenwongsa, Pisit and Sayan Prishanchit 1990, *Underwater Archaeology in Thailand II: Ceramics from the Gulf of Thailand,* Bangkok: Department of Fine Arts.

Chaudhuri, Kirti N., 1985, *Trade and Civilisation in the Indian Ocean,* Cambridge and New York: Cambridge University Press.

Chen Da-sheng, 1995, 'Chinese Influence on Archaeological Finds in South East Asia', in Rosemary Scott and John Guy (eds.), *Southeast Asia & China: Art, Interaction, and Commerce,* London: Percival David Foundation of Chinese Art; Singapore: Sun Tree Publishers: 55-63.

Chhabra, Bahadur Chand, 1935, 'Expansion of Indo-Aryan Culture during Pallava Rule, as Evidenced by Inscriptions', *Journal of the Asiatic Society of Bengal,* vol. I: 1-64.

———, 1935a, 'Identification of "Śrī Visnuvarman" of the Perak Seal', *Journal of the Greater India Society,* vol. II: 71-5.

———, 1956, 'Ancient India and South-East Asia', *Indo-Asian Culture,* vol. 4, no. 3: 301-7.

Cho, Hungguk, 1995, 'Early Contacts between Korea and Thailand', *Korea Journal* 35: 1 (Spring 1995): 106-18.

——— 2000, 'The Trade between China, Japan, Korea and Southeast Asia in the 14th Century through the 17th Century Period', *International Area Review,* vol. 3, no. 2 (winter 2000).

Ch'oe, Sang-su, 1983, 'Korea-Indonesia Relations: Visit of a Java Envoy in the 15th Century', *Korea Journal* 23: 4 (April 1983): 71-2.

Chong, Yang-mo 1981, 'Ceramic Wares Recovered off the Coast of Korea', *Arts of Asia* 11: 4 (July-August 1981): 104-12.

Christie, Jan Wisseman, 1988-9, 'The Sanskrit Inscription Recently Discovered in Kedah, Malaysia', *Modern Quaternary Research in Southeast Asia*, vol. 11: 39-54.

———, 1990, 'Trade and State Formation in the Malay Peninsula and Sumatra 300 B.C.-A.D. 700', in J. Kathirithamby-Wells and J. Villiers (eds.), *The Southeast Asian Port and Polity: Rise and Demise*, Singapore: Singapore University Press: 39-60.

———, 1993, 'Texts and textiles in "Medieval" Java', *Bulletin de l'Ecole Francaise d'Extreme-Orient*, vol. 80: 181-211.

———, 1998, 'Javanese Markets and the Asian Sea Trade Boom of the Tenth to Thirteenth Centuries AD', *Journal of the Economic and Social History of the Orient*, vol. 41: 344-81.

Chun Hae-jong, 1968, 'Sino-Korean Tributary Relations in the Ch'ing Period', in John K. Fairbank (ed.), *The Chinese World Order*, Cambridge Mass: Harvard University Press: 63-89.

Coedes, George, 1956, 'Indian Influences upon Siamese Art', *Marg*, vol. 9: 30-9.

———, 1957, 'Nouvelles données sur la dynastie Śailenda de java et ses origins', in Z.V. Togan (ed.), *Proceedings of the Twenty-second Congress of Orientalists*, Istanbul, 1951, Leiden, vol. II: 317-32.

———, 1964a, 'Les états hindouisés d'Indochine et d'Indonésie', *Historie du monde* 8.2, Paris: E. de Boccard.

———, 1964b, 'Some Problems in the Ancient History of the Hinduized States of Southeast Asia', *Journal of Southeast Asian History*, vol. 5: 1-14.

Coomaraswamy, Ananda K., 1972, *History of Indian and Indonesian Art*, Delhi: Munshiram Manoharlal.

Day, Tony, 2002, *Fluid Iron: State Formation in Southeast Asia*, Honolulu: University of Hawaii Press.

Deng, Gang, 1997, *Chinese Maritime Activities and Socioeconomic Development, c. 2100 B.C.-1900 A.D.*, Westport, Connecticut and London: Greenwood Press.

———, 1999, *Maritime Sector, Institutions, and Sea Power of Premodern China*, Westport, Connecticut and London: Greenwood Press.

———, 2003, 'The State and Market in China's Maritime Sector', paper presented at the 9th Conference on Chinese Maritime History, Taipei, 12-14 March 2003.

Diem, Allison I., 1998-2001, 'The Significance of Pandanan Shipwreck Ceramics as Evidence of Fifteenth Century Trading Relations within Southeast Asia', *Bulletin of the Oriental Ceramic Society of Hong Kong*, no. 12.

Donkin, Robert Arthur, 1999, *Dragon's Brain Perfume: An Historical Geography of Camphor*, Leiden: Brill.

Drewes, Gerardus Willebrordus Joannes 1968, 'New Light on the Coming of Islam to Indonesia?', *Bijdragen tot de Taal-, Land- en Volkenkunde*, vol. 124: 433-59.

Duyvendak, Jan Julius Lodewijk , 1937, *Ma Huan Re-examined*, Amsterdam: Noord-Hollandsche Uitgeversmaatschappij.

———, 1938, 'The True Dates of the Chinese Maritime Expeditions in the Early Fifteenth Century', *T'oung Pao*, vol. 34: 341-412.

Eredia, Gedinho de, 1997, *Eredia's Description of Malaca, Meridional India and Cathay, Translated from the Portuguese with Notes by J.V. Mills and New Introduction by Cheah Boon Kheng*, Kuala Lumpur: Malay Branch of the Royal Asiatic Society Reprint 14.

Evans, Ivor Hugh Norman, 1927, 'Notes on the Remains of an Old Boat found at Pontian', *Journal of the Federated Malay States Museums*, vol. 12/4: 93-6.

Fairbank, John K., 1968, *The Chinese World Order: Traditional China's Foreign Relations*, Cambridge Mass.: Harvard University Press.

Fatimi, S.Q., 1963, *Islam Comes to Indonesia*, Singapore: Malaysian Sociological Research Institute.

Ferrand, Gabriel, 1919, 'Le K'ouen-louen et les anciennes navigations interocéaniques dans les mers du sud', *Journal Asiatique*, 11th series, vol. 13.2: 239-333, vol. 13.3: 431-92 and vol. 14: 5-68 and 201-41.

Flecker, Michael, 1999, 'The 13th Century Java Sea Wreck—Bulk Iron and Ceramics from China', Proceedings of the Fujian Ceramics Conference, Singapore/Chicago.

———, 2000, 'A 9th-century Arab or Indian Shipwreck in Indonesian Waters', *The International Journal of Nautical Archaeology*, vol. 29: 199–217.

———, 2001, 'A 9th-century AD Arab or Indian Shipwreck in Indonesia: First Evidence for Direct Trade with China', *World Archaeology* 32, 335-54.

Francis, Peter, 2002, *Asia's Maritime Bead Trade: 300 B.C. to the Present*, Honolulu: University of Hawai'i Press,

Gibson-Hill, Carl Alexander, 1952, 'Further Notes on the Old Boat found at Pontian, in Southern Pahang', *Journal of the Malayan Branch of the Royal Asiatic Society* 25.1: 111-33.

Glover, Ian and Julian Henderson 1995, 'Early Glass in Southeast Asia and China', in R. Scott and J. Guy (eds.), *Southeast Asia & China: Art, Interaction, and Commerce*, London: Percival David Foundation of Chinese Art; Singapore: Sun Tree Publishers: 141-70.

Goddio, Franck, Stacey Pierson and Monique Crick, 2000, *Sunken Treasure: Fifteenth Century Chinese Ceramics from the Lena Cargo*, London: Periplus.

Gommans, Jos and Jacques Leider (eds.), 2002, *The Maritime Frontier of Burma: Exploring Political, Cultural and Commercial Interaction in the Indian Ocean World, c. 1000-1800*, Amsterdam: KNAW and Leiden: KITLV.

Gordon, Alijah, 2001, *The Propagation of Islam in the Indonesian-Malay Archipelago*, Kuala Lumpur: Malaysian Sociological Research Institute.

Gotuaco, Larry, Rita C. Tan and Allison I. Diem, 1997, *Chinese and Vietnamese Blue and White Wares Found in the Philippines*, Philippines: Bookmark Inc. Makati.

Graaf, H.J. de and G. Th. Pigeaud (tr.), M.C. Ricklefs (ed.), 1984, *Chinese Muslims in Java in the 15th and 16th centuries*, Melbourne: Monash papers on Southeast Asia No. 12.

Green, Jeremy, Rosemary Harper and Vidya Intakosi, 1986, *The Maritime Archaeology of Shipwrecks and Ceramics in Southeast Asia and the Ko Si Chang Three Shipwreck Excavation*, Victoria: Australian Institute of Marine Archaeology.

Groom, Nigel, 1981, *Frankincense and Myrrh: A Study of the Arabian Incense Trade*, London and Beyrouth: Longman and Librairie du Liban.

Guy, John S., 1986, *Oriental Trade Ceramics in Southeast Asia 9th to 16th Century*, Singapore: Oxford University Press.

———, 1987, *Ceramic Excavation Sites in Southeast Asia: A Preliminary Gazetteer*, Adelaide, Art Gallery of South Australia: Research Centre for Southeast Asian Ceramics, papers 3.

———, 1993-4, 'The Lost Temples of Nagapattinam and Quanzhou: A Study in Sino-Indian Relations', *Silk Road Art and Archaeology*, vol. 3.

———, 1998, *Woven Cargoes: Indian Textiles in the East*, London: Thames and Hudson.

Hadimuljono and C.C. Macknight 1983, 'Imported Ceramics in South-Sulawesi', *Review of Indonesian and Malay Affairs*, 1983, 17: 66-91

Hall, Kenneth R., 1977, 'The Coming of Islam to the Archipelago', in Karl Hutterer (ed.), *Economic Exchange and Social Interaction in Southeast Asia*, Ann Arbor, Center for South and Southeast Asian Studies, University of Michigan: 213-32.

———, 1985, *Maritime Trade and State Development in Early Southeast Asia*, Honolulu: University of Hawai'i Press.

Hall, Kenneth R. and J.K. Whitmore, 1976a, *Explorations in Early Southeast Asian History: The Origins of Southeast Asian Statecraft*, Ann

Arbor: Center for South and Southeast Asian Studies, University of Michigan, Michigan Papers on South and Southeast Asia No. 11.

———, 1976b, 'Southeast Asian Trade and the Isthmian Struggle 1000-1200 A.D.', *Exploration in Early Southeast Asian History*: 303-40.

Hamashita Takeshi, 1988, 'The Tribute System and Modern Asia', *Memoirs of the Research Department of the Toyo Bunko*, no. 46: 7-23.

Harrisson, Tom, 1958, 'The "Ming gap" and Kota Batu, Brunei (with an appeal for help)', *Sarawak Museum Journal*, vol. 8, no. 11 (new series): 273-7.

Hasebe, Gakuji, 1991, 'Historical Relations between Japan and Vietnam in the Area of Trade in Ceramics', The National Committee for the International Symposium on the Ancient Town of Hoi An (ed.), *Ancient Town of Hoi An*, Vietnam Social Sciences, vols. 1-2.

Hazard, Benjamin H., 1973, 'Creation of the Korean Navy During the Koryo Period', *Transactions of the Royal Asiatic Society-Korea Branch* 48: 10-28.

———, 1976, 'The *Wako* and Korean Responses', in James B. Parsons (ed.), *Papers in Honor of Professor Woodbridge Bingham: A Festschrift for His Seventy-fifth Birthday*, San Francisco: Chinese Materials Center, Inc.

Ho, Chuimei, 1994a (ed.), *New Light on Chinese Yue and Longquan Wares: Archaeological Ceramics Found in Eastern and Southern Asia, A.D. 800-1400*, Hong Kong: Centre of Asian Studies, The University of Hong Kong.

———, 1994b, 'Problems in the Study of Zhejiang Green Glazed Wares with Special Reference to Lo Kho Khao and Laem Pho-Payang, Southern Thailand', in Chuimei Ho (ed.), *New Light on Chinese Yue and Longquan Wares*, Hong Kong: Centre of Asian Studies, The University of Hong Kong: 187-212.

Honda, Hiromu and Noriki Shimazu, 1993, *Vietnamese and Chinese Ceramics Used in the Japanese Tea Ceremony*, Singapore: Oxford University Press.

Horridge, G. Adrian, 1982, *The Lashed Lug Boat of the Eastern Archipelago, the Alcina MS and the Lomblen Whaling Boats*, Greenwich: National Maritime Museum, Monograph 54.

Hourani, George Fadlo, 1951, *Arab Seafaring in the Indian Ocean in Ancient and Early Medieval Times*, Princeton: Princeton University Press.

Howitz, Pensak Chagsuchinda, 1977, 'Two Ancient Shipwrecks in the Gulf of Thailand: A Report on Archeological Investigations', *Journal of the Siam Society* (Bangkok) 65, no. 2 (July 1977): 1-22.

Hultzsch, Euger Julius Theodor, 1913, 'Note on a Tamil Inscription in Siam', *Journal of the Royal Asiatic Society*: 337-9.

———, 1914, 'Supplementary Note on a Tamil Inscription in Siam', *Journal of the Royal Asiatic Society*: 397-8.

Hurgronje, Christiaan Snouck (tr. A.W.S. O'Sullivan), 1906, *The Achehnese*, Leiden: Brill.

Hutterer, Karl (ed.), 1977, *Economic Exchange and Social Interaction in Southeast Asia: Perspectives from Prehistory, History and Ethnography*, Ann Arbor: Center for South and Southeast Asian Studies, University of Michigan.

———, 1978, 'Prehistoric Trade and the Evolution of Phillippine Societies: A Reconsideration', in Karl Hutterer (ed.), *Economic Exchange and Social Interaction in Southeast Asia*: 177-96.

Iioka, Naoko, 2003, 'A Survey of Japanese Materials Concerning To-sen', paper presented at Asia Research Institute Graduate Symposium, National University of Singapore, October 2003.

Ishii, Yoneo, 1971, 'Seventeenth Century Japanese Documents about Siam', *Journal of the Siam Society* (59:1): 161-74.

———, 1988, 'Thai-Japanese Relations in the Pre-Modern Period: A Bibliographic Essay with Special Reference to Japanese Sources', in Chaiwat Khamchoo and E. Bruce Reynolds (eds.), *Thai-Japanese Relations in Historical Perspective*, Bangkok: Innomedia.

———, 1990, 'The Ryukyu in Southeast Asian Trade in the 15th and 16th Centuries', in K.M. de Silva, Sirima Kiribamune and C.R. de Silva, (eds.), *Asian Panorama: Essays in Asian History, Past and Present*, New Delhi.

———, 1992, 'The Rekidai Hōan and some Aspects of the Ayutthayan Port Polity in the Fifteenth Century', *The Memoirs of the Toyo Bunko*, vol. 50: 81-92.

———, 1998, *The Junk Trade from Southeast Asia, translated from the Tō-sen Fusetsu-gaki 1674-1723*, Singapore: Institute of Southeast Asian Studies.

Jacq-Hergoualc'h, Michel, 2002, *The Malay Peninsula: Crossroads of the Maritime Silk Road (100 BC-1300 AD)*, tr. Victoria Hobson, Leiden: Brill.

Jörg, Christiaan J.A. and Flecker, Michael, 2001, *Porcelain from the Vung Tau Wreck: the Hallstrom Excavation*, Singapore: Sun Tree Publishing.

Karashima, Noboru, 1995, 'Indian Commercial Activities in Ancient and Medieval Southeast Asia', paper delivered at the Conference of the International Association of Tamil Research.

Kern, Johan Hendrik Caspar, 1907, 'Concerning Some Old Sanskrit Inscriptions in the Malay Peninsula', *Journal of the Straits Branch, Royal Asiatic Society*, vol. 49: 95-101.

Kiralfy, Alexander, 1944, 'Japanese Naval Strategy', in E.M. Earle (ed.), *Makers of Modern Strategy: Military thought from Machiavelli to Hitler*, Princeton: Princeton University Press.

Kobata, Atsushi and Matsuda Mitsugu, 1969, 'Ryukuan Relations with Korea and South Sea Countries', *Ryukyuan Relations with Korea and South Seas Countries: An Annotated Translation of Documents in the* Rekidai Hôan, Kyoto: Atsushi Kobata.

Krause, Friedrich, 1915, 'Fluss- und Seegefechte nach Chinesischen Quellen aus der Zeit der Chou- und Han-dynastie und der Drei Reiche', *Mitteilungen der Seminar für orientalischen Sprachen*, vol. 18: 61.

Kulke, Hermann, K. Kesavapany and Vijay Sakhuja (eds.), 2009, *Nagapattinam to Suvarnadwipa: Reflections on the Chola Naval Expeditions to Southeast Asia*, Singapore: Institute of Southeast Asian Studies.

Lee Chor Lin, 1995, 'Textiles in Sino-South East Asian Trade: Song, Yuan and Ming Dynasties', in R. Scott and J. Guy (eds.), *Southeast Asia & China: Art, Interaction, and Commerce*, London: Percival David Foundation of Chinese Art: Singapore: Sun Tree Publishers: 171-86.

Lee, Hyoun-jong, 1977, 'Military Aid of the Ryukyus and other Southern Asian Nations to Korea: During the Hideyoshi Invasions', *Journal of the Social Sciences and Humanities* 46 (December 1977): 13-24.

Leong Sau Heng, 1990, 'Collecting Centres, Feeder Points and Entrepots in the Malay Peninsula c. 1000 B.C.-A.D. 1400', in J. Kathirithamby-Wells and J. Villiers, *The Southeast Asian Port and Polity: Rise and Demise,* Singapore: Singapore University Press: 17-38.

Lo Jung-pang, 1955, 'The Emergence of China as a Sea Power in the Late Sung and Early Yuan Periods', *Far Eastern Quarterly*, 14: 489-503.

———, 1958, 'The Decline of the Early Ming Navy', *Oriens Extremus,* no. 5: 149-68.

———, 1969, 'Maritime Commerce and Its Relation to the Sung Navy', *Journal of the Economic and Social History of the Orient,* vol. 12: 57-101.

———, 1976, 'The Termination of the Early Ming Naval Expeditions', in James B. Parsons (ed.), *Papers in Honor of Professor Woodbridge Bingham, a Festschrift for his Seventy-fifth Birthday*, San Francisco: Chinese Materials Center: 95-103.

Lombard, Denys, 1990, *Le carrefour javanais; essai d'histoire globale*, 3 vols, Éditions de l'École des Haute Études en Sciences Sociales.

Lombard, Denys and Jean Aubin, edited, *Marchands et hommes d'affaires asiatiques dans l'océan Indien et la mer de Chine, XIIIe-XXe siècle*, Paris: EHESS.

Loofs-Wissowa, Helmut, 1991, 'Dongson Drums: Instruments of Shamanism or Regalia? A New Interpretation of their Decoration May provide the Answer', *Arts Asiatique*, XLVI: 39-49.

Majumdar, Ramesh Chandra, 1927 (1985 rpt.), *Champa: history & culture of an Indian colonial kingdom in the Far East, 2nd-16th century* A.D., Delhi: Gian Pub. House.

———, 1933, 'Les rois Śailendra de Sunarnadvīpa', *Bulletin de l'École Française d'Extrême-Orient*, XXXIII: 121-41.

———, 1934a, 'The Śailendra Empire up to the end of the 10th Century', *Journal of Greater Indian Society*, 1: 1-27.

———, 1934b, 'The Struggle between the Śailendras and the Cholas', *Journal of the Greater India Society*, 1: 71-91.

———, 1937-8, *Ancient Indian Colonies in the Far East, Vols. I and II—Suvarnadvipa*, Dacca: A.K. Majumdar.

Manguin, Pierre-Yves, 1983, 'Comments on the Concept of Trans-Peninsular Routes, SPAFA', Final Report Consultative Workshop on Archaeological and Environmental Studies on Srivijaya (T-W3), 29 March-11 April 1983, Bangkok.

———, 1984, 'Relationships and Cross-influences between South-East Asian and Chinese Shipbuilding Traditions', Supplementary Report for SPAFA, Appendix 5g, Consultative Workshop on Research on Maritime Shipping and Trade Networks in South-East Asia.

———, 1985a, *Sewn-plank Craft of Southeast Asia: A Prelimary Review*, Greenwich: National Maritime Museum, Archaeological Series 10.

———, 1985b, 'Research on the Ships of Srivijaya', Report for SPAFA Consultative Workshop on Archaeological and Environmental Studies, Jakarta, Padang.

———, 1985c, 'The introduction of Islam into Champa', *Journal of the Malaysian Branch Royal Asiatic Society*, vol. 58, part 1: 1-29.

Manguin, Pierre-Yves., A. Mani and Geoff Wade (eds.), 2011, *Early Interactions between South and Southeast Asia: Reflections on Cross-Cultural Exchange*, Singapore: Institute of Southeast Asian Studies.

Marr, David G. and A.C. Milner (ed.), 1986, *Southeast Asia in the 9th to 14th Centuries*, Singapore: Institute of Southeast Asian Studies & Research School of Pacific Studies, ANU.

Marrison, G.E., 1951, 'The Coming of Islam in the East Indies', *Journal of the Malayan Branch of the Royal Asiatic Society*, 24, 1: 31-7.

McKinnon, Edmund Edwards, 1996, 'Medieval Tamil Involvement in Northern Sumatra, c11-c14 (The Gold and Resin Trade)', *Journal of the Malaysian Branch of the Royal Asiatic Society* 69: 1.

Meacham, William, 1984-5, 'On the improbability of Austronesian Origins in South China', *Asian Perspectives*, vol. 26 (1): 89-106.

Menzies, Gavin, 2002, *1421: The Year China Discovered the World*, London: Bantam Press.

Mikami Tsugio, 1983, 'Ceramic Road Economic and Cultural Relations between East and West as seen through the Seaborne Trade in Ceramics', in Yamamoto Tatsuro (ed.), *Proceedings of the 31st International Congress of Human Sciences in Asia and North Africa, Tokyo and Kyoto*, 1983.

Miksic, John N. 1995, '14th Century Chinese Glass Found in Singapore and the Riau Archipelago', in R. Scott and J. Guy (eds.), *Southeast Asia & China: Art, Interaction, and Commerce,* London: Percival David Foundation of Chinese Art: Singapore: Sun Tree Publishers: 252-73.

Miksic, John N. and Yap Choon Teck, 1992, 'Compositional Analysis of Pottery from Kota Cina, North Sumatra: Implications for Regional Trade during the Twelfth to Fourteenth Centuries A.D.', *Asian Perspectives,* vol. 31, no. 1: 57-76.

Mills, John Vivian Gottlieb, 1974, 'Arab and Chinese Navigators in Malaysian waters in about A.D. 1500', *Journal of the Malaysian Branch of the Royal Asiatic Society*, 47. 2: 1-82.

———, 1979, 'Chinese Navigators in Insulinde about 1500', *Archipel* 18: 69-93.

Momoki Shiro, 1998a, 'Dai Viet and the South China Sea Trade: From the 10th to the 15th Century', *Crossroads,* vol. 12, no. 1.

———, 1998b, 'Was Champa a Pure Maritime Polity?: Agriculture and Industry Recorded in Chinese Documents', paper presented at 1998 Core University Seminar, Kyoto University and Thammasat University, Eco-history and Rise/Demise of the Dry Areas in Southeast Asia, Kyoto University, Japan, 13-16 October 1998.

———, 1999, 'Was Dai Viet during the Early Le Period (1428-1527) a Rival of Ryukyu within the Tributary Trade System of the Ming', in Nguyễn Thê Anh and Ishizawa Yoshiaki (eds.), *Commerce et Navigation en Asie du Sud-Est (XIV-XIX Siecle),* Paris: L'Harmattan,

Mori, Katsumi, 1972, 'The Beginning of Overseas Advance of Japanese Merchant Ships', *Acta Asiatica* 23: 1-24.

Mukherjee, Rila, 2012, *Oceans Connect: Reflections on Water Worlds across Time and Space*, Delhi: Primus Books.

———, 2011, *Pelagic Passageways: The Northern Bay of Bengal before Colonialism*, Delhi: Primus Books.

Nakamura, Rie, 2000, 'The Coming of Islam to Champa', *Journal of the Malaysian Branch Royal Asiatic Society,* vol. 73, pt. 1: 55-66.

Needham, Joseph, Wang Ling & Lu Gwei-Djen, 1971, *Science and Civilisation in China,* vol. 4, part III, Civil Engineering and Nautics, Cambridge: Cambridge University Press.

Nicholl, Robert, 1979, 'Brunei and Camphor', *Brunei Museum Journal* 4.3: 52-74.

Othman bin Mohd Yatim, 1984, 'Foreign Ceramics discovered in Peninsular Malaysia', *Studies in Ceramics,* Jakarta: Pusat Penelitian Arkeologi Nasional: 215-23.

———, 1988, 'Discoveries and Research on Ancient Ceramics in Peninsular Malaysia', *SPAFA Digest* 9 (2): 2-8.

Pearson, Michael, 2011, 'History of the Indian Ocean: A Review Essay', in *Wasafiri*, vol. 26, no. 2, pp. 78-99.

Pelliot, Paul, 1933, 'Les grands voyages maritimes chinois au début du XVe siècle', *T'oung Pao* 30: 237-452.

———, 1935, 'Notes additionalles sur Tcheng Houo et sur ses voyages', *T'oung Pao* 31: 274-314.

Phillips, George, 1885-6, 'The Seaports of India and Ceylon Described by Chinese Voyagers of the Fifteenth Century', *Journal of the North China Branch of the Royal Asiatic Society* 20 (1885): 209-26 and 21 (1886): 30-42.

Poujade, Jean, 1946, *La route des Indes et ses ravires,* Paris: Payot.

Prakash, Om and Denys Lombard (eds.), 1999, *Commerce and Culture in the Bay of Bengal, 1500-1800,* New Delhi: Manohar.

Ptak, Roderich, 1987, 'The Transportation of Sandalwood from Timor to China and Macao, *c.* 1350-1600', in Roderich Ptak (ed.), *Portuguese Asia: Aspects in History and Economic History (Sixteenth and Seventeenth Centuries),* Stuttgart: Franz Steiner Verlag Wiesbaden GmbH: 87- 109.

———, 1990a, 'Notes on the Word "Shanhu" and Chinese Coral Imports from Maritime Asia, *c.* 1250-1600', *Archipel* 39: 65-80.

———, 1990b, 'Die Andamanen und Nikobaren nach chinesischen Quellen (Ende Sung bis Ming)', *Zeitschrift der Deutschen Morgenländischen Gesellschaft* 140.2: 243-73.

———, 1990c, 'Pferde auf See: Ein vergessener Aspekt des maritimen chinesischen Han-dels im frühen 15. Jahrhundert', *Journal of the Economic and Social History of the Orient*, 34: 199-233.

———, 1991a, 'China and the Trade in Tortoise-Shell (Sung to Ming Periods)', in R. Ptak and D. Rothermund (eds.), *Emporia, Commodities and Entrepreneurs in Asian Maritime Trade, c. 1400-1750*, Stuttgart: Franz Steiner Verlag Wiesbaden GmbH: 195-229.

———, 1991b, 'China and Portugal at Sea: The Early Ming System and the *Estado da Índia* Compared', *Revista de Cultura*, 13/14: 21-38.

———, 1992, 'The Northern Trade Route to the Spice Islands: South China Sea-Sulu Zone-North Moluccas (14th to early 16th century)', *Archipel* 43: 27-56.

———, 1993a, 'Piracy along the Coasts of Southwest India and Ming China: Comparative Notes on Two Sixteenth Century Cases', in Artur Teodoro de Matos and Luís Filipe F. Reis Thomaz (eds.), *As relações entre a Índia portuguesa, a Ásia do Sueste e o Extremo Oriente. Actas do VI Seminário Internacional de História Indo-Portuguesa* (Macau, 22 a 26 de Outobro de 1991) (Macau / Lisbon): 255-73.

———, 1993b, 'China and the Trade in Cloves, *circa* 960-1435', *Journal of the American Oriental Society* 113.1: 1-13.

———, 1994a, 'Merchants and Maximization: Notes on Chinese and Portuguese Entrepreneurship in Maritime Asia, *c.* 1350-1600', in R. Ptak and K.A. Sprengard (eds.), *Maritime Asia: Profit Maximisation, Ethics and Trade Structure, c. 1300-1800*, Wiesbaden: Harrassowitz Verlag (South China and Maritime Asia 2): 29-59.

———, 1994b, 'Sino Japanese Maritime Trade, *circa* 1550: Merchants, Ports and Networks', in Roberto Carneiro and A. Teodoro de Matos (eds.), *O século cristão do Japão. Actas do Colóquio Internacional Comemorativo dos 450 Anos de Amizade Portugal-Japão (1543-1993)*, Lisbon: 281-311.

———, 1994c, 'Images of Maritime Asia in Two Yuan Texts: *Daoyi zhilüe* and *Yiyu zhi*', *Journal of Sung-Yuan Studies* 25 (1995): 47-75.

———, 1995, 'Asian Trade in Cloves *circa* 1500: Quantities and Trade Routes—A Synopsis of Portuguese and Other Sources', in Francis A. Dutra and João Camilo dos Santos (eds.), *Proceedings of the International Colloquium on the Portuguese and the Pacific. University of California, Santa Barbara, October 1993*, Santa Barbara: Center for Portuguese Studies, University of California, Santa Barbara: 149-69.

———, 1996, 'Glosses on Wang Dayuan's *Daoyi zhilüe* (1349/50)', in Claudine Salmon (ed.), *Récits de voyages des Asiatiques. Genres, mentalités, conception de l'espace*, Paris: École Française d'Extrême-Orient: 127-45.

———, 1998a, 'Possible Chinese References to the Barus Area (Tang to Ming)', in Claude Guillot (ed.), *Histoire de Barus. Le Site de Lobu Tua*. Bd. 1: Études et documents, Cahiers d'Archipel 30 (Paris: École des Hautes Études en Sciences Sociales): 119-47.

———, 1998b, *China and the Asian Seas: Trade, Travel and Visions of the Other (1400-1750)*, Aldershot, etc.: Ashgate Publishing Ltd.

———, 1998c, 'Ming Maritime Trade to Southeast Asia, 1368-1567: Visions of a System', in R. Ptak, C. Guillot and D. Lombard (eds.), *From the Mediterranean to the China Sea*, Wiesbaden: Harrassowitz Verlag: 157-92.

———, 1998d, 'From Quanzhou to the Sulu Zone and Beyond: Questions Related to the Early Fourteenth Century', *Journal of Southeast Asian Studies* 29.2 (1998): 269-94.

———, 2000a, 'Camphor in East and Southeast Asian Trade, *c.* 1500: A Synthesis of Portuguese and Asian Sources', in Anthony Disney and Emily Booth (ed.), *Vasco da Gama and the Linking of Europe and Asia*, New Delhi: Oxford University Press: 142-66.

———, 2000b, 'The Eastern Rim of Southeast Asia in Late Medieval and Early Modern Chinese Sources', *Nanyang xuebao* (Journal of the South Seas Society) 55: 22-47.

———, 2003a, 'Seltene Vögel für China: Papageien', in Loris Kakadus (Song bis Ming), R. Ptak, Jorge M. dos Santos Alves and C. Guillot (eds.), *Mirabilia Asiatica*, Wiesbaden: Harrassowitz Verlag: 151-74.

Purvis, Frank Prior, 1919, *Ship Construction in Japan: Ancient and Modern*, Transactions of the Asiatic Society of Japan, Yushodo Booksellers Ltd.

Ramchandran, A. 1996, *The Cultural History of the Lower Krishna Valley: Its Contacts with Southeast Asia*, Jaipur: Publication Scheme.

Ray, Haraprasad, 1991, 'Bengal's Textile Products Involved in Ming Trade during Cheng Ho's Voyages to the Indian Ocean and Identification of the Hitherto Undeciphered Textiles', in R. Ptak and D. Rothermund (eds.), *Emporia, Commodities and Entrepreneurs in Asian Maritime Trade c. 1400-1750*, Stuttgart: Franz Steiner Verlag Wiesbaden GmbH.: 81-93.

———, 1991, 'Bengal's Textile Products involved in Ming Trade during Cheng Ho's Voyages to the Indian Ocean and Identification of Hitherto Undeciphered Textiles', in Roderich Ptak and Dietmar Rothermund (eds.), *Emporia, Commodities and Entrepreneurs in Asian*

Maritime Trade, c. 1400-1750, Stuttgart: Franz Steiner Verlag, pp. 81-93.

———, 1993, *Trade and Diplomacy in India-China Relations: a study of Bengal during the Fifteenth Century*, New Delhi: Radiant Publishers.

Ray, Himanshu Prabha, 1989, 'Early Maritime Contacts between South and Southeast Asia', *Journal of Southeast Asian Studies* 20 (1): 42-54.

———, 1994: *The Winds of Change: Buddhism and the Maritime Links of Early South Asia*, New Delhi: Oxford University Press.

———, 1996, 'Seafaring and Maritime Contacts: An Agenda for Historical Analysis', *Journal of the Economic and Social History of the Orient*, vol. 39: 422-31.

———, 2003, *The Archaeology of Seafaring in Ancient South Asia*, Cambridge: Cambridge University Press.

Ray, Himanshu Prabha and E.A. Alpers (eds.), 2007, *Cross Currents and Community Networks: The History of the Indian Ocean World*, New Delhi: Oxford University Press.

Ray, Himanshu Prabha and Jean-François Salles (eds.), 1996, *Tradition and Archaeology: Early Maritime Contacts in the Indian Ocean*, New Delhi: Manohar, rpt. 2012.

Reid, Antony, 1988, *Southeast Asia in the Age of Commerce 1450-1680*, vol. 1: *The Lands below the Winds*, New Haven: Yale University Press.

———, 1993a, *Southeast Asia in the Age of Commerce 1450-1680*, vol. 2: *Expansion and Crisis*, New Haven: Yale University Press.

———, 1993b (ed.), *Southeast Asia in the Early Modern Era: Trade, Power and Belief*, Ithaca, New York: Cornell University Press.

———, 1993c, 'Islamization and Christianization in Southeast Asia: The Critical Phase 1550-1650', in A. Reid (ed.), *Southeast Asia in the Early Modern Era*, Ithaca, New York: Cornell University Press.

———, 1995 (comp.), *Witnesses to Sumatra: a travellers' anthology*, Kuala Lumpur: Oxford University Press.

———, 2000a, 'The Islamization of Southeast Asia', in Anthony Reid, *Charting the Shape of Early Modern Southeast Asia*, Chiang Mai: Silkworm Books, 15-38.

———, 2000b, *Charting the Shape of Early Modern Southeast Asia*, Chiang Mai: Silkworm Books.

———, 2000c, 'The Rise and Fall of Sino-Javanese Shipping', in Anthony Reid, *Charting the Shape of Early Modern Southeast Asia*, Chiang Mai: Silkworm Books: 56-84.

Richards, Dick, 1995, *South-East Asian ceramics: Thai, Vietnamese, and Khmer*, Kuala Lumpur: Oxford University Press.

Ricklefs, Merle Calvin, 1979, 'Six Centuries of Islamization in Java', in Nehemia Levtzion (ed.), *Conversion to Islam*, New York: Holmes and Meier: 100-28.

Rogers, Michael C., 1991, 'Notes on Koryo's Relations with *Sung* and *Liao*', *Chindan hakpo* 71-72 (1991: 12): 310-35.

Roxas-Lim, Aurora, 1987, *The Evidence of Ceramics as an Aid in Understanding the Pattern of Trade in the Philippines and Southeast Asia*, Bangkok: Chulalongkorn University, Institute of Asian Studies (Asian Studies Monograph 36).

Sadler, Arther Lindsay, 1937, 'The Naval campaign in the Korean War of Hideyoshi', *Transactions of the Asiatic Society of Japan*, 2nd Series, no. 14: 179-208.

Sakai, Robert K., 1968, 'The Ryukyu (Liu-Ch'iu) Islands as a Fief of Satsuma', in John K. Fairbank (ed.), *The Chinese World Order*: 112-34.

Sang-won, Jeon, 1974, *Science and Technology in Korea: Traditional Instruments and Techniques*, Cambridge Massachusetts: MIT Press.

Sarkar, Himansu Bhusan, 1971, *Corpus of the Inscriptions of Java (Up to 928 A.D.)*, 2 vols., Calcutta: K.L. Mukhopadhyay.

———, 1986, 'The homeland of Kaundinya I of Funan and Traditions about his Marriage', *Journal of the Institute of Asian Studies* (Madras) vol. 4, no. 1 (September 1986): 21-31.

Sastri, K.A. Nilakanta, 1932a, 'A Tamil Merchant Guild in Sumatra', *Tijdschrift voorIndische Taal-, Land- en Volkenkunde*, vol. 72: 314-327.

———, 1932b, 'The Takua-Pa (Siam) Tamil Inscription', *Journal of Oriental Research* (Madras), vol. 6, no. 4: 299-310.

———, 1935-7, *The Colas*, Madras: University of Madras, 2 vols.

———, 1944, 'The Tamil Land and the Eastern Colonies', *Journal of the Greater India Society*, vol. XI: 26-8.

———, 1949, 'Takuapa and Its Tamil Inscription', *Journal of the Malayan Branch of the Royal Asiatic Society*, vol. XXII, no. 1: 25-30.

Satow, Ernest Mason, 1885, 'Notes on the Intercourse between Japan and Siam in the Seventeenth Century', *Transactions of the Asiatic Society of Japan*, no. 13: 189-210.

Schottenhammer, Angela, 2001 (ed.), *The Emporium of the World: Maritime Quanzhou, 1000-1400*, Leiden; Boston, Mass.: Brill (Sinica Leidensia, v. 49).

Scott, Rosemany and John Guy, 1995, *South East Asia & China: Art, Interaction & Commerce*, London: Percival David Foundation of Chinese Art: Singapore: Sun Tree Publishers.

Scott, William Henry, 1981, 'Boat-Building and Seamanship in Classic Philippine Society', *SEAMEO Project in Archaeology and Fine Arts Digest 6*, 2: 15-33.

Sen, Tansen, 2003, *Buddhism, Diplomacy and Trade: the Realignment of Sino-Indian Relations, 600-1400*, Honolulu: University of Hawai'i Press.

———, 2006, 'The Formation of Chinese Maritime Networks to Southern Asia, 1200-1450', *Journal of the Social and Economic History of the Orient*, vol. 49, no. 4, pp. 421-53.

Shultz, Edward J., 1988, 'Koryo's Envoys to China: Early 12th Century', *Han-kuo hsueh-pao* 7: 247-66.

Sjostrand, Sten, 1997, 'The "Xuande" Wreck Ceramics', *Oriental Art* 43: 7-14.

Smith, Ralph B., 1979, 'Check-list of "Heger Type I" Bronze Drums from South East Asia', in R.B. Smith and W. Watson (ed.), *Early South East Asia*, Oxford, New York and Kuala Lumpur: Oxford University Press: 509-16.

So, Billy K.L., 1994, 'The Trade Ceramics Industry in South Fukien during the Sung', *Journal of Sung & Yuan Studies* 24: 1-19.

———, 2000, *Prosperity, Region, and Institutions in Maritime China: the South Fukien pattern, 946-1368*, Cambridge, Mass.; London: Harvard University Asia Center.

So Kwan-wai, 1975, *Japanese Piracy in Ming China during the 16th Century*, East Lansing.

Solheim, Wilhelm G. II, 1975, 'The Nusantao and South China', *Journal of the Hong Kong Archaeological Society* (Hong Kong) 6 (1975): 108-15.

———, 1992, 'Nusantao Traders beyond Southeast Asia', in I. Glover, P. Suchitta and J. Villiers, *Early Metallurgy, Trade and Urban Centres in Thailand and Southeast Asia*: 199-212.

———, 2000, 'Taiwan, Coastal South China and Northern Viet Nam and the Nusantao Maritime Trading Network', *Journal of East Asian Archaeology*, vol. 2, nos. 1-2 (2000): 273-85.

Sørensen, Per, 1986, 'Kettledrums of Heger 1 Type: Some Observations', in Ian Glover and Emily (ed.), *Southeast Asian Archaeology 1986*, Oxford: BAR International Series 561.

Spenser, George W. 1988, 'Indian Trade Diasporas and Chola Maritime Expansion', *Journal of the Institute of Asian Studies* (Madras), vol. 6, no. 1: 1-13.

Subbarayalu, Yellava, 1998, 'The Tamil Merchant-Guild Inscription at Barus: A Rediscovery', in Claude Guillot (ed.), *Histoire de Barus: Le Site de Lobu Tua—I Études et Documents*, Paris: Cahier d'Archipel.

Subrahmanyam, Sanjay, 1999, 'Persianization and "Mercantilism", in Bay of Bengal History, 1400-1700' in Prakash and Lombard (eds.), *Commerce and Culture in the Bay of Bengal, 1500-1800*, pp. 47-85.

Sung, Shee, 1995, 'The Trade and Culture Relations between China and Koryo during the Northern Sung', *Chinese Culture* 36: 2 (June): 65-74.

Tan Yeok Seong, 1962, 'Chinese Element in the Islamisation of South east Asia: A Study of the Strange Story of Njai Gede Pinatih, the Grand lady of Gresik', Chang Kuei-yung et al. (eds.), *International Association of Historians of Asia: Second Biennial Conference Proceedings*, Taipei: 399-408.

Tao, Jing-shen, 1988, 'Relations Between the Sung, the Liao, and Koryo', *Two Sons of Heaven: Studies in Sung-Liao Relations*, Tucson: The University of Arizona Press.

T'ien Ju-kang, 1981, 'Cheng Ho's Voyages and the Distribution of Pepper in China', *Journal of the Royal Asiatic Society*, no. 2: 186-97.

Tibbets, Gerald Randall, 1956, 'The Malay Peninsula as known to the Arab Geographers', *Malayan Journal of Tropical Geography*, vol. 9: 21-60.

———, 1971, *Arab Navigation in the Indian Ocean before the Coming of the Portuguese*, Oriental Translation Funds, New Series XLIII, London: Royal Asiatic Society of Great Britain and Ireland.

———, 1973, 'Comparison between Arab and Chinese Navigational Techniques', *Bulletin of the School of Oriental and African Studies*, 36 (1): 97-108.

———, 1979, *A Study of the Arabic Texts Containing Material of Southeast Asia*, Leiden: E.J. Brill.

Tsao Yung-ho, 1982, 'Pepper Trade in East Asia', *T'oung Pao*, 68.4-5: 221-47.

Turnbull, Stephen, 2002, *Samurai Invasions: Japan's Korean War 1592-98*, London: Cassell & Co.

Turnbull, Stephen and Wayne Reynolds, 2002, *Fighting Ships of the Far East (1): China and Southeast Asia 202 BC-AD 1419*, Oxford: Osprey Publishing.

———, 2003, *Fighting Ships of the Far East (1): Japan and Korea AD 612-1639*, Oxford: Osprey Publishing.

Underwood, Horace H., 1979, *Korean Ships and Boats*, Yonsei University rpt. originally published in *Transactions of the Royal Asiatic Society: Korea Branch*, vol. 23 (1934).

Van Leur, J.C., 1955, *Indonesian Trade and Society: Essays in Asian Social and Economic History*, The Hague and Bandung: W. van Hoeve.

Vogel, Hans Ulrich, 1993, 'Cowry Trade and Its Role in the Economy of Yünnan: From the Ninth to the Mid-Seventeenth Century', *Journal of the Economic and Social History of the Orient*, vol. 36, pt. I: 211-52 and pt. II: 309-53.

Wade, Geoff, 1998, 'A Maritime Route in the Vietnamese Text *Xiêm-la-quôc Lô Trinh Tâp-luc* (1810)', in Nguyễn Thê Anh and Yoshiaki Ishizawa (eds.), *Commerce et navigation en Asie du Sud-Est, XIVe-XIXe siècle*, Paris & Montréal (Québec): l'Harmattan.

———, 2003, 'Ming China and Southeast Asia in the 15th Century: A Reappraisal', paper presented at the Workshop on Southeast Asia in the 15th Century: The Ming Factor, 1-2 May 2003, Singapore.

Wake, Christopher, 1997, 'The Great Ocean-going Ships of Southern China in the Age of Chinese Maritime Voyaging to India, Twelfth to Fifteenth Centuries', *International Journal of Maritime History* (St. John's, Newfoundland), vol. 9, no. 2: 51-81.

Wang, Gungwu, 1958, 'The Nanhai Trade', *Journal of the Malaysian Branch of the Royal Asiatic Society*, (1958:2): 1-135. Reprinted by Times Academic Press, Singapore, 1998.

Wang, Gungwu, 1964, 'The Opening of Relations between China and Malacca 1403-05', in J.S. Bastin and R. Roolvink (eds.), *Malayan and Indonesian Studies: Essays Presented to Sir Richard Windstedt*, London: Oxford University Press.

———, 1968a, 'The First Three Rulers of Malacca', *Journal of the Malaysian Branch of the Royal Asiatic Society*, vol. 41: 1: 11-22.

———, 1968b, 'Early Ming relations with Southeast Asia: A Background Essay', in John K. Fairbank (ed.), *The Chinese World Order*, Cambridge Mass.: Harvard University Press: 34-62.

———, 1970, 'China and Southeast Asia 1402-1424', in J. Chen and N. Tarling (eds.), *Social History of China and Southeast Asia*, Cambridge: Cambridge University Press.

Weeraprajak, Kongkaew, 1989, 'The Earliest Sanskrit Inscriptions Found in Malaysia', *Sinlapakon*, vol. 33, no. 4 (September-October 1989): 30-8.

Welch, David J. and Judith R. McNeill, 1989, 'Archaeological Investigations of Pattani History', *Journal of Southeast Asian Studies*, vol. 20, no.1: 27-41.

Wheatley, Paul, 1959, 'Geographical Notes on some Commodities Involved in Sung Maritime Trade', *Journal of the Malayan Branch of the Royal Asiatic Society*, vol. XXXII: 5-140.

———, 1961, *The Golden Khersonese*, Kuala Lumpur: University of Malaya Press.

———, 1975, 'Satyānṛta in Suvarṇadvīpa: From Reciprocity to Redistribution in Ancient Southeast Asia', in J.A. Sabloff and C.C. Lamberg-Karlovsky (eds.), *Ancient Civilization and Trade*, Albuquerque: University of New Mexico Press: 227-38.

Whitmore, John K., 1977, 'The Opening of Southeast Asia, Trading Patterns through the Centuries', in Karl Hutterer (ed.), *Economic Exchange and Social Interaction in Southeast Asia*, Ann Arbor: Center for South and Southeast Asian Studies, University of Michigan: 139-54.

Wicks, Robert S., 1992, *Money, Markets and Trade in Early Southeast Asia: the Development of Indigenous Monetary Systems to AD 1400*, Ithaca: Southeast Asia Program, Cornell University.

Wiethoff, Bodo, 1963, *Die chineische Seeverbotspolitik und der private Überseehandel von 1368 bis 1567*, Hamburg.

Wolters, Oliver William, 1967, *Early Indonesian Commerce: A Study of the Origins of Srivijaya*, Ithaca: Cornell University Press.

Yang, Qin-Zhang, 1990, 'South-Song Stone Anchors in China, Korea, and Japan', *The International Journal of Nautical Archaeology and Underwater Exploration* 19: 2 (1990): 113-21.

Yokokura, M., 1992, 'Dongson Bronze Drums from Thailand', *Journal of Southeast Asian Archaeology*, no. 12: 97-104.

Yoon, Moo-byong, 1977, 'The Sea Route of the Sunken Ancient Vessel on the Seabed off Sinan', *Korea Journal* 17: 11 (November 1977): 18-23.

Yun, Yong-I, 1998, 'Ceramics from Tadohae Shipwrecks', *Koreana*, vol. 12, no. 2.

CHAPTER 5

The Vietnamese Coastline: A Maritime Cultural Landscape

CHARLOTTE MINH HÀ PHAM

The Maritime Cultural Landscape of Vietnam

An overview of the maritime history of pre-colonial Vietnam demonstrates how boat-building traditions can reflect social, cultural, political and economical contexts and how they result from cultural and/or technological exchanges. The central idea of this paper is that a maritime perspective can provide new elements to understand Vietnam's history and state formation and that through boat studies, complementary data can be gathered to offer a holistic interpretation of the ancient seafaring and maritime-oriented cultures. Overall, this paper aims at creating a livelier and more practical picture of the maritime activities that occurred along the coast of Vietnam in the fascinating maritime trade context during the past two millennia.

Vietnam's history is most commonly addressed from a land perspective, focusing on agrarian expansion where the sea and maritime activities are seldom considered. Yet, historians like Hall (2008), Wheeler (2001), Whitmore (2006) and Li (2006) have eloquently discussed the role or position of Vietnam in the maritime trade context. Through the idea of looking at boat traditions, I would like to further follow their lead by considering water and the coastal highway as essential elements in this complex cultural landscape.

In Vietnam, one is never far from water. It borders the 3,260 km long coast and it has two major deltas that create an extended network of waterways and channels. In the north, the Red River delta forms an extensive flat agricultural land and a riverine network occupying a nodal position for exchange between the coast of the Tonkin Gulf and the hinterland of south China while the Mekong delta in the south is a low-level plain subject to intense flooding that enriches the plains in minerals and makes them favourable for rice cultivation. In between these two, the coastal plain is a narrow corridor of a width of 50-120 km bordered on the west by the plateau of the Annamitic Chain that resembles a dragon-like spine of about 1,000 km length, and on the east by the perilous South China Sea. There, the plains are criss-crossed by downstream river networks and the inward curving central coast receives the north-east winds upfront as well as violent typhoons four to five times a year. The sea is notorious for its danger, characterized by heavy storms and treacherous shoals, reefs and sand banks near the Hoang Sa (Paracel) and Truong Sa (Spratley) Islands that await the weary captains, who need to navigate close to the coast to avoid being shipwrecked. However, the small islands of Con Dao, Ly Son and Cu Lao Cham offer shelter, fresh water and refitting supplies to the ships that can navigate along them.

This region particularly well-suited to maritime exploitation and dependence on marine resources, is also strategically located on the trade routes between southern China and the Malayo-Siamese isthmus. Natural elements contribute greatly to this vital crossroads in maritime trade. The trade winds and currents dictate the direction of the voyages and thus the cultural exchanges, while the monsoon regime forced merchants, travellers, soldiers, monks or ambassadors to stop in Vietnam's harbours for several months at a time, where they mingled with local seafarers and inhabitants. The region reaped benefits from this geographical position by selling its own products and by offering in its harbours shipping services, boat repairs, warehousing, accommodation, food, markets, etc., while the rulers could also gain from taxing ships and merchants. This strategic location and the topography demonstrate the important presence of water, which in turn implies the inherent use and reliance on boats in the country. As Wheeler pointed out:

> . . . before the twentieth century, waterways were the preferred and often the sole mode of transportation. . . . When faced with a formidable mountain wall, Vietnamese, a coastal people, simply passed around it, in boats,

thereby subverting whatever limits the mountains may have imposed in the first place. (2003: 3)

Moreover, boats were not only used as a means of transportation; but also played an essential part in the country's militaristic endeavours and defence. Several battles were conducted on water-based battle fields (Lê Dinh Thong, 1990, 1992). Furthermore, Vietnam is a land of wet-rice cultivation and of fishing: activities intimately related with waterways through which boats are the primary means of livelihood. Boats constitute a living space, an environment for social activities and communication and are assigned different roles in the Vietnamese daily life; 'boat houses' are quite common to fishermen who live on rivers and lagoons and can also be organized in floating villages. Boats can also form the basis of important floating markets, as seen even today in the Mekong delta, or can be small floating shops where all the selling and buying activities take place on them. Boats and life along the river or on the water are also celebrated in the folklore. Ceremonies, funeral rites, courtship rituals or festivals involving boats are still practised, and the art of 'water puppetry' is a source of great Vietnamese pride. The construction of the boat itself involves different rituals (Cadière, 1902) such as giving offerings to the Whale Deity or to the Sir Fish. Social conventions, include even today, taboos and rules to observe so as to avoid upsetting the gods and spirits (Claeys, 1939, 1942).

During the American War, the American Advanced Research Project Agency recorded in South Vietnam 'approximately 180 individual boats of about 60 different types' in a volume entitled *The Blue Book of Coastal Vessels* (1967: 12). However, there was no attempt to explain the reasons for such a diversity. Present-day Vietnam hosts fifty-four ethnic groups, belonging to six major language families. This intrinsically multicultural context is the result of Vietnam's strategic location at a cultural and trade crossroads but is also the product of a long exchange and migration since the dispersal of the Austronesian ethno-linguistic group during the Neolithic (Bellwood and Glover, 2004) and of various cultural influences that have shaped Vietnam's cultural landscape, ranging from the Chinese in the north, the Indian/Khmer from the west, the Malay world from the east to Persians or even Europeans in the last centuries. Nowadays, since the people's living standards are improving, boat-building traditions are slowly disappearing or changing. Yet there is still much to be inferred from their shapes, their construction sequences and from their evolution and stories (Pham et al., 2010). A boat is not just a means of transportation or the reflection of technological capabilities and achievements, and its shape and technology cannot be reduced only to environmental or functional factors. A boat can reflect a whole cultural trend and its socio-economic context. They are mirrors to culture, a reflection of various cultural components that influence its shape, construction and use. 'Their meaning is much broader than timbers and technology' (Adams, 2006: 6).

Addressing boat diversity and ubiquity in the Vietnamese context and taking into consideration the environment as well as historical events and cultural context and exchanges, it clearly appears that boat traditions are part of a complex cultural weave where specific traditions could be hard to isolate, most particularly when taking in consideration the constant migratory character of the Vietnamese people over the last century and the related consequences of the French and American wars. However, in this paper, the two main trends of influences that are most clearly decipherable in boat traditions will be put forward: the Chinese influence and the Malay world influence. From the first millennium CE until 1802, when the Emperor Gia Long unified the country as we know it today, two essential stories unfolded in parallel in Vietnam. These two parallel stories are addressed here as they complement each other in understanding the fate of both major states; the Dai Viêt and the Champa polities. As the story goes, the southern provinces of the Cham were slowly overwhelmed by the Dai Viêt expanding southwards, yet this story is usually recounted through an ethnocentric and land-based perspective, and usually justified by military incentives rather than economic ones until recently at least. Taking into consideration the fact that the mountains needed to be crossed, and that the 'coastal highway' was a more convenient and essential route, the landscape witnessed an endless power confrontation between the two groups over almost 2,000 years. Thus, the boat traditions in Vietnam, their role, and their evolution, can contribute towards the telling of these two parallel stories and might show shifts in power to underline the fact that the story is not so linear following a north-south axis but involves a larger ecological and cultural sphere.

History of Northern Vietnam Reflected in Boat Traditions

Prehistory

Two types of 'primitive' boats have survived in the contemporary record that can be related to the earliest times of northern Vietnam: dugouts and sea-going rafts. In terms of archaeology, there is clear evidence of the use of dugouts as boat-shaped burial coffins belonging to the Dong-so'n culture. This culture flourished between 1000 BCE-CE 200 and was an agrarian society based on rice culture and game hunting, also excelling in metallurgy. A maritime aspect of the Dong-so'n culture is that they buried their dead in boat-shaped coffins (Bellwood and Glover, 2004) that carried the soul to the other world, thought of as being made out of water also called 'the nine streams' or the 'gold river' (Do Thi Thanh Thuy et al., 2006: 78). This practice is not rare in Vietnam and is shared with other ethnic groups who still follow the same burial procedures and belong to the same language group (Muong, Tais) (Cuisinier, 1948). To date, 171 boat-shaped coffins have been recovered from forty-four different waterlogged archaeological sites (Bui Van Liem, 2005). A very recent find (Bellwood et al., 2007), the 'Dông Xa boat' (Hung Yen province), dated to 40-50 BCE is a log-boat, re-used as a coffin. This latest find is significant in boat-building history because it shows a locked mortise and tenon plank-fitting technique which 'to our knowledge, this technology in its precise plank-edge form is not reported from non-nautical contexts anywhere in the Old World' (Bellwood et al., 2007: 13). The tenon and mortise sizes and shapes, compared with Mediterranean ones, reflect the riverine nature of the Vietnamese craft and indicates dugout and wooden vessel construction from the earliest times.

Bronze casting in Vietnam emerged during the middle of the second millennium BCE and reached its peak around 500 BCE. The Dong-so'n ceremonial kettledrums are found in almost all of Southeast Asia, from north-east Thailand to Malaysia, to remote islands of Indonesia and as far as the Easter Island (Bellwood and Glover, 2004). This distribution suggests an extensive network of commercial value and therefore, trading fleets and merchant vessels. These drums are decorated with beautiful boat depictions and Sorensen concludes that they 'most likely represent craft which were particularly suitable for river transport of men and goods, perhaps also used for inshore navigation but less suitable for seagoing expeditions' (1986: 195). Unfortunately these depictions were never thoroughly investigated with a naval architect's eye, so we have no idea of how far they could have sailed, how much load they could have carried or even if these boats were ritual representations or were actually used inshore or at sea.

Sea-going rafts are still seen today along the coast of the province of Thanh Hoa but are fast disappearing, their floats being replaced by styrofoam and their hulls being fitted with small diesel engines and long tail motors. Rafts were used as early as 3000 BCE by the first wave of Austronesian-speaking migrants who reached Taiwan (Ling Shun-Sheng, 1956) and similarities have been observed between the rafts of Sam Son (Thanh Hoa) and the ones of Formosa (Worcester, 1966: 93-6). While traditional rafts have disappeared from the Taiwanese landscape, it is possible that rafts in Vietnam survived because of the availability of material, their adaptability to

Figure 5.1: Rafts of Sam Son, Thanh Hoa province (© C. Palmer).

the environment, as well as due to their tradition (Aubaile-Sallenave, 1987: 45). Origins, uses and evolution of the sea-going rafts were similarly never thoroughly addressed and require urgent attention.

Chinese Domination

The turn of the first millennium CE marks a significant cultural change for northern Vietnam. The Dong-so'n culture was encompassed by the Han and from 111 BCE onwards the region entered a phase of a thousand years of Chinese domination. During almost a millennia, the Chinese imposed the basis of a new administrative system, as also their language, and Buddhism and developed the 'maritime silk route'. This domination led to distinct development of northern Vietnam as opposed to the other emerging polities of Southeast Asia. Located at the heart of the early maritime trade, the newly-named commandery of Giao Chi, acted as China's commercial hub. The commerce between central Vietnam and China for aromatic woods thrived from the fifth century BCE, stopping along the northern Vietnamese coast located at the top of a triangle between South China, Hainan and Champa. Giao Chi was also a strategic connecting point between the maritime and land routes. Due to the difficult conditions of navigation in the Gulf of Tonkin because of huge hidden rocks along the coast (Li, 2006: 84), the maritime routes went east of Hainan Island to Fujian and Guangdong, while a path across the Truong Cordillera connected to Laos or northern Cambodia overland. During the first millennium, the coastal maritime route that linked South China with Southeast Asia developed and northern Vietnam was characterized by inter-regional trade, not only with Chinese regions but with other coastal regions in Southeast Asia. This period of prosperous exchange is linked to the development of coastal navigation, which also linked riverine sites with sites in the Giao Chi prefecture in the Red River delta (Nishimura, 2005: 105).

The Gulf of Tonkin region was an extension and an integral part of an area called the Jiaozhi Ocean (Jiaozhi Yang), an active trading zone located right in the heart of the more ancient Western Sea Route up to the fifteenth century, and frequented by Muslim traders from South, West and Southeast

Asia. This trading zone included the Guangxi coast facing the Tonkin Gulf, coastal Dai Viêt, northern Champa and Hainan Island. (Li, 2006: 83)

Additionally, the Giao Chi region had a reputation among the Chinese of being a rich land, which produced an abundance of valuable goods, especially sub-tropical products such as rhinoceros horns, elephant tusks, kingfisher feathers, and pearls. Hence, the Viêt people not only enjoyed fertile paddy fields but also were privileged by an advantageous geography which enabled them to communicate and trade with people in the southern territories (Hoàng Anh Tuan, 2007: 12). The harbour of Luy Lau, a crucial Buddhist centre (Nguyên Tai Thu, 1997), was a convenient port of call for monks from India, Sri Lanka or Central Asia. There, mulberry trees sustained the raising of silkworms, and the harbour became an important cultural and commercial centre favoured by foreign merchants, monks and scholars as well.

While long distance would be carried by foreign merchants, local travel between Vietnam and south China would have been carried out by smaller ships or boats, a specialty of the Viêt sailors according to Wang Gungwu. (Li, 2006: 85)

Unfortunately, there are no documents to suggest the type of boat used by the local Vietnamese involved in this important trade network. Nevertheless, by considering the strong Chinese influence over the commandery over a thousand years, it is not surprising to find some boats that bear exactly the same general construction characteristics of the Chinese tradition in contemporary boat records.

The main characteristics of the early Chinese boat tradition include a shell-first construction, a flat bottom with the midship towards the stern, and a transom bow. The entire boat was constructed with iron nails and the hull was compartmented with bulkheads which created watertight partitions that are a typical of Chinese boatbuilding. They bore an axial rudder, could be propelled by a long sculling oar called *yuloh* and when in the form of a sailing vessel, were rigged with the famous battened lug sails. It is widely acknowledged that before the Song dynasty, the Chinese vessels were essentially fluvial junks (Manguin, 1980: 276). It is only after the tenth century that they started to create large sea-going fleets that reached its high point with the treasure fleet of Admiral Zeng He in the fourteenth century. Fluvial fishing junks of the Ha Long Bay seen in the 1940s (Pietri, 1943: 103), the salt and lime transporters on the Red River (flat bottom, iron nails, axial rudder), but also the trading ships of Nghe An, the *ghe ghia* in Cua Lo (a fishing ship constructed with iron nails) or the small watercraft even today in the Ha Long Bay (Pietri, 1943: 103, 95, 81, 83), are samples of Vietnamese boats that were constructed according to this 'northern tradition' (Pham et al., 2010).

Figure 5.2: The *ghe manh* of *Nghe An*, with beamy aft, high stern, main frame aft of midships, bold sheerline, bulkheads, axial rudder and cotton Chinese sails with battens (Pietri 1943: plate LVI).

Kunlun Ships and Foreign Influence

In northern Vietnam today, there are, however, other boat-building features that are quite distinct from the Chinese tradition, such as a slender hull, a V-shaped bottom, lack of bulkheads, lateral rudders and the fact that the construction and fastening relies on wooden pegs rather than on iron nails (Pham et al., 2010). References in the early twentieth century, describe the *tra co* with a slender hull like the boats from the central region, fastened with treenails, with a keel and a very inclined helm, slightly different from the axial Chinese rudder. The *thuyen luoi* was said to have had a higher stem and stern posts and no bulkheads like most of the boats found in Vietnam while the *ghe cau* seen in Dong Hoi, blend Chinese and a Southeast Asian tradition. They were constructed with hardwood dowels, with a double chine planking and a bottom plank shaped into a point and bent upwards at the two ends to form a false stem and a false sternpost. It also exhibits Chinese features like the main frame that is noticeably aft of amidships, and the hull that is structured with bulkheads, and bears an axial rudder (Pietri, 1943: 80). If not a result of constant migrations over the past centuries, it is most likely that these features, which are more related to a general Southeast Asian tradition and are common in central Vietnam and the Malay world, may parallel the amazing cosmopolitan scene then on the sea during the first millennium CE.

At that time, although the Chinese, and later the Arabs/Persians and Indians, controlled the trading networks, the principal long-distance carriers were the 'south sea people' or *Kunlun*, a term 'probably used for the maritime peoples of Indochina and later extended to the Indonesian population' (Nguyên Thê Anh, 1996: 108) or to the Malay people coming from Palembang and then from the great seafaring empire of Srivijaya. Chinese documents from the third and eighth century attest to these huge ocean-going ships (Needham, 1971: 465-70; Manguin, 1980, 1983). These were larger and sturdier than any other kind, with a capacity of 500 to 1,000 tonnes, carrying about 1,000 passengers and being of about 35-50 m in length. Their construction technique was to lash the planks together and secure them with wooden dowels. Their hull was pointed with a symmetrical stem and stern, and V-shaped with a keel that would make them sturdier in the open sea. They were very sea-worthy, with multiple sheathing, multiple masts with lugsails and a bowsprit, with lateral rudders, and without bulkheads or iron nails, features which really made them distinct from the Chinese tradition. It is possible that these huge ships influenced Chinese boat-building, which started with large sea-going ships by the thirteenth and fourteenth centuries, retaining some of these foreign features while keeping their essential riverine junk features (Manguin, 1993). Although some of the Southeast Asian features can be clearly identified in boat traditions in northern Vietnam today, contrary to the Chinese, Vietnam did not develop its ship technology to make huge seafaring vessels. Its political and economic context result in the fact that Vietnam remained with a boat tradition that would not surpass the needs for regional and coastal travel and that it would not develop into a sea-going fleet.

Figure 5.3: The ghe cau of Dong Hoi in the north, bears features from both the Chinese and the Southeast Asian tradition (Pietri, 1943: plate LV).

From the Independence to the Present

With a new millennium came the independence of Vietnam, which started with a significant naval battle: the Bach Dang Battle in CE 938. With a very simple but ingenious tactic, the hero Ngô Quyên destroyed the Chinese armada: the heavy and large ships were lured up the mouth of the river in the bed of which stakes had been planted, that were invisible at high tide. When the tide receded, the small Vietnamese flotilla of light and easily manoeuvrable boats counter-attacked ferociously until the tide ebbed, impaling the enemies' ships on the stakes, blocking them in a forest of poles and enabling the Vietnamese troops to annihilate their enemies with burning arrows (Lê Thanh Khoi, 1992: 188). This strategy was re-used by General Tran Hung Dao against the Mongols in CE 1288.

The new Ly Dynasty (1012-1225) then established the first Vietnamese state: the Dai Viêt or the greater land of the Viêt. The on-going trade business between Southeast Asia, China and India led to inevitable participation of Dai Viêt in commercial exchanges (Manguin, 2000: 153). It took part in the major maritime trade system by developing harbours such as Van Don that was inaugurated in 1149. Van Don was an internationally designed military and commercial port which welcomed merchants from China, India and Siam. Conditions were favourable for building a naval fleet for resistance and shipyards had a production capacity of hundreds of big ships with up to hundred oars per year (Do Thi Thanh Thuy et al., 2006: 12). The new strength of the Dai Viêt and its reliance on its newly-developing navy was proven by two major battles in the eleventh century that won it three provinces from its southern Cham enemies (in 1069, the Dai Viêt troops went down to sack the city of Vijaya with a fleet of 200 vessels) and that settled the frontier with China that stands still today. Between 1075 and 1077, the troops and the navy of Ly Thuong Kiet confronted the Song in an important naval battle on the Nhu Nguyêt river (Lê Thanh Khoi, 1992: 162).

Independence from Chinese domination was hence followed by a period during which the national dynasty developed. It was essentially characterized by a will to solidify the state with the establishment of political, military and administrative powers. The state continuously pushed back the Chinese and the Vietnamese sway grew stronger with each victory against this redoubtable empire and against the southern enemies of Champa and Angkor. The focus of the state was on developing the agricultural potential (Whitmore, 2006: 108-10) and on inland and up-river development (land routes for gold, silver and spices) and most essentially towards the politics of defence (strategy, ingenuity, tactics, military devices) and politics of expansion (through rivers, coast and land). This underlines the fact that the Dai Viêt accorded importance to its navy and that military strategies depended on naval ingenuity to gain significant victories. Therefore, their boats were essentially made for transporting troops and going to war. Military accounts clearly describe this Vietnamese tendency of fitting the boats with different devices and weapons for attack and defence (*Binh Thu Yeu Luoc* thirteenth century CE, *An Nam Chi Luoc* fourteenth century CE, *Quan Trung Tu Menh Tap* fifteenth century CE). However, in terms of sea-going fleets, during the entire second millennium CE, Dai Viêt's periodic endeavours to actively take part in the maritime commerce at sea or to develop long-distance trade and high-seas fishing never succeeded.

Literary sources often comment on the lack of an important Vietnamese fleet. 'There is little evidence of Vietnamese doing business outside their own regions, or taking to the sea on trading expeditions' (Reid, 2000: 138) a fact that has been attributed to a certain 'Vietnamese detachment' from the sea. Other reasons were also suggested by foreigners in the seventeenth to nineteenth centuries like the priest Alexandre de Rhodes (1883: 181) or 'Richard' (Pinkerton, 1808: 736) who quite negatively explained the lack in terms of a poor mastering of navigation, a disinterest in marine industry and in the trade sector, a prohibition of the rulers from leaving and travelling abroad and finally, the frailty of their flexible boats and their inability to resist fierce waves or tremendous storms. Paradoxically the maritime skills of the Vietnamese were also often highly praised. John Crawfurd who wrote in 1825 said 'I know no people of the East so well fitted to make expert mariners from their hardiness, their activity and their prompt and cheerful habits of obedience' (Lamb, 1970: 263). Even so, it is admitted that 'they were not involved in any form of trade outside their country, all imported products were delivered by foreign merchants and exports were shipped in the same way' (Mantienne, 2003: 530).

As a matter of fact, the various attempts to develop overseas fleets were quite often hindered by the overall context, where shifts in politics and international commerce trends influenced the direction of Dai Viêt's trade and hence its naval attempts and failures. For example, the development of the first official standing Chinese navy overtook Dai Viêt in terms of ship-building (CE 1132). Similarly the Cham harbours of Kauthara and Panduranga attracted all the merchant ships, while recurrent attacks from neighbours also impacted the fate of the Vietnamese potential fleets. Even when the Trân dynasty (1225-1400) saw an opportunity to take a share in the maritime trade with the fading of the great seafaring empire of

Srivijaya, the Mongols intervened. The Trân began their accession by a triple push back to the Mongols, who were decisively defeated in 1288, reproducing at Bach Dang the same strategy previously used against the Chinese. These distractions prevented the Viêt to impose themselves in the maritime trade. Later, King Ho Quy Ly (1336-1407) also saw the benefits of developing the ship-building industry but was cut-off short by another Chinese domination that lasted twenty years (1407-27). During the subsequent Lê dynasty (1428-1527) the state reached a certain balance and strength; however, this stability did not survive the reigns of the last rulers due to internal quarrels. In the fifteenth century Dai Viêt was still a mainstream trading power in Southeast Asia which gave weight to its conquest of the south. Traffic multiplied on the south China Sea due to an increase in the number of exchanged goods (Manguin, 2000: 153) and the fierce competition between the Chinese, Japanese and Indian merchants. However, the bureaucracy and Confucian tendencies of the Lê dynasty in the sixteenth century definitely ended all attempts of creating a strong outgoing navy. The later major internal strife between the Trinh and the Nguyen Lords (*c.* 1627-73) showed great dependence on a fleet as well as an impetus for building French-like large vessels; an art that the new emperor Gia Long himself supervised and in which the Vietnamese excelled (Li, 2004: 120) but the naval capability did not develop further after the reign of Thieu Tri (1841-7).

Although the lack of a substantial navy can be blamed on external factors, it can also be explained by internal reasons. As Huard and Durand (1954: 229) suggest, 'neglecting sea and mountain, Vietnamese focused all their historical efforts towards one sole aim: the conquest of rice plains'. Therefore, 'if the Vietnamese navy seldom went out of its territorial waters, it is not because of an absence of technical means, but rather because of a main focus on rice cultivation'. Although this statement follows an essentially agrarian and land-based history, it is a fact that rather than looking upon the world and on high-waters exploration, the Dai Viêt's foci since its independence were on sustaining their growing demographics and on expanding their lands, notably by developing their weaponry, war vessels and military. Ship-building was developed for military purposes and naval tactics for defence and coastal raids. Subsistence was based on rice, coastal fisheries or riverine products, and the local Vietnamese had no need for high-seas fisheries and exploitation of marine resources. The state was self-sufficient based on a tax regime and forced labour, and did not rely directly on external trade. In any case, the monsoon brought the trade goods to the coast, reducing the incentive for the Vietnamese to go to the sea themselves, while the state could simply tax foreigners' ships and trade. Finally, the navy was state-dependent, and there were no big private ship-builders (Huard and Durand, 1954: 227-9). All these elements support the idea that the boat history of the Dai Viêt is fluvial and coastal and that it developed for military purposes and troop transportation.

History of Central and Southern Vietnam Reflected in Boat Traditions

Champa is not a centralized kingdom, not even a federation, but consisted of several separate entities, whose interrelationships varied from time to time (total separation, alliance, peace, hostility, trade) (Vickery, 2005: 39) and which thrived at different periods of time (CE 192-1802) in the central region of Vietnam. The Cham people are believed to be of Malayo-Polynesian descent, and were part of an 'Indianized' culture that built temples to Shiva, used Sanskrit, followed Hinduism and constructed impressive temple complexes. Their dead were placed in urns, but the remains were then consigned to the sea (Higham, 1989: 233), which indicates that the people's roots may be found in the previous Sa Huynh culture which had a skilled navigational tradition. The Cham were not only experts in navigation over water but also in land transport trading slaves and aromatics, and are also particularly known for being 'pirates' (Lê Thanh Khoi, 1992: 109). Their activities were infamous to travellers in the South China Sea. Even as late as 1599, long after the destruction of the capital of Vijaya, sea travellers complained of Cham raids (Wheeler, 2003). The Cham ability to strike quickly and ferociously using their unparalleled naval expertise enabled them to establish and control a network of ports that owed allegiance to their kings. Contacts with all neighbouring nations were quarrelsome; 'the Khmer were originally friendly toward the Cham, but this relationship soured after the 9th century and they became firm enemies' (O'Reilley, 2007: 136). The opposite happened with the Malay with whom the Cham finally entered into a commercial relationship. As with the Chinese, Cham kings paid regular tributes and sent envoys to the court, and 'tributary relations came themselves to resemble a kind of commerce' (Hardy et al., 2009: 112). Their plundering reputation and acts of piracy formed the core component of the Cham political economy as they actually relied on this 'plundering dynamic' to maintain their sovereignty and supplement their income (Hall, 1989). While the Dai Viêt was tributary to the trade network, the Cham played an important part in it, ensuring a significant position as middlemen in the Nanhai trade. Their lack of unity was their downfall although some capitals remained secondary entrepôts on the main international route.

Prehistory and the Stitched Tradition

The ancestors of the Cham, the Sa Huynh culture, was characterized by a particular mortuary tradition of cremating the dead and interring the ashes in painted jars, and also has cultural traits which suggests that they are part of the groups associated with the migration of the Austronesian-speaking groups. Sites related to this culture have been found all along the central coast and are dated from between 1000 BCE to CE 200. It is believed that 'Sa Huynh people' settled in Vietnam during the first millennium BCE, coming from a homeland in Borneo (Vickery, 2005: 13) as they were competent navigators. Archaeological investigations have discovered glass, cornelian and agate beads which clearly involved an early overseas trade network with India (Bellina, 2003), while jade artefacts—characteristic of their production—have been found in various peninsular Southeast Asian locations. These artefacts (two-headed animal jade earrings) have been the subject of recent studies (Hung et al., 2007) that identified a jade source in Taiwan, confirming the trading network and maritime voyages of the Sa Huynh craftsmen.

The emblem of the Austronesian speaking group's navigation skills is a boat with an outrigger. Its construction method implied lashing planks together to make the hull fast, which evolved in what is called the lash-lug tradition (Horridge, 1982) considered to be a tradition common to the whole Austronesian range. The difference between the lashed boats of Southeast Asia and the sewn boats of the Western Indian Ocean is that in the former, the stitches are discontinuous and that they are only seen on the inside (Manguin, 1993: 260).

Even if there is substantial archaeological evidence around Southeast Asia to attest to this early 'Austronesian' tradition (third to fourteenth century), in Vietnam, however, there is no evidence whatsoever of the use of outriggers. However, for the stitching tradition, excellent descriptions of the *cinga, sinja, thuyen gia* (Cadière, 1921; Paris, 1942) or *gay you* (Pâris, 1843): a coastal stitched-plank vessel used for trade between Siam and central Vietnam till the nineteenth century, date back to the late seventeenth century (Vachet, 1675). Today, the *ghe nôc* where *ghe* means boat and *nôc* means fish trap, is a small riverine sample of this stitched tradition that still survives in the channels near the ancient imperial city of Hue.

Figure 4: Gay you (Paris, 1843: plate 47).

The Question of the Cham Boats

Although the Cham are renowned as excellent seafarers, there is unfortunately very scanty evidence on the types of boats that they used to plunder the seas. Only two undated carvings exist (My Son and An Thinh quarry) and similarities with the boats represented on the Borobudur relief in Java have been suggested (Paris, 1939, 1941: 335). The Borobudur ships are the earliest representations of the boats that plied in the region; all the nine ships seem to be stitched; the largest ones have a prominent stem- and stern-post, a bipod or tripod mast with a square sail, a bowsprit, a double quarter rudder and a double outrigger. The four smallest ships have no outrigger. However, these ships were not clearly related to any cultural group (Manguin, 1980: 274) and even if the 'Cham carvings' show affinities with Javanese traditions, they lack the outboard galleries for oarsmen and the outriggers that are obvious features of most of the Borobudur ships (Burningham, pers. comm., 2011). These carvings could also be affiliated to the depictions seen in East Timor (Lape et al., 2007) which suggests a broad 'Austronesian' style, however, at this stage of research no substantial conclusion can be drawn.

Figure 5.5: Carving in the quarry of An Tinh (© A.V. Shweyer).

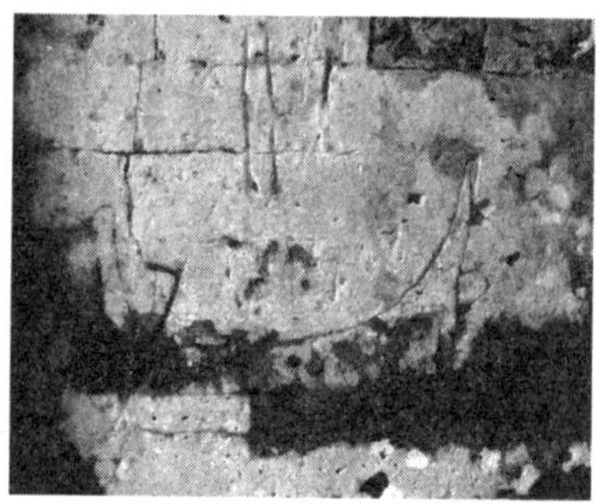

Figure 5.6: My Son temple B6 (© Tran Ky Phuong).

Another representation that hints at Cham boats is found in Cambodia, on the relief of the Bayon in Angkor Thom. Dated to *c.* 1185 it represents a battle on the Tonle Sap between the Khmer and the Cham. Discussion on the veracity of the event is ongoing (Vickery, 2005: 59-72). The boats appear like small flat-bottomed river crafts, probably local and certainly fluvial and cannot be related to a specific Cham boat tradition.

The Southeast Asian Tradition

From the twelfth to fourteenth century, the Cham states were quite powerful and in the last quarter of the fourteenth century they very nearly conquered all of Vietnam (only after the failure of that adventure was Dai Viêt clearly dominant, Vickery, 2005: 23). The Cham port of Thi Nai rose in the mid-twelfth century and thrived on the trade between eastern Java and China. The destruction of Srivijaya's hegemony also allowed the re-emergence of the Cham coast as a commercial power, and its ports became more prominent as ports of call on the way to China. The states stimulated in part by this commercial energy became in turn major consumers of international trade goods (ceramics, silk, cotton).

In terms of boat technology, there is archaeological Southeast Asian evidence for that specific period of time that attests to an evolution from the stitched tradition to a fully-dowelled construction method (Manguin, 1993: 265). The boats correspond to a Southeast Asian boat-building tradition and share construction features with the previously-mentioned 'Kunlun' ships, except that the planks are fastened with wooden pegs and not stitches. They still bear for the most part, a V-shaped hull, a keel and a lateral rudder, and this tradition completely corresponds to most boats seen today in the contemporary record of central Vietnam (Pham et al., 2010). The *ghe bau* is a typical example, yet it cannot be accounted for as a typical Cham boat. There are, since the nineteenth century (Pâris, 1843; Paris, 1942; Pietri, 1943), extensive literary descriptions of these large coasters that plied along central Vietnam for fishing, trade and goods transportation. They have loosely been assimilated to the Malay word *proa*, based on linguistics (Nguyên Boi Lien et al., 1991). However, the word *proa* just like *ghe bau* is a generic term for different kinds of sailing vessels and cannot really support any cultural or technological exchange. Even if they do share characteristics, an in-depth comparative study is necessary to connect the boat traditions from Vietnam with the ones of the Malay. Yet the Malay and the Cham certainly entertained tight relationships and traded extensively with one another and the geographical distribution of

Figure 5.7: Construction in central Vietnam (© C. Palmer).

Figure 5.8: A typical *ghe bau* from Annam (Pietri 1943: plate XLII).

the *ghe bau* corresponds to the area once occupied by the Cham (Li, 1998: 114).

Around the tenth century, the inauguration of the Dai Viêt harbour of Van Don and the development of inland routes connecting Angkor to northern Vietnam pushed the Malay and the Cham into becoming allies to impose themselves on the trade network. This interaction is important in terms of boat technology even if

> it is quite possible that a number of the naval raids against Vietnam attributed to the Chams during this period were actually initiated by the semi-autonomous Malay sea nomads who used Cham ports as their bases of operation. Expeditions were undertaken to acquire both material wealth and manpower, in the form of slaves. This wealth was subsequently distributed among the participants of the expeditions, the warriors and seamen who in return acknowledged the Cham rulers' authority. Successful plundering expeditions were thereby a mean of reinforcing the image of Champa's sovereign as the source of his allies' prosperity. . . . (Nguyên Thê Anh, 1996: 115)

The South China Sea Tradition

The golden age of maritime trade along the South China Sea corresponds to the appearance of a new tradition in the archaeological record. In the recent past due to the development of maritime archaeology about twenty shipwrecks were identified in the entire region, bearing features that seem to blend different regional boatbuilding traditions together (Manguin, 1993). It was a highly cosmopolitan context in which different types of boats plied the seas that seemed to have produced hybrid ships, which blended Chinese features with the Southeast Asian features of the contemporary *Jongs* of the Majapahit. Characteristics include the V-shaped hull, the keel and a thin pointed bow of the Southeast Asian tradition, as also the partitioning of the hull into compartments following the Chinese tradition. Yet, these bulkheads are not watertight and the frames shared the structural strength. Additionally, these ships usually have iron nails like the Chinese ones but also wooden dowels in some instances and their steering systems are either Chinese with an axial rudder or Southeast Asian with a lateral rudder. Examples, are the Pattaya wreck, the wreck of Phu Quoc, the wreck of Bukit Kajas and that of the Ko Si Chang 3 (Flecker, 2007). This cluster of characteristics is combined in various ways in all these shipwrecks that are dated between the fourteenth and sixteenth century. It terms of context, these vessels may have been the result of the Ming ban on private overseas trade (1371-1569). 'It is possible that displaced Chinese merchants who moved to Southeast Asia at that stage may have been the first to order ships built in this manner' (Wade, 2003: 5). It triggered the rise of Thailand in the ceramic trade as well as Vietnamese productions. The predominance of hybrid ships in the Gulf of Thailand and along the coast of peninsular Malaysia mirrors this surge in Thai production (Flecker, 2007: 81). At that period of time,

> Southeast Asia played a crucial role in the maritime trade which affected Europe and Asia firstly by being the source of the spices, and secondly because it was through the Southeast Asian port polities—'the leading regional centres of economic life, political power and cultural creativity' —that this trade flowed. (Wade, 2003: 10)

Boats in Vietnam today and even specimens like the *ghe bau* or the small stitched *ghe nôc* actually witness this international mix by also bearing Chinese features in their construction methods. These features may be the result of the important Chinese diaspora that settled in central and south Vietnam. Further research should be conducted to contextualize and explain the technological evolution of the boat-types seen in this region. This would also pinpoint the manner in which the histories of the Dai Viêt, of Champa and of neighbouring polities and kingdoms are tightly interrelated through the maritime network.

Independent Assemblages

Vietnam also has independent and unique traditions and boat characteristics that need to be investigated. The origin and evolution of these technological features have never been studied, yet they might hint at ship-building achievements that were specific to the local people.

Innovation or adaptation, Vietnamese or Cham, and nowadays ubiquitously found in the entire country, the basket-boat is a specific type of watercraft unique to the Vietnamese context (Pham, forthcoming). Although its invention was attributed to a Viêt general who was fighting the Chinese in the tenth century (Huard and Durand, 1954: 226), it may also find its roots in the early times of the Cham in central Vietnam. Actually, the geographical distribution of an endemic boat tradition that mixes wood and basket can be related to the ancient Cham borders before the tenth century (Moréchand, 1955: 311). Basket-boat construction reached its zenith in the form of these large mixed hulls coasters that answered the most pressing needs of cargo loads and travel distances, joining the characteristics and advantages of a strong wooden structure and a flexible worm-resisting bamboo hull adapted to the environment.

These constructions led to the invention of other features that are also unique to Vietnam such as the bow-board and the sliding rudder in the stern-post. As these woven bamboo hulls cannot bear an opening to let the centreboard slide, an element was fitted on the stem-post to support the action of the rudder and to oppose the leeway. The rudder also slides into the stern-post. The main reason for these sliding elements is to enable the boat to adapt to the irregularity of the coast and to bring it ashore easily.

Since the late nineteenth century, these unique mixed hulls found in the region between Danang and Quy Nhon were described as the

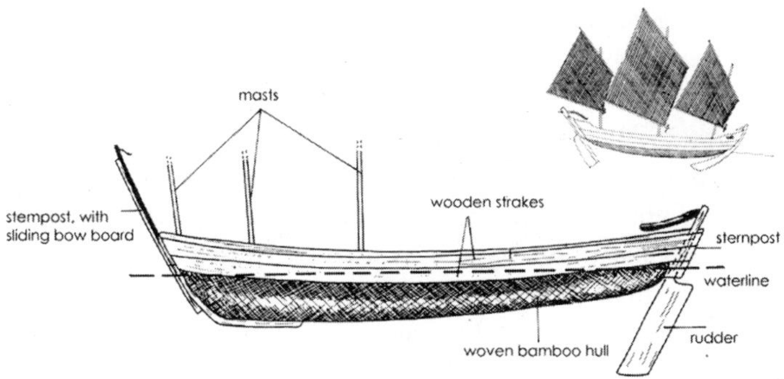

Figure 5.9: Mixed hulls; *ghe gia* of Quy Nhon (after Aubaile-Sallenave 1987: 5) and a small *ghe nang* (Paris 1942: fig. 5).

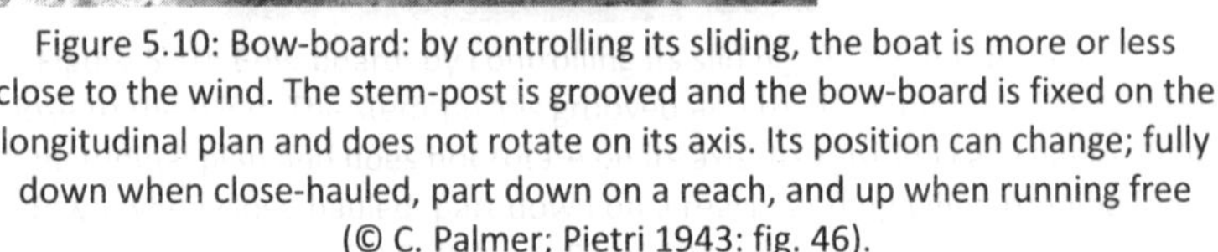

Figure 5.10: Bow-board: by controlling its sliding, the boat is more or less close to the wind. The stem-post is grooved and the bow-board is fixed on the longitudinal plan and does not rotate on its axis. Its position can change; fully down when close-hauled, part down on a reach, and up when running free (© C. Palmer; Pietri 1943: fig. 46).

most amazing coasters of the South China Sea. They were referred to as *ghe nang*, *ghe gia*, *ghe cau* but also *ghe bau*. Pietri (1943: 61) and P. Paris (1942: 356) describe some *ghe bau* with a mixed hull while Audemard (1971: 17-19) describes a *gai bao* as completely wooden. This is also the case with the *ghe gia*, which can be both according to its location. This confirms the fact that these are generic names that are not particular to one type of constructed vessel. Unfortunately, even though small basket-boats and small mixed hulls are still seen along the coast of former Champa, the coasters have completely disappeared.

The ingenuity of Vietnamese boat-builders was praised by authors who looked at the diversity of floating crafts of Vietnam in detail (Pham et al., 2010). However, their origins, evolution and cross-cultural context are seldom addressed in order to understand their features, shapes and designs. Future work will hopefully be conducted not only to identify the specific boat traditions of the region or to answer questions relative to the size, cargo and sailing distances but also to set them in a context to further the cross-cultural interchanges that result from the thriving maritime trade and cosmopolitan character of the South China Sea.

Conclusion

This paper aims to initiate a perspective where the role of boats could be put forward in the unravelling of the respective histories of the Dai Viêt and the Cham. This is only the beginning of a new dimension that put forward to set boat technology into a social, economic, political and cultural context. Yet it underlines the fact that comprehending state formation from a cultural, ecological and technological per-spective in which the sea is not a boundary but a 'coastal highway' will challenge the classic linear North to South story of the Dai Viêt encompassing central Vietnam. It will also account for radical-social changes during its conquest of Champa territories. The maritime component of the Vietnamese environment, the strategic location of the coast and the exploitation of the waterways shaped alliances and conflicts between the Dai Viêt, the Cham but also with the Chinese, the Malays or the Europeans. The maritime activities, the maritime trade and the water travels in turn result in cultural exchanges and technological adaptations that can be investigated though boat studies. This approach could add a maritime perspective to the cross-cultural diversity and interchanges in central Vietnam that have been recently addressed by historians to finally put forward Vietnam's central location in the maritime trade and cultural network of Southeast Asia. Although the Vietnamese people were often considered 'poor sailors afraid of the sea' and did not develop important sea-going fleets, their traditional boat constructions paradoxically show great ingenuity, manifesting the skill to blend technologies and innovate in a subtle way as seen in the mixed hull constructions or as succinctly demonstrated in Mantiennes's description of the part-

Chinese part-European ships built in the arsenal of Saigon in the early nineteenth century (2003: 531). This indicates the potential of independent unique naval traditions that need to be taken into consideration while addressing cultural and technological exchanges in the region. Chinese boatbuilding was influenced by Southeast Asian ships, and technological evolutions were not unilateral. Hence, addressing boat-types in Vietnam could also help identify the role and influence of this coastline on Southeast Asian boat traditions, which acted not only as repository of cultural and technological exchanges but also as a cradle and source of interconnectedness. Additionally, boats, that were vehicles to commercial, cultural, political and religious exchanges, were not only central to the overall development of maritime Southeast Asia but were also instrumental in the local connected histories of the region. The Dai Viêt used the coastal highway in the conquest of southern territories, the Cham used the water to impose their sovereignty in the region and inland waterways connected an apparently fragmented landscape, connecting highlands and lowlands as well as inbound trade with international trade without the need to master the sea with a great fleet. Rulers and locals knew how to exploit water connections, locations and resources to position themselves in a network that went through or connected different landscapes into a single system and which also linked people at different levels, from foreign merchants on the coastline to highlanders in the plateau to mandarins in the citadels. So if Vietnam's narratives until now were based on military endeavours, agricultural development and commercial relations, this maritime perspective would add a water constituent to the story that flows beyond these orientations and blends in spheres that are usually considered separately.

REFERENCES

Adams, Jonathan, 2006, 'From the Water Margins to the Centre Ground', *Journal of Maritime Archaeology*, 1 (1): 1-8.

Aubaile-Sallenave, Françoise, 1987, *Bois et bateaux du Vietnam*, *Collection Ethnosciences n°3*, Paris: Centre National de la Recherche Scientifique, Selaf.

Audemard, Louis-Théophille, 1971, *Les Jonques Chinoises, Volume X: Les Bateaux d'Indochine*, Rotterdam: Museum voor Land en Volkenkunde en het Maritiem Museum «Prins Hendrik».

Bellina, Bérénice, 2003, 'Beads, Social Change and Interaction Between India and South-east Asia', *Antiquity*, 77: 285-97.

Bellwood, Peter, Judith Cameron and Nguyên Van Viet, 2007, 'Ancient Boats, Boat Timbers and Locked Mortise-and-tenon Joints from Bronze/Iron-age Northern Vietnam', *International Journal of Nautical Archaeology*, 36 (1): 2-20.

Bellwood, Peter and Ian Glover (eds.), 2004, *Southeast Asia, from Prehistory to History*, London: Routledge Curzon.

Bui Van Liem, 2005, 'A Study of Boat-shaped Coffins from Dong Son Sites in Vietnam', *Indo-Pacific Prehistory Association Bulletin*, 25: 117-19.

Cadière, Léopold, 1902, 'Cérémonie pour la construction d'une jonque; Les coutumes populaires de la vallée du Nguôn-Son', *Bulletin de l'Ecole Française d'Extrême Orient*, 2 (4): 373-6.

———, 1921, 'Un voyage en "Sinja" sur les côtes de Cochinchine au XVIIème siècle', *Bulletin des Amis du Vieux Hué*, (Janvier-Mars): 15-29.

Claeys, Jean-Yves, 1939, 'Les chants des pêcheurs d'Annam', *Bulletin de l'Institut Indochinois pour l'Etude de l'Homme*, 5 (fascicule 1): 149-53.

———, 1942, 'L'Annamite et la mer, Conférence du 21 mars', *Bulletin de l'Institut Indochinois pour l'Etude de l'Homme* (fascicule 1): 48-53.

Cuisinier, Jeanne, 1948, 'Monographie des Muongs', *Travaux et mémoires de l'Institut d'Ethnologie*, XLV: xx-618.

De Rhodes, Alexandre, 1883, *Divers voyages et missions en la Chine et autres royaumes de l'Orient avec son retour en Europe par la Perse et l'Arménie*, Lille: Desclée, De Brouwer et Cie (rpt.).

Do Thi Thanh Thuy, Nguyên Thu Trang, Nguyên Thi Phuong and Nguyên Thanh Hoa, 2006, *Report on Maritime Waterways in Vietnam*, ASEAN-COCI Symposium on Maritime and Waterways, Terengganu, Malaysia: ASEAN.

Flecker, Michael, 2007, 'The South China Sea Tradition: The Hybrid Hulls of South-East Asia', *International Journal of Nautical Archaeology*, 36 (1): 75-90.

Freudenreich, L. Benjami et al. (eds.), 1967, *The Blue Book of Coastal Vessels, South Vietnam*, The Advanced Research Projects Agency (DOD), Columbus: Battelle Memorial Institute, Remote Area Conflict Information Centre.

Hall, Kenneth R. (ed.), 2008, *Secondary Cities and Urban Networking in the Indian Ocean Realm, c. 1400-1800*, Lanham: Lexington Books.

Hall, Kenneth R., 1989, 'The Politics of Plunder in the Cham Realm of Early Vietnam', in R. Van Niel (ed.), *Art and Politics in Southeast Asian History: Six Perspectives*, Honolulu: Southeast Asian Studies, Center for Asian and Pacific Studies, University of Hawaii at Manao: 5-16.

Hardy, Andrew, Mauro Cucarzi, and Patrizia Zolese (eds.), 2009, *Champa and the Archaeology of My Son (Vietnam)*, Singapore: National University of Singapore Press.

Higham, Charles, 1989, *The Archaeology of Mainland Southeast Asia; from 10,000 BC to the fall of Angkor, Cambridge World Archaeology*, Cambridge: Cambridge University Press.

Hoàng Anh Tuan, 2007, *Silk for Silver: Dutch-Vietnamese Relations, 1637-1700*, vol. 5, *TANAP Monographs on the History of the Asian-European Interaction*, Leiden: Brill.

Horridge, Adrian, 1982, *Lashed-lug boats of the Eastern Archipelagoes*, vol. Monograph 54, Greenwich: National Maritime Museum.

Huard, Pierre and Maurice Durand (eds.), 1954, *Connaissance du Viêt Nam*, Ecole Française d'Extrême Orient (Hanoi), 43 vols, vol. 8, *Connaissance de l'Indochine*, Paris: Imprimerie Nationale.

Hung, Hsiao-Chung et al., 2007, 'Ancient Jades Map 3000 Years of Prehistoric Exchange in Southeast Asia', *Proceedings of the Academy of Science*, 104 (50): 19745-50.

Lamb, Alistair, 1970, *The Mandarin Road to Old Hué: Narratives of Anglo-Vietnamese Diplomacy from the 17th Century to the Eve of the French Conquest*, London: Archon Books.

Lape, Peter V., Sue O'Connor, and Nick Burningham, 2007, 'Rock Art: A Potential Source of Information about Past Maritime Technology in the Southeast Asia-Pacific Region', *International Journal of Nautical Archaeology*, 36 (2): 238-53.

Lê Dinh Thong, 1990, 'La marine Vietnamienne avant l'arrivée des Français', in H. Coutau-Bégarie (ed.), *Marins et Océans*, vol. III, Paris: Economica, http://www.stratisc.org/pub_mo3_LEDINHTHON.html [Accessed on 30 November 2007].

———, 1992, 'Stratégie et science du combat sur l'eau au Vietnam avant l'arrivée des français', in H. Coutau-Bégarie (ed.), *Evolution de la pensée navale*, vol. II, Paris: Economica, http://www.stratisc.org/PN2_PENSEEVIET.html [accessed on 23 February 2008]

Lê Thanh Khoi, 1992, *Histoire du Viet Nam, des origines à 1858*, Paris: Sudestasie.

Li, Tana, 1998, 'An Alternative Vietnam?: The Nguyên Kingdom in the Seventeenth and Eighteenth Centuries', *Journal of Southeast Asian Studies*, 29 (1): 111-21.

———, 2004, 'Ships and Shipbuilding in the Mekong Delta *c.* 1750-1840', in N. Cooke, and T. Li (ed.), *Water Frontier: Commerce and the Chinese in the Lower Mekong Region, 1750-1880*, Singapore: Rowman & Littlefield & Singapore University Press: 119-34.

———, 2006, 'A View from the Sea: Perspectives on the Northern and Central Vietnamese Coast', *Journal of Southeast Asian Studies*, 37 (1): 83-102.

Ling Shun-Sheng, 1956, 'The Formosan Sea-going Raft and Its Origin in Ancient China', *Bulletin of the Institute of Ethnology*, 1: 25-54.

Manguin, Pierre-Yves, 1980, 'The Southeast Asian Trading Ship: An Historical Approach', *Journal of Southeast Asian Studies*, 11 (2): 253-69.

———, 1983, 'Relationship and Cross Influences between Southeast Asian and Chinese Shipbuilding Traditions', *9th Conference of the International Association of Historians of Asia*, Manila, Philippines, 21-5 November 1983: 1-21.

———, 1993, 'Trading Ships of the South China Sea', *Journal of the Economic and Social Society of the Orient*, 36: 253-80.

———, 2000, 'Les cités-états de l'Asie du Sud-Est côtière', *Bulletin de l'Ecole Française d'Extrême Orient*, 87: 151-82.

Mantienne, Frédéric, 2003, 'The Transfer of Western Military Technology to Vietnam in the Late Eighteenth and Early Nineteenth Centuries: The Case of the Nguyên', *Journal of Southeast Asian Studies*, 34 (3): 519-34.

Moréchand, Guy, 1955, 'Caractères économiques et sociaux d'une région de pêche maritime du Centre Viêtnam (Nha-Trang)', *Bulletin de l'Ecole Française d'Extrême Orient*, 47 (1): 291-352.

Needham, Joseph, 1971, *Science and Civilisation in China*, vol. 4: *Physics and Physical Technology/Part III: Civil Engineering and Nautical Technology*, Cambridge: Cambridge University Press.

Nguyên Boi Lien, 1991, 'Tran Van An and Nguyên Van Phi, Bau Junk in Hoi An, Quang Nam Region', *Ancient Town of Hoi An*, Ha Noi: Society Science Publisher: 141-5.

Nguyên Tai Thu (ed.), 1997, *History of Buddhism in Vietnam*, vol. 5, *Cultural heritage and contemporary change, Series IIID, South East Asia*, Washington: Council for Research in Values and Philosophy.

Nguyên Thê Anh, 1996, 'Indochina and the Malay World: A Glimpse on Malay-Vietnamese Relations to the Mid-nineteenth Century', *Asia Journal*, 3 (1): 105-31.

Nishimura, Masanari, 2005, 'Settlement Patterns on the Red River Plain from the Late Prehistoric Period to the 10th Century AD', *Indo-Pacific Prehistory Association Bulletin*, 25 (Taipei Papers, vol. 3): 99-107.

O'Reilley, Dougald, 2007, 'Early Civilisations of Southeast Asia', *Archaeology of Southeast Asia*, Lanham: AltaMira Press.

Pâris, François-Edmond, 1843, *Essai sur la construction navale des peuples extra-européens, ou Collection des navires et pirogues construits par les habitants de l'Asie, de la Malaisie, du Grand Océan et de l'Amérique, dessinés et mesurés pendant les voyages autour du monde de L'Astrolabe, La Favorite et L'Artémise*, 2 vols., Paris: Arthus Bertrand.

Paris, Pierre, 1939, 'Recherche de parentés à quatre embarcations d'Indochine', *Bulletin de l'Institut Indochinois pour l'Etude de l'Homme*, (fascicule 2): 209-20.

———, 1941, 'Les bateaux des bas-reliefs khmers', *Bulletin de l'Ecole Française d'Extrême Orient*, 41: 335-61.

———, 1942, 'Esquisse d'une ethnographie navale des pays Annamites', *Bulletin des Amis du Vieux Hué*, 4 (Octobre-Décembre): 352-450.

Pham, Charlotte Minh Hà (forthcoming), 'A Unique Boat Building Tradition: Vietnam's Basket Boats', *The Institute of Nautical Archaeology Annual*.

Pham, Charlotte Minh Hà, Lucy Blue and Colin Palmer, 2010, 'Traditional Boats of Vietnam, An Overview', *International Journal of Nautical Archaeology*, 39 (2): 258-77.

Pietri, Jean-Baptiste, 1943, *Voiliers d'Indochine*, Saigon: Société des Imprimeries et Librairies Indochinoises (SILI).

Pinkerton, John (ed.), 1808, *A General Collection of the Best and Most Interesting Voyages and Travels in all Parts of the World*, History of Tonquin from the French of Richard, Paris, 1778, vol. 9, London: Strahan Preflong Printers Street: 708-71.

Reid, Anthony, 2000, 'Economic and Social Change, *c.* 1400-1800', in N. Tarling (ed.), *The Cambridge History of Southeast Asia. Volume one & two: From Early Times to c. 1800*, Cambridge: Cambridge University Press: 116-60.

Sorensen, Per, 1986, 'Kettledrums of Heger I Type: Some Observations', I. Glover and E. Glover (ed.), *Southeast Asian Archaeology*, Oxford: BAR International Series, # 561: 195-200.

Vachet, Bénigne, 1675, *Mémoire pour servir à l'histoire générale des Missions, Relations des Missions et Voyages des Evesques Vicaires Apostoliques et de leurs Ecclesiastiques des années 1672, 1673, 1674 et 1675*, Paris: Victor Goupy, rue Garancière.

Vickery, Michael, 2005, 'Champa Revised', Asia Research Institute Working Paper, no. 37, March 2005, www.ari.nus.edu/sg [accessed on 20 April 2010].

Wade, Geoffrey, 2003, 'The Pre-Modern East Asian Maritime Realm: An Overview of European-Language Studies', Asia Research Institute Working Paper Series, no. 16, www.ari.nus.edu/sg [accessed on 15 December 2009].

Wheeler, Charles, 2001, 'Cross-cultural Trade and Trans-regional Networks in the Port of Hoi An: Maritime Vietnam in the Early Modern Era', Dissertation presented to the Faculty of the Graduate School of Yale University in candidacy for the Degree of Doctor of Philosophy.

———, 2003, *A Maritime Logic to Vietnamese History? Littoral Society in Hoi An's Trading World c. 1550-1830*, vol. Seascapes, Littoral Cultures, and Trans-Oceanic Exchanges, 12-15 February 2003, Library of Congress, Washington D.C.: www.historycooperative.org/proceedings/seascapes/wheeler.html, [Accessed on 21 April 2008].

———, 2006, 'One Region, Two Histories: Cham Precedents in the History of the Hoi An Region', T.T. Nhung and A. Reid (eds.), *Viet Nam: Borderless Histories*, Wisconsin: The University of Wisconsin Press: 163-93.

Whitmore, John K., 2006, 'The Rise of the Coast: Trade, State and Culture in Early Dai Viet', *Journal of Southeast Asian Studies*, 37 (1): 103-22.

———, 2008, 'The Disappearance of Van Don: Trade and State in Fifteen Century Dai Viet—A Changing Regime?', Conference on A Mini Mediterranean Sea—Gulf of Tongking through History, National University of Australia and Southeast Asia Study Institute (China, 14 and 15 March 2008).

Worcester, George Raleigh Gray, 1966, *Sail and Sweep in China*, London: Science Museum.

CHAPTER 6

Mariners, Merchants, Monks: Sri Lanka and the Eastern Seas

SOMASIRI DEVENDRA

Preamble: Legends as History

In the 1930s and 1940s, when I was still in kindergarten, Sri Lanka was planning for independence from Britain. Our freedom struggle was not as proactive as the one in India from where we drew inspiration. Post-war independence, however, was anticipated and nationalist fervour strongly influenced the Buddhist schools which had grown in opposition to missionary schools and we were swept along by this swell. While we still sang English nursery rhymes around the piano in our singing classes, out in the playground, we embraced traditional Sinhala songs, games and dances which, though new to us urban middle-class children, struck a responsive chord that still reverberates.

One such song, particularly relevant to the theme of this paper, took the form of a question and response and went thus:

	Translation
Oliňda thibennē . . . Koi koidēsē?	Where, O where is the *Oliňda* plant found?
Oliňda thibennē . . . Bangali dēsē	In the land of Bengal is the *Oliňda* found.
Genath sadannē . . . Koi koi dēsē?	And where, O where is it brought and grown?
Genath sadannē . . . Sinhala dēsē.	To the land of the *Sinhala* is it brought and grown

These verses are from a rural, pre-colonial past and preserved in medieval Kandy, the last kingdom of Sri Lanka. It describes a board game, the *Oliňda keliya.* Said to have been originally played by courtiers using pearls, it was later adopted by villagers who, lacking pearls, substituted the shiny red-and-black seeds of the *Oliňda* (*Abrus precatorius,* commonly Crab's eye, Jequirity, Rosary Pea, etc.) on carved ebony boards (*Oliňda poruwa*), specifically during the Sinhala and Tamil New Year, which dawns in mid-April (so it probably had a ritual significance). The plant is toxic, and the seeds were used for weighing gold as they are of a uniform weight (1/10th of a gram).

Thus, when an independent Bangladesh emerged as a modern state, my generation recognized the name from childhood. Is *Oliňda* found in Bengal, now? From information provided by Deepak Acharya, Anshu Shrivastava, Sanjay Pawar and Garima Sancheti under the heading 'Abrus Precatorius: Herb from Patalkot, India' on website: http://www.disabled-world.com/medical/alternative/herbal/abrus-precatorius.php#ixzz1a1OeJHty the following information has been gleaned: It is native to India and was introduced to the warmer regions of the world (Cal, 2004*).* It is indigenously found throughout India, even at altitudes up to 1,200 m on the outer Himalayas. It is now naturalized in all tropical countries (Dwivedi, 2004). It grows in other tropical climates such as India, Sri Lanka, Thailand, the Philippine Islands, South China, North America, tropical Africa and the West Indies as well. It also grows in all tropical or sub-tropical areas (Inchem, 2004, no reference provided). It is used as an ornament throughout North America. Thus the plant is found in India and, it can be presumed, Bengal.

The history of Sri Lanka abounds in references to *Vaňga desa,* the land of Bengal. While we have prehistoric settlement sites in Sri Lanka, more than 100,000 years old and that remains of the anatomically modern man *c.* 35,000 years BP, we became the island we are now around 7,000 years ago and the new island came to be settled by Indian colonists much later. Historical legend places the date as 543 BCE based on when the Buddha attained *parinibbāna.* Thus, history, as written by and about the settlers, only begins 2,600 years ago. Like most legends, this does not stand up to objective analysis: the second-century Buddhist monk-chroniclers used the date of the Buddha's *parinibbāna* as the date on which, miraculously, history began. On this date, (we are told) Prince Vijaya and 700 companions landed at Tambapanni in the north-west of the island. What is relevant for the subject of this paper is the story of Vijaya, as related in the *Mahāvaṁsa,* the Great Chronicle. It begins in *Vaṅga desa*:

In the country of the Vangas, in the Vanga capital there lived once a king of the Vangas. The daughter of the king of the Kalingas was the king's consort. By his spouse the king had a daughter and the soothsayer prophesized her union with the king of beasts. Very fair she was and very amorous and for shame the king and queen could not suffer her. (Geiger, 1912/ rpt., 2003: 51)

The princess, a free spirit, lived up to the prophesy, joining a caravan travelling to Magadha, which was attacked in the Lata country (now Gujarat) by a lion who took her, and from whom she had twins, a boy and a girl. The son, Sinhabahu, finally engineered an escape, and the mother and children headed back to Vanga. He killed his father, the lion, and, in time, was raised to the throne of Vanga, but he renounced it, going back to Lata to build a city, Sihapura, from where he ruled with his sister as his wife. They had many children but the eldest is Vijaya, one of a pair of twins, '. . . who was of evil conduct and his followers were even like himself and many intolerable deeds of violence were done by them' (Geiger, 1912/2003: 53).

Unable to face the people's wrath, the king disowned him and set them all adrift on a ship. The ship reached Suparaka (now Sopara, near Mumbai), where Vijaya's men behaved in much the same way and were banished again. Sailing down the west coast of India he landed in Sri Lanka. Defeating the indigenous ruling tribe, he established his own dominance and married the daughter of the Pandu king of Madura, south India.

However, the marriage proved to be childless and Vijaya left no progeny. The kingdom was offered to Panduvasudeva, his unmarried nephew. Meanwhile, in India, Pandu, a Sakya prince who had been warned about the destruction of the Sakya clan (the clan of Prince Siddhartha who became the Buddha), had left his home and had gone '. . . to another tract of land on the further side of the Ganga and founded a city there and ruled as king.' Pandu had a daughter, Baddakaccana, 'a woman made of gold, fair of form and eagerly wooed' by seven kings. Pandu, unhappy with all of them and following the soothsayers' advice, placed her with her retinue on board a 'ship' upon the Ganga, saying 'Whosoever can, let him take my daughter'. The ship made its landfall at Gonagamaka (now Trincomalee) from where the princess and her retinue proceeded westwards on foot, 'robed as nuns', till they were identified as a royal party. Eventually, she married Panduvasudeva, and from this union sprang the Lion Kings of Sri Lanka.

This is the story in essence. The most interesting aspects of it are that Sri Lanka had been occupied by an urbanized people at the time of Vijaya's arrival; that Vijaya, Panduvasudeva and Baddakaccana can all be traced to Vanga desa; and that Trincomalee, in the Bay of Bengal, makes its first appearance very early in historical writings. Its oldest recorded name is Gokarna in Pali.

Introduction

I have related this story to show Sri Lanka's umbilical link with the Bay of Bengal and, more importantly, its hints at two routes of migration over the Indian Ocean, i.e. one from Gujarat following the coast southwards to the Gulf of Mannar to reach the north-western coast of Sri Lanka; and the other from somewhere up the Ganga, traversing the Bay of Bengal in a southerly direction to reach the north-eastern coast of Sri Lanka.

This brings me to the Bay of Bengal itself and I would like to pose the following question: How does one define it? Certainly, maritime space cannot be defined only in terms of geography or the environment. The word 'only' is important. First, the sea exists (the Bay is but a part of it), and man's achievements based upon his mastery of it follows. Unless one takes due note of geography and environment, one is in danger of losing focus. The maritime space that is the Bay of Bengal is a stage; the very stage upon, and across which interaction between cultures and peoples took place.

Therefore, it is necessary that we agree on what this stage is: in fact, to attempt to define it as a physical entity.

Perhaps, in our deliberations, we should remember that the Bay does not begin and end upon its shores. From the maritime and nautical perspective, the Bay of Bengal is essentially a body of water; and all interaction between countries and cultures could take place because of the existence of ships that could stitch them together across that space. The sea was the stage on which every drama we talk of today was played and the ships provided the infrastructure. The point I make is that the 'maritime space' that is our focus is a body of water which we learnt to make use of. Certainly, it cannot be defined *only* in terms of geography or the environment but, equally, it cannot be defined without appreciating its unique geographical position, environment and character, all of which impinged on the littoral countries.

The view that all the seas of the world are one is particularly relevant to those of us who are islanders. To Sri Lankans, all interaction with those not living in our country could take place only by sailing the seas. The *Mahā muhuda* (the Great Ocean) surrounds us and we do not think of any part of the sea as a special maritime space. However, we recognize that a part of the sea between India and Sri Lanka is shallower than the sea that washes the greater part of the latter's shores. We think of the Western Sea, the Eastern Sea and the Southern Sea. The Arabian Sea (along the eastern shore of which Vijaya sailed south) and the Bay of Bengal (down which Baddakaccana sailed southwards) were parts of these: we had no Northern Sea. There was no reason to differentiate the Bay from the Eastern Sea; our view of it was as a part of the *Mahā muhuda* which lay to the east. We had much to do with the Bay, but to make contact with any country along its shore or way beyond it to the countries farther east, we had to sail across the Eastern Sea. The Bay, lacking a clearly defined southern border, was a part of the Eastern Sea and, hence, for the seafarer, it did not form a different sea. It is along the routes of the seafarers that intangible links bound Sri Lanka to countries fringing the Bay and it is these routes that made us a part of the cultural continuum that is the Bay. To end these introductory remarks, the bounds of the Bay can be defined visually on a map (Figure 6.1) which graphically depicts its international, multi-cultural and multi-lingual character.

Figure 6.1: Regions and cultures on the rim of the Bay.

Sri Lanka's Eastern Sea

The Bay of Bengal would have been viewed differently by each nation or region abutting it. For the nation states of Myanmar and Bangladesh and the Indian states of Bengal, Orissa, Andhra, and Tamil Nadu, it would be 'The Sea', the only one that washes its shores. This is not so for the island states of Sri Lanka and Sumatra (I cannot comment on the Andamans), and the farther appendages of mainland Asia—Malaysia and Thailand—which lie to its far south. This factor would naturally have coloured their perceptions: while they were part of the Bay's dynamic, they were not caught in its gravitational pull to the extent that Myanmar, Bangladesh and the Indian regions are. Thus, Sri Lanka's own view of the Bay was influenced not so much because it was its westernmost limit as by the fact that the ports fringing it were a part of the Eastern Sea.

The Bay, in fact, has no maritime boundary but is now deemed, for convenience alone, to be separated from the Indian Ocean by a line drawn on the chart linking Sri Lanka's southernmost point to the northernmost point of Sumatra. These two islands, therefore, represent the southernmost limits of the Bay (Figure 6.2).

These two factors, i.e. its position *vis-à-vis* the Bay of Bengal and the Indian Ocean, mark Sri Lanka as a geographical punctuation mark between the eastern and western halves of the northern Indian Ocean. Additionally, there are the limitless deeps of the *Mahā muhuda* to the south, studded with countless islands, and the shallow Palk Strait to the north, which played a seminal role from the earliest

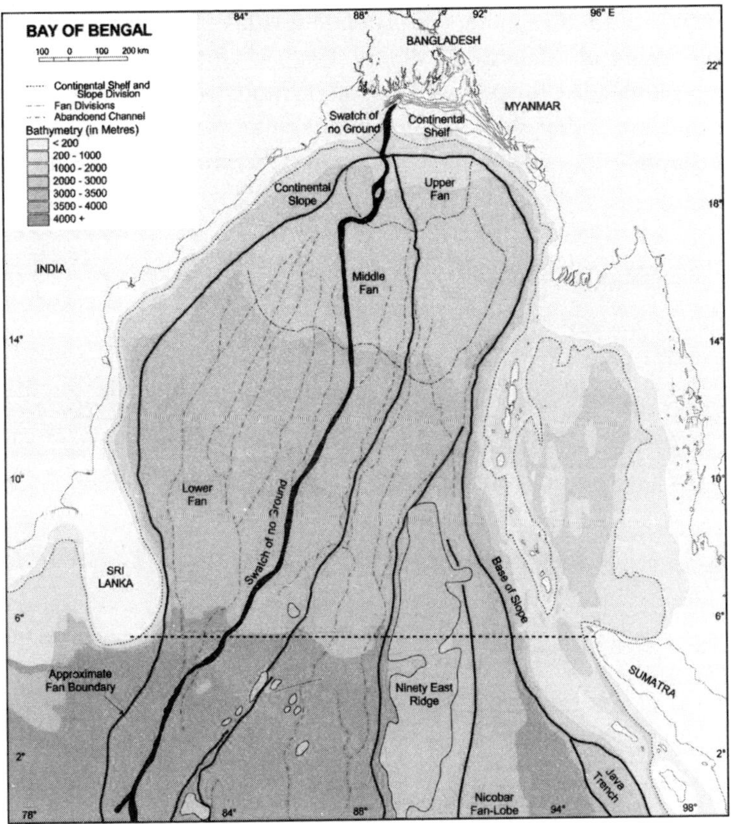

Figure 6.2: Southern limit of the Bay.

days. For Sri Lanka, surrounded by the Ocean, the Bay was a part of its eastern sea, not an entity itself. Thus, any maritime activity which involved the Bay also involved Sri Lanka. An example, from Dutch times (Figure 6.3) is the inter-Asian trading network built-up by the Dutch East India Company, Vereenigde Oost-Indische Compagnie (VOC) on a Batavia-Galle baseline from which shipping spread northwards into the Bay of Bengal and the China Sea.

In more ancient times, shipping between Sri Lanka and the lands to the east was of two types: coastal and cross-oceanic. Coastal shipping engaged in trade with eastern and southeast Indian states, extending to Bangladesh (and up-river). The other was cross-oceanic shipping that either struck across the Bay to Myanmar or further eastwards to Singapore, Thailand, Sumatra and thence through the Straits of Malacca to distant Cathay. Goods and passengers being offloaded for portage over the Isthmus of Kra and boarding a ship in another shipping area were also known and some related archaeological evidence has been found (Chaisuwan, 2011: 83-112).

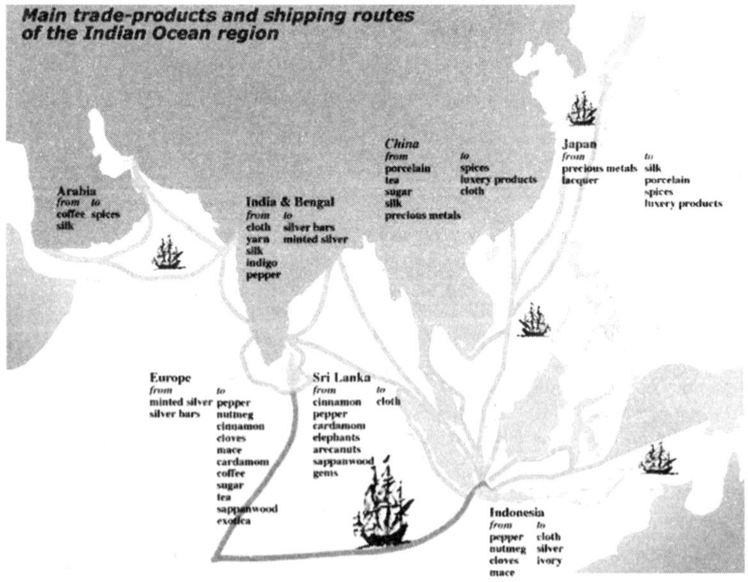

Figure 6.3: Dutch inter-Asian trading network.

Mariners, Merchants, Monks

Under these three categories we can include all persons who traversed the Bay of Bengal and beyond, carrying with them trade goods, technologies, ideas and philosophies. These three single words can be expanded almost infinitely but I would like to briefly define these three types of persons as follows.

Under 'Mariners', I include shipbuilders; their technology and their adaptation of neighbouring technologies; sailors and navigators; who created ports and their infrastructure; and, importantly, ships and sailors who made their landfall in our ports: in other words, people who made interaction a physical possibility.

Under 'Merchants', I include those who utilized the possibilities thus created, proving that travel was financially viable; those who brought communities together by the exchange of trade goods; and those who established regular contact between countries and made travel possible as passengers.

Under 'Monks', I include men and women who used the possibilities thus created to carry and disseminate intangible goods—ideas, knowledge, culture and philosophy—perhaps the most enduring legacies that travelled the seaways. Buddhist pilgrims, particularly to India, are also included here, as are the many craftsmen and scholars who accompanied monks on their missionary voyages.

Naturally, these are not watertight compartments and so there will be some overlap. In presenting my ideas, I will start in reverse order: monks first followed by merchants, but with some overlap between them. They are necessary to provide a context to this paper but my sources are the work of others from whom I have learnt. However, when it comes to mariners I deal with my own research, fieldwork and ideas. It is in this sphere that I believe I can contribute something to this volume.

Monks

It is, of course, Buddhist monks and nuns that I speak of, for Buddhism was the major religion of Sri Lanka. Tradition has it that King Devānāmpiyatissa, a contemporary of the Indian king

Dharmāśoka, had requested the latter to send Buddhist monks to the island to spread the word of the Buddha. He, in fact, requested that he be re-consecrated by Dharmāśoka whose expanding kingdom he did not underestimate. The *Mahāvaṁsa* has it that the monks arrived not by sea but by levitation at the royal hunting ground of Mihintale on the day that the king was on a hunt. Says the *Mahāvaṁsa*, they 'rose in the air . . . coming hither . . . alighted on the pleasant Missaka-mountain' (today's Mihintale). Here the two met and the *Mahāvaṁsa* records what may well be the first I.Q. test in the world. The monk tests the king's intelligence through a series of questions to judge his ability to understand the teaching. The conversion of the king and his people follow. A recent publication (Goonatilake, 2010: 33) quotes an Indian source as follows:

> Mahinda, the son of Asoka, on his way to Sri Lanka according to Indian archaeologists appears to have travelled by sea through the South Indian port of Kavirapattinam (Kaverippumpattinam). In the spread of Buddhism to south India Mahinda was 'greatly helped' by Aritta, the uncle of Devanampiyatissa, probably (in) the village near Madura called Arrittapatti, with Brahmi inscriptions of Asoka's time attesting to this. (Ramachandran, 1992: 2-3)

Personally unacquainted with the work referred to, I take the quote at face value, for this would place Mahinda in a Bay of Bengal maritime context, as being the first of the monks I speak of. That he did come by sea is entirely feasible: the *Mahāvaṁsa*, though silent about his journey, is quite clear about the arrival by sea of his sister, the *theri* Sanghamitta, who came to establish the *bhikkhuni* ordination, bearing with her a sprig of the original *bodhi* tree at Bodh-Gaya under which the Buddha achieved enlightenment. Its history has been meticulously recorded and it continues to be venerated at present. An even more interesting side of the story is the ship itself which had conveyed *theri* Sanghamitta to the port of Jambukola(pattana), in the north of the present city of Jaffna. After the *bhikkhunis* had taken up residence at the nunnery called *upasikavihara*, Sanghamitta built three buildings on the premises, says the *Mahāvaṁsa*.

> . . . in one of these great buildings she [theri Sanghamitta] caused the mast

of the ship that had come with the great Bodhi-tree to be set up, in one the rudder, and in one the helm, from these they were named. (Geiger, 1912/2003: 133-4)

That ships were familiar to even the writers of the Chronicles is evident as also the fact that Indian ships were fitted with the rudder-and-tiller. Another fact of nautical interest is that ships were not berthed at but anchored off the coast, and goods and passengers came ashore by other means. Both Dharmāśoka in India and Devānāmpiyatissa in Sri Lanka, waded up to the ship (and vice versa) with the *bodhi* tree on their heads to place it on board or receive it. This manoeuvre is commented on later in this paper. The fact that monks were familiar with ships and travel by sea from the earliest days is made abundantly clear here.

There are, naturally, many references to travel to the seats of Buddhism. That they travelled by sea has to be assumed, and it is likely that they changed vessels at different ports. The ships they travelled in were not passenger but cargo ships where goods were landed and others taken on board. So there would have been several legs to a journey and journeys could take many months with breaks in between. Kaveripattinam, or the Poompuhar of today, has already been noted and references to other, more northern ports follow. But it was Bodh-Gaya that was the magnet. Travel there by sea and river was certainly possible though it was earlier assumed that:

The development of sea routes connecting Sri Lanka with the more northern ports of the more eastern coast of India probably took place well after the development of routes linking Sri Lanka with places in the western coast of India. . . . It is only with reference to a period around the middle of the first millennium that it is possible to speak with confidence about a sea route linking Sri Lanka with the mouth of the Ganges being in operation. (Gunawardena, 1990: 32)

More recent archaeological work has shown that by the early centuries there emerged a 'single looping network' of sea travel from lower Bengal to Sri Lanka. (Ray, 2006: 113-43)

As travel by sea had been achieved, it is a reasonable assumption that ships (or boats or sea-going rafts) did carry goods and passengers from one point to another. This is not to say that there was an established route linking the southern and northern Indian ports together. Travel would not have been continuous, but from point to point, partly overland and partly by sea, with long breaks in-between. Sea routes, in 'bookish' parlance, ignore many realities familiar to seamen. The plausible conclusion is that north-south travel involving the use of watercraft, at least in part, was in existence and this implies that sea travel along the Coromandel coast was not uncommon. The first links between Sri Lanka, monks and travel by sea had, thus, been forged early on and was to become a commonplace activity for Buddhist monks who, it must be remembered, were steeped in a missionary tradition from the time that the Buddha instructed 'Go forth ye monks. . . .'

Many are the references to Sri Lankan monks in India and even Indian monks in Sri Lanka, a sample of which are given here. Mahanama, a first-century pilgrim to Bodh-Gaya, had left an inscription that was seen in the fourth century by the Chinese commentator, Wang Xuance (Seneviratne, J. 1915: 75, 77-123). A fourth-century king, Meghavarna, sent gems from Sri Lanka to King Samudragupta to build a monastery where Sri Lankan monks would reside. It was more than a monastery. It was more akin to the learning centres of Nalanda and Vikramashila, and was maintained by the Sinhalese. The Chinese pilgrim, Xuanzang (Barua, 1979), gives us a description of it in the seventh century. A Sanskrit inscription mentions the visit of Prakyatakirtti, a Sinhalese pilgrim of royal descent in the seventh or eighth century. Another inscription attributable to the ninth-tenth century mentions a Buddhist image carved by the Sinhalese Udayasiri at Mahabodhi. It mentions that the large number of Sinhalese pilgrims present contributed to the upkeep of the temple. Many other sources can be quoted but I will end with the reference by the thirteenth-century Tibetan monk, Dharmavasin, to three hundred Sinhalese monks at Bodh-Gaya and the fact that only they were allowed to sleep within the courtyard of the main temple.

With Buddhism still flourishing in Andhra Pradesh, there are many references to Nagarjunakonda. The suffix *-konda* is *kanda* or hill in Sinhala and I have myself climbed Thotlakonda on a visit to Visakhapatnam, and seen the second-century remains of a Buddhist monastery there. Not too far from here was Bavikonda, which was another monastery where a large urn that is believed to have contained the relics of the Buddha, was found. Mahayanism made its appearance in India under Nagarjuna with whom Aryadeva, a Sinhalese, was associated. The Theravada Buddhist establishment in Sri Lanka had split into several schools—the Mahavihara, Abhayagiri and Jetavana—and the adherents of each school were to be found along the East Indian littoral. In Nagarjunakonda (or ancient Vijayapuri) there were at least two Sinhalaviharas: one for the monks of the Mahavihara, called Mahaviharavasivihara, and another called Chuladhammagiri. The prefixes *maha-* and *chula-* are revealing. A Sinhalavihara was built in the third century by an unknown donor, and an *upāsaka*, Bodhisiri, added a shrine for the *bodhi* tree.

> An inscription records a grant by Bodhisiri for the monks of Tambapanna (Sri Lanka) who converted (*pasadakanam*) Kashmir, Gandhara, China, Chilata, Tosali, Avamta, Vanga, Vanavasi, Yavana, Damila Palura and the island of Tambapanni. (Goonatilake, 2010: 32)

The inscriptional record of Buddhist contacts with Andhra continues till even the fourteenth century, with a mention in the Gadaladeniya inscription (near Kandy) of renovations carried out at Amaravati by a Sinhala monk, Dhammakirti.

Perhaps, for Sri Lankan Buddhists, the most important event was the arrival here of the Sacred Tooth Relic of the Buddha. The *Dhātuvaṁsa*, a chronicle of the Relic, speaks of a Prince Dantakumara, son of the king of Ujjeni, who, while in Kalinga to worship at Dantapura, fell in love with Hemamali, daughter of the king of Kalinga. They brought the relic hidden in the princess' hair, to Sri Lanka. They travelled in disguise from Tamralipti by a trading vessel. The Relic became the Palladium of the kings of Sri Lanka and its fame spread all over the Buddhist world. Many desired it: the Chinese claim to have captured it more than once and the Portuguese claim to have captured and destroyed it. Countless numbers of replicas were made and sent all over the world but the original is still believed to be in Kandy.

The movement of monks and pilgrims was two way. Instances of Indian monks travelling to Sri Lanka are on record. Perhaps the best known was Buddhaghosa who translated the Sinhalese written record of the Buddha-word back into Pali. The *Tripiṭaka*, which had survived some centuries as it was orally transmitted, had been written down in Sinhala in the second century BCE. At this time a great drought drove most monks away from the country. Kanchipuram and Madurai in south India, according to Buddhaghosa, were still major centres of Pali scholarship. Others who made an impact were Sanghamitta, who converted the king to Vaitulyavada, a form of Mahayana; and Buddhatta, from the land of the Cholas who, in the fifth century, composed many works at the Abhayagiri monastery. In the seventh century, Buddhists were expelled from Kanchipuram and Vajrabodhi, from Pandya country, passed through Sri Lanka, bound for China. When Rajaraja Chola ruled Sri Lanka in the tenth century, south Indian monks made their mark there. Dipankara Thera, Buddhamitra, and Mahakasyapa travelled in the twelfth century, as also Anuruddha from the Pandya region. King Parakramabahu II, patronized Dharmakirti, also of Pandya region in the thirteenth century. This travel was essentially religious in character, meaning that it was only for purposes of learning, building of temples and monasteries and missionary activities. However, culture, technology and the arts followed the monks and a regular two-way communication ensued. When Sanghamitta came to Sri Lanka, Dharmāśoka sent with her:

> . . . persons from royal families, and eight from families of ministers, and moreover eight persons from brahman families and eight from families of traders and persons from the cowherds likewise and from the hyena and sparrow-hawk clans (from each one man) and also from the weavers and the potters and from all the handicrafts. . . . (Geiger, 1912/2003: 128)

There still are families in Sri Lanka who claim descent from them. This role—of a core of specialists in various trades accompanying the monks—was one that Sri Lanka was called upon to play when she assumed the mantle of being the centre of Theravada Buddhism. By this time, developments in the Indian social fabric had effectively marginalized Buddhism and Sri Lanka became the natural repository of the southern tradition. Mahayana sects were found in Sri Lanka, too, and some used the island as a springboard to countries further east. The coming of Sanghamitta with this retinue transformed Sri

Lanka which had been developing a distinctive cultural persona of its own, although it had started out as a colony of north Indian settlers. This event changed the trend and the country was drawn back into the mainstream of north Indian culture—by now, a Buddhist culture. Sri Lanka did continue to develop a culture of its own but the link with Buddhism kept it harnessed to India. When Buddhism lost its hold in India, a more vernacular version of the Buddhist culture came into being, particularly after the Buddha-word was set down in writing in the second century BCE. This development achieved three things: it put an end to the absolute dependence on the oral transmission of the Teachings; it was written down in Sinhala and not Pali; and it made the history of Sri Lanka (as recorded in the *Mahāvaṁsa*) part of Buddhist scripture.

Thus, when Sri Lanka became the repository of Theravada, it was this tradition that was expounded to the Southeast Asian countries of Myanmar, Thailand, Cambodia, Laos, Java, the Celebes and beyond. The Sinhala Buddhist culture spread over these areas from ninth to fifteenth centuries until the arrival of the Portuguese which disrupted the organic development of this region. As in the case of India, only a sample of the information is given here. In the eleventh and twelfth centuries, when Bagan in Myanmar reached pre-eminence, an explosion in building activity began, and the dominant external style emulated was that of Sri Lanka. The writing, too, began to follow that of the *Mahāvaṁsa*, which, in turn encouraged existing vernacular languages and styles to develop. The Myinkaba Kubuauk-gyi temple of the twelfth century in Bagan was painted with many scenes of the life of the Buddha, and episodes from the *Mahāvaṁsa*. The latter include scenes of the Buddha's visits to Sri Lanka, the *arahats* Mahinda and Sanghamitta, and the kings Dutugemunu, Vasabha, Siri Sangabo and Buddhadasa. The latest king depicted is Vijayabahu I, who was the last king of Sri Lanka before the building was built (Figure 6.4).

Sinhalese forms of architecture and sculpture permeated other countries like Thailand, Cambodia, Laos and Vietnam. Stupas and Buddha images imitated Sinhalese models and, in some cases, were imported from or gifted by Sri Lanka. The Sihinga Buddha image in Thailand was gifted by the thirteenth-century king Parakrama-

Figure 6.4: Dutugemunu and his elephant Kandula, a *Mahāvaṁsa* story.

bahu II. The Sukhothai city there was rebuilt in the fourteenth-century by Sinhalese craftsmen who were sent by King Bhuvanekabahu IV. Less than a century before the arrival of the Portuguese, a group of Burmese monks were sent to Kalyani (Kelani) for instruction and higher ordination. From Burmese records we know that there was a serious drought prevailing in Sri Lanka, which prompted their early return—a fact not mentioned in any Sri Lankan record.

In most of these countries the order of monks were re-cast in the Sinhalese model. Many monks took up residence in these countries and Sinhala Nikāyas were formed. It followed that Sri Lankan-style monasteries and *viharas* were built, and many are still venerated. An early example is the Ratu Boko (eighth-ninth century) monastery in Java. Apart from epigraphical evidence, the architecture and landscaping bears unmistakable parallels with the Abhayagiri monastery in Anuradhapura. Borobudur, notwithstanding connections with Mahayana and Tantra, is now being thought of as an extension of Sri Lankan Buddhism.

The sea-borne Theravada tradition from the south met the Mahayana adherents in Southeast Asia. Mahayana, Hinduism and remnants of animism were what the Theravada monks encountered. What prevailed cannot now be ascertained as the results were not uniform. It is likely that a degree of competitiveness between the two branches of Buddhism resulted.

From the seventeenth to the nineteenth centuries, the Myanmar, Thai, Lao, Shan and Cambodian courts adopted the Sinhalese Theravada Buddhist models in ceremony, literature, law and monastic life. As in Sri Lanka, this led to the development of vernacular learning and the sidelining of Sanskrit. Increased levels of literacy and a greater demand for a national literature resulted. The influence of the *Mahāvaṁsa* cannot be overestimated. In fact, there is a Cambodian *Mahāvaṁsa*, which carries material not included in the existing copies of the original here.

One southeastern Buddhist country, however, had a very significant impact on Sri Lanka. This was Thailand which returned the very teachings that the latter had nurtured in that country. Thailand had received the teachings from Dharmāśoka himself at about the same time that they reached Sri Lanka. There was a well-developed artistic Hindu-Buddhist tradition of art, heavily influenced by Thai native genius. When Sukhothai was expanding the Sinhala style influenced the Chiang Saen school of art of Lanna Thai (Guruge, 1990: 251). A *Sangharaja* from Sri Lanka was invited to take up residence in Sukhothai and the ruins of the monastery still stand.

The construction of this monastery is the theme of one of the most important epigraphical records of Thailand. This is, in fact, one of the earliest inscriptions in the Thai script. This inscription records the growing influence of Theravada Buddhism to whose propagation the king, under the guidance of the scholar-monk, had devoted the utmost effort, energy and attention.

As mentioned above, a group of Thai monks had received their higher ordination (*upasampadā*) in Sri Lanka in CE 1423 and, on their return, had formed the Siamese sect which was destined to play a major role in Sri Lanka. After the fifteenth century, Buddhism began to fade away in Sri Lanka and on more than one occasion, there were fewer senior monks than the number required to perform the higher ordination ceremony, or to teach younger novices. After monks brought from Arakan failed to resuscitate the Sangha, it went into decline. Under a change of dynasty, the new king, Narendrasinha, was appealed to by a self-taught monk, Saranankara, to get senior monks from other lands. The king himself had no maritime capability as the ports and seas were now under Dutch control: nevertheless, he asked the Dutch for help and they responded by making available a ship. This time the country of choice was Thailand but after formalities were completed, the news came that the Sri Lankan king had died, so the mission was aborted by the Thai king. However, two years later, the new Sri Lankan king, Kirti Sri Rajasingha, sent another mission to Thailand which was successful in its mission. In May 1783, Upali Thera and twenty-four other monks, accompanied by five ambassadors reached the Kandyan capital with a letter from the Thai king and six Sinhalese monks received the higher ordination in July. Among them was Saranankara himself. Buddhism of the same tradition that had been introduced to Thailand was now re-planted on Sri Lankan soil by Thai monks. Three years later, another delegation arrived, bringing Buddhist texts that were, by then, lost in this country. Till today, the Siamese sect remains the largest and most influential, and the only one that was established under royal patronage. Sri Lanka had now reaped the benefits of what it had sown.

Merchants

Much has been said about merchants already. Buddhist monasteries developed along trade routes and growing urban centres. They were located at strategic points on the trade routes, and Buddhist symbols were adopted for coins, seals and pottery, thereby facilitating trade (Ray, 1986).

The material goods that were traded will not be dealt with here. It is a subject that requires thorough research and as several respected writers have done so, it will not be dealt with even in a summary form. The nautical aspects of merchant shipping will be dealt with: where and how merchant shipping developed in the Bay of Bengal.

When did merchant shipping develop in the Bay? Most writers look at the Indian Ocean from the west. It is taken for granted that Indian Ocean trade and shipping, began in the Arabian Sea, progressed up to Sri Lanka and then stopped. Sailing beyond this became possible only after the 'discovery' of the monsoon cycle. Consequently, in India, shipping first developed along her western coast, which happens to be the Arabian Sea's eastern boundary. Indian shipping on the eastern coast developed much later. I intend to look at this from another angle altogether. My point of dissent is based upon common sense and material evidence. How can one venture out to sea if one does not know that winds blow in season, that stars rise and set (as do the sun and moon), and that they do not change their positions in relation to each other? Shepherds who tended their flocks by day, caravan travellers who crossed the desert by night and fishermen afloat or ashore knew this, although they did not know the reason why. Pliny, the Roman author and naturalist, met the ambassadors from Sri Lanka who arrived in Rome in the time of Claudius, one of whom told him that his father had visited China several times. Not only did they do so before Hippalus (credited with 'discovering' the monsoon for the Western world), but they knew what he, perhaps, did not. We do know that they had commented on different ways in which the stars appeared over Rome, particularly remarking on the difference in the position of the Great Bear and Pleiades, the fact that Canopus was much brighter in the Sri Lankan sky, and that the sun was always to the south and, therefore, shadows in the Roman latitudes always pointed north (Weerakkody, 1997). Coming as they did from a country where astrology was a serious study, this is not surprising. India had, in fact, worked out a 'longitudinal grid' over Indian skies for astrological purposes; one meaning of the Sanskrit word *lanka* was the 'meridian' of that grid, and the prime meridian passed over the middle of Sri Lanka. This was knowledge that had been garnered over centuries or even millennia.

The importance of Hippalus' so-called discovery of the monsoons was that, it was the work of a man who gathered this 'exotic' knowledge and had recognized a pattern that could be used as a planning tool. He has to be admired for the way in which he analysed why sailors sailed to 'the beat of a different drum'; but he did not 'discover' the monsoons for the whole of the known world, nor did this lead to new shipping routes. In various ways, the alternating monsoons were known and made use of: for example, the Sri Lankan knowledge of the *yala* and *maha* seasons in relation to agriculture. These were determined by the two monsoons: one which brought heavy rains (the water of which was tapped and stored for controlled use after the rains), and the other which brought less and was used to rain-feed crops. Sri Lanka's successful hydrological civilization was built on this knowledge of the monsoon winds. In other countries affected by the monsoons, similar knowledge must have existed.

Once the cycle was known to the Arabian Sea sailors, they could use it to go beyond Sri Lanka, but their ships had to develop the necessary rigging and sea-keeping qualities for long-haul voyages. Thus, it was a combination of the knowledge of the monsoon cycle and the development of larger and sturdier ships that made voyaging around Sri Lanka to the Eastern Sea viable. Knowledge of the movements of stars was the other dimension. In the Mediterranean, the use of stars was known to sailors, but only for direction-finding and not for position-fixing. Hence, these sailors could not make much use of the unfamiliar skies of the Indian Ocean. It was the Arabs, who had honed their knowledge of stellar movements by years of study of the clear desert skies who made it possible to sail the latitudes, but this was later.

So far, only the impact of the monsoons in the Arabian Sea has been considered, with a solitary reference to Sri Lanka. However, what the monsoons meant to Sri Lanka was different from what it would have meant to the different regions of the eastern and western coasts of India, and of the Bay. Even today, the monsoon cycle sets the rhythm for many activities there and several of these date back far into the past. Knowledge, from a seaman's perspective is implicit in the Jātaka stories, and specifically in the *Suppāraka Jātaka*. Dates of these stories vary: many prior to Dharmāśoka while others are derived from collections of folk stories such as the *Pañcatantra*. Dates will not be debated here but it is essential to note that merchant-shipping far beyond the coast was taken for granted in times earlier than the purported 'discovery' of monsoon winds by Hippalus in the mid-first century around which time Ptolemy recorded his findings. Archaeological evidence from Sri Lanka includes two potsherds dated to the second century BCE, which show line drawings of ships. One, found in Anuradhapura (Figure 6.5), shows a line drawing of a ship with a mast and quarter rudders (i.e. steering oars), and the other (Figure 6.6), from Hambantota in the south, shows an even more sophisticated ship, with sails hoisted, and structural features that may point to a ship-building culture to the east of Sri Lanka.

These are ships, not rafts. If such ships could sail for profit, and be seen often enough for potters to remember their outlines, some 250 years before Ptolemy and before Hippalus 'discovered' the monsoons, then one must re-think the story of shipping in the Indian Ocean eastwards of Sri Lanka. Gunawardena (1990: 28) says of the first century CE:

> . . . it seems likely that by this time mariners proceeding to Java, Sumatra and Malaya had begun to use the monsoon winds to sail directly across the Bay of Bengal. This change in the methods of navigation was of special significance for trade and travel and for Sri Lanka in particular. (Sylvan) Levi tended to believe that the Satavahanas dispatched their trading ships through Sri Lanka.

Obviously, they had the ships, they had the trade, they knew the routes and they could read the stars: *ergo* they knew when and where the winds blew. And the monsoon winds blew as environmental conditions—not man—dictated.

Leaving the Arabian Sea, our earliest shipping route was to India. It is a shallow sea, and the distance was not great but it had to be sailed across. It was no voyage of discovery as fishermen from both sides knew of each other. A common chank-fishing culture existed on both shores from prehistoric times. Neither coast was *terra incognita* to them. Travel by log raft was and is common, and the area of operations extends northward today to Visakhapatnam. A

Figure 6.5: Potsherd from Anuradhapura.

Figure 6.6: Potsherd from Godawāya.

second-century BCE rock engraving of a raft (Figure 6.7) forms part of an inscription, which records the donation of a cave to the Sangha by a Bharata merchant, which survives at Duvegala, in Polonnaruwa. It can easily be recognized as a craft in use today.

There is a literary reference, too. Describing the exodus of Buddhist monks to south India during the troubled times in the reign of Vatthagamami (133-77 BCE) the *Sammohavinodan* refers to an unusual kind of raft that was supposedly used.

> The raft which was constructed at the port of Jambukola is said to have 'three decks' (*tibumakam*). The lowest deck, which tended to be immersed in water, was evidently not used. The travellers occupied the second deck while their belongings were kept on the third. The voyage was considered to be so perilous that. . . . (Gunawardena, 1990: 26)

The description is of an entirely plausible form of sea-going raft: the lowest 'deck' was the raft itself, the second would have been raised a couple of feet above it and the third may have formed a roof over the travellers. In fact, rafts from across the Bay of Bengal are not infrequently storm-driven to Sri Lanka's eastern shore and, one occasion, I was able to get a photograph from Trincomalee (Figure 6.8).

One can see the bottom 'deck', the second and the third, but the last does not cover the whole of the second. There was no one on board when the raft was washed ashore but there were pieces of Burmese-language newspapers that indicated its origin. The raft was intact. As usual, villagers quickly stripped it of the larger bamboos

Figure 6.7: A shaped-log raft, with mast, engraved at Dūvēgala.

Figure 6.8: A Burmese bamboo raft washed ashore at Trincomalee.

of which it was constructed as these were larger than those easily available in the country.

I have dealt with the shipping between Sri Lanka and the east coast of India under the section 'Monks' and, hence, will speak of the more eastward areas of the Eastern Sea. Our sources are, again, Buddhist and Chinese but the content is nautical. By the early fifth century, sea routes with Asia and China were well established. Apart from Faxian who took a ship from Sumatra, there was Gunavarman, a Kashmiri monk, who had spent some time in Sri Lanka before he took a ship to Java through the Malacca Straits. There are also references to two groups of Sri Lankan nuns who travelled to China and established the *bhikkhuni* order. They were taken there by a mariner Nandi. This event led, in fact, to the preservation of the *bhikkhuni sāsana* since the order declined in Sri Lanka and was not re-established under royal patronage as the order of monks was. In fact, in Sri Lanka, the very idea of nuns was looked at askance. In China, the order took root and spread to adjoining countries where, though in a Mahayana context, the *bhikkhuni sāsana* flourished. A couple of decades ago, a handful of nuns from Sri Lanka travelled to Korea and were admitted to the order there. They have since returned and public opinion is fast accepting them in the mainstream.

Yijing, in his Memoir on Chinese pilgrims, provides information on routes from Southeast Asia to Tamralipti or Tamluk in the north of the Bay of Bengal. One linked the Malacca Straits with Sri Lanka, a second linked the Malay peninsula with Tamralipti. Yijing gives details of his own voyage from Sumatra to Lie-tcha. On the second leg of the voyage the ship dropped anchor at the Nicobar islands and he gives a description of the people there. From here he reached Tamralipti in half a month. This was the third route. He comments that it involved many stops due to the vagaries of winds and unknown currents conditions. The fourth route took the monk Daolin from Malaya to Java, and from there to the Bay (whether via the Straits of Malacca or not is not known) and to the Nicobar Islands, and then reaching Tāmralipti after many years.

The information presented by I-tsing is particularly relevant and useful since it indicates that Sri Lanka was connected by sea routes not only with ports in the southern, western and northeastern regions of the Indian subcontinent but also with Southeast Asian kingdoms like Ho-ling, Dvaravati, and Fu-nan and through them with China, thus creating an extensive network which facilitated the movement of merchants and goods, as well as of pilgrims, scholars, texts, images and other sources of cultural influence. Li Chao . . . speaks of visits paid by Sri Lankan vessels to Vietnam and China every year. . . . (Gunawardana, 1990: 33)

What emerges from Yijing's Memoir is the availability of ships from port to port; something that indicates frequent trading voyages to different destinations. It is a pity that there is no similar description of sea routes involving Myanmar. We know the routes only because of the monks who travelled by them but hardly anything about the many ports or the goods that were carried in relays from one port to another.

However, we do have a riveting description of a sea-borne punitive raid by Parakramabahu I of Sri Lanka on the kingdom of Ramaňňa (Arakan) involving, trade interests. There had been traditionally exchanges of gifts between Sri Lanka and Ramaňňa. Certain types of elephants were in great demand in Sri Lanka and the Sri Lankans may have been middle-men in the elephant trade. Whatever the reasons, Ramaňňa stopped the trade and Sri Lanka tried to prevent

Ramañña from buying them from the neighbouring Kamboja. Sri Lankan envoys were arrested, their merchandise confiscated and the relations soured. Sri Lanka built a fleet and sailed for Ramañña, and a skirmish occurred there.

The *Cūlavaṁsa*, the continuation of the earlier *Mahāvaṁsa*, carries a most illuminating account of the logistics of a punitive raid to Burma, stemming from a dispute involving the trade in elephants. The incident in question is supported by a contemporary inscription recording the grant of land and privileges to the leaders of the expedition. It makes a reference to *hatan nav* (lit. warships) but it is uncertain whether they were a kind of ship specially fitted out for war, or ships constructed for the expedition. The latter is more likely following the *Cūlavaṁsa* description of their construction:

> . . . gave the order without delay to make ready ships of various kinds, many hundreds in number. Now all the country round about the coast was one great workshop occupied with the building of the ships taken in hand. When within five months he had all the ships well built he assembled them . . . (at) Pallava-vanka . . . he had provisions supplied for a whole year . . . and abundant weapons of war such as armour . . . *gokanna* arrows . . . for defence against elephants, also different kinds of medicines preserved in cow-horns for dealing with venomous wounds caused by poisoned arrows . . . remedies for curing the poison of infected water . . . iron pincers for extracting iron arrow-heads, . . . lastly also skilful physicians. . . . (*Cūlavaṁsa,* Pt. II: 64-6)

This description, which indicates knowledge of the requirements for storing a ship for an offensive campaign, is more important for the reference to ships of various kinds being built on the seashore. It is a pointer to ship-building without the need for inland shipyards, to the ability to mobilize a large work-force capable of undertaking the building of a large fleet, and even to the possibility that the ships were of the outrigger-equipped type and capable of being built on the beach—that they were, in fact, *yathra dhonis*. Even leaving room for exaggeration, this account rings true in terms of the building of an expeditionary force. The account continues, and even records the loss at sea of the majority of the fleet. There are other, equally credible accounts of attacks at sea between local warring factions and other expeditions that intervened in south Indian politics. All of these indicate the knowledge of naval strategy in offensive operations.

Today, I see two more significant aspects of interest in this account. The large number of ships lost with no excuses given or demonic forces blamed is a detail of interest: it possibly buttresses the credibility of the account. Another is the need to research ships capable of carrying even a few elephants on board: however, even the Dutch took an elephant to Holland. At the rock-cut cave site of Ajanta in western India, elephants are shown in boats in the *Sinhala Avadāna*, an illustration of an incident in the *Valahassa Jātaka*.

Mariners

With mariners, one comes to the nautical as opposed to the maritime dimension of interaction across the Eastern Sea. I will try to refrain from overly referring to the Western Sea and to keep the focus on the area this study is concerned with. Further, I am aware that most scholars who have made Sri Lanka the focus of their studies have concentrated on the Western Sea, and less on the Eastern and Southern Seas. What has been written of the Eastern Sea has been confined to culture, religion, literature and travel. A different perspective is called for in keeping with the aims of this volume, and I would like to make a start.

In this section—unlike in the two preceding sections—I will not draw on the work of others but present my own work on the subjects of nautical archaeology and naval architecture. Nautical archaeology, (a branch of maritime archaeology) is not, as often believed, concerned only with shipwrecks. A simple clarification is offered in www.nauticalarchaeologicalsociety.org (accessed September 2011, and 28 November 2011):

> Few people in Britain live more than a few miles from an example of our maritime past. It is not just our seas, but our rivers, canals and lakes, and the facilities such as ports, warehouses and factories that make up that heritage. It is however, much more than that. It includes the people who used, made, crewed and built that heritage—without them the ships could not sail, factories would produce nothing and great voyages of exploration would not have happened.

Naval architecture, on the other hand is concerned with the design of water-borne transport, whether meant for marine or freshwater use, in civilian or military roles. It responds to the technical, environmental and material limits within which the desired vessel must be built and operated. Today it involves basic and applied research, design, development, design evaluation and calculations during all stages of the life of a marine vehicle. In pre-modern times, these stages were not followed: the way a ship was built followed a design that had grown over centuries—or even millennia—in response to the very factors modern naval architecture responds to. Ship-building under the old methods still exist, and that is why naval architecture is often called more a craft than a science.

Nautical Archaeology

In keeping with the theme of the volume, I consider it apt to include here extracts from a Report I was asked to submit on, what was then a proposal, to build a port at Hambantota. It has now been built but what I had to say on the impact on the heritage of the proposed location is as good a place as any to start on the subject of nautical archaeology. I did not confine my report to the site as the land and sea around the proposed port, but expanded it to include history, macro-history, archaeo-history and nautical archaeology. These extracts come as close as possible to a nautical archaeological study of southern and eastern Sri Lanka, without becoming a complete study in itself. This was a report for policy-makers and not an academic paper.

Extract 1

The line between pre-history and history is drawn between *before* and *after* the availability of written records, irrespective of their accuracy. Sri Lanka became an island 7,000 years ago. No written records exist of the preceding period. None exists either for the *c.* 6,400-year period between that date and the sixth century BCE when the legendary Prince Vijaya arrived here from India. The legend memorializes the arrival of Indian settlers in the island. Later, but still within the first millennium BCE, Buddhism became the dominant religion. Monks in monasteries began recording happenings in the country from that date. History in Sri Lanka, therefore, commences from the sixth century BCE.

For the purpose of this project, the macro-historical parameter is that Hambantota was a part of the Ruhunu-rata, one of the three major divisions of the country (the Ruhunu, Maya and Rajaratas) during the ancient and medieval periods. Ruhuna was second in importance, often the refuge of rulers who lost control over the main Rajarata region, which was the focus of the attention of the monk-chroniclers who maintained written historical records. These rulers were able to recoup and win back their lost territory. Foremost among them were Dutugemunu, Vijayabahu I and Parakramabahu I—all hero figures in the written records. From Hambantota, Ruhuna stretched westwards to Beruwala, and eastwards and northwards to Trincomalee. It was, therefore, an area with a long coastline and, consequently, a rich maritime history. It existed alongside the Rajarata as a largely independent principality, with its own kings and princes for most of this period, although it was not given the emphasis it deserves in the Rajarata-centric histories. Whatever lacunae there are in the subjective historical records are, however, filled in by archaeology which deals with material remains.

The archaeo-historical parameter of this study is the maritime context. All shipping that traversed the northern Indian Ocean rounded the island. Sailing across the ocean, essentially for trade, involved using one monsoon for the outward passage and the other for the return. To ride out the 'wrong' monsoons, havens were needed, preferably sheltered ports, from where trading could be carried on. For this, the hinterland should have industrial and manufactured goods, surplus agricultural produce, entrepôt opportunities, regulated markets, and communities. Ruhuna offered these in its many river mouths, headlands, bays, coves and inland lagoons. The better ones developed into fully-fledged commercial harbours. Ports were loci of merchants and seamen. They were managed by them though the officers of the ruling kings imposed port regulations, customs duties and salvage laws—for all of which contemporary archaeological evidence is available.

The last parameter is nautical archaeology. This involves the nature of shipping using the southern Ruhuna seaboard, the area where they came from and their destination, the facilities that they required in ports, their structure, the nature of the sea they sailed in, the dangers they faced and their remains (if any). Together, these parameters covering the hinterland, the coastline and the sea, define the archaeological and historical context for the present paper.

Extract 2

Much archaeological excavation and analysis has been done on the subject of industrial and commercial sites and will not be repeated here. Those that need to be noted for the purposes of this report are the large number of metal-smelting furnaces discovered, dating back to the first century CE. Foremost among them were the steel-smelting furnaces. This country has a very old tradition of steel manufacture, and the product was considered of very high quality. In the early 1990s, Gill Juleff (2001: 43-8) discovered and excavated furnaces of high-carbon crucible steel at Samanalawewa, 'produced directly and in substantial quantities in sophisticated frontal smelting furnaces driven by wind pressure'. This steel was produced for export and would have been transported by boats along the Walawe Ganga to southern ports.

In 1992, excavations conducted in Tissamaharama (Akurugoda) revealed five settlement layers with furnaces. Hans-Joachim Weisshaar and W. Wijeyapala commented thus in their interim report: 'Numerous crucibles and several furnaces revealed . . . a workmen's quarter. Clear traces of copper and/or bronze were evident. Large amounts of slag came to light; the metal production was of considerable importance, and lasted for several centuries.' Slag heaps, incidentally, are found all over Hambantota and adjoining areas.*

During the same series of excavations, definite (though small) evidence of gold melting was found along with a glassy slag, evidence of surplus lead oxidizing and reacting with the underlying ceramic sherds. Evidence of bead manufacture was common. Very large

* The full study is dealt with in the Final Report (Weisshaar, Roth and Wijeyapala, 2001: 5-41) in the chapter on Akurugoda.

quantities of glass, agate, amethyst, rock-crystal, garnet, carnelian and rose-quartz had been produced. From the discovery of some of them in raw material form, it is surmised that beads were imported, processed and re-exported. Beads of shell and horn have also been found.

Osmund Bopearachchi (2001: 97-109), in his study of southern port sites, excavated 'more than twenty' furnace structures, and extended his search to the very large number of coins, seals, sealings, lead objects, intaglios and beads. These items are used for obtaining dates by comparing them with others of the same kind from other sites here and abroad. One particular hoard comprised 75,000 Roman (or pseudo-Roman) coins.

Whether these large quantities were meant for local consumption or not, the conclusion to be drawn is the same: this area was a thriving settlement for many centuries. The finds listed above were found only in the course of excavations or explorations, but there is no doubt that Hambantota—placed between the capital city (Tissamaharama) and two ports of significance (Godawaya and Kirinda)—was not an uninhabited area but one with settlements, industry and trade.

These extracts cover important aspects which impinge on the Eastern Sea. First, the Ruhuna kingdom, stretching from Beruwala on the western coast and following the coast up to Trincomalee on the east, had the longest coastline. It was a kingdom with a maritime slant: its eyes were turned seawards just as the eyes of the Rajarata were turned inwards. A country with a long coastline does not become a magnet for seafarers for this reason alone. There must be places to lay-up while awaiting the desired monsoon winds, there must be communities and traders with commercial interests, the hinterland must be developed industrially and agriculturally, and water must be available in plenty. Ruhuna had all these and seafarers began to call at its ports. Gunawardana (1990: 28) has noted the link between the evolution of larger, long-haul ships, and the rise in importance of ports south of Mantai. Sailors from the west began to venture further south in search of newer destinations and, by the thirteenth century, it had all but ceased to be. Arab merchants were already established in Colombo by the ninth century but it is more than possible, from the pattern of Roman coin hoards in the south and up-river, that Roman ships sailed around the islands: in fact, Roman coins (smaller bronze coins alone) minted purely for use outside Rome have been found in large quantities, indicating that this had been another industry in the south. After Islam, Arabic cross-oceanic sailing expanded exponentially. Plotting their positions by a combination of star sights from the 'kamal', deduced reckoning, day's run and compass, every time they touched land they recoded its latitude. Arab maps, which combined all previously plotted sites show how ships could sail across the Arabian Sea to Beruwala. There are thirty locations plotted along the coast from Beruwala to Trincomalee, attesting to the commercial interest in this kingdom (Figure 6.9).

From Trincomalee, Arab ships used the favourable monsoon to sail across the Eastern Sea to the Bay of Bengal and beyond. It follows that they would have had settlements and I had the fortune to locate one, which was ideally suited for ships to lay-up, with plenty of sweet water in the inner harbour of Trincomalee—presently called Nicholson's Cove. Here we have the site of a very specifically Arab maritime colony which had been continuously occupied for at least

Figure 6.9: Positions plotted by Arab sailors shown on a Mercator projection.

200 years. From a seaman's point of view, this is an ideal spot for sailors to ride out the inter-monsoonal storm period till the wind changed to enable them to sail the rest of the way across the Bay of Bengal. Nicholson's Cove is a narrow inlet, sheltered by parallel hilly ridges from the winds, with a shelving beach where ships could be beached for repairs, and a plentiful supply of sweet water (Figure 6.10).

Unfortunately, during the Second World War, the availability of water made the British military authorities choose this site for a large camp: it is then that they discovered three gravestones of which two were readable, one of them being the one I reported on and the other of the matyr Qadi 'Afifu'd-Din 'Abdu'llah son of 'Abdu'r-Rahman son of Muhammed son of Yusuf al-'Alawi' who had died on 16 August CE 1405. The third, also discovered by me, is too defaced to read. The sweet water wells that had proved to be a magnet to both the Arabs and the British, still exist (Figure 6.11).

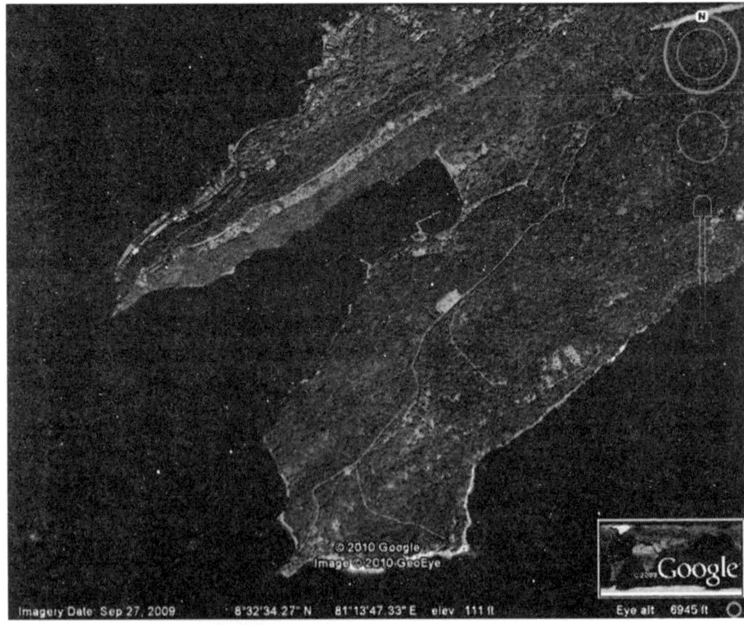

Figure 6.10: Satellite image of Nicholson's Cove, Trincomalee.

Figure 6.11: Photo of surviving well.

From elsewhere in the Ruhuna, ships from what is now Indonesia had carried on a brisk trade across the Eastern Sea. Soon after Sri Lanka was annexed as a Crown Colony of Britain, Sir Alexander Johnston, President of the Vice-Admiralty Court, attempted to codify customary law customs governing mercantile shipping. Johnston, writing about the first Arabic inscription found here, made several interesting footnotes, one of which bears repetition here (Johnston, 1827: 547):

> One of the principal Arabic works on medicine which they introduced into Ceylon was the work of Avicenna; they also introduced Arabic translations of Aristotle, Plato, Euclid, Galen, and Ptolemy, extracts of which were frequently brought to me while I was in Ceylon by the Mohammedan priests and merchants, who stated that the works themselves had originally been procured from Baghdad by their ancestors and remained for some hundred years in their respective families in Ceylon, but had been subsequently sold by them, when in distress, for some considerable sums of money to some *merchants who traded between Ceylon and the eastern islands* (emphasis mine).

Sri Lankan ports, though under the control of the king and his officials for administrative, customs, salvage, etc., were, in terms of operational matters, more in the hands of the merchants. In the same paper, Johnston describes the 'The maritime laws and usages, which prevail amongst the Hindu and Mohammedan mariners and traders who frequent Ceylon . . . may be classed under four heads' (Johnston, 1827: 548). His classification is revealing:

(1) Those that carry on trade in small vessels between the coasts of Malabar, Coromandel, and the island of Ceylon;
(2) those which prevail amongst the Mohammedan mariners and traders of Arab descent between the coasts of Malabar, Coromandel and the island of Ceylon;
(3) those which prevail amongst the Arab mariners and traders who carry on trade in very large vessels between the eastern coasts of Africa, Arabia, the Persian Gulf, and the island of Ceylon;
(4) those which prevail amongst the Malay mariners who carry on trade between the coasts of Malacca, the eastern islands, and Ceylon.

He adds the equally revealing comment:

> The first are in some degree modified by the tenets of the Hindu religion and by Hindu law. The second, the third, and the fourth are modified in a great degree by the tenets of the Mohammedan religion, and Mohammedan law. (Johnston, 1827: 548)

Prevailing customary law was, therefore, compounded by such factors as size of the ship, the sailing routes, and religion. Altogether, his observations are very thought-provoking.

I surmise that the first international ports (as opposed to the ports that serviced coastal-shipping) were those which were linked to trade routes that stretched, at least halfway across the Indian Ocean. Mantai may have been one of the oldest because while there was a need for merchandise to cross from the Arabian Sea to the Bay of Bengal, most of the ships that called there from the west were not constructed to navigate the Mannar or Pamban passages. Cargo had, therefore, either to be portaged along land routes or transhipped on local craft from Mantai to ports on the northern coast and beyond. Gunawardena (1990: 30-1) comments:

> Hence even by the middle of the first millennium, voyages from the Red Sea to places like Java in the eastern extremity of the Indian Ocean will have

been unusual. This probably meant that patterns of shipping and trade in the eastern part of the Indian Ocean were distinct and autonomous to a certain degree—a situation that emphasized the commercial importance of Sri Lanka due to its strategic situation in the middle of the Indian Ocean. The comments that Procopius made on problems of Eastern trade suggest that Persian and Ethiopians went only as far as Sri Lanka where they awaited the arrival of cargoes of silk and other merchandise from further east. Ships from the western sector of the Indian Ocean and those from the eastern sector were now meeting in Sri Lanka.

P. Ragupathy (Pl. 148: page unnumbered) has mapped the distribution of jetty ports and fishing camps in Jaffna (Figure 6.12) and it is possible that some of them had served coastal shipping linking the Mantai with the Bay of Bengal through the Mannar passage.

The writ of the king in power extended to ports and shipwrecks. Some interesting epigraphical evidence for this exists. To quote a few examples, Parakramabahu I (twelfth century) erected an inscription in the Tamil language, concerning salvage. This was at Nayinativu in the extreme north (Indrapala, 1963: 70):

> . . . the foreigners should come and stay at Uratturai (Uratota), that they should be protected and that foreigners from many ports should come and gather at our ports; as we like elephants and horses, if the vessels bringing elephants and horses to us get wrecked, a fourth (share of the cargo) should be taken by the treasury and the (other) three parts should be left to the

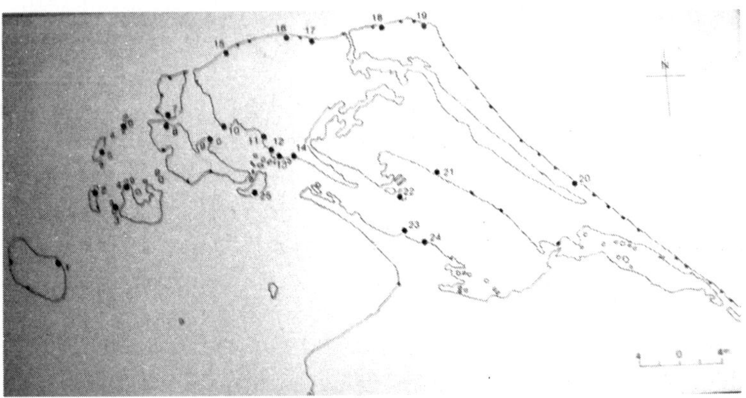

Figure 6.12: Jetty ports and fishing camps in Jaffna peninsula.

owner; if vessels with merchandise get wrecked, an exact half should be left to the owner. . . .

Another in Devundara (now Dondra) speaks of customs, bribery and smuggling (Paranavitana, 1953: 69-70):

. . . apart from the levying of such imposts as have been approved by the Maha-Pandithe, illegal imposts shall not be levied. To those coming from foreign countries, means shall not be afforded to avoid the payment of imposts and duties that are due, which they do by establishing places of business, corrupting royal officers by means of presents and keeping with friends the merchandise smuggled from their own countries. . . .

It would appear that many things do not change. Finally, there is the Galle trilingual inscription engraved in China and set up in Galle in the thirteenth century by Zheng He. It merits mention as the languages in which it is written are Chinese, Persian (in Arabic script) and Tamil. As the Nayinativu inscription is also in Tamil, it is generally accepted that the *lingua franca* of South Asian sailors was Tamil: after all, these inscriptions were meant for the eyes of sailors. However, this observation has no bearing on the vexed question of whether the inhabitants of that area were Tamil-speaking or not.

Ports that were frequented from time to time by cross-oceanic shipping—such as Mantai, Colombo, Galle, Godawaya, and Trincomalee—each became important from the coming together of several factors, flourished for a while, and then lapsed to becoming of regional importance only. In ancient and medieval times, they were often the mouths of rivers that provided access to the interior and archaeological evidence still exists: the walls of the port city at Mantai (Figure 6.13), the remains of watercraft dated to the fourth century BCE and ninth century CE upriver at Colombo (Figure 6.14); a large Arab stone anchor dated (^{14}C date refined using the OxCal programme to 430 +/- 80 BP) to 1310 and 1650 CE) (Figure 6.15); an inscription regarding the income from the port and a recently-discovered shipwreck with raw material for the bead-making industry of the Ruhuna. Coastal shipping and regional ports probably had no built infrastructure. Neville Chittick (1980: 14) has observed that 'Ports have come and gone throughout the last two thousand years; there seems to be a curious, but presumably fortuitous flourishing of such ports with a cycle of 200-300 years'.

Figure 6.13: Aerial photograph of the Mantai site.

Figure 6.14: Fourth-century BCE log-boat from Kelani River.

Figure 6.15: Arab stone anchor with wooden flukes from Galle.

Some sites, though, retained their utility on even a minor scale after their heyday as major ports had ended. But what did these smaller ports look like? Chittick (1980: 14) elucidates this position very clearly:

> Under the influence of the modern model, we tend to think of the ideal port as a largely enclosed expanse of deep water, suitable for the construction of quays alongside which ships were moored. This is a type evolved in north-western Europe, originally because of the heavy swells found there and the nature of the beaches. . . . In much of the Indian Ocean region . . . the circumstances are different. The winds are comparatively moderate, steady and predictable. . . . The beaches, at least in the west . . . have an almost flat foreshore below a steep, sandy beach. Boats can therefore be conveniently beached at high tide on the foreshore, unloaded onto men's shoulders and carried up the beach when the tide recedes. Vessels are consequently built in a fashion to make such beaching possible. Quays and lighters are, in general unnecessary. Only when there is inadequate shelter is it necessary for ships to anchor and unload cargoes into small boats. Such adequate shelter is, however, available in long stretches of the coast . . . provided either by a coral fringing reef or an off-shore island or an inlet or creek, or even by a headland, used on either side, according to the duration of the monsoon. . . .

His observations fit the smaller port sites perfectly, and the absence of alongside berthing and the presence of a headland fit Galle and Colombo, too.

Naval Architecture

The question that has now to be answered is whether Sri Lanka participated in Indian Ocean shipping. To look at the outrigger-equipped fishing craft which are all that remain of a tradition of sea-going craft, one would doubt that we had any ships that sailed over the Eastern Sea. It is not surprising that Toussaint (1966: 4-5) was moved to observe that:

> The Sinhalese people never looked towards the sea and the navigators whom history records were always foreigners. The outriggers themselves are of foreign origin, and it is not in Ceylon that we shall really comprehend the ocean's story.

But studies into Sri Lankan shipping have progressed beyond Toussaint although it is true enough that to 'really comprehend the ocean's story', one cannot look at Sri Lanka alone. That apart, my own studies into our ships and watercraft built upon those by Hornell, Vitharana, Kentley and Kapitan, have convinced me that there was an area of the Indian Ocean—of which Sri Lanka was the centre—where a type of watercraft with unique attributes was in use. The other countries involved were the Andamans and Minicoy (in Lakshdweep). In Sri Lanka, this nautical culture, which I call the Oru culture, was the dominant culture: 'dominant', because there were other cultures, too, on the island. Hornell (1943: 40), who once served as an advisor to the Sri Lankan Department of Fisheries, remarked:

> No greater contrast can be found in small craft designing than that between the types used on opposite sides of the Gulf of Mannar, South of latitude 9° N. On the Indian, or Tamil, side the catamaran or boat canoe alone are employed; on the Sinhalese side, the outrigger canoe is the national and dominant design, the catamaran being used only in the northern, or non-Sinhalese part of the island and by migrant Tamil fishermen in Colombo.

What he means by catamaran is the Oru: the English word is a corruption of the Tamil word *kattumaram*, which is the name for a shaped-log raft, while the Oru is a log-boat married to a single outrigger. The Oru was the dominant design in the Sinhalese areas. In the Tamil areas to the north of Mannar, the *kattumaram*, the *teppam* (both log rafts) and the *vallam* (in Sri Lanka, this is a log-boat without an outrigger though it is a generic term in India) were common. Large *vallam* were imported from India, where the log was transformed in the way that Hornell has described. What matters is that there were large, ocean-going cargo carriers both in the north and the south that continued to be built and sailed up to 1930. Admittedly, the northern shipbuilders built ships that were basically not developed within the island but the fact remains that there was a healthy tradition of ship-building and seafaring. The men of Valvettithurai, on the north-eastern tip of Sri Lanka, built and sailed the ships while the owners and financiers were Chetties from South India (Figure 6.16).

Figure 6.16: Jaffna *Thoni* at Colombo harbour.

In the nineteenth and twentieth centuries the cargo ships of the north, *thonies*, participated in the British inter-Asian shipping network to good effect. I was able to get information from a website www.valvanilla.com (see Note below) where the operations are described thus:

Most of them (i.e. *thonies*), while being built and operated by sailors from Valvettithurai, were owned by the wealthy Chetty families from Tamil Nadu. The rest were owned by the Chetty traders who had settled in Valvettithurai since the opening of secure sea lanes in the Indian Ocean by the Portuguese (from Arab & Far Eastern pirates. They might have been there since before Cholas' time). Building and maintaining large ocean-going vessels in those days required a large sum of capital; it can be afforded by only few families who had already well established themselves as reputed trading families. These vessels, up to Second World War, plied the sea-routes the Tamils had used for centuries before. They made ports-of-call in south India,

Visakhapatnam to Cochin (occasionally even Calcutta), Rangoon, Far Eastern destinations, ports in the Middle East (such as Aden). In Ceylon itself, they made frequent trips to Galle and ports in between. They carried rice, spices, roof tiles, timber (teak, sandalwood, etc), palmyra products, dried fish, tobacco products, etc.

In 1938, an American had spotted one, the Annapooraniyamal (Figure 6.17) and admired her lines so much that he purchased it and sailed her from Colombo to Boston with a crew of five from Jaffna. The same source quoted above describes her as being

. . . a cargo vessel modelled on the popular British frigate-type ship; it was known for its speed and manoeuvrability,

The *Gloucester Times* of August 2,1938 had this to say:

. . . resembles the ghost of His Majesty's ship Bounty returning to the seas. . . . The craft itself, a 90-foot affair, was built at Jaffna some nine years ago on the lines of the British man-o-war which ever hit into that area at the beginning of the 19th century. That model was the much the same as the 'Bounty' on which a crew mutinied and became white settlers of Pitcairn Island. The natives have never changed the mould, and though larger ones are built, the sch. Annapoorani as it was known, is the popular cargo ship plying the trade in the Indian Ocean.

Figure 6.17: The 'Annapooraniyamal/Florence C. Robinson' at Boston.

It is more than probable that this was the longest recorded trip made by an Asian-built sailing ship. The ship was registered as the 'Florence C. Robinson' with Lloyds.

(This website went off the Net soon after I had sourced it in 2008. However, I had downloaded the material and also found a reference on a Blogsite which gave further details. In April 2009, I wrote a feature article, 'Westward Ho!' quoting all details, one of three such articles about each of the three Sri Lankan ship-building cultures.)

The shipping tradition of the south was totally different although it, too, produced ocean-going cargo ships. It would be redundant to repeate my investigations as they have recently been published at length (Devendra, 2010: 313-401) and since expanded (Devendra, 2011: 109-32). However, my studies show that the Oru culture was a vernacular naval architectural idiom based upon a dual-element form, i.e. either a log-boat and a single outrigger or twinned log-boats. I present here the line of development from dugout log to seagoing cargo ship.

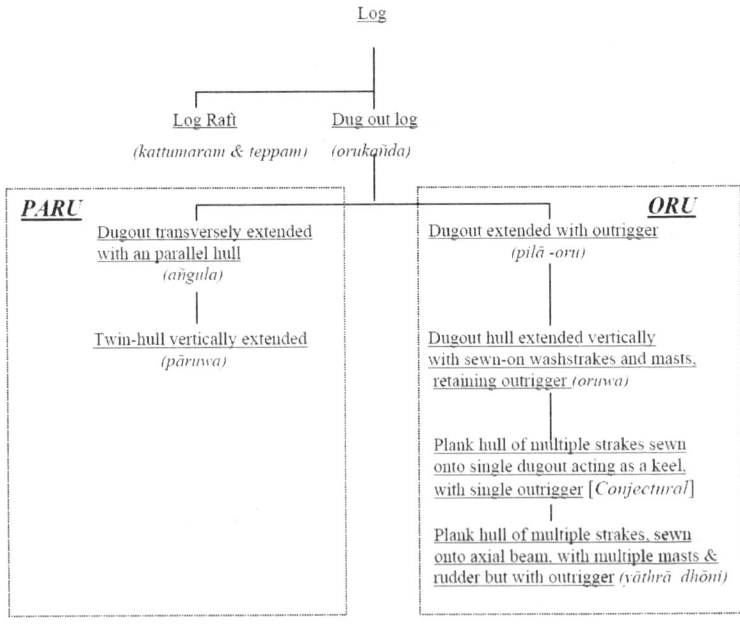

Development of watercraft within the *Oru culture* (Sri Lanka)

It is worth noting that the twin-hull form did not progress beyond inland waters and as a solitary marine craft: a beach seine net carrier. In the Pacific, the larger voyaging vessels were the large double-hulled type, which suited long voyages. Similarly, the Oru did not expand transversely by building an elevated platform that spanned the space between the hull and the outrigger for the carrying of passengers and goods—as had been done in the eastern islands of New Guinea and the Pacific—but had only a rudimentary platform for the use of fishermen's gear. Neither did the second outrigger which characterized the Indonesian ships that sailed to East Africa and Madagascar. Nevertheless, a quantum leap from fishing boat to cargo ship was achieved and I was able to trace the 'missing link' to Kerala. The result was the *yathra dhoni* (Figure 6.18): originally with a single square sail and quarter rudder but later with main and mizzen masts carrying square-headed lug-sails, and a jib set on a short bowsprit, and fitted with a rudder and tiller.

Throughout all these morphological changes, one feature remained unchanged: the single outrigger attached with two booms. This was to be the signature of the *yathra*, perhaps the largest (and only) single outrigger cargo ship to sail the seven seas. Although the last one was built in 1935, it was wrecked on a reef in the Maldives. That *yathra* sailed from Ceylon—Dodanduwa near Galle, was their

Figure 6.18: A *yathra dhoni*, beached.

last home port—to India is well recorded and Paris (Figure 6.19) gives a detailed drawing of one which he says is common to the Coromandel coast and Sri Lanka.

Folk songs, preserved among the fishermen place the *yathra* further east near Malacca. One reads the following in translation:

> Now listen: Malacca is a far-off country.
> We bring the telescope on deck and scan the seas around us.
> We turn the ship towards *Sinhala desa*
> And decorate the ship for our arrival.

(Recorded by Vitharana: 1992. Free translation by me)

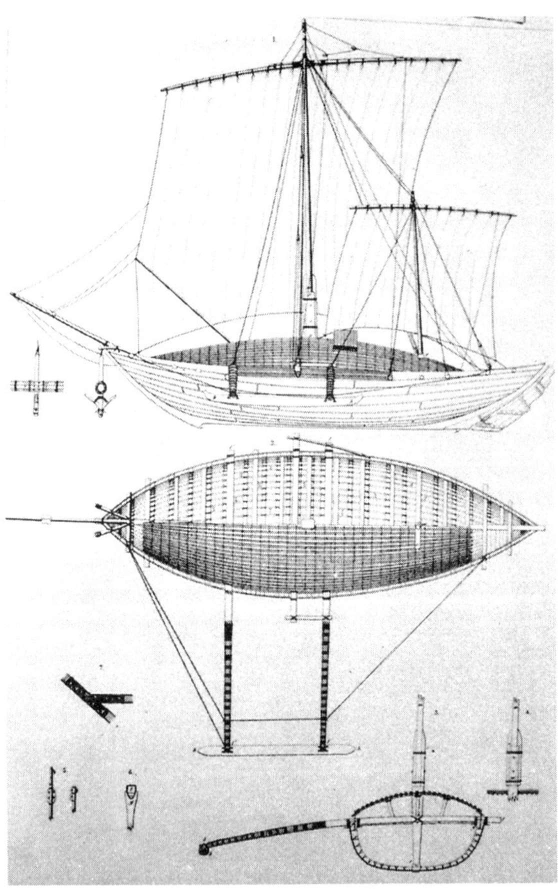

Figure 6.19: Drawing of a *yathra dhoni* by Paris.

The Oru and the *yathra*, were the true vernacular craft of Sri Lanka, while the hybrid vessels of the north speak to us of a more adventurous tradition.

Epilogue

I have proposed new ways of looking at certain orthodox views on certain subjects, which, I hope, will be seriously considered. Winding up, therefore, I shall present yet another dimension that historians generally do not consider relevant.

Experimental archaeology is rapidly coming of age. The website www.oxbowbooks.com describing *Experimentation and Interpretation: The Use of Experimental Archaeology in the Study of the Past* (ed. Millson, Dana, 2011), says: 'Now that archaeology has moved beyond the focus of the processual/post-processual debates of the 1970s and 1980s, which pitted science against the arts, archaeologists have more freedom to choose how to 'do archaeology'. This approach can analyse all the known information about an artefact, replicate it on full scale, and test its viability under the conditions prevailing at the time. The most recent example, in Sri Lanka is that of the monsoon-powered, linear, steel-smelting furnaces discovered by Gill Juleff upriver from Godawaya. Juleff, having uncovered a number large enough to assume a factory-scale production of steel for export, rebuilt a damaged one and, using the traditional lore unearthed, successfully smelted high-carbon steel. Her work made the cover of *Nature.* Similarly, at sea, Thor Heyerdahl's *Kon-tiki* and *Ra* made headlines. I now present are two examples of experimental archaeology involving ships that sailed the Eastern Sea.

Gunawardana (1990: 29), whose work I have great respect for (albeit disagreeing with some of his conclusions), says:

> Pierre-Yves Manguin's argument (Manguin, P-Y. 1980:273) that double outriggers of the Indonesian type were not suited for transoceanic navigation is certainly apt.

Manguin certainly knows Indonesian 'lashed-lug' boats and cannot be held responsible for not being aware of the evidence—such as that which I now present—since it was not available to him at the time that he voiced this opinion.

In the early years of the present century, serious nautical archaeologists turned towards building authentic, full-sized replicas of ancient and medieval ships, and sailed them according to the manner in which they were believed to have been sailed in the same environment. Nick Burningham, an Australian who built two: one was a replica of the VOC *Dufken*, the first known Dutch ship to find its way from Jakarta to Australia in 1606. She was a *jacht* (scout), 'a fast, lightly-armed ship probably intended for small valuable cargoes or privateering' (www.duyfken.com), built in 1595. I was fortunate enough to witness her being built at the Western Australian Maritime Museum and to board her at Galle in 2002 when she was on the Batavia-Galle leg (a thirty-one day's sail) of her voyage home via Mauritius and the Cape to the Texel, following the old VOC sea-routes. Given below is a picture of her (Figure 6.20) and of the route she took (Figure 6.21).

The other ship built by Burningham was totally different. She was built by 'a team of experienced Indonesian shipbuilders . . . practiced in constructing ships using traditional building techniques. They are based in the Kangean Islands, some 60 miles north of Bali'.

Figure 6.20: Replica of the 'Duyfken'.

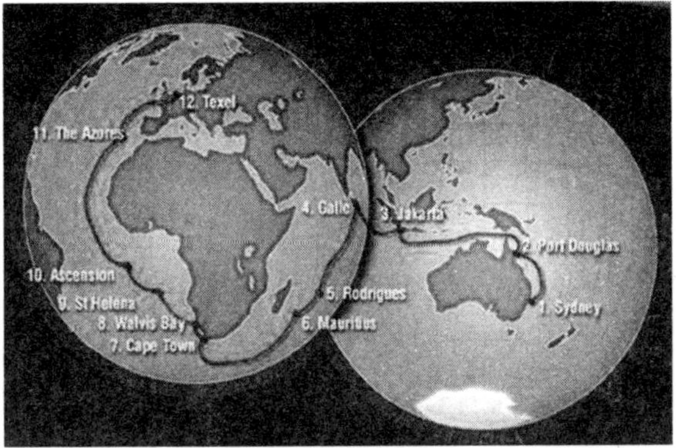

Figure 6.21: The voyage of the 'Duyfken'.

(www.borobudurshipexpedition.com) 'The intention is to develop a reconstruction of the type of large outrigger vessels depicted at Borobudur in a form suitable for ocean voyaging and recreating the first millennium Indonesian voyaging to Madagascar and Africa.' The ship left Jakarta on 16 August 2004, sailed south towards Cocos/Keeling to pick up the Trades, sailed a long distance to Seychelles where she arrived on 29 September and, after a seventeen-day stay, reached Madagascar on 14 October: a total of forty-two days sailing time to cross the Indian Ocean. A picture of the ship (Figure 6.22) and a map of her voyage to Ghana (Figure 6.23) are worth seeing, and the two websites quoted are essential reading for those who would comment on ships of days gone by.

Given the performances of the two ships across the Indian Ocean, one sees that Manguin's assessment of the capabilities of outrigger ships has to be reconsidered. My intention in including new information as concluding remarks, is to show that historians and archaeologists cannot write the ocean's history, without getting under the skin of 'those who go down to the sea in ships'. In all fairness, however, I must stress that the two replica ships were experimenting with the different routes: the former following the port-to-port route of a homeward-bound merchantman and the latter a cross-oceanic unbroken passage of a voyaging ship. The difficulties faced by the *Duyfken*, because of the nature of her chosen route is best illustrated by the trace of her track (Figure 6.24) as she approached Galle from

Figure 6.22: The replica 'Borobudur ship'.

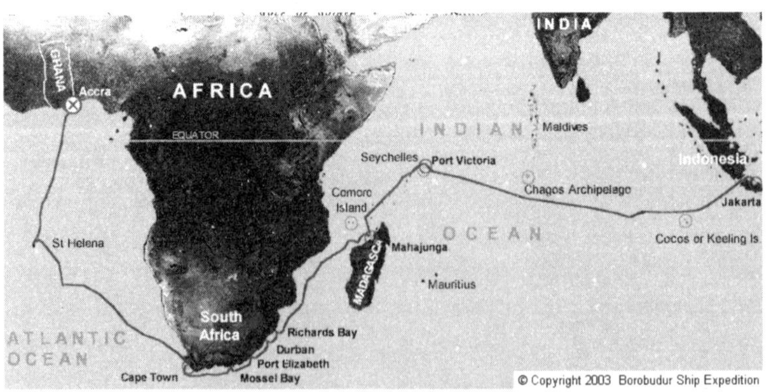

Figure 6.23: The route followed by the 'Borobudur ship'.

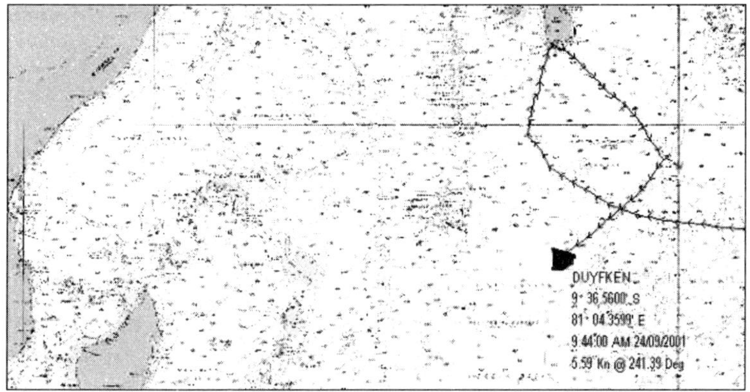

Figure 6.24: 'Duyfken's' track entering and leaving Galle port.

the westward and departed east, causing her to 'cross her track'; which was necessary as she was dependent on the prevailing wind.

My intention in presenting these examples is to stress the need for multi-disciplinary research; and to express the hope that many untapped fonts of knowledge will soon form other parameters of maritime historical and archaeological studies.

Acknowledgements

I have included in the Bibliography only those sources that I actually dealt with, although the subject matter calls for a much longer list. I have also included the handful of websites that I have accessed. My grateful thanks are due to all these sources for enhancing my own education in the process of writing this paper. I must particularly thank two sources: the first being Susantha Goonatilake whose *A 19th Century Clash of Civilizations: The Portuguese Presence in Sri Lanka* I have freely dipped into and I thank him for the permission granted. With this recent book available, which had all the important details that I would normally have to collect from myriad sources, I have been spared a lot of work.

The other is (the late) Prof. R.A.L.H. Gunawardena's much reprinted paper 'Seaways to Seiladiba: Changing Patterns of Navigation in the Indian Ocean and their Impact on Pre-colonial Sri

Lanka', which, I consider the best written on this subject. Of course, there are places where I do not agree with him and it is my loss that I could not discuss these with him. I would, therefore, like to dedicate this paper to his memory.

REFERENCES

Barua, Dipak K., 1979, *Buddha Gaya Temple: Its History*, Gaya: Buddha Gaya Temple Management Committee.

Bopearachchi, Osmund, 2001, 'Ancient Sri Lanka: New Archaeological Date of the Trade between Rome and China', in Leelananda Prematilleke, et al. (eds.), *Men and Monuments: D.T. Devendra, A Centennial Tribute,* Colombo: Central Cultural Fund, Sri Lanka: 97-109.

Chaisuwan, Boonyarit, 2011, 'Early Contacts between India and the Andaman Coast in Thailand from second century BCE to eleventh century CE', in Pierre-Yves Manguin, A. Mani, and Geoff Wade (eds.), *Early Interaction Between South and Southeast Asia*, Singapore: Institute of Southeast Asian Studies and New Delhi: Manohar, 83-112.

Chittick, Neville, 1980, 'East Africa and the Orient: Ports and Trade Before the Arrival of the Portuguese', *Historical Relations Across the Indian Ocean,* Paris: UNESCO: 13-22.

Devendra, Somasiri, 2011, 'Sailing on a String and a Prayer: The ORU Culture in Sri Lanka and the Indian Ocean', in Lotika Varadarajan (ed.), *Gujarat and the Sea,* Darshak Itihas Nidhi: 109-32.

———, 2010, 'Ships- and Shipbuilding in Sri Lanka, with Particular Reference to a Vernacular Naval Architectural Idiom', in M.A.T. de Silva (ed.), *Evolution of Technological Innovations in Sri Lanka,* Colombo: Vijitha Yapa Publications: 313-401.

———, 2009, 'Westward Ho!', *Sunday Times*, 19 April 2011, Colombo: Wijeya Newspapers Ltd.

Dwivedi, R.S., 2004, 'Un-nurtured and Untapped Super Sweet Non-sacchariferous Plant Species in India' (see below for Internet reference).

Geiger, Wilhelm, 1912, *The Mahavamsa: The Great Chronicle of Ceylon*, London, rpt. 2003, Dehiwela: Buddhist Cultural Centre.

———, 1912, *Culavamsa, being the More Recent Part of the Mahavamsa,* part II, rpt. 1953, Colombo: Ceylon Government Information Department.

Goonatilake, Susantha, 2010, *A 19th Century Clash of Civilizations: The Portuguese Presence in Sri Lanka*, Colombo: Vijitha Yapa Publications.

Gunawardana, R.A.L.H., 1990, 'Seaways to Seiladiba: Changing Patterns of Navigation in the Indian Ocean and their Impact on Precolonial Sri Lanka', *Sri Lanka and the Silk Road of the Sea*, Colombo: Sri Lanka National Commission for UNESCO, Central Cultural Fund: 25-44.

Guruge, Ananda W.P., 1990, 'The Sri Lankan Factor in the Development of the Art of Sukothai and Lanna Tai', in S. Bandaranayake et al. (eds.), *Sri Lanka and the Silk Road of the Sea*, Colombo: Sri Lanka National Commission for UNESCO, Central Cultural Fund: 245-52.

Hornell, James, 1943, 'Fishing and Coastal Craft of Ceylon', *The Mariner's Mirror*, vol. 19, no. 1, January: 40.

Indrapala, K., 1963, 'The Nayinativu Tamil Inscription of Parakkramabahu I', *The University of Ceylon Review*, Colombo: University of Ceylon: 70.

Johnston, Sir Alexander, 1827, 'A Cufic Inscription found in Ceylon', *Transactions of the Royal Asiatic Society of Great Britain and Ireland*, 1, 1: 547-8.

Juleff, Gillian, 1955, 'An Ancient Wind-powered Iron Smelting Furnace in Sri Lanka', *Men and Monuments: D.T. Devendra. A Tribute*, Colombo: Central Cultural Fund: 43-8.

Kapitan, Gerhard, 2009, *Records of Traditional Watercraft from South and West Sri Lanka*, BAR International Series 1931 and NAS Monograph Series No. 2, Portsmouth.

Kentley, Eric and R. Gunaratne, 1987, 'The *Madel Paruwa*: Sewn Boat with Chine Strakes', *The International Journal of Naval Archaeology and Exploration*, 16, 1: 35-48.

Manguin, Pierre-Yves, 1980, 'The Southeast Asian Ship: An Historical Approach', *Journal of Southeast Asian Studies*, vol. XI, no. 2: 266-76.

Paranavitana, Senarat, 1953, 'The Shrine of Upulvan at Devundara', *Memoirs of the Archaeological Survey of Ceylon*, vol. VI, Colombo: Department of Archaeology: 69-70.

Paris, François-Edmond, 1843, *Essai sur la construction navales des peuples extra-europeens*, Paris: Arthus Bertrand.

Ragupathy, P., 1987, *Early Settlements in Jaffna*, Madras: Mrs T. Ragupathy.

Ramachandran, T.N., 1992, *The Negapattinam and other Buddhist Bronzes in the Madras Museum*, Madras: The Director of Museums.

Ray, Himanshu Prabha, 2006, 'Inscribed Pots, Emerging Identities: The Social Milieu of Trade', in Patrick Olivelle (ed.), *Between the Empires:*

Society in India 300 BCE *to 400* CE, New York: Oxford University Press, 2006: 113-43.

———, 2003, *The Archaeology of Seafaring in Ancient South Asia,* Cambridge: Cambridge University Press.

———, 1986, *Monastery and Guild: Commerce under the Satavahanas*, New Delhi: Oxford University Press.

Seneviratne, J., 1915, 'Chino-Sinhalese Relations in the Early and Middle Ages', translated from M. Sylvain Levi's article in Journal Asiatique, *Journal of the Ceylon Branch of the Royal Asiatic Society* XXIV, 1: 77-123.

Toussaint, Auguste, 1966, *History of the Indian Ocean,* London: Routledge and Kegan Paul.

Vitharana, V., 1992, *The ORU and the YATHRA: Traditional Outrigger Craft of Sri Lanka,* Dehiwela: Sridevi Press.

Weisshaar, Hans-Joachim, H. Roth, and W. Wijeyapala, 2001, *Ancient Ruhuna: Sri Lankan-German Archaeological Project in the Southern Province,* Mainz am Rhein: Verlag Phillip Von Zabern.

Weerakkody, D.P.M., 1997, *Taprobane: Ancient Sri Lanka as known to Greeks and Romans,* Turnhout: Brepols.

Internet Sites Referenced and Dates Accessed

www. cal.vet.upenn.edu/poison/plants/pprosar.htm [viewed on 22.12.2004]
www.ias.ac.in/currsci/jun10/articles19.htm [viewed on 23.12.2004]
www.disabled-world.com [September 2011, and 28.11.11]
www.nauticalarchaeologysociety.org [September 2011, and 28.11.11]
www.valvanilla.com [See Note embedded in text]
www.duyfken.com [September 2011, and 29.11.11]
www.borobudurshipexpedition.com [September 2011 and 29.11.11]
www.oxbowbooks.com [22.10. 2011, and 29.11.11]
www.cf.hum.uva.nl/galle [Regularly and on 29.11.11]

CHAPTER 7

The Rhythms of the Economy and Navigation along the Ganga River

MURARI JHA

Each river is a special little world (Febvre, 1932: 302)

Introduction

The Ganga River historically functioned as the highway of empires, and as such, provided an arena for economic and political activities along its water course. It facilitated the mobility of people with varied and variegated aims. The very act of traversing the fluvial course of the Ganga presents us with a case of close interaction with the natural environment where a sailor had to face the weather, wind patterns, currents and shoals and, as a result, also the hazards of shipwreck. How did the Gangascape influence social and economic organizations along the river? How did travel commence on this aquatic highroad of the empire and to what end?

The Ganga River as a unit of historical analysis has often been glossed over in the existing South Asian historiography. Historians have considered empires and regions but the Ganga River which ensured their survival often skipped their attention. In the past, the river sustained a large population by providing food and nourishment. Even in contemporary times, the river meets the food requirements of around 500 million people with the cereals and grains produced in the Ganga plain. Indeed, without the Ganga River and its perennial water course which ensured irrigation and fertility, the prosperity of the regions and the continuation of empires would have been unthinkable. It is not surprising, therefore, that the successful Indian empires of the Mauryas, Guptas, Afghans, Mughals and the British were all located on the Ganga plain. A proper treatment of this issue needs more space than can be allocated in one paper, yet I shall take this opportunity to raise some issues and problems concerning research on the Ganga River (Figure 7.1).

This paper, therefore, has a modest aim. It tries to shed some light on the economy and navigation along the Ganga River until the early modern period. Its geographical focus lies primarily in the more humid and wet parts of the Ganga plain. It discusses the functional aspect of the Ganga River, treating it as a geographical unit with which people interacted closely to fulfil their economic and political interests. The first section of the paper situates the Ganga River in a historical perspective, and looks at some political and economic patterns in *la longue durée*. The second section gives a detailed

Figure 7.1: Eighth-century image of Ganga from Udaigiri in Orissa now in the Patna Museum. By the fifth century the river Ganga acquired an anthropomorphic form and was sculpted on the door frames of temples along with the river Yamuna.

description of the sailing rhythms in the Ganga organized by the Dutch captains of the fleet plying between the Hugli and the Patna factories during the first half of the eighteenth century. The Dutch sources closely observe the sailing patterns in the river. There is no reason to believe that the local people or other Europeans sailing in the Ganga would have followed entirely different sailing patterns and would have encountered a newer set of challenges than the Dutch sailors did. On the issues of navigation in the Ganga, the Dutch sources provide fascinating details. Thus, we can safely generalize the Dutch sailing experiences on the river for others who were also making use of this fluvial highroad. A discussion of the vigorous economic and political activities carried out in and around this river enables us to analyse the nature of interaction on the Ganga plain during the early modern period.

The Ganga River System

The Ganga River rises in the Himalayas at Gomukh in the Gangotri glacier, the highest in the region and surrounded by snowy peaks of 20,000 to 24,000 ft high. From this glacier, the Bhagirathi and Alaknanda flow southwards and form the early courses of the Ganga River (Colebrook, 1979, vol. XI: 443). Both these rivers are joined by other Himalayan streams such as the Mandakini, Dhauli Ganga and Pindar. The Bhagirathi and Alakhnanda meet at Devprayag and the river is called by the name of Ganga after their confluence (Bell, 1832, vol. IV: 469; Jain et al., 2007: 336; Law, 1976: 31). After flowing through the northern and relatively arid plain the Ganga meets the Yamuna River at Allahabad and their confluence is known as Prayag (literally, the place of sacrifice). Prayag is considered to be sacred in the Hindu tradition where the ancient Kumbh pilgrimage, a great bathing festival attended by millions of pilgrims, is organized at an interval of every twelve years (Neville, 1928: 151-2; Smith, 1882: 54-5). As the Ganga takes an eastward course through the semi-arid and humid plain, the rivers such as the Ghagghar, Son, Gandak and Kosi join it in successive order. The middle and lower reaches of the Ganga thus have the appearance of a funnel, and streams from the north and south add to the swell of the river. These tributaries link different areas of the Ganga plain to the Ganga highway and facilitate communication networks on which men, military and merchandise moved. Needless to say, the availability of such arteries of communication influenced society, economy and polity throughout the course of history. The existence of fluvial roads and innumerable river confluences clearly distinguish the semi-arid and humid parts from the drier zones of the Ganga plain.[1]

The Ganga River System in the Early Historic Period

Recent archaeological evidence suggests human settlements and well-developed agriculture in the seventh and sixth millennia BCE at sites such as Lohuradeva near Gorakhpur, located on the banks of the Rapti and Rohani, tributaries of the Ganga (Chakrabarti, 2006: 217). In the Ganga basin, perhaps the most significant change in the mid-first millennium BCE was in the settlement pattern. A settlement hierarchy is in evidence in northern India by 400 BCE, with the largest sites, surrounded by monumental earthen ramparts, dominating the major arteries of communication (Erdosy, 1995: 108). At the bottom of the scale were nucleated village settlements inhabited by agriculturalists and herders. In between were minor centres and towns, which have revealed data for the manufacture of ceramics and lithic blades, and finished and unfinished beads, as well as for metal smelting. Several of these towns were fortified, the ramparts serving defensive purposes and also demarcating cities from the surrounding landscape.

During the fourth century BCE, there were riverine cities such as Kampilya, Varanasi, Pataliputra (Patna) and Champa conveniently located at the upper, middle and lower reaches of the Ganga. There is considerable information available from Jain and Buddhist sources as well as in the Chinese pilgrims' travel accounts on the commercial voyages organized on the Ganga, often reaching up to the Malay archipelago, from at least the third century BCE to the seventh century CE (Darian, 2001; Ray, 1987-8: 79-89). During ancient times, the Ganga plain was looking outwards towards the sea and to the outer world, as the river provided easy communication networks. The numerous river channels of north India fed into the Ganga riverine traffic, which ultimately joined the overseas trade via Champa and Tamralipti in the ancient period.

Steven Darian has studied the economic role of the Ganga in the ancient period. He suggests that during the pre-Christian centuries, sea-faring merchants from eastern Bihar traded in northern Bihar or Mithila through the Kosi River. These merchants vended commodities such as betel nuts, sugar, *ghee* or clarified butter, rice, cloth and jewels (Darian, 1970: 68). As most of the rivers in northern Bihar were navigable, such trading networks were easily maintained (Pandey, 1963: 204). Apart from the Kosi River of north Bihar, the Gandak and the Gogra found mention in ancient texts such as the *Śatapatha Brāhmaṇa* and the last-named is referred to by Megasthnese as 'Solomattis'. The Gogra also finds mention in the literary source *Raghuvaṁśa* belonging to the Gupta period. Information on merchants' activities are hard to come by in these texts but navigation in these rivers appears to be indisputable (Forster, 1798: 82-5).

Several rivers of north Bihar were navigable throughout the year and functioned as feeders to the Ganga riverine traffic (Darian, 1970: 68). However, this was not the case with southern rivers such as the Son, which rises in the Mekal Hills, flows more than 400 miles north-north-east and joins the Ganga to the west of Patna (O'Malley, 1924: 6).[2] Although Pandey suggests that the Son was navigable throughout the major part of the year, we know from other sources that the river had only limited navigability during the rains and could only be reached up to Daudnagar to the south-west of Patna. Indeed, the rivers to the south of the Ganga offered limited navigation while many rivers to the north offered excellent navigation facilities throughout the year.

The riverine communication channels certainly added to the commercial traffic in the Ganga. During the early modern period, the vigorous commercial activities of the Asian, Portuguese, Dutch and English merchants along the Ganga was a re-enactment of the economic role of the river during the ancient period. It is yet to be fully understood as to why the Ganga, which had been the highway during the ancient period, again assumed a central position in the trade and economy of the region in the early modern period. Rather than showing a linear pattern, the economic history of the Ganga plain seems to be moving in a cyclical order.[3] As happened in many other parts of the world, the forces from outside the region played an important role in transforming the economic and political landscapes of the Ganga plain.

The Ganga River System in the Early-Modern Period

During the early-modern period, the river channels along the Ganga played an important role in facilitating communication and commercial traffic. To this end the hydrological circuit of the landscape of the Ganga plain could be seen as a system functioning according to the geographical and environmental conditions, and the economic needs of the region (Chakrabarti, 2001: 38). When harnessed properly this hydrological circuit or riverine network facilitated economic and political developments.

The plain assumed its central role again from the early second millennium CE, as a fresh wave of migrants from Central and West Asia settled on the scene. The new horse-riding immigrants not only brought mobile resources but also ensured the long-distance overland connection between the Ganga plain and Central Asia (Abu-Lughod, 1989: 170-84). The architects of the Delhi Sultanate, the Afghans and the Mughal empire-builders, the founders of successor states after the weakening of the Mughal empire and finally the emergence of the British—all seem to have been re-enactments of experiences of the early historic empire-builders who pinned themselves down in the Ganga plain for imperial expansion and consolidation. It is not yet satisfactorily demonstrated as to why an all-Indian empire should be rooted in the Ganga plain. Once their control over the productive regions around the Ganga is weakened, the empire is in disarray. This was what happened with the Mughal empire. Thus, control over the Ganga River and its plain was essential for the survival of any empire which claimed to have control over a large part of South Asia. It is evident that apart from the high agricultural output, the region aptly served the empires with its excellent communication system provided by numerous river channels. Such communication networks could easily be exploited for exercising political control and administrative authority. At the same time, the river system was equally prone to be exploited by fissiparous elements who were bent on defying imperial control. The centrifugal elements could be kept in check as long as the imperial state had resources and the power to do so. Once their ability to wield this power and authority eroded, the loosely confederated *zamindars* (landholders) and chieftains were eager to throw off the yoke of imperial control.

The Ganga was used for military exploits and expeditions by imperial forces. It has been suggested that during the Mughal period, for political integration and for the marching of soldiers, the eastern land route from Agra to Bengal was often substituted for the relatively easy communication lines offered by the Ganga and Yamuna rivers (Gommans, 2002: 103). For military and logistical purposes, the river played a crucial role in ensuring supplies after the Mughal army crossed the Yamuna and reached the Ganga plain. The beasts of burden and the warhorses needed to be fed. Hence, the requirements of fodder could easily be met from the productive and fertile land along the banks of the river. Apart from meeting the requirements of food and fodder, the river also facilitated the march of the army. In the humid conditions of eastern India, the Mughal warhorses proved to be quite ineffective, especially after Rajmahal, which served as a natural terminus for the Mughal armies marching to the east. They had to rely on other forms of warfare, mainly the riverboats and the infantry (Gommans, 2002: 25-8). In the Bengal delta the Mughals had to shift their seasoned cavalry techniques to riverine warfare. In this area, the Mughals depended upon the *bara bhuyan* or twelve largely autonomous chiefs, drawn mainly from the Afghan ethnic stock, for the supply of ships and the Mughal river fleet or *nawara*. The Mughals compensated them with the so-called *nawwara-jagirs* (Gommans, 2002: 165). Thus, the Ganga served as the military highway to assert political control but it equally served those who wanted to defy it. The Afghans did not relent with the allocation of *nawwara-jagirs* and, by the late seventeenth century, captured many of the Mughal towns in Bengal, including Rajmahal (Wilson, 1895: 147-8). Though the Afghan uprising was quelled, the danger of such attacks continued to linger.

Apart from its use as the military and strategic communication line, the Ganga was also exploited for commercial purposes by merchants.

River navigation was easy and convenient for the merchants trading in bulk goods. The Mughals tried to regulate river traffic through the system of the *dastak* or passport. Merchants travelling through north Indian rivers had to take a *dastak* from the place of their journey. In order to get a free passage, they had to show the *dastak* at every customs-post or *chabutra* situated on the river (Saran, 1973: 305).

In the first half of the seventeenth century, Sebastien Manrique, a Portuguese traveller travelling from Dacca to Patna through the Ganga, reports six customs-posts at Rajmahal and these were charged with issuing and checking the passes of river-boats (Manrique, 1927: 135). Similar traffic could be noticed, though to a lesser extent, on the Gandak which flows into the Ganga opposite Patna (Deloche, 1994, vol. II: 22). Rivers such as the Burhi Gandak, Baya (an overflow of the Great Gandak), Baghmati and Tiljuga provided communication channels through which the local marts and production centres were interlinked. The Burhi Gandak River was navigable all through the year for boats of 1,000 maunds while the Baghmati, an affluent of the Burhi Gandak, could be traversed by boats of 400 to 500 maunds except in a very dry season. During the rains, the Baghmati connected the Ganga valley and southern Nepal. The rivers linked the important marts and the sub-divisional headquarters of Darbhanga, Samastipur and Madhubani. Apart from these towns, Naraya in the Phulparas *thana* was an important mart which handled local and Nepalese grain traffic. Rusera, owing to its location on the Burhi Gandak which gave access to the Ganga River near Munger, used to be a great mart before the opening of the railways (Kerr, 1904: 5-9; Deloche, 1994, vol. II: 23).

There were other riverine channels known as *khal* and *dhar* in the region, and during the wet season they were more convenient for travel and transport than the roads. During the nineteenth century, the northern parts of the Bhagalpur district were easily navigable through the rivers of the Supul (contemporary Supaul) and Madahpura (Madhepura) divisions. The many small channels of these divisions joined the Kosi River. Through the Kosi, these divisions connected to the Ganga opposite to Colgong or Kahalgaon. Some of the *parganas* of the Bhagalpur district like Nisankpur Kura were sending most of their produce through the *dhars* or *khals* such as the Parwan, Dandasari and Daus. The boat route to *pargana* Chhai was through the Ghugri and Kalbabya branches of the Ganga. There was a great mart, Sibganj, on the banks of the Kalbabya, which was swept away in 1868 as a result of the northward shift of the river. Thus, a new trade centre, Karik, about 6 miles downstream further north-east, had emerged (Hunter, 1976: 31). Clearly, the shifting river course determined the rise and decline of many of the riparian marts and trade centres. Fluctuating fortunes of trade centres notwithstanding the fluvial channels provided them connectivity to the Ganga and further access to the larger towns and port cities. The above instances of connectivity between the remote areas and the principal towns through the fluvial channels come from nineteenth-century sources. In previous centuries, too, these channels and river routes served important commercial and economic roles.

The Rhythms of Sailing in the Ganga: The *Pattenase Togt* of the Dutch

As we have already noted, the Ganga was used as a route for trade and travel during the ancient period but we lack any systematic record which could give us detailed information about the organization of voyages before the arrival of the European companies. The sailing journals of the Dutch fleet's journey to Patna called *Pattenase Togt* fill this lacuna and offer us a sumptuous picture to visualize the rhythms of sailing in the Ganga. In the following paragraphs we discuss the Dutch sailing rhythms in the Ganga and the locality/toll posts on the river banks, which were often made the points for night halts. We also account for the hazards of navigation, and the frequent communication between the officials of the Dutch factories at Hugli and Patna and the captains of the fleet on the river. It can safely be assumed that the rhythms of sailing by the Dutch might not have been qualitatively different from that of other Asian and European merchants out on similar voyages on the Ganga, especially in terms of the use of particular types of boats, exploitation of the winds and current patterns (Figures 7.2 and 7.3).

Figure 7.2: Country boats continue to be used on the Ganga, as evident from this view of the River Ganga at Gandhi Ghat, Patna.

Figure 7.3: Boats at Gandhi Ghat.

The Ganga as a Trade Route

The Dutch were already sending their Patna fleet upriver, at least since the mid-seventeenth century when they established their factory at Patna. Around 1670, at the time of the Dutch physician and draftsman, Nicolaus de Graaff's trip to Patna, the number of boats in the fleet appears to be rather modest, twenty boats in all (De Graaff, 1701: 91). By the third decade of the eighteenth century the number of boats in the fleet increased, sometimes reaching up to 112 boats. The fleet made two round voyages between Hugli and Patna every year. Clearly, it can be taken as an indication of the growing commerce of the Dutch East India Company or *Verenigde Oost-Indische Compagnie* (VOC) from Patna. Below we will briefly discuss how the Dutch fleet was organized on this riverine route, what instructions were given to the crew and which the main riverine stopovers between Hugli and Patna were.

Periodically, the captain of the Patna fleet was issued a document, called *instructie* or instruction by the Hugli Council on the conduct of sailing, as well as on the precautions to be taken while on the river. If the same captain continued in service to organize the Patna fleet, there was little need to give him instructions every time he set sail. Thus, the instruction was normally given to a new captain who was in-charge of the fleet for the first time. The instruction to a new captain had only a slight addition while the contents of the rest of the document remained unchanged. This is evident from the instructions given to Captain Jacob Willem van den Brughen in 1730 and few years later to Lieutenant Captain Jan Geldsak, the new captain of the Patna fleet (NA, VOC, Inv. nr. 8765: 1046, 1046-80; Inv. nr. 8777: 694-750, Inv. nr. 8762: 195-230).[4]

In the instructions issued on both these occasions, we find particular emphasis on the order in which different boats were to be placed in the fleet. The instruction reads, 'When you have boarded the fleet with all your crew, you have to start your journey in the name of God, having placed the vessels with merchandise, ammunition and supply in good order in the middle of the escort' (NA, VOC, Inv. nr. 8777: 701).[5] Clearly, the safety of the cargo and ammunition boats was the foremost concern of the Hugli Council. These two sets of instructions hardly differ from each other except for the name of the captain and the prominent crew to whom the documents were addressed. There were a number of guidelines to which the captain and crew of each fleet were ordered to adhere to. Let us discuss some of the guidelines issued by the Hugli Council in the *instructie* of 1730. The captain of the fleet was instructed to set sail without any delay or unnecessarily loitering here and there, in course of the journey as was done by English and indigenous merchants. If the weather permitted, they should set sail as soon as the day broke and continue the journey till half an hour before sunset. Afterwards, they should halt at a place which the *daroga* (chief officer/head of the police) Kesari Singh decided upon (NA, VOC, Inv. nr. 8765: 1047-8). The service of the *daroga* was crucial for ensuring the safety of the fleet. Being a local, he knew best where to halt for the night. In 1730, in the fleet of Captain Jacob Willem van den Brughen, Kesari Singh, whose title suggests his Rajput or Bhumihar identity, acted as the *daroga* who decided where the fleet should make a stopover for the night. The *daroga* was not the only one from the local society. Among the crew and soldiers, there were other locals. Thus, the captain was given clear instructions to ensure that no one, particularly Europeans, should enter the kitchen boat of the local steersmen and rowers and not interfere with their dietary habits. If a European touched their food, they would not eat it but would throw it away in the river and desert the fleet.

Wherever the fleet with more than a hundred crew members and soldiers made a stopover it created an opportunity for petty traders selling foodstuffs to cater to the necessities of the amphibious folks in the fleet. Thus, the captain was instructed to make sure that his crew and soldiers did not behave in a hostile manner, use violence against the 'blacks' or take goods from the petty traders without paying for them. Such acts would create problems not only with the authorities but also with the small traders. The latter would stop coming to the fleet with foodstuff which might endanger the provisioning of the fleet, causing great inconvenience (NA, VOC, Inv. nr. 8765: 1048-9). All these points suggest a fair degree of interaction between the fleet and the local people along the Ganga. However, interactions with indigenous boats sailing in the river could be a source of difficulty too. Therefore, a strict warning was given to the captain not to take any strange boat into the convoy, which might create issues with the customs officials and also jeopardize the safety of the Company's goods in the fleet. Besides, the captain was ordered not to let his crew or soldiers buy any slaves. The reference to the presence of petty traders and foodstuff-sellers at different places along the banks of the Ganga probably suggests that the Dutch were not their only clients. These foodstuff-sellers were servicing probably hundreds, if not thousands, of other traders and travellers who passed through the river everyday.

Normally a fleet consisted of anywhere between twenty-five to fifty different types of boats and sometimes the number crossed a hundred. Some of the sailing journals, which are in the form of the *dag register* or diary, and the instructions issued to the captain of the fleet give the number of boats and crew members of the fleet. In 1729, an instruction letter given to Jacob van der Helling mentions the number of different types of boats in the fleet as one hundred and fourteen. Among the crew and soldiers, three hundred and twelve were European while the local employees, including soldiers numbered forty-six. It is further reported that the number of Europeans was thirty-four less than the previous year (NA, VOC, Inv. nr. 8762: 227-30). In 1733, Jan Geldzak sailed to Patna with forty-nine boats while, in 1734, Jan van Ingen commanded thirty boats. In the same year, another fleet consisted of thirty-three various sorts of boats (NA, VOC, Inv. nos. 8776: 786, 8777: 688, 745-6, & 8778: 485).[6] A report of 1734 has seventy-nine Europeans and seventeen local employees on a thirty-three boat fleet. Amongst the seventy-nine Europeans there were fifty-nine soldiers or *gemeene soldaten*. Among the seventeen local, there were six *pions* or soldiers and one *daroga*. In the same year, another larger fleet with sixty-three boats had 109 Europeans, including eighty-three military and forty-four local servants of which eighteen were soldiers (NA, VOC, Inv. nr. 8777: 687, 744-5).

Perhaps the boats used in the Ganga were locally made and the building materials, such as good timber, were locally procured. The Flemish artist Balthazar Solvyns (1760-1824) spent several years in Calcutta and his drawings present a visual record of the late eighteenth-century boats of Bengal (Hardgrave, Jr. 2001). In the sailing journals we only have casual remarks about the boat-building places. In the delta, 'Bagorganjs' has been mentioned as a great centre for indigenous boat-building. It is reported that a large number of big and small boats were built throughout the year at this place. Here one could also purchase the required materials for the building of indigenous barks. The Dutch captain Lubertas Vermeer(?), who was in-charge of the survey of the delta to find new sailable channels and routes through the Sundarbans to Patna in order to avoid shallow waters at Morcia, got his boats' anchors and ropes made at this shipyard of Bagorganjs. It is not clear from Captain Vermeer's testimony whether this shipyard was producing boats only for the riverine traffic or whether seaworthy vessels for the long haul or coastal traffic were also built (NA, VOC, Inv. nr. 8772: 1469-71). Another report, 'Memoritje van alle zodanige Vaarthuijgen' or the memoranda of the boats used by the VOC in the Bengal directorate, gives us the types and the sizes of the boats employed in the Ganga River. The following table gives a picture of the types of boats.

Table: Listing boats sailing on the Ganga (NA, VOC, Inv. nr. 8762: 267)

	Enlisted men on the boat	Length (in feet)	Width (in feet)	Depth of the hull (in feet)	Year of induction (wat jaar aangeland)
Sloops:					
Den amphioenkramer	11	60	18	6½	1707/very bad
Het twedegeluij	10	60	18	8	1720/bad, damaged by worms
D' Jager	11	60	18½	7½	1728/repaired
Voltha	10	60	18½	8	1729/good
Pantjallangs:					
D' weroname	10	61	18	7	1720/bad
D' Leydsaamheid	10	56	17½	6½	1720/bad
Galjoots:					
D' Visscher	14	75	23	8	1726/repaired
D' Putter	14	75	23	8	1726/repaired
Rowing and sailing boats:					
Pattena	–	50	14	6½	1726/good
D' Ganges	–	65	16½	4	1727/good
Bassura					
D' Grote Bassura	–	115	12	–	1720/very bad
D' Kleene Bassura	–	84	10	–	1724/bad

Rhythms of Production around Patna in the Ganga Plain

In the Ganga plain in a normal monsoon year, two crops, i.e. autumn or *kharif* and winter or *rabi*, were produced. The winter crops of marketable variety included wheat and oilseed, which were harvested by April-May and entered into the market. The autumn crops such as paddy, cotton and sugar cane which ripen in December-January were sold in the local markets. Some of the commodities produced from these crops could be stored and preserved for a relatively longer period of time, the peasants and local merchants waited for a better price for their goods, till the second half of the year when communication by rivers was easier. During the lean season of navigation, especially in the first half of the year when communication with the delta was relatively difficult, the price of commodities such as rice tended to increase in the importing markets of Calcutta (Datta, 2000: 214). At the onset of the monsoon when river traffic eased, it offered relatively smooth communication to the market towns and the marketable crops could fetch an even better price from the merchants trading to relatively distant markets (Chatterjee, 1996: 52-3). The Dutch Patna fleet started to operate towards the end of the monsoon as it was easy to navigate the swollen Ganga then. Until the approach of the monsoon, the Dutch and other merchants at Patna could purchase and store their merchandise to be shipped towards Bengal from July/August.

Thus, it appears that the rhythms of navigation and traffic in the river closely followed the rhythms of production and trade. For example, as Anand Yang has shown, one of the main winter or *rabi* crops of Bihar in the nineteenth century (harvested in March-April) such as oilseed dominated the commercial traffic towards Calcutta from July throughout the monsoon and even during later months. During this period, oilseeds and rice together constituted more than half of the traffic on the Ganga. Furthermore, while *ghee* (clarified butter), indigo, sugar, hides, wheat, saltpetre and oilseeds flowed down the stream, commodities such as rice, opium and tobacco made up the upstream traffic beyond Patna towards the North-Western Provinces (Yang, 2000: 30). From a petition written on 30 June 1816 by 17 Bihari merchants seeking an exemption from the obligation of taking the *rawannah* (passport) at Patna, we know that they purchased mustard seeds, linseed, *ghee*, *mutter* (peas), cloth, etc., in Tirhut, Bhagalpur and Purnia districts, and took their merchandise through the Ganga River to Murshidabad for sale. The petition claims that these 17 merchants annually paid Rs. 1 lakh as customs duty at the Murshidabad customs house where they also took the *rawannah*. A payment of Rs. 1 lakh as customs duty at the rate of 5 per cent makes a total transaction of Rs. 2 million by these merchants. This suggests that there existed rich commercial traffic linking the interiors of the Bihar *subah* with large markets such as Murshidabad and Calcutta in the Bengal delta (BL, P/111/68). Such commercial traffic must have existed during the previous centuries as well.

In the eighteenth century, however, textiles, opium and saltpetre were important commodities for the Dutch Patna fleet, and their production rhythms were well-synchronized with the traffic rhythms in the Ganga. Cotton was a *rabi* crop, which means that it was ready for harvesting latest by December-January. Afterwards, the moist weather of winter was most suited for processing the raw cotton to make thread and for weaving. Thus, much before the arrival of the monsoon, the bulk of textiles was ready for sale in the Patna market. Similarly, poppy being a *rabi* or winter crop, its finished product or opium matched the traffic rhythm perfectly.

The Tirhut *sarkar* of the Bihar *subah* produced prodigious quantity of saltpetre. Saltpetre constituted the chief ingredient for manufacturing gunpowder. This salt occurred on the surface of the land. The profession of scraping and collecting of this commodity had traditionally been assigned to a caste known as *Loneahs* who commenced their operation of collecting saltpetre from November every year (Stevenson, 1833: 23). After collecting the crust the *Loneahs* used to sell this raw material to the middleman or *paikars* who treated this substance by boiling it in water in large earthenware pots and then letting it cool (Chaudhuri, 1978: 339).[7] After this process the salt crystallized along the edges of the earthen pots. By repeating this procedure a refined variety called *dobara* with 80 to 85 per cent nitre could be obtained (Jacobs, 2006: 123; van Dam, 1932: 33). There was another variety called *dhoah* which was re-dissolved and crystallized and the final product called *kalmi* or *dobara-cabesaa* contained up to 95 per cent nitre. This variety was produced by a few rich indigenous merchants who could supply it to the Calcutta bazaar (Stevenson, 1833: 26-7; Om Prakash, 1985:

59). Other indigenous merchants lacked the resources to produce the highly-refined quality known as *kalmi*. The Dutch, therefore, produced this *kalmi* or *dobara-cabessa* variety at their refining units, using copper cauldrons instead of earthen pots. When the output could not keep pace with the demand, the VOC shipped second-grade *dobara* with an 80 to 85 per cent nitre content to Europe and refined it in the Netherlands (Jacobs, 2006: 123). The entire procedure from the collection of the raw material from the earth's surface to refining it for sale was done in the winter season and this commodity was ready to be shipped before the dispatch of the Patna fleet.

The Patna fleet was generally divided into two *smaldelen* or fleets and both these fleets made one round voyage in a year, particularly in the latter half. The first fleet or *smaldeel* left for Patna between July/August and the second left Hugli for Patna latest by September. The upriver journey must have been propelled by the eastern winds which prevailed during these months. For the downstream voyage, it was expected by the Hugli Council that both the *smaldeel* or fleets should return to Hugli by the end of November when the eastern winds slackened. For instance, Samuel Martinus' fleet left Hugli on 15 August 1728 and reached Patna on 2 October, thus spending one month and seventeen days on the upriver journey and traversing a distance of about 500 miles. For the downstream journey, his fleet started from Patna on 10 November and arrived at Hugli on 21 November (NA, VOC, Inv. nr. 8760: 33-66).[8] In 1733 Jan Geldzak's fleet made an early return voyage from Patna, starting on 13 September and reaching Hugli on 23 September. Sometimes when the Patna fleet returned even during mid-November it faced little or no difficulty in sailing downstream and in fact, Samuel Martinus' fleet reached Hugli in just eleven days, on 21 November. This was the general sailing pattern of the Patna fleet on the Ganga.

There were many important halting places along the Ganga between Hugli and Patna and, at different points, the Mughals or the local chiefs had customs posts. Between Hugli and Rajmahal, there were important places such as Aziemgens, Morcia, Nerangabaad, Derriapour and Dobera (NA, VOC, Inv. nr. 8765: 1059-60). After Rajmahal, the important places included Sakrigali, Gangapoursaat,

Schabaad or Shahabad, Chanda, Tjyndpour, Jahangeera, Munger, Singia, Laalpour, Surajgarha, Rouanella, Derriapour, Nawada, Fatuha and Patna. We have many instances of shipwreck, difficulty in taking the boats across because of the shallow waters, and sand-banks and strong currents at places such as Sakrigali, Gangapoursaat, Jahangeera, Munger, Rouanella, and so on. At many places there were islands that posed further difficulties for navigation.

Problems of Navigation in the Ganga River

Navigation in the Ganga was not free from hazards. Reefs, sandbanks, shallow water and strong currents posed threats to the boats (Figures 7.4 and 7.5). In the months of September and October the monsoon gradually weakens but these months are rife with periodic cyclones and storms which posed additional threats to the boats. Thus, the fleet had to deal with all these hazards in the course of their up and down river voyages. In the Dutch sources there are references to many accidents and loss of cargoes while sailing upriver against the

Figure 7.4: Plaque in St. Luke's Church, Patna for those killed in a hurricane on the Ganga in 1842 indicates the dangers of navigation in the Ganga.

Figure 7.5: St Luke's Church in Danapur cantonment on the banks of the Ganga, Patna built in 1827-30.

stream. In the Ganga danger always lurked and boat-wrecks occurred quite frequently.

At Sakrigali, there was a strong current and it posed a serious threat to boats sailing upriver. Here the boats had to be taken to another bank by crossing the currents of the channel and this was done by towing them with ropes and pulling them across. The same procedure of towing and dragging across the current of the channel was often repeated at Barari near Bhagalpur (NA, VOC, Inv. nr. 8776: 791).[9] At this place the Chandan River drained into the Ganga which gave additional force to the stream, and made navigation difficult and hazardous. Junctions of rivers such as the Burhi Gandak in Munger and the Kiul at Surajgarha created difficult points for the river boats to cross. In August 1733, when Lieutenant Jan Geldzak was on the upriver journey, one of the merchant boats of the fleet was wrecked because of the very strong current along the channel near Shahabad above Sakrigali. Geldzak made all efforts to trace the wreckage of the boat which had drifted quite far away. Sergeants such as Herman Velting and Cornelis van Aken as also the *daroga*, who were sailing behind the wrecked boat, told Geldzak that the *manjhi* (boatman) Ramoth, a local employee of the VOC, had handled the boat carelessly and it had, therefore, drifted along the strong current and got wrecked on a sandbank near the shallow waters. The Patna officials were informed that some merchandise such as pepper, mace and cinnamon, was washed away in the incident (NA, VOC, Inv. nr. 8776: 793-4). Apart from the dangerous streams, cyclonic weather and storms formed other sorts of navigational hazards. A major incident of shipwreck was reported on 20 October 1730 at Rouanella when the fleet under the command of Jacob van Helling was only a few miles away from reaching Patna. Bad weather of cyclonic winds, a constant downpour and the resultant strong currents in the river caused the massive destruction of almost all the boats in the Dutch fleet (NA, VOC, Inv. nr. 8762: 78-9). During this turbulent weather, it is reported that the British, with their hundred or so merchant boats, stayed put between Jangiera and Coedercatta (both places to the east of Munger). Whether they sustained any damage is not reported (NA, VOC, Inv. nr. 8762: 83). It appears from selected boat journals that major incidents involving shipwreck occurred mainly on the upstream journey. The downstream journey was comparatively smooth and fewer incidents of these kind were reported.

Reefs posed another threat to the boats. There were reefs along Sakrigali, Bhagalpur, Jahangeera and Sitakund both places to the east of Munger. At these points outcrops of southern hills had encroached upon the Ganga and these posed grave dangers to boats. At Teliagarhi near Gangaprasad, it was reported in October 1734 that the channel had become unsailable because it received torrents mixed with lac from the mountains. Therefore, some *pions* were sent to explore another route through Purnia's territory (NA, VOC, Inv. nr. 8778: 508-9).[10] Throughout the journey, taking soundings of the water was a routine practice and after ascertaining the depth of the channel or 'canael' did the fleet trek further. Some soldiers and the *daroga* were regularly employed for this purpose and they used to sail forward with some *Pollewaers* and reported on the river's conditions to the fleet captain. These precautions minimized the possibility of boat accidents to some extent.

Communication along the Journey

While on the river, the Patna fleet maintained frequent communication with the Hugli Council and the Patna factory by regularly sending and receiving letters and messages. The possibility of being able to communicate from different locations on the river ensured better coordination between the fleet and the Dutch factory. Such communication also ensured the better safety of the fleet and a timely supply of cargoes to the factory at Hugli. Whenever an incident involving shipwreck occurred, the captain of the fleet immediately informed the Dutch authorities at Hugli and Patna. Also, the authorities at Hugli and Patna were intimated when the fleet entered Bihar or Bengal in its upstream and downstream journey. In 1733 when Jan Geldzak was only a few miles away from reaching Patna on 2 November, he received a letter from the Hugli Council dated 22 October. It took less than two weeks for a letter from Hugli to reach the location of the fleet on the river. How was this fast communication network operated?

When Jan Geldzak's fleet was near Kahalgaon on its upstream journey on 17 August 1733, the captain received a letter sent by the Patna officials signed on 4 August and delivered by two trusted *pions*. The *pions* also gave the message that local trouble-makers had prepared themselves to obstruct the fleet of the Company (NA, VOC, Inv. nr. 8776: 796).[11] As there is no mention of an incoming fleet from the direction of Patna, it appears that the two *pions* themselves brought this letter from Patna either overland or via the river route. On 4 August 1733, Geldzak wrote a letter to the Hugli Council via Casset (Persian *qaseed* or courier) informing the Dutch authorities about the carelessness of Manjhi Ramoth which had led to the shipwreck and loss of cargo. A few months later Geldzak made another upstream journey with the second fleet of the season and when the fleet reached Gangaprasad he informed the Patna officials through an express Casset about his safe arrival in Bihar territory. When Geldzak advanced much farther from Munger, he wrote a letter to the Hugli Council from the customs house of Kathgola. In his downstream journey from Patna when Geldzak reached Salempour Coukie (customs post) he sent a letter to the Hugli

Council informing the Dutch authorities of his safe arrival in the Bengal territory through a fast rowing boat, as he put, 'pr: Express Casset een roijvaartuijg' (NA, VOC, Inv. nr. 8776: 830). In this case the courier seems to be using a rowing boat. It appears that the Casset was a safe and fast means for sending and receiving letters and messages. Apart from using the service of Casset the Dutch captains of the Patna fleet frequently employed *pions* to get intelligence about the prevailing political situation along the Ganga. These *pions* were also used to spy on the local chieftains and *zamindars* and reported about their military standing such as on the number of artillery and cavalry commanded by each chieftain.

Conclusion

The Ganga River was bountiful in terms of ensuring the productivity of the land along its flood plains. The fertility and productivity of the region depended both on local factors and on demand from external stimuli, since the river was linked from early times to maritime networks in the Bay of Bengal. It is the interaction between the two spheres that made the Ganga plain a source of wealth, though this is an issue that has not been adequately explored by historians.

After the establishment of the Delhi Sultanate we find a new impetus to economic growth as the Ganga plain became more closely connected to the economies of Central and West Asia and the Mediterranean. During the same time we find the emergence of several towns and cities along the Ganga River. Patna (former Pataliputra) became an important town in the sixteenth century once again. The process of the region's integration with the wider world economy further peaked as Europeans started participating in Asian commerce. In the form of bullion, external stimulus came once again and it had a catalytic effect on the economy and on the growth of towns and cities.

During the seventeenth and eighteenth centuries the Ganga plain profited from agricultural expansion and the growing maritime contacts with the outside world. Local merchandise found markets not only in different parts of Asia but these were also transported to Europe. The commercial activities of the Dutch and English East India Companies connected the region with the ever-widening global economy. The Patna fleet of the Dutch conveyed the commodities of Bihar to Hugli. After the goods were collected at Hugli they were transhipped to overseas markets. The economy of the region responded positively to demands and absorbed a growing amount of precious metals. In the entire process from the production to transportation of goods, the economic role of the Ganga was central. It was the wealth creating capacity of the river which sustained the empires. It seems that in the early modern period the Ganga served the empires in a similar way as it had done to the Mauryas and the Guptas. The long distance mercantile activities marked both the ages. In the early modern period the Ganga redeemed its ancient glory when merchants had left its bank and ventured out to overseas voyages.

NOTES

1. We find the modern tripartite geographical division of the Ganga plain into the upper, middle and lower plains to be grossly unsatisfactory. Such division fails to explain historical processes which gravitated between the two competing environmental zones of the Ganga plain. My ongoing PhD research at Leiden raises some questions about the problems of the modern geographical division of the Ganga plain.
2. The late eighteenth-century English traveller William Hodges visited the beautiful mosque at Maner on the Son River.
3. My current PhD research at Leiden University engages with these problems in more detail.
4. Nationaal Archief (henceforth, NA), Verenigde Oost-Indische Compagnie (henceforth, VOC), Inv. nr, 8765: 1046, 1046-80 contain the instruction given to Jacob Willem van den Brughen and crew of the Patna fleet in the year 1730. Another instruction given to Jan Geldzak's Patna fleet in the year 1734 can be found in NA, VOC, Inv. nr. 8777: 694-750. Compare, for similar contents of the instruction issued to Jacob van der Helling and the other crew of the Patna fleet in 1728, NA, VOC, Inv. nr. 8762: 195-230. Daroga Kesari Singh appears in the instructions of 1728 and 1730, and he seems to have been in the employ of the VOC till around that period.
5. NA, VOC, Inv. nr. 8777: 701. 'Waneer uE dan niet alle de manschapp in de vaartuijgen gestapt zijn zullen uE de reyse met goed ordre plaatsend de negotie ammonitie provisie vaartuijgen int midden van het escorte in godes Name aanvangen.'

6. NA, VOC, Inv. nr. 8776: 786 for Jan Geldzak's fleet consisting of forty-nine diverse types of boats; NA, VOC, Inv. nr. 8778: 485 for Jan van Ingen's fleet; NA, VOC, Inv. nr. 8777: 688 for another fleet of thirty-three boats in 1734. In the same year another fleet left with sixty-three different types of boats. See, NA, VOC, Inv. nr. 8777: 745-6.
7. Chaudhuri uses the term *assamies* for those who extracted and refined saltpetre in Bihar.
8. NA, VOC, Inv. nr. 8760, 'Dagregister gehouden door den Capitain Samuel Martinus Hogerwerf, gedurende den Optogt naar Pattena in het Jaer 1728' (Diary kept by the captain Samuel Martinus Hogerwerf during the upriver journey to Patna in the year 1728), pp. 33-66 (by mistake the scribe entered p. 59 twice instead of writing it as 69 which resulted in double pagination for some pages).
9. NA, VOC, Inv. nr. 8776, for Sakrigali see, p. 791, for Barari see, p. 797 'Met den light moest ik even boven Barrarij alle vaartuijgen met drie touwen onder kragt van volk door een zeer sterke stroom laten slepen.' (In order to cross the very strong current above Barrarij, at sunrise I had to get all the boats dragged by the men using three ropes.).
10. NA, VOC, Inv. nr. 8778: 508-9. For the rocks of Jahangeera which caused several accidents in the Ganga, see Nicolaus de Graaff, *Reisen van Nicolaus de Graaff*, p. 95.
11. NA, VOC, Inv. Nr. 8776: 796. Captain Geldzak reports, ''s morgens om half zeven stak ik wederom de Ganges over en ontvang uijt handen van twee vertrouwde pions een missive van de Pattenase bediendens gedagtekend den 4 Aug: nevens het mondeling berigt dat nevens in den weg eenige nadeelige preparatien tegens 's Ed. Comps. smaldeelen wierden gemaakt'. (In the morning at half past six I crossed over the Ganga and received a letter dated 4th [of] August from the Patna's employees from the two faithful pions who also verbally told me that some detrimental actions were being prepared against the honourable Company's fleet [by the local *zamindars*])

REFERENCES

Archival Sources

National Archives, The Hague:
NA, VOC, Inv. nr. 8760

NA, VOC, Inv. nr. 8762
NA, VOC, Inv. nr. 8765
NA, VOC, Inv. nr. 8772
NA, VOC, Inv. nr. 8776
NA, VOC, Inv. nr. 8777
NA, VOC, Inv. nr. 8778

The British Library, India Office Records, London

BL, P/111/68, Behar and Benares Revenue Proceedings (Customs), Camp Culwar Zillah Shahabad, 3 August 1816.

Published Sources

Abu-Lughod, Janet L., 1989, *Before European Hegemony: The World System AD 1250-1350*, New York: Oxford University Press.

Bell, James, 1832, *A System of Geography: Popular and Scientific or A Physical, Political and Statistical Account of the World and its Various Divisions*, Glasgow: Archibald Fullarton and Co., vol. IV.

Chakrabarti, Dilip K., 2006, *The Oxford Companion to Indian Archaeology*, New Delhi: Oxford University Press.

———, 2001, *Archaeological Geography of the Ganga Plain: The Lower and the Middle Ganga*, New Delhi: Permanent Black.

Chatterjee, Kumkum, 1996, *Merchants, Politics and Society in Early Modern India, Bihar: 1733-1820*, Leiden: E.J. Brill.

Chaudhuri, Kirti Narayan, 1978, *The Trading World of Asia and the English East India Company 1660-1760*, Cambridge: Cambridge University Press.

Colebrooke, Henry Thomas, 1979, 'On the Source of the Ganges, in the Himadri or Emodus', *Asiatic Researches comprising History and Antiquities, the Arts, Sciences, and Literature of Asia*, vol. XI, Delhi: Cosmo Publications (rpt. of 1818).

Darian, Steven G., 1970, 'The Economic History of the Ganges to the End of Gupta Times', *Journal of the Economic and Social History of the Orient*, vol. 13, no. 1, January: 62-87.

———, 2001, *The Ganges in Myth and History*, Delhi: Motilal Banarsidass.

Datta, Rajat, 2000, *Society, Economy and the Market: Commercialization in Rural Bengal, c.1760-1800*, New Delhi: Manohar.

De Graaff, Nicolaus, 1701, *Reisen van Nicolaus de Graaff, na de vier gedeeltens des Werelds, als Asia, Africa, America en Europa: Behelsende een Beschryving van sijn 48 jarige Reise en aanmerkelykste voorvallen, die hy heeft gesien en die hem zyn ontmoet. ... Als ook een nette, dog korte Beschryving van China ... Hier agter is by gevoegd d' Oost-Indise spiegel, zynde een Beschryving van deselve Schryver van geheel Oost-Indiën ...*, Hoorn: Feyken Ryp, Boekdrukker over 't Stadhuis.

Deloche, Jean, 1994, *Transport and Communications in India: Prior to Steam Locomotion*, vol. II: *Water Transport*, tr. James Walker, New Delhi: Oxford University Press.

Eaton, Richard M., 2004, *The Rise of Islam and the Bengal Frontier 1204-1760*, New Delhi: Oxford University Press (fifth impression 2006).

Erdosy, George, 1995, 'City States in North India and Pakistan at the Time of the Buddha', in F.R. Allchin (ed.), *The Archaeology of Early Historic South Asia*, Cambridge: Cambridge University Press: 99-122.

Febvre, Lucien, 1932, *A Geographical Introduction to History*, in collaboration with Lionel Bataillon, E.G. Mountford and J.H. Paxton trans., London: Kegan Paul, Trench, Trubner & Co., Ltd..

Forster, George, 1798, *A Journey from Bengal to England, through the Northern Part of India, Kashmire, Afghanistan, and Persia, and into Russia, by the Caspian-Sea*, in 2 vols., vol. I, London: Printed for R. Faulder.

Gommans, Jos, 2002, *Mughal Warfare: Indian Frontiers and High Roads to Empire, 1500-1700*, London & New York: Routledge.

Hardgrave, Jr., L. Robert, 2001, *Boats of Bengal: Eighteenth Century Portraits of Balthazar Solvyns*, New Delhi: Manohar.

Hodges, William, 1999, *Travels in India during the years 1780, 1781, 1782 and 1783*, New Delhi: Munshiram Manoharlal.

Hunter, William Wilson, 1877, *A Statistical Account of Bengal*, vol. XIV, District of Bhagalpur and the Santhal Parganas, London: Trübner & Co. (Indian rpt., 1976).

Jacobs, Els M., 2006, *Merchants in Asia: The Trade of the Dutch East India Company during the Eighteenth Century*, Leiden: CNWS Publications.

Jain, Sharad K., Pushpendra K. Agarwal and Vijay P. Singh, 2007, *Hydrology and Water Resources of India*, Dordrecht/The Netherlands: Springer.

Kerr, J.H., 1904, *Final Report on the Survey and Settlement Operations in the Darbhanga District, 1896 to 1903*, Calcutta: Bengal Secretariat Press.

Kulke, Hermann and Dietmar Rothermund (eds.), 1986, *A History of India*, London & New York: Routledge, 4th edn., 2004.

Law, Bimla Churn, 1976, *Historical Geography of Ancient India*, Delhi: Ess Ess Publications.

Manrique, Fray Sebastien, 1927, *Travels of Fray Sebastien Manrique, 1629-1643*, ed. C. Eckford Luard, Oxford: Hakluyt Society, vol. II.

Nevill, H.R., 1928, *Allahabad: A Gazetteer being Volume XXIII of the District Gazetteers of the United Provinces of Agra and Oudh*, Allahabad: The Superintendent, Government Press, United Provinces.

O'Malley, L.S.S., 1924, *Bihar and Orissa District Gazetteers: Patna*, Patna: Bihar and Orissa Govt. Print (revised edn. by J.F.W. James)

Pandey, Mithila Sharan, 1963, *The Historical Geography and Topography of Bihar*, Delhi: Motilal Banarsidass.

Prakash, Om, 1985, *The Dutch East India Company and the Economy of Bengal, 1630-1720*, Princeton: Princeton University Press.

Ray, Himanshu Prabha, 1987 & 1988, 'Early Trade in the Bay of Bengal', *The Indian Historical Review*, vol. XIV, nos. 1-2 (July & January): 79-89.

Saran, Paramatma, 1973, *The Provincial Government of the Mughals, 1526-1658*, London: Asia Publishing House.

Smith, George, 1882, *The Geography of British India: Political & Physical*, London: John Murray, Albemarle Street.

Stevenson, J., 1833, 'On the Manufacture of Saltpetre, as Practiced by the Natives of Tirhut', *The Journal of the Asiatic Society of Bengal*, vol. II.

Thapar, Romila, 1966, *A History of India*, Harmondsworth: Penguin Books.

Van Dam, Pieter, 1932, *Beschryvinge van de Oostindische Compagnie*, Tweede Boek, vol. II, 's-Gravenhage: Martinus Nijhoff.

Wilson, C.R., 1895, *The Early Annals of the English in Bengal, being the Bengal Public Consultations for the First Half of the Eighteenth Century*, vol. I, London: W. Thacker.

Yang, Anand A., 2000, *Bazaar India: Markets, Society, and the Colonial State in Gangetic Bihar*, New Delhi: Munshiram Manoharlal.

CHAPTER 8

Telling the Story of History: Remembering the Historical Links between India and Southeast Asia from the Eighth Century to the Present

FARISH A. NOOR

History, Stories, and Storytelling: How Cultural Maps Remain Narrative and Virtual

> Men make history, and the leading members of the revolutionary generation realised that they were doing so, but they could never have known the history they were making. . . . What in retrospect has the look of a foreordained unfolding of God's will was in reality an improvisational affair in which sheer chance, pure luck—both good and bad—and specific decisions made in the crucible of political crises determined the outcome. . . . If hindsight enhances our appreciation for the solidity and stability of the (historical) legacy, it also blinds us to the stunning improbability of the achievement itself.[1]
>
> Joseph J. Ellis, *Founding Brothers: The Revolutionary Generation*

History from the time of Thucydides to the present remains a case of narratives and storytelling. The history of nations are basically the stories they tell of themselves, by themselves and to themselves in the process of self-presentation and representation, with the aim of securing for themselves an identity that they can call their own.

Yet we need to remember that history—as stories—remains the most contested of the humanities and social sciences; and, in the wake of Foucault, we know that it is upon the site of historical narrative that all forms of power are enacted, all sorts of epistemic orders are erected, and all kinds of claims are made and contested. History is also the site of political power-contestation, and the historical subject, as Foucault has noted, is not some innocent soul whose moral writ is bare but rather a subject that has been forged and shaped by the workings of both political and epistemic power. History is never innocent, and seldom untainted by such claims to power and knowledge.

Compounding matters is the fact that history-telling is a process that takes off in the immediate present, while remaining wilfully and selectively blind to the aspects of the past that might complicate that present. In the countries of South and Southeast Asia today, history-writing has come within the purview of the modern post-colonial nation state; itself a hybrid offspring of that fateful uneven encounter between East and West, and which has left present-day South and Southeast Asians with a long-lasting legacy of Western (if not colonial) knowledge and episteme.

Our histories are *national* histories, and they tell the story of nations that are seen and cast as unique, particular and distinct from one another: Yet the post-colonial historian seldom delves deeper into a past where the basic epistemic tools that guide his hand were perhaps absent altogether. How do we write a history of South and Southeast Asia without the aid of a compass that tells us where is south and north in the first place? How do we write a history of the proto-states that lived and breathed before there were even such things as borders and frontiers, prior to the advent of the modern state, and nationality, and citizenship? Can we, today, even begin to imagine the writing of a history that does not bring in its long train of scholarship such accoutrements?

What we seem to be lacking in the region—and by this I refer to the lands across the expanse of the Indian Ocean—is a deconstructive account of history, i.e. a history that demonstrates and even highlights the constructiveness of history and historical identities. Our national histories are written on the solidly-cast iron railing of linear progression that takes us from some mythical point of genesis in the past to some teleologically predetermined destination in the future; with no veering off the set course and no stops along the way.

The official histories of so many post-colonial Asian nation states seem ill at ease with the realities of contingency, irony, chance and accidentalism. The official historian seeks to sweep all such instances of irregularity under the carpet, as a conductor may wish to dim the dissonant chord of a singular instrument with the overpowering bellow of the orchestra as a whole. A cursory overview of the official histories of South and Southeast Asia may offer some instances of this conformist logic at work. In the official histories of countries like Pakistan and Malaysia, the pre-Islamic past is treated with extreme caution, for the reality of that pre-Islamic past may threaten the Islamic reality of the present. Here the fear of the pre-Islamic other lies not in the fact that the pre-Islamic other is so different, but rather in the fact that he is so alike—*and thus a reminder of the simple fact that our ancestors were non-Muslims once.*

In the official histories of countries like Indonesia, on the other hand, narrow ethno-nationalism has sought to lay claim upon every aspect of the nation's culture and to make the claim that all that there is, and all that is Indonesian, is necessarily the result of a local genius, that is *sui generis*. Indonesian nationalists lay claim to things like *batik* and *gamelan* music as essentially (in the Aristotelian sense, almost) Indonesian—while conveniently forgetting that the myths and stories that make up much of Indonesian culture is in fact South Asian in origin. It is one of the greater ironies that Indonesia—which today claims copyright over *batik* and *gamelan* at the expense of its neighbours in the region—has a national airline named after *Garuda*, a semi-divine figure of Indian mythology. Yet the myopic eye of the nationalist historian does not flinch, or even note the irony of the situation.

The official histories of South and Southeast Asia are myopic, narrow and selective simply because they are national histories that serve other ends than those of history and story-telling. In most of the countries of the region, our national histories serve the ends of power-related nationalist discourses, providing the raw material for ideological projects aimed at nation-building, boundary-policing and exteriorizing the Other. It ought not to come as a surprise, therefore, if these official histories do not and cannot take us further than where some of us may want to be taken to.

This then raises the related question: If official histories are by their nature and intent limited, narrow and myopic histories, then can there be any other sources from which we can cull together a history—a story—that is more open, contingent, nuanced and plural in its content and message? Can history be liberated from the shackles of ideology and politics, and be made to serve the ends of a creative and inclusive story-telling instead? Before we even begin to look for such instances of liminal alternative histories, perhaps we ought to back-track a little and revisit the region we are talking about, at a time when nationalism had yet to rear its ugly, narrow head.

Remembering our Common Identity: A Glance at Southeast Asia during the Hindu-Buddhist Period

> India gave her mythology to her neighbours, who went to teach it to the whole world. She gave to three-quarters of Asia a God, a religion, a doctrine, an art. She carried her sacred language, her religion, her institutions to Indonesia, to the limits of the known world and from there they spread back to Madagascar and perhaps to the coast of Africa. . . .[2]
>
> Levi, 1938: 30

It seems commonsensical by today's standards to assert that our ancestors lived at a time where the concept of nation states, political boundaries, racial difference and citizenship were alien to them. We—the people of South and Southeast Asia today—are the descendants of communities and nations that were open to external influences to a far greater degree than we perhaps realize, and this is borne out by the fact that the culture, religions and vocabularies that were used in the ancient past demonstrate an easiness with cosmopolitanism that would embarrass most of us today. In *re-membering* our past, we need to somehow imagine what it was like to live then, in an age free of narrow political identities and loyalties.

To remember our past, we need to recall names and places, as well as geographical configurations that have passed from memory. There was once a land called *Suvarnabhumi,* whose western shores were turned towards the Indian Ocean, facing the eastern shores of the

Indian subcontinent. Like two faces reflected by a common mirror between them, the developments on both sides of this great watery divide mirrored each other, bearing witness to the rise and fall of kingdoms and empires. It was towards this fabled land of gold, spices and aromatic woods that generations of Indian navigators steered their vessels, braving the monsoon winds and turbulent waters, hoping to make landfall in order to be able to return home with their hulls full of bounty (Levi, 1929; Nilakanta Sastri, 1938; Wang Gungwu, 1958).

The oldest statues of the Buddha that have been found in Southeast Asia remain as oblique indicators of the seafaring lives of the first mariners who came to the region from India by sea. Many of these statues—influenced by the Amaravati school that flourished in India up to the fourth century—feature the image of the Buddha standing upright with long, flowing robes that fall from his shoulders to the ground. The gentle, sweeping flow of the folds of the Buddha's robe are no mere accident for this image happens to be that of the Buddha Dipankara (The Calmer of the Seas), whose very name can be traced to the word *dvipa* (island) and who was worshipped as the protector of seamen (Dupont, 1954). The *Brihatkatha*, *Kathakosa*, as also the Buddhist Jatakas refer to Bengali merchant-princes and fortune-hunters sailing eastwards from Tamralipti (Tamluk) in the Bengal region for Suvarnadvipa (Sumatra) and returning home with riches aplenty.

The region of Southeast Asia has been called by many names: Greater India, Farther India, and the land below the wind. Sanskrit records refer to it as Suvarnabhumi—the land of gold—and place it firmly within the frontiers of the world as it was then known to the South Asians. However, facts remain and endure despite the efforts of even the most determined revisionist, and geography remains a mute testament to the realities of times long forgotten. The Indian Ocean was (and remains) the vast corridor that kept these two lands apart and together at the same time, and what began as a sporadic series of trading expeditions across this ocean eventually developed to be a continuous traffic of human bodies, goods and commodities, as well as ideas and doctrines. As a result of this transcultural contact and exchange, the social and cultural terrain of Southeast Asia was visibly altered due to the incorporation of Indian designs and motifs, traces of which remain till today in the plastic and utilitarian arts of Southeast Asia, from the ubiquitous Indon-Malay *keris* (dagger) to the design structure of boats and sailing vessels in the archipelago (Coomaraswamy, 1927; Ghosh, 1935; Hornell, 1920; Kempers, 1933; Krom, 1931; Noor, 2000).

The South Asians who came to the Southeast Asian archipelago[3] were neither colonialists (in the Western sense) nor conquerors and the arrival of the South Asians, as George Çoedes (1962, 1968, 1992) has argued, could not be compared to Chinese colonization that was happening at the same time or the arrival (and subsequent colonization and conquest) of the Europeans who came centuries after.

> The coming of the Indians to Southeast Asia cannot be compared to the arrival of the Europeans to America, for in this part of the world the new-comers were not strangers discovering new lands. At some time that we must try to date, following circumstances that we can attempt to imagine, the sporadic influx of traders and immigrants became a steady flow that resulted in the founding of Indian kingdoms practising the arts, customs and religions of India and using Sanskrit as their sacred language. (Çoedes, 1968: 14-15)

What took place in Southeast Asia during the pre-Islamic and pre-colonial eras can only be understood in the context of an age where geo-political boundaries were fluid, porous and inter-penetrating; and local developments took place against a backdrop of transcultural exchange and translocal evolution.

Our concern here is not to elaborate upon the often contested and contentious claims of numerous scholars who have tried to locate the precise date for the beginning of the 'Indianization' process.[4] Most accounts tend to agree that the Indianization process was already underway between the second and third centuries, and evidence of Indianized societies and polities in Southeast Asia can be found from the fourth to the fifth—precisely the time when the Gupta[5] dynasty of India had reached its peak and was spreading its cultural and political influence abroad from the Bay of Bengal. Chinese records testify to the existence of small Hindu-Buddhist polities on the Malay peninsula around the second century, while Sanskrit inscriptions there do not go back any further than the fourth.[6] In the territories that make up present-day Malaysia, evidence of Hindu-Buddhist influence and Indianization go back to the second and third centuries. Historical records and religious texts from both India and China refer to the presence of established Hindu-Buddhist kingdoms like Langkasuka-Kadaran, Tambralinga and Takkola.

The arrival and settlement of Hindu and Buddhist traders, scholars and missionaries in Southeast Asia contributed vastly to the development of the Hindu-Buddhist polities there, and also further entrenched the process of Indianization that eventually gave much of Southeast Asia its normative political, economic and religious culture—traces of which can still be seen today.

However, it would be wrong to conclude that the Indianization of the Indon-Malay archipelago was simply a process of passive absorption of all that was Indian, Hindu or Buddhist. This would negate or undermine the role of local genius and the agency of the rulers and peoples of the archipelago themselves, who were never passive recipients of these news ideas, beliefs, values and customs from abroad. Coedes' account of the Indianization process between the second to fifth centuries points to a far more complex process (or processes) that operated on a number of different registers simultaneously. The Khmer ruler Yasovarman I (889-900) for instance, opened his court to a number of religious teachers and priests from the Vaishnavite, Shaivite and Buddhist traditions, and his adoption of these beliefs was selective and deliberate.

Nor should we assume that the traffic of ideas, goods and people between India and Southeast Asia was always moving in one direction. The Indon-Malay world not only interacted with the Indian subcontinent, but there were also instances when ambitious Malay rulers would turn their attention westwards to India to fulfil their dreams of power and glory: The twelfth-century medieval chronicles of Sri Lanka, for instance, record the invasion of the island by a Malay ruler from Nakhon Si Thammarat named Chandrabhanu. Not only did Chandrabhanu's army defeat the forces of the Sinhalese rulers of Polonnaruwa, they also managed to claim the prized relic of the Buddha that was in the possession of the Polonnaruwa kingdom. Following their victory the Malays then established their own kingdom in the northern part of the island (close to the Jaffna region) and the dynasty only met its end in the early thirteenth century when the son of Chandrabhanu was killed by the Pandyan king of south India (Hussainmiya, 2001: 1-2).

The end result of this long process of transcultural exchange was the construction of new categories of identity and belonging, a reworking of social norms and values, and the construction of a new epistemic order that actually contributed to the further evolution and development of Hinduism and Buddhism, as they filtered through the prisms of the local and vernacular. It was thanks to this process of Indianization that South and Southeast Asia were brought closer together, to the point where a common linguistic, religious, architectural and aesthetic culture was shared by the communities that spanned the Indian Ocean. This long process of cultural transmigration and exchange in turn paved the way for the coming of Islam to Southeast Asia from South Asia; it is for this reason that Islam's arrival on the shores of the Malay Peninsula, Sumatra and Java can aptly be described as the second moment or episode in the long drama of the Indianization of the Malay archipelago.

More Stories to Tell: How the Story of India's Proximity to Southeast Asia is Recounted in the Popular Religious Narratives of Indonesia and Malaysia

We will take the account of the long-shared history between South and Southeast Asia recounted above as the working premise for what we wish to address next: namely, the manner in which the image, memory and understanding of India has been kept alive not in the official histories of countries like Indonesia or Malaysia but in the popular narratives of religious movements instead. We do so to underscore the point that history does not have to be official in order to have a voice and to resonate in the hearts and minds of others, but it has to have relevance and meaning for it to signify anything to those who share those narratives.

Here our focus will be on the semi-sacred narratives of Muslims in Southeast Asia. Others have looked at the continuity of shared sacred geographies between South and Southeast Asia. While such continuities prevail in the lived normative realities of Buddhist and Hindu life in the region, the same sort of continuities also exist in the normative quotidian of many Muslims who see India and South Asia in general as a special place that has a unique significance for them.

That this is the case with many Muslims who live beyond the shores of India is not surprising for India's outward cultural expansion has taken place on a number of registers, and has led to the creation of a wide range of Indian-originated Muslim movements and schools of thought that are now present across the world: As Dietrich Reetz (2006) has shown, India has been the home for a number of Muslim groups whose expansion has exceeded the political frontiers of India proper: The Deobandis, Tablighis and Ahmadis (both Qadiani and Lahori) have become major transnational players on the global stage of Muslim politics and society, and other Indian-originated movements such as the Barelvis and Ahl-e Hadith—though not nearly as widespread as the former—are now visibly present in neighbouring countries such as Pakistan and Bangladesh.

The movement that we would like to focus our attention upon is the Tablighi Jama'at, which has been described by some scholars as perhaps the biggest lay missionary movement of any religion in the world today (Masud, 2000). Formed in India in the late 1920s in the wake of other transnational Indian movements such as the Khilafat movement,[7] the Tablighi Jama'at remains a fascinating subject for study. The origins of the Tablighi Jama'at go back to the Indian Deobandi movement that was started by Maulana Muhammad Qassim Nanotawi and Maulana Rashid Ahmad Gangohi at the Deoband seminary in 1867. Like the Deobandis, the Tablighis were conservative fundamentalists who were inspired by the reformists of the Wahhabi movement from Saudi Arabia. Unlike the Deobandis who were educationists, the Tablighis were missionary-activists who sought to transform Muslim society and bring Muslims back to the path of true Islam. The movement was formed in the late 1920s by Maulana Muhammad Ilyas Kandhalawi (d. 1944), whose family was closely linked to the Deobandi leadership and its sister school, the Mazahiru'l-Ulum in Saharanpur.

The Tablighi Jama'at was formed at a time of intense rivalry between Muslims and other faith communities in India. The movement sought to purify Indian Islam of non-Islamic influence, and tried to win back Muslims who had been converted by Christian and Hindu revivalist movements in the country. For this reason, it was often criticized by other religious groups who regarded it as a subversive force that intended to weaken the Indian nation from within. In order to deflect criticism from its activities, the Tablighi Jama'at rejected the use of violence and opted to remain apolitical. Unlike the Deobandis, the members of the movement avoided direct confrontation with Hindu or Christian groups. Barbara Metcalf (2002) notes that the Tablighi Jama'at could be compared to the Western Alcoholics Anonymous movement that started around the same time. Both organizations sought to reform their followers from within and sought to improve their moral qualities while regulating their public behaviour (Metcalf, 2002: 8). Rejecting politics and political activism of any kind, the movement emphasized its peaceful (*sukun*), passive and gradualist approach instead. Members of the movement were expected to take part in communal activities and join in their missionary efforts. They were expected to spend one night a week, one weekend a month, forty days a year and 120 days at least once in their lives with the members of the movement.[8]

The Tablighi Jama'at movement spread all over the world from Europe to Asia, and was held together by its close internal linkages and networks. In time, it penetrated into many guilds, business communities and elite networks as well. In most cases, however, its members were ordinary Muslim males from the lower levels of society. The movement has always been able to attract such followers due to its emphasis on the egalitarian ethos of Islam. By the end of the twentieth century, the regular congregation of Tablighis in Raiwind, Pakistan and Tungi, Bangladesh, could attract several million followers, making it the second biggest gathering of Muslims after the annual pilgrimage to Mecca.

Here, we are less interested in the complex debates about the Tabligh's interpretation of Islam, or whether its normative praxis accords with Muslim orthodoxy. Needless to say, as with many other Muslim minority groups, the Tabligh has also been accused of unorthodox beliefs and praxis by fellow Muslim detractors.

However, what is of interest to us is how, India looms large in the narratives and literature of the Tablighis in Southeast Asia as a master signifier in the movement's discourse, serving as one of the primary nodal points that sutures and seals the discursive economy of the movement, giving it its identity and coherence over time and space.

That India is special for the Tablighis is hardly surprising considering its Indian origins and the fact that much of what passes as normative Tablighi behaviour has been shaped by the cultural and historical features of India itself. But this has been a bone of contention for the Tablighis who have been constantly criticized and vilified as an Indian Muslim invention of Islam, and who are seen as deviating from the norms and standards set by Arabic Islam hailing from the Hijaz and North Africa. How and why the Tablighis persist in their Indocentric view of Islam and Muslim history is itself a fascinating subject of study for it provides us with one important instance of collective history discourse-production that is being done on an unofficial, non-state register.

Elsewhere we have looked at how the Tablighi Jama'at has held a certain appeal to Muslims in countries like Malaysia, Thailand and Indonesia on account of the normative praxis of Islam in the movement that are seen as familiar to those of the archipelago (Noor, 2009, 2010a, 2010b, 2010c). For thousands of ordinary Muslims in Southeast Asia—many of whom may happen to be third or fourth generation South Asian migrants and part of the wider Indian Muslim diaspora themselves—India is seen as one of the most important centres for the production of Muslim knowledge and scholarship, and this perception is one that is predictably enhanced even further in the writings of Tablighi authors.

This Indocentric world view is borne out in the vernacular writings of the Tablighis of Southeast Asia in particular, and comes in the form of the easy-to-read pamphlets and booklets that they use as instructional tools for themselves and their new members/ converts. As the Tablighis have grown accustomed to being attacked on a regular basis by other Muslims, who regard them as some sort of 'Indian aberration', it is understandable that much of their own writing is designed to explain and justify why they see India as being the cradle of Islam and humanity. To illustrate what we mean by this Indocentric world view, we now turn to one of the texts in question written by the Indonesian Tablighi teacher, Ustaz Yudha al-Hidayah.

Ustaz Yudha al-Hidayah's work *Ada Apa Ke India?* (*Why Go to India?*, 2008) is one of those Tablighi tracts that again serves a number of purposes: it re-states the centrality of India and its importance in the calculations of the Tablighis; defends the Indocentric world view of the Tablighis against the criticisms of the Salafis and other Muslims who see the Arabian Peninsula as the natural home of Islam; and, of course, provides ample justification for the Tablighis' frequent pilgrimages to India—which, presumably, comes in useful when the Tablighis confront their detractors as well as their wives whenever they need to perform the *khuruj* to the subcontinent. Al-Hidayah begins his tract by repeating many of the questions and criticisms that have been levelled against the Tablighis for their attachment and attraction to India. He rhetorically poses the queries thus:

> *Kok belajar agama ke India bukankah pusat agama ada di Arab kerana Rasululloh SAW berasal dari sana? Ada juga orang yang berkata: Orang orang Tabligh hajinya di India?*
> *Orang Tabligh dihubung dengan aliran sesat dan agama yang ada di India yakni dengan Ahmadiyyah dan dengan Hindu, dsb.* (Al-Hidayah, 2008: 10)
>
> Why, they ask, do we study religion in India when the heart of our religion lies in Arabia, as the Prophet came from there? And others may ask: Do the Tablighis perform their pilgrimage [*hajj*] in India then? The Tablighis have been wrongfully associated with the sects and religions of India, such as the Ahmadis and the Hindus.

The Ustaz is on hand trying to allay these concerns and he begins by noting that the centre of the Muslim world has, over time, shifted from one locality to another: *Pusat agama yang selalu berpindah sejak zaman sahabat* (The centre of our religion has shifted from one age to another, Al-Hidayah, 2008: 13). Citing a plethora of writings—including the predictions of Nostradamus (Al-Hidayah, 2008: 14)—he notes that the centre of the Muslim world has moved from Arabia to Baghdad, and later to Ottoman Turkey and Mughal India. Furthermore he argues that the notion that the best place to study Islam is the Arabian peninsula is a myth, and that there are many other places where one can be trained to be a savant in things Islamic:

> *Jadi sejak dahulu tidak harus belajar agama di Arab. Mitos belajar agama di Arab (Makkah dan Madinah) sebenarnya tak betul, kerana untuk menjadi Qori yang terbaik, lebih bagus belajar di Mesir. Seorang Ulama di Yaman yakni Sheikh Sulaiman telah katakan: Jika pingin belajar mahdzab/fiqih datanglah ke Hadramaut atau di Tarim, sedangkan kalau mau belajar Hadis yang terbaik ini ialah di Saharanpur, India.* (Al-Hidayah, 2008: 15)
>
> In fact, since the very beginning, there was never any real need for us to study religion in Arabia. The myth that one has to study in Mecca and Medina is false, for if one wanted to learn to become a true *Qori* the best place to do that has always been Egypt. And Sheikh Suleiman, a Sheikh from Yemen, once noted that if one wished to learn about the different schools of legal thought, then one ought to travel to Hadramaut or Tarim, and if one wanted to learn more of *Hadith*, then the best place for that would be Saharanpur, India.

In his effort to underscore the centrality of India for Muslims, al-Hidayah takes the reader on an excursion and presents him with a series of historical proofs that back-date the coming of Islam to India. He recounts a number of episodes in Semitic history that place India at the centre of the world—literally—and posits the view that India was the cradle of humankind and the place where Adam first stepped foot on the earth:

> *India adalah awal kehidupan manusia... Pahamlah kita bahawa Nabi Adam AS adalah manusia pertama di dunia sehingga beliau diturunkan di India maka India adalah negeri pertama kali ada kehidupan manusia.* (Al-Hidayah, 2008: 49)
>
> India was where humankind first began. . . . Know that the Prophet Adam was the first among humans, and it was in India that he was brought to earth for the first time. And so India is the first place on the earth where there was human life.

Al-Hidayah continues along the same vein and notes that it was from India that the Prophet Adam performed the pilgrimage (*hajj*) on foot a thousand times, making him the first Prophet who performed the *tashkil* (*khuruj*) across India (Al-Hidayah, 2008: 66-7). He notes that the great flood during the time of the Prophet Noah took place in India (Al-Hidayah, 2008: 53-5), and that the black stone (*hajar aswad*) of the *Ka'abah* was found in India and taken by the Prophet Abraham himself to Mecca (Al-Hidayah, 2008: 70, 73-4).

With these claims under his belt, al-Hidayah hopes to lay to rest the accusation that the Tablighis have turned their *qiblat* in the direction of India for he insists that long before Islam had arrived in Arabia and was brought to the Bedouin of the desert, Allah's prophets had already walked the earth of India and that many of the key events in Abrahamic history took place on this subcontinent. What better credentials and reputation could be bestowed upon India then, when one considers that it was the cradle of the Abrahamic tradition, home to the Prophets and the first place where God's message to humankind was delivered?

The rest of the tract goes on to praise the virtues of Islam in India, and to commend the pious labours of the subcontinent's Muslims. Al-Hidayah notes that before the Muslims of India began their missionary work, there was no communal form of missionary activity among Muslims anywhere, and that the Muslims of India have re-activated the spirit of missionary zeal that once animated the first Muslims who lived during the time of the Prophet himself:

> *Sebelum orang India sebarkan kerja dakwah kaum Muslimin tak ada dakwah ijtima'iat.* (Al-Hidayah, 2008: 16)
>
> Before the work of the Muslims in India there was no *dakwah ijtima'iat* anywhere in the Muslim world.
>
> *India telah merubah cara perjuangan umat Islam sebagaimana cara Rasululloh SAW menegakkan agama yakni dengan cara dakwah... India membangkitkan semangat dakwah ummat Islam yang telah mati, kerana ajakan ajakan para Muballigh yang hanya kepada ibadah sahaja.* (Al-Hidayah, 2008: 21)
>
> India has changed the way in which the Muslims strive, akin to the manner in which the Prophet himself first preached our religion, that is through the method of *dakwah*. India has reawakened the spirit of the Muslim *ummah* that was dead, for the calling of the *Muballighs* was focused solely on devotion.

This is why, al-Hidayah argues, the Tablighis continue to see India as the place where the spirit of Islam is at its strongest and where they need to go in order to recharge their convictions and determination to continue their work and never to relent. Furthermore, he argues that the life and culture of India is ideally suited (*cocok*) to the life of the Tablighis due to the modesty of its people and their culture right down to their cuisine—which seems less inclined to induce a Muslim to sloth and slumber:

> *India negeri yang cocok dengan perjuangan haq, disana makanannya sangat sederhana dengan satu model saja. Jika makan briani, makan briani saja. Jika salen hanya salen dengan satu jenis sayur. Jika dhal, hanya dhal dengan roti. Berbeda dengan negara Arab yang sudah datang kemewahan padanya.*
> (Al-Hidayah, 2008: 41)

> India is the place that is most ideally suited for our work, which is the struggle for truth (*haq*); for there the food is balanced and moderate in quantity. If it's *biriyani* (rice), then it's only *biriyani* that you will eat; if it's *salen*, then it's just *salen* with one type of vegetable; if it's *dal*, then it will only be *dal* with bread. That is so different from the Arab countries where wealth has overcome them.

Having thus defended the virtues of *biriyani* and *dal* against the rich and debilitating diet of the richer Arabs, al-Hidayah rounds off his argument by waxing eloquent on the virtues of the Indian Tablighis whom he had met on his many trips to India: their frugal and stoic character, their humility and their steadfast determination to carry on their *dakwah* work without complaint or concern for themselves, or the future.

Al-Hidayah's tract shares a number of familiar concerns that we have touched upon earlier, including the concern to defend the reputation of the Tablighis and their attachment to India. It is important to note that the most serious criticism of the Tabligh that he identifies is the claim that they have turned their back on Arabia and the Arab lands, and have made India the *qiblat* of their lives. This charge has always been taken very seriously by the Tablighis for obvious reasons, one of them being the desire to distance themselves from other Indocentric Muslim movements such as the Qadiani Ahmadis, for whom the pilgrimage to Qadian is a central tenet of their beliefs, as laid out in the *Tazkirah* of Mirza Ghulam Ahmad.[9]

The rhetorical devices that al-Hidayah employs—reconstructed myths of genesis, and accounts of the Prophets Adam, Abraham and Noah in India—are intended to backdate the coming of Islam to India, giving historical as well as moral justification for the elevation of the subcontinent's standing in the eyes of the Tablighis, who see it as the cradle of man and Islam alike. Though not openly confrontational towards the Arabs—notwithstanding some uncharitable remarks on the richness of Arab food and the worldliness of the rich Arabs—the tract, nonetheless, shores up its argument by taking pre-emptive measures against any claim to Arab superiority or authenticity. And like many Tablighi tracts, its primary purpose is as a tool of education and instruction for the many Tablighis who will, eventually, make their way to India to perform the *khuruj* there.

The tract *Baedeker* or *Rough Guide to India* offers little in terms of knowledge and information about India and its diverse peoples and cultures. Again, it has to be remembered that such tracts serve the purpose of compelling and channelling the actions of the Tablighis within the regulated confines of their communal life, which happens to be an exclusively homo-social Muslim space shared with other brother Tablighis. It is not surprising, therefore, to note that there is no mention at all of the Hindus of India, or the simple fact that India has *always* been a Hindu-majority country. But, then again it should be added that the Tablighis who travel to India do so not in the spirit of religious ecumenicalism. They are, instead visiting the land where Adam first set foot upon the earth, and where Abraham and Noah passed by as well.

From Java To India: The Foregrounding of India in the Popular Religious Discourse of the Javanese/Indonesian Tablighi Jama'at

By recounting the story of India as seen via the lens of the Tablighi Jama'at above, we have shown that history does not always have to be seen or taken entirely as an academic exercise or academic production. The Tablighis' account of the special history of India as the home of their faith may beg a series of other related questions—

those pertaining to the authenticity of their sources or the correctness of their claims—but from the perspective of discourse analysis, what matters more is what this discourse tries to do, and the discursive strategies and effects they are meant to have upon those who inhabit that discursively-constructed universe.

It is clear that for the Tablighis of Indonesia and the rest of Southeast Asia, India has a history, one that is uniquely and closely tied to their movement as well. They seem less bothered by the fact that the post-colonial histories of Indonesia and Malaysia have severed the links to India and South Asia as they foreground the present reality of these modern nation states while denying connections with/to the past. In the world of the Tablighis of Indonesia at least, India has always been close, and never more than a stone's throw away from Java. Furthermore, as we have seen in the narrative recounted earlier, not only is India close to Southeast Asia, it also happens to be home—home to the Tablighis, home to the Southeast Asians and home to Islam.

To date, however, narrative accounts of such trans-oceanic contact and communication have received very little attention from official historians who seem to neglect the worth of such alternative (sometimes liminal, sometimes subaltern) historical narratives. Why is this? As we have suggested at the beginning of this paper, the tendency to subsume all local histories under the broad banner of the official history of the nation is one that is politically and ideologically motivated, but one that also carries a cost, as in the manner in which other alternative narrative accounts of history have been sidelined, bypassed or silenced altogether.

However, if we were to attempt a more comprehensive (though not necessarily totalized and exhaustive) account of history as storytelling, we ought to take on board the multiple storylines that together make up the complex picture of trans-oceanic contact and exchange between these two land masses that span the Indian Ocean. The history of the Indian Ocean communities is a complex one, as it has created a complex and complicated assembly of peoples and cultures that resist totalization and/or neat compartmentalization. Although official histories need to record what is relevant and important as far as the requirements of the nation state is concerned, we also need to remember that official histories are themselves partial histories that tell only a part of the story.

And if the official histories of India, Indonesia, Malaysia, etc., tell only the story of the nation, by the nation and to the nation today, we should remember that outside these official narratives of knowledge and power there stand other narratives (far less official but certainly relevant and resonant for others) that tell of different accounts of the past and present. The official histories of the nation states that line the shores of the Indian Ocean today, are limited, particular and, in many respects, exclusive histories; but parallel to them are narrative traditions that tell the story of never-ending contact and sustained collective identity-production. The Tablighi Jama'at's account of India, its history and its historical relevance to the Tablighis of Southeast Asia is one such example of the story of history-writing and history-telling being told. And though the official histories of countries like India and Indonesia may see these states as entities apart, the two are brought together in the sweeping, inclusive narrative of the Tabligh as a common homeland to a community of the faithful and pious.

NOTES

1. Joseph J. Ellis, *Founding Brothers*, pp. 4-5.
2. The French Orientalist scholar Sylvain Levi (b. 1863-d. 1935) was famed for his study of Sanskrit texts and ancient Indian history. His earliest works were on Indian Classical literature and drama, and he later became the vice-president of the Société Asiatique that was based in Paris, France.
3. Debates still rage on till today about the exact routes that were used by Indian traders (and later brahmana missionaries) as they made their way to Southeast Asia. Scholars and historians have attempted to track down the routes that were used by looking at the names of places and settlements as they were recorded in ancient texts, but most of these findings have proven to be inconclusive. As Çoedes (1968) notes:

   the information we can draw from the Indian place names transplanted to Farther India is not very conclusive, for these names often appear for the first time in writings of a later date, and the choice of names like Champa, Dvaravati, Ayodhya and other famous cities of Puranic legend does not necessarily prove the Gangetic origin of those who transplanted them to foreign lands. Place names that are less well known offer better evidence. One can, for example, establish a relationship between Taruma, which the earliest Javanese inscriptions place on the western part of that island, and a locality of the same name located near Cape Comorin (now Kanyakumari). Likewise the use of the name Ussa (Odra, i.e. Orissa) for Pegu and of Shikshetra (i.e. Puri) as an only name for Prome in Burma certainly indicates a relationship between these states and Orissa. The name *Kalinga* resembles that of Kling used by the Malays and the Cambodians to designate Indians. The appellation *Talaing*, applied to the Mons by the Burmese, seems to indicate that at a certain epoch Telengana, of the Madras region, was in particularly active relations with the Mon country. Following the same line of thinking we can recall the presence of ethnic names originating in the Dravidian line among the Karo Bataks of Sumatra: Chola, Pandhya, Pallava, Malayalam. (p. 30)

While it is still impossible to prove conclusively from which part of India that Indian influence was first brought to Southeast Asia, it is clear that by the third and fourth centuries there was a substantial volume of traffic between the Eastern coastal states of India and the Indon-Malay archipelago as well as mainland Southeast Asia.

4. Çoedes (1968), drawing on material found in various archaeological studies, argues that the traces of Indian influence in Southeast Asia can be found even before the rise of the Aryan states and kingdoms in India. But these traces of Indian influence cannot be described as transcultural exchange in any real sense of the word: they rather point to parallel developments in both regions that were happening at the same time. It is still difficult, if not impossible, to pinpoint the exact date when the Indianization process began. One of the earliest documents of any scholarly merit is the ancient Pali text, the *Niddesa*, which dates to the first centuries of the Common Era. According to Çoedes (1968: 16), the *Niddesa* contains several Sanskrit references to locations that Sylvain Levi has identified as belonging to Southeast Asia. Çoedes' own prudent and cautious estimation is that the 'Indian colonization (of Southeast Asia) was intense in the second and third centuries CE and came to fruition in the fourth and fifth centuries.' (p. 19)
5. The Gupta dynasty of India (CE 320-550) emerged after nearly a century of internal chaos and strife in India following the assassination of the last of the Mauryan kings in 184 BCE. By the fifth century, Gupta

influence had extended to the Bengal region, and the Bay of Bengal became, by extension, the springboard from which Gupta power—and Indian cultural influence—would spread further abroad.

6. Çoedes (1968: 18) notes that 'none of these findings can be dated before the time of Ptolemy (second century CE). Ptolemy's geographical nomenclature for trans-Gangetic India was full of place names with Indian-Sanskrit correspondences.'
7. The Khilafat movement began as a reaction among Muslims worldwide to the perceived threat that the Ottoman Caliphate was about to be dismantled in the wake of the First World War. Regardless of the wishes and ambitions of the Turkish nationalists, the Young Turks' aim of dismantling the Caliphate was a traumatic event for Muslims worldwide who regarded the Ottoman Porte as the centre of Muslim political power worldwide. Since the sixteenth century the Ottoman Empire had recognized Muslim kingdoms all over the world and had sent economic and military aid to those in distress from North Africa to Southeast Asia. The prospect of losing this centre of power was seen as a major blow to Indian Muslims in particular. Consequently Indian Muslim activist leaders like Maulana Mohammad Ali Jouhar began to call on India's Muslims to rise up against the British for the latter's role in the slow destruction of the Caliphate. Describing the British as infidel enemies of Islam who wished to destroy the last bastion of Muslim political power, Maulana Mohammad urged Muslims to come together to fight against British colonial rule and to support the Ottoman Sultan. Maulana Mohammad was supported by other Indian Muslim leaders like Maulana Shaukat Ali, Maulana Ahmed Ansari, Hazrat Mohani, Hakim Ajmal Khan and Maulana Abul Kalam Azad in setting up the All-India Khilafat Committee in Lucknow, Uttar Pradesh, in 1919. In 1920, the All-India Khilafat Committee published its *Khilafat Manifesto* which called on Indian Muslims to rally to the defence of the Ottoman Caliphate and placed the responsibility for the survival of the Caliphate on the shoulders of the British government. Cognisant of the power and influence of the Khilafat Committee, the Indian nationalist leaders of the Indian National Congress sought to work with them in a demonstration of pan-Indian solidarity with their fellow Indian Muslims. In 1920, the Congress formally aligned itself with the Khilafat movement and the Khilafat movement's cause was endorsed by Congress leaders like Mahatma Gandhi. Gandhi urged the Muslims of India to work with the Congress in the combined

struggle to free India from colonial rule and to protect the Caliphate at the same time. The Congress also endorsed and supported the Khilafat movement's campaign to improve the standard of education for Indian Muslims, which culminated in a number of educational initiatives such as the setting up of the Jamia Millia Islamia University in Delhi in 1920. By this time, Indian Muslim leaders like Maulana Abul Kalam Azad and Hakim Ajmal Khan were working closely with Gandhi and the Congress, and also urging the Muslims of India to support the Congress in its nationalist struggle. Working through the formal and informal networks of communication that connected the domains of the British empire, delegations were sent by the Indian Khilafat Committee across India, and to Burma, Malaya, Singapore and beyond.

8. Metcalf (2002: 9). Like the Deobandis, the Tablighis also had an ambiguous relationship with Sufism. They rejected many of the traditional practices and beliefs of the Indian Sufi *tariqas* on the grounds that they were contaminated by alien Hindu practices and ideas, but also sought to use Sufi methods and rituals when it suited them. Metcalf (2002) notes that 'among the Tablighis the holiness associated with the Sufi *Pir* was in many ways defused into the charismatic body of the *jama'at* so that the missionary group itself became a channel for divine intervention.' (p. 11) Like the Deobandis, the Tablighi Jama'at attempted to reproduce the strong *Pir-Murid* bonds in the Sufi *tariqas* within their own organizational structure, making it a very strong and intimately-linked organizational network that would be able to straddle enormous geographical distances. The Tablighis also adapted another feature of the Indian Sufi *tariqas*: the (sometimes extreme) veneration of the Prophet Muhammad and his life history. In Tablighi Jama'at circles, *Hadith* and *Surah* literature concerning the Prophet was and is of great importance.
9. The Tablighis' loathing for the Ahmadis is understandable by virtue of the similarities rather than the differences they share. With the exception of the Ahmadis' stand on the revered status of Ghulam Mirza Ahmad as a Prophet, the Ahmadis and Tablighis obviously share the same vocabulary, symbols, rites and rituals of Islam. The fact that the Tablighis and Ahmadis both view India as a special place complicates matters for the former, and renders them vulnerable to the charge that they are as Indo-centric as the latter, though for different reasons.

REFERENCES

Al-Hidayah, Ustaz Yudha, 2008, *Ada Apa Ke India? Negeri Yang Enjoy*, ed. Ustaz Abu Kisty, Addai Press.

Bernet Kempers, August Johan, 1933, *The Bronzes of Nalanda and Hindu-Javanese Art*, Leiden: Brill.

Çoedes, George, 1962, *The Making of Southeast Asia*, California: University of California Press.

———, 1968, *The Indianised States of Southeast Asia*, ed. Walter F. Vella and tr. Susan Brown Cowing, Honolulu: University of Hawai'i Press.

———, 1992, *Sriwijaya History, Religion & Language of an Early Malay Polity*, Kuala Lumpur: Malaysian Branch of the Royal Asiatic Society.

Coomaraswamy, Ananda, 1927, *History of Indian and Indonesian Art*, Leipzig: Karl W. Hiesemann.

Dupont, Pierre, 1954, *Les Buddhas dit d'Ararmavati en Asie du Sud-est*, Proceedings from the XXIII International Congress of Orientalists, Cambridge: Cambridge University Press.

Ellis, Joseph J., 2002, *Founding Brothers: The Revolutionary Generation*, New York: Vintage Books.

Ghosh, Devaprasad, 1935, 'Migration of Indian Decorative Motifs', *Journal of Greater Indian Studies*, London, 2: 32-47.

Hornell, James, 1920, 'The Origins and Ethnological Significance of Indian Boat Designs', *Memoirs of the Asiatic Society of Bengal*, Calcutta, 8.

Hussainmiya, B.A., 2001, 'The Malays in Sri Langka', *Borneo Bulletin*, 4 August: 1-2.

Krom, Nicholaas J., 1931, 'Antiquities of Palembang', *Journal of Greater Indian Studies*, 3: 24-37.

Levi, Sylvain, 1929, 'Les Marchands de Mer et leur role dans le Bouddhisme Primitif', *Bulletin de l'Association Francaise des Amis de l"Orient*, Paris, October: 19-39.

———, 1938, *L'inde Civilisatrice: Apercu Historique*, Paris: Librairie d'Amérique et d'Orient.

Masud, Muhammad Khalid (ed.), 2000, *Travellers in Faith: Studies of the Tablighi Jama'at as a Transnational Islamic Movement for Faith Renewal*, Leiden: Brill.

Metcalf, Barbara D., 2002, *Traditionalist Islamic Activism: Deoband, Tablighis and Talibs*, ISIM Papers IV, Leiden: International Institute for the Study of Islam in the Modern World (ISIM).

Nilakanta Sastri, Kallidaikurichi Aiyah, 1938, 'The Beginnings of Intercourse Between India and China', *Indian Historical Quarterly*, Delhi, 14: 380-9.

Noor, Farish A., 2000, 'From Majapahit to Putrajaya: The Kris as a Symptom of Civilisational Development and Decline', *Journal of Southeast Asia Research*, School of Oriental and African Studies, London, November, 8, 3: 239-80.

———, 2009, 'The Tablighi Jama'at as a Vehicle for (Re)Discovery: Conversion Narratives and the Appropriation of India in the Southeast Asian Tablighi Jama'at Movement', in Michael Feener and Terenjit Sevea (eds.), *Islamic Connections: Studies of Muslim South and Southeast Asia*, Singapore: Institute for Southeast Asian Studies (ISEAS) Press: 195-219.

———, 2010a, 'On The Permanent Haj: The Tablighi Jama'at in Southeast Asia', *Southeast Asia Research*, School of Oriental and African Studies, London, 18: 4.

———, 2010b, 'At Home Across the Ocean: The Role of the Indian Muslim Diaspora in the Spread of Islamist Networks across South and Southeast Asia', *Peace and Security Review*, Quarterly Academic Journal of the Bangladesh Institute of Peace and Security Studies, June: 87-119.

———, 2010c, *The Arrival and Spread of the Tablighi Jama'at in West Papua (Irian Jaya), Indonesia Today*, Rajaratnam School of International Studies (RSIS) Working Papers Series no. 191, Nanyang Technical University, Singapore, February.

Reetz, Dietrich, 2006, *Islam in the Public Sphere: Religious Groups in India, 1900-1947*, Delhi-Oxford: Oxford University Press.

Wang Gungwu, 1958, The Nanhai Trade: A Study of Early Chinese Trade in Southeast Asia, *Journal of the Malayan Branch of the Royal Asiatic Society*, 31, 2: 1-135.

CHAPTER 9

Trade, Religion and Politics: Portuguese Activities in the Bay of Bengal, 1632-1840

PIUS MALEKANDATHIL

Portuguese settlers who expanded their trading centres along the water space of the Bay of Bengal in the lure of profitable ventures used their unique position to successfully negotiate with the Portuguese power centre on the west coast of India as also with local authorities but, more significantly, with Christian missionaries sent on evangelical assignments. Unlike the crown-sponsored official expansion that the Portuguese made along the west coast of India, the expansion by Portuguese private traders along the Bay of Bengal was nebulous and amorphous, making each Portuguese settlement along the east coast of India evolve as distinctively different from one another, despite their being called the 'shadow empire' (Winius, 1983; Campos, 1998; Malekandathil, 2010). The long chain of mercantile settlements along the Bay of Bengal often set-up by private Portuguese traders, adventurers and renegades, and less integrated with the Portuguese power centre in Goa, created and stamped an altogether different perception and image of Portuguese activities in the East.

The northern zones of the Bay of Bengal, stretching from coastal Orissa and Bengal, and going up to Pegu and the Arakan littoral, witnessed the emergence of a network of Portuguese settlements of varying size and economic importance with three major focal points. On the one hand, there evolved a circuit with Hugli as the core centre (Hartmann, 1994: 258) and Balasore,[1] Pipli,[2] Angelim,[3] Tamboly,[4] Banja,[5] Jampardo,[6] Cajosy,[7] Jessore,[8] Portupara,[9] Chinchura,[10] Barnagor,[11] Chandernagore,[12] Calcutta[13] and Bottocana[14] as feeder satellite mercantile settlements. On the other hand, there emerged another circuit with Dacca[15] as the core area and a web of feeder secondary mercantile settlements of the Portuguese evolving in Norikul,[16] Chandipur,[17] Seripur,[18] Tasgão,[19] Cambalim,[20] Balva,[21] Sypur,[22] Ossompur,[23] Cassimbazar,[24] Serampur,[25] and Ossunabar.[26] The third circuit revolved around Chittagong,[27] (which was earlier under the Arakans) as the core area, and Concão,[28] Jamalcão,[29] Dianga,[30] Angaracale,[31] and Rangamati,[32] operating as satellite supporting mercantile units. The increasing demand in Lisbon and in Brazil for the saltpetre and textiles of Bengal created a circuit connecting Bahia and Lisbon with the ports of Bengal in the eighteenth century, pumping, in return, Bahian tobacco into the markets of Bengal, which was further taken to inland consumption centres. The wealth deriving from trade sustained many of the religious activities of the Augustinians and the Jesuits in Bengal. In turn, the various religious orders appropriated a great amount of authority in the region, with the Augustinian superior wielding a political position and the powers of a magistrate for the local inhabitants of Bandel, and challenging the jurisdiction of even the Jesuit bishop of Mylapore and, at times, the authorities in Goa.

The Indo-Portuguese descendants of Bengal provided a supportive social base for the English in the initial days of their establishment, allowing the latter to draw wives, fighting soldiers and commercial intermediaries from them, and resulting in a radical ethnic mutation that suited the English colonial agenda. The ethnic mutation of Luso-Indians into Anglo-Indians became rampant with the establishment of the diocese of Calcutta in 1832, which increasingly tried to dissociate the Portuguese descendants from the jurisdiction of the diocese of Mylapore that was controlled by the Portuguese *Padroado*. This paper looks into the changing meanings of Portuguese activities in the northern zones of the Bay of Bengal where due to their distance from the Portuguese power centre of Goa, they managed to define their own course of commercial, religious and political life that suited the various exigencies of the times.

Historical Setting

In the initial years of the seventeenth century, the Portuguese settlements along the northern zones of the Bay of Bengal represented a variety of activities ranging from thriving trade to assertions of political ambitions, from modest and legitimate pursuits of profit to an avaricious desire for wealth-accumulation, coupled with elements of piracy and criminality. On the one hand, there was a chain of Portuguese mercantile settlements in Mughal Bengal with Hugli established by Pedro Tavares in 1580 (Wicki, 1970: 649),[33] on the basis of a *farman* issued by Akbar evolving as the core centre of their commercial activities in western Bengal (Collis, 1995: 88; Campos, 1998: 21, 51, 54-6). Akbar's *farman* gave a great degree of legitimacy to the settlement of Hugli and others in its vicinity, as they had initially been established by private traders, smugglers and adventurers (Wicki, 1960: 697).[34] In course of time Hugli (later Bandel) pushed Satgaon, which was located on the banks of the silting river Saraswati, to the background (Abu-l Fazal, 2006: 128, 133). The Portuguese in Hugli, whose number increased to 7,000 in 1632 (Rego, 1955, vol. XI: 184), used to pay an amount of 100,000 *tangas* or rupees as customs duty to the Mughals (Campos, 1998: 56).

With the conversion of Dacca into the capital of Bengal in place of Rajamahal and Gaur (Collis, 1995: 88; Thekkedath, 1988: 452), many Portuguese began to flock to this city and its vicinity, augmenting the size and number of Lusitanians engaged in trade in eastern Bengal. Meanwhile, there appeared a large multitude of Portuguese adventurers and freebooters linked with the king of Arakan, who combined in themselves trade and military activities with Chittagong as their focal point (Abu-l Fazal, 2006: 137).[35]

Chittagong, located outside Mughal control, was the greatest port (*porto grande*) of the region, to which a large number of Portuguese private traders, renegades, freebooters and adventurers from the Lusitanian pockets of Cochin, Goa and Coromandel moved from 1530s onwards. Banking upon the Mughal leniency towards the Portuguese, particularly during the time of liberal rulers like Akbar and Jahangir, and against the background of the Mughal-Jesuit dialogues happening at Agra, Fatehpur Sikri and Lahore (Malekandathil, 2007), many Portuguese adventurers started appropriating enclaves and territories lying on the frontier regions of the Mughals and the Arakanese for themselves (Collis, 1995: 88). One of the most evident cases was the island of Sandwip. It was a major source for salt-trade in Bengal (Campos, 1998: 67), and was captured and attached as a tributary island to the Portuguese settlement of Chittagong by Domingo Carvalho and Manoel de Mattos in 1602 and, later, by Sebastião Gonsalves Tibau from 1607 till 1616 (Collis, 1995: 88-9; Campos, 1998: 67, 156). Similarly, Filippe de Brito e Nicote, obtained from the king of Arakan, Xilimixa (Salim Shah?), the port of Siriam in Pegu in return for the military help rendered to the latter and, eventually, he established a kingdom in Pegu (Danvers, 1991: 20-2; Collis, 1995: 88; Campos, 1998: 70, 78).

The developments between 1602 and 1616 give the impression that Portuguese adventurers in the north-eastern zones of the Bay of Bengal were moving towards a political project and territorial acquisitions in the area, making Chittagong and Pegu their power bases (Danvers, 1991: 20-21; Collis, 1995: 87-8; Campos, 1998: 71). Besides these three strands of political and commercial endeavours, there was a sizeable segment of Portuguese adventurers involved in piracy and criminality in the eastern pockets of the Bay of Bengal, either independently or in the company of Arakanese pirates, who, in turn, used to sell their stolen cargo through the legitimate markets of western Bengal and Orissa, including Tamluk, Hijli and Pipli. François Bernier says that this region was the

> place of retreat for fugitives from Goa, Ceylon, Cochin, Malacca and other settlements in the Indies, held formerly by the Portuguese; and no persons were better received than those who had deserted their monasteries, married two or three wives, or committed other great crimes. These people were Christians only in name; the lives led by them were most detestable, massacring or poisoning one another without compunction or remorse and sometimes assassinating even their priests, who . . . were too often no better than their murderers. (Bernier, 1989: 174-5)

Taming and disciplining the Portuguese traders and adventurers scattered over the northern zones of the Bay of Bengal became the major task of the various religious orders that established houses and colleges in many of the Portuguese enclaves of this region. Though the Augustinians, the Jesuits, Franciscans and Dominicans established various houses in different parts, it was the Augustinians, who actually enjoyed a privileged position in Bengal and its vicinity. By this time they had been sent as major negotiators to the frontier zones of the Portuguese sea-borne empire, including Safavid Persia and Ottoman Turkey. It was Dom Alexis de Menezes, the Augustinian Archbishop of Goa and later the viceroy of *Estado da India* who began to send Augustinian friars to Safavid Persia, Ottoman Turkey and Bengal (Malekandathil, 2003: 517-19; Rego, 1955: 202-22; Hartmann, 1994: 198). As Bengal at that point of time was under the ecclesiastical jurisdiction of the diocese of Cochin, the Jesuits, Franciscans and the Dominicans sent to Bengal were dispatched from Cochin, while the Augustinians were sent to Bengal from Goa and were to report directly to the Augustinian provincial there (Rego, 1955: 185; Thekkedath, 1988: 458-78; Malekandathil, 2001: 91-6)[36] and not to Cochin.

The Augustinians set-up several churches all over Bengal and in course of time, due to the vast distance to Goa, they elected a provincial commissario to look after the ecclesiastical matters of Bengal. For all practical purposes, he was the prelate major of the region, wielding a great amount of power (Rego, 1955: 186). The direct control of Bengal by the Augustinians of Goa bypassing the diocesan administrative structures of Cochin and later of Mylapore (since 1606) was a part of the strategy to link the active economy and wealthy terrains of Bengal that were lying on the peripheries of the empire with the core power centre at Goa through missionary personnel. Even when many of the Jesuits, Franciscans and Dominicans left quickly for Cochin from many of their bases in Bengal due to the conflicts that broke out between the Portuguese and the Arakanese over the issues of the territorial acquisitions that the Lusitanian adventurers had made in Arakan's areas of interest between 1602 and 1615, the Augustinians continued to work among the Portuguese traders (Rego, 1995: 184) renegades and adventurers converting themselves into the connecting link between the peripheral geographies of Bengal and the power centre of Goa.

Incorporation of the Province of Bengal into Wider World of Trade

The Portuguese traders of Bengal played a decisive role in the commodity movements through both the water-channels and land-routes. While one strand of trade moved to the heartland of Delhi administration through the Grand Trunk Road, which was in operation since the time of Sher Shah, another moved through the Ganga. It should be mentioned here, specially, that the expansion of Portuguese commerce in Bengal, particularly in eastern Bengal, went hand-in-hand with the intensified clearance of forests, the settling down of people and the extension of wet rice cultivation under the leadership of Sufi *pirs* in the sixteenth and seventeenth centuries. Sylhet (located near Dacca), whose origin and growth is associated with the Sufi *pir* Shah Jalauddin (Khan, 2004: 103-5) had a settlement of a considerable number of Portuguese *casados* (Hambye, 1997: 470), which evidently shows the networking that had evolved by this time between the emerging cultivational group of Muslim pioneers and the trading segment of the Portuguese.

Dacca, located closer to most of the newly-reclaimed rice-cultivating pockets of eastern Bengal and developed by Muslim holy men, had a great concentration of Portuguese traders and many converted Indian Christians, which the Augustinian document of 1720 estimates as running into several thousands (Rego, 1958: 25-6). The commodities, particularly rice, from the expanding paddy cultivating zones of Bengal, moved to the local markets established by Muslim pioneers (Eaton, 1995: 214-15) from where they were carried to the rice-deficient zones of the Indian Ocean by Portuguese merchants. By the end of the sixteenth century, rice formed a sizeable cargo that was frequently taken from Bengal to Cochin.[37]

In 1590, about 900 *candis* of rice was brought from Bengal to Cochin by the Portuguese *casados* (Biblioteca Nacional de Lisboa {BNL}, 1980: fol. 25). A lot of rice from Bengal and Pegu reached Cochin as return cargo between 1592 and 1597, when the annual average of rice import in Cochin was 386,830 kg (Taboado: fol. 7-15; Malekandathil, 2010: 176). Thomas Best also refers to rice being taken from Bengal to Pegu by a Dutch vessel in 1613 (Foster, 1995: 153-4). There was another circuit in which rice from Bengal was taken by the Portuguese *casados* to Maldives where it was exchanged for cowries and this was, in turn, taken back to Bengal, Pegu and Tennaserim where cowries were used as a monetary medium (Correa, 1921: 129-30; Sanceau, 1978: 482; Ptak, 1987:

123-8; Bernier, 1989: 437). Though Bengal supplied a large bulk of textiles, silk, saltpetre moving from Patna through the Ganga, long pepper, opium and lac, by middle of the seventeenth century sugar became a major commodity that was taken frequently to Golkonda, the Karnatic terrains, Arabia and the Persian Gulf regions (Bernier, 1989: 437-46).

There was a feeble strand of commerce going to China through the land-route; however, a major segment of Portuguese trade from Bengal moved to China via the Portuguese enclave of Macao. The Indo-Portuguese families appropriated a major share of trade between Bengal and Macao in the eighteenth century (Cunha, 2006: 390). Very often their trading circuits merged with the circuits between Spanish America and Spanish Philippines, facilitating their emergence as sizeable carriers of bullion to Bengal. By 1805-6, the value of Bengal's exports to China was *sicca* rupees 70,79,641, out of which about 50 per cent was opium (Pinto, 2003: 14). Saltpetre, silk, cotton textiles and long-pepper were the major items that were carried from the Bengal ports to Goa and then to Lisbon and Brazil. Bengal was the largest supplier of saltpetre to the Portuguese. Later, when saltpetre was discovered in the high mountains of Bahia in Brazil in 1694, the viceroy of Goa was asked to send three or four saltpetre workers from Bengal to Brazil for the purpose of making gunpowder from it. The crown sent repeated letters to the viceroy of Goa in 1700 and 1702 asking for saltpetre workers from Bengal who were not so 'old, feeble and sick' to endure the long voyage to Brazil (Anthony, 2004: 66-7).

Textiles formed another major commodity taken from Bengal to Lisbon and many of the Portuguese enclaves were located in the heartland of textile manufacturing like Dacca and Sripur. Dacca produced a variety of muslins like *abrawns, allaballies, budduncoss, dories, jamdanies, mulmuls, nyansooks, sarbatis, seerbund, sublimes, tanjibs, terridams, hummums, sarkalis, cossaes, seerhandconnas* and handkerchiefs, while Sripur produced *chowtahs, totally, soosess* and so on (Mitra, 1978: 151-3). When the Portuguese tried to introduce textile weaving in Para in Brazil, attempts were made to collect skilled weavers from Bengal.

As early as in 1588 the crown had asked the Portuguese viceroy of

Goa to send spinners and weavers, if possible couples up to twelve in number, for teaching the Brazilians the art of cloth-manufacturing. In 1750, the crown made attempts to set-up a colony of weavers from Bengal and Coromandel in Bahia in Brazil. The crown asked the viceroy to send married couples of weavers and dyers of cotton and muslin fabrics from Coromandel and Bengal to Bahia for the purpose of establishing a weavers' settlement in the Brazilian state of Para. Weavers from Bengal were specially preferred as they produced good quality calicoes, *chitos*, *lenços* and *cassas*. They were also supposed to take looms, spinning wheels, seed-removers and other accessories along with them. The weavers and dyers were offered travel expenses, cash for the purchase of tools, landed estates in Para in Brazil, religious freedom, concession in taxes and duties, etc. Moreover, the herbs and roots that were used for dyeing in the textile producing regions of the Bay of Bengal were also to be sent to Brazil, and efforts made to see whether these species were available in Maranhão. Fr. Francisco de Assumpção, the superior of the Augustinians in Bandel who had the power of a magistrate was given the task of identifying the most skilled weavers from Bengal and sending them to Para, while the archbishop of Mylapore was asked to identify and send the right labour force from Coromandel (Anthony, 2004: 39, 63-4).

In the eighteenth century, the ports of Bengal formed a major outlet for trade in opium, which the Indo-Portuguese merchants carried to Macao. Seeing the profit that the opium trade brought to Indian ports, the Portuguese authorities encouraged the cultivation of poppy in Brazil. For this purpose, they collected a detailed account of the cultivation of poppy and the making of opium from Bengal and sent to Brazil (Anthony, 2004: 39, 107). It was through the Jesuit priest, Luis de Gões, who was the brother of Pero de Gões, donor of the captaincy of Paraiba do Sul in Brazil, that tobacco was first introduced in India (Anthony, 2004: 228). In the mid-seventeenth century François Bernier refers to the dealers of tobacco in Bengal (Bernier, 1989: 441). By 1675, Bahian tobacco was introduced into India in the form of snuff made in Lisbon and, eventually tobacco was used in India for chewing, smoking and sniffing. The Indo-Portuguese traders used to take tobacco to Bengal and, by 1750, the

Portuguese traders had drafted a plan to launch a trading company in Bengal to obtain saltpetre and textiles from Bengal with proceeds from tobacco. Though the Portuguese officials did not show much interest in it, some native merchants joined together to form the Bengal Trading Company for the same purpose (Anthony, 2004: 249-50, 272 n. 66). Between 1675 and 1775, the use of tobacco became widespread in many places in India including Bengal, which in turn necessitated the networking of the ports of Bengal with Goa, Bahia and Lisbon. In later centuries, cultivation of tobacco spread to Bengal and its neighbouring regions.

By the 1730s the centre of commercial activities shifted from the Hugli-Bandel region to Calcutta, which had a sizeable Portuguese settlement since 1690. The subsequent shifting of the British headquarters to Calcutta also opened up a lot of commercial opportunities to the Indo-Portuguese merchants of Bengal. By the 1790s Manoel de Souza, one of the leading brothers of an Indo-Portuguese family, had his commercial base in Bengal while his other brother, Antonio de Souza, conducted business in Madras and the third, Miguel de Lima e Souza operated in Bombay, thereby playing a vital role in the trade emanating from the three presidency towns (Pinto, 2003: 72-3). Their nephews, Jose Barreto Senior, Jose Barreto Junior and Antonio Lourenço Barreto, were leading Indo-Portuguese merchants of Calcutta in the 1790s. The business house of the Barretos formed one of the fifteen agency houses of Calcutta that besides controlling the country trade of Bengal, also extended financial support to the production of silk, indigo, sugar and opium, and supplied indigo to the English. They had their own banks, marine insurance companies, and acted as the main suppliers of opium to Macao (Pinto, 2003: 73-6). João de Faria and his son, Rogerio de Faria, also emerged as leading traders of Bengal from the Indo-Portuguese community. Their business house in Calcutta known as Bruce, Faria and Co. thrived on the opium trade with China from 1796 and, later, the Farias extended their trading activities to Surat, Bombay, Portugal, Brazil and Mozambique (de Souza, 1991: 6-8).

The Indo-Portuguese traders of Bengal had, by this time developed a parallel strand of trade connecting Bengal with Macao on the one side, and with Mozambique and Bahia on the other. Because of the Portuguese policy of liberalization of trade, Brazilian ships were permitted to enter Portuguese and non-Portuguese ports, including Mecca, Surat, Goa, Bengal and China (Philomena Sequeira Antony, 2004: 171). In 1795, two vessels made a triangular commercial trip involving Bengal-Bahia and Lisbon, carrying 1,511 volumes of textiles and 1,417 volumes of textiles respectively. In 1796 another ship from Bengal carried 1,433 volumes of textiles and sold 315 volumes in Bahia. The rest was taken to Lisbon (Philomena Sequeira Antony, 2004: 188-9). In 1802 São Francisco Xavier, a Lisbon-based ship, was given the licence to conduct trade with Madeira, Rio de Janeiro and Bengal, while in 1803, three vessels were given licences to conduct trade between Rio de Janeiro and Bengal. The Brazilian port of Rio de Janeiro and the Indian port of Bengal were the chief destinations for the ships despatched from Lisbon between 1809 and 1815 (Pinto, 2003: 216-17). The Luso-Brazilian traders frequenting Calcutta and Madras from 1798 to 1821 were the major suppliers of bullion to Bengal and the Coromandel (Pinto, 2000; Lapa, 1989: 394-6; Russell-Wood, 2001: 191-211).

Bengal textiles formed a major cargo taken to Lisbon. About twelve boxes of silk were taken from Bengal to Lisbon in 1787 and 875 bales in 1788. In 1802, the size of Bengal's textile trade with Lisbon amounted to 1,496 bales and twenty-nine packets, which rose to 1,788 bales and fifty packets in 1811. In 1816, four ships from Bengal carried 9,545 bales and 260 packets of cloth (Pinto, 2003: 142). It is interesting to note that some Lisbon ships moved only to Bengal and between 1803 and 1826, about twelve ships were sent from Lisbon to Bengal alone for trade (Pinto, 2003: 92). For the return voyage, they used to take from Bengal a variety of cargo including indigo, saltpetre, silk and textiles, among which [textiles?] prominent were the *tincal, hummums, casas, bastas, mulmuls, jarras, abachis, bolsaquis, coupis, caridaris, dongris* and the *dimitrys* of Dacca and Balassore, the *dusiquesais, fotas, lencos, sutrumals, cramaci, pacaquis de mulmul, bandana, chapa, susins, surhatcanas, sanas, nansuis, sursaquers, jarindams, janjeb de dacca, japonis, hamoramatis, coluna, hazari,* etc. (Pinto, 2003: 93).

Tail Wagging the Dog

The total destruction of the Portuguese settlement of Hugli in 1632 by the forces of Shah Jahan, and the eventual deportation of about 4,000 Portuguese to Agra along with the Augustinian and diocesan priests (Rego, 1955: 184; Maclagan, 1932: 99-105), was a serious blow to the Portuguese severely shattering their confidence levels. Though the Augustinians came back in 1633 on the offer of 777 *bighas* of land from the Mughals and began a new settlement in Bandel (Rego, 1955: 185; Josson, 1921: 78-81)[38] the Portuguese settlers of West Bengal could not maintain their earlier high profile visibility. Unlike the Jesuits from the province of Malabar who did not have enough resources and personnel to continue their work in Bengal, the Augustinians from Goa, with access to larger resources and support from the power centre, could easily build churches and religious houses in Bandel and other places in Bengal. They also managed to mobilize resources from the Indo-Portuguese settlers of the province of Bengal for the building of churches and religious institutions, which were also used as mechanisms for linking the Portuguese adventurers and traders of Bengal with the power centre of Goa. Obviously, this scheme received uninterrupted funding.

In this process, the Augustinian superior of Bandel was made the vicar general of the bishopry of Mylapore and was authorized till 1797 as a magistrate to decide all cases pertaining to the Christians, except those involving capital punishment (Thekkedath, 1988: 464; Hambye, 1997: 451). Through a network of churches and chaplains, the Augustinians extended the legal frames of the Portuguese into the diasporic Portuguese settlements of Bengal, inviting these settlers through their religious teachings to revert to the values and ideals of the larger Portuguese mainstream agenda. The long chain of churches that the Augustinians established were around the three major centres mentioned above. Through the repeated ecclesiastical exercises and spiritual journeys of the Augustinians, as well as their spiritually taming devices, the Portuguese settlers were in course of time integrated with the churches that they had built among them, which ultimately revolved around their major centre at Hugli-Bandel (Rego, 1958: 23-5).[39]

Dacca, the capital of Bengal, was the core area for diverse Portuguese settlements in the heartland of the muslin trade and the Portuguese mercantile settlements of Manaswar, Narandia, Pulgari, Tezgaon (in the suburbs of Dacca), Norikul, Chandipur and Sripur were integrated with the principal Portuguese base at Dacca (Rego, 1955: 25-7) through the spiritual itineraries and church institutions of the Augustinians.

By the time the Augustinians reached Chittagong, the Portuguese adventurers, mercenaries and pirates had developed an unholy alliance with the king of Arakan, whereby they resorted to a wide variety of activities in which piracy was a major component. The taming and spiritual disciplining of the Portuguese settlers around Chittagong formed the major task of the Augustinians and the Indo-Portuguese settlements of the extreme north-eastern frontier of the Bay of Bengal like Dianga, Angarcale, Chiroto, Bondasil, Rangamati and Hossumpur (Usumdupur) (Rego, 1955: 25-7), which were loosely integrated with the power base of Goa through the agency of these Augustinian missionaries, represented the only vestige of linkage that they could then think of with the *Estado da India* structure.

For all practical purposes, many of the Portuguese settlers in the north-eastern peripheries of the *Estado* were operating independently of Goa. Their major source of wealth was slave-raiding, occasional piracy and arms-selling to the native rulers. As Fr. Sebastian Manrique says, by 1641, the Magh and the Portuguese had captured about 18,000 people and brought them as slaves to Chittagong from lower Burma and northern Orissa (Collis, 1995: 77-92; Bernier, 1989: 175-6, for details of slave trade). The eastern part of the Bay of Bengal had earlier been the heartland of Portuguese piracy, which accelerated with the support of the king of Arakan, and continued till the capture of Chittagong by Shaista Khan, a general in the Mughal army in 1665. Shaista Khan managed to dissociate a major segment of these Portuguese adventurers from the service of the king of Arakan by offering them land grants and encouraging them to enter his service. The Feringhi (Portuguese) Bazar of Dacca was one such settlement of the Portuguese who had switched sides to Shaista Khan (Manucci, 2005: 117; Bernier, 1989: 181-2).

However, the Augustinians could not integrate these settlers with Goa in the way that the early colonial masters desired. With increasing power accumulation and wealth concentration, the Augustinian monks who went to Bengal to spiritually discipline the Portuguese renegades and adventurers began to be increasingly lured by the commercial and lucrative milieu of the adventurers themselves, almost creating an atmosphere of the tail wagging the dog.

The Augustinians, particularly the Augustinian prior of Bandel enjoyed a political position in the community of the Portuguese-settlers and, eventually they came into conflict with the bishop of Mylapore who claimed ecclesiastical jurisdiction over Bengal, which the Augustinians were reluctant to concede. They also had problems with the Jesuits operating in Chandernagor. It was against this background that Francis Laynes, the Jesuit bishop of Mylapore, made an episcopal visit to Bengal in 1712 and placed the unyielding Augustinians of Bandel under interdict in 1714. The king of Portugal issued orders in 1704 to expel the trouble-making Augustinians from Bengal (Hambye, 1997: 451-6). Thus the situation of Bengal almost looked like the 'tail wagging the dog' phenomenon.

Religious Processes and the Ethnic Mutation of the Indo-Portuguese

With the evolution of Bengal as the seat of English power, there was a long and steady process of ethnic mutation of the Luso-Indians into Anglo-Indians in the region. It began with a complex process by which the Indo-Portuguese were absorbed into the English space, initially as commercial collaborators, fighting soldiers and as wives for the Englishmen. Since the establishment of the English base in Calcutta, there was a large-scale migration of the Indo-Portuguese from their various enclaves in Bengal to Calcutta, where the number of Catholics increased from 10,000 in 1724 to 25,000 in 1774 (Hambye, 1997: 460), out of whom the Indo-Portuguese were 3,181 in 1837 (Campos, 1998: 198).

At a time when the English were stabilizing their position in Bengal, these Indo-Portuguese acted as their supportive social base. Many of them also acted as their commercial intermediaries, while a considerable number were inducted into the English army as a fighting force. In the late 1750s, there were about 180 Luso-Indians of Bengal fighting as soldiers for the English (Campos, 1998: 191). As marriageable English ladies were not available in India at that point of time, the English East India company servants who followed either Anglicanism or Presbyterianism began to take wives from the Indo-Portuguese community. Marriages between the English company servants and the Luso-Indians became so frequent and rampant that the company officials began to object (Hambye, 1997: 461; Long, 1869: 90, 113-14).

The nuanced process leading to ethnic mutation was further accelerated by a religious development that reduced the hold of the Portuguese *padroado* priests over the Indo-Portuguese settlers of Bengal. From the last part of the sixteenth century, the spiritual needs of the latter were looked after by various religious orders working under the Portuguese ecclesiastical system of *padroado* (Boxer, 1969: 229; Sa, 2007: 258), the principal among them being the Augustinians.

In fact, the *padroado* rights and duties were initially given to the Order of Christ, which was one among the four military religious orders of Portugal (Santiago, Avis, Hospital and Christ) involved in the fight against Islam in the context of the Crusades. The Order of Christ, which was founded by King Dinis in 1319 to replace the Order of the Knights of Templars after its suppression by the Pope, had channellized a great amount of the wealth of the Templars for sponsoring Portuguese voyages of geographical discoveries in the Atlantic. Since the time of Prince Henry the Navigator, who was the Grand Master of the Order of Christ, a chain of voyages leading to these discoveries became an important activity of the Order of Christ, which was eventually given the spiritual jurisdiction over the 'lands, islands and places' hitherto discovered or yet to be discovered by the Portuguese by the Pope. After the death of Henry, the headship of the Order of Christ was incorporated into the Portuguese crown. A series of Papal Bulls like *Dum diversus* (1452), *Romanus Pontifex* (1455) and *Inter Caetera* (1456) were issued to the Portuguese rulers, handing over spiritual authority in the newly discovered areas to them.

From the first decade of the seventeenth century, ecclesiastical activities in Bengal were exclusively managed by the Augustinians operating under the *padroado* system. In fact, the *padroado* system gave the responsibility of evangelization in the newly discovered territories to the Portuguese crown, as a result of which the king of Portugal got the right to select and present his own men as prelates and superiors to the posts of bishop and monastic heads (Pallippurathukkunnel, 1982: 3-4; Sa, 2007: 255-80; Costa, 2005: 71-88). However, for all practical purposes, the *padroado*, which was set-up for better conduct of the evangelization work and serving God, became a pliable tool in the hands of the Portuguese for implementing their mercantilist designs and for carrying out the expansion of Portuguese power and influence in areas where the power of weapons would not succeed in the normal course. The defects in the functioning of the *padroado* system later made Pope Gregory XV set up the *Propaganda Fide* (literally, 'propagation of faith') in 1622, entrusting a major portion of Asia to this ecclesiastical administrative arrangement. However, in 1838, the *padroado* was suppressed by the Pope, despite severe opposition from the Portuguese crown, and the strained relationship between Rome and Portugal continued up to 1886 (Dominic, 1972: 102-3).

It was through the *padroado* missionaries, particularly the Augustinians, that the scattered Portuguese settlements of the province of Bengal were connected and integrated with the power centres of Goa and Lisbon. Now, with the occupation of Bengal, the English began to see the continued presence of Portuguese religious missionaries in the region as a menace to their political authority. This political challenge raised in the religious space of Bengal was ably responded to by them by getting a few of the Augustinian priests (five in number) who were working among the Indo-Portuguese settlers converted to Anglicanism, the religion of the new masters. These converted priests were allowed to work in Bengal as Anglican priests (Hambye, 1997: 461-2). The ex-Augustinians eventually dissociated many of the Indo-Portuguese from Portuguese *padroado* hold and helped them to get aligned with the new masters of the land.

The English in Bengal wanted to have *Propaganda Fide* missionaries to challenge the hold of the *padroado* missionary priests over the

Indo-Portuguese settlers of the Bay of Bengal. Negotiations for getting missionaries agreeable to the English were initiated in Rome and London and, finally, Rome put an end to the ecclesiastical rule of Bengal by the Portuguese *padroado* missionaries and introduced a new diocese in Calcutta in 1834 under the *Propaganda Fide* in its stead (Moraes, 1972: 157). This was followed by the sending of an Irish Jesuit priest, Robert St. Leger, as bishop to the newly-formed diocese of Calcutta (Apostolic Vicariate) (Campos, 1998: 126). The Portuguese priests and the Luso-Indians vehemently opposed this move of handing over ecclesiastical authority to the *Propaganda Fide* saying that it was an encroachment on the age-old *padroado* rights of the king of Portugal (Rego, 1956: 150-67).

Through these English and Irish Jesuits, the Indo-Portuguese settlers were eventually dissociated from the Portuguese *padroado* priests, which, in turn, helped the English colonial authorities to easily penetrate into the affairs of this community and create a supportive and pliable social base out of them. The dissemination of English education and way of life instead of the Portuguese culture and language speeded up this process of the ethnic mutation of the Luso-Indians. The result was the eventual construction of a new category of Anglo-Indians out of them. The Portuguese *padroado* could not prevent this mutation process and the erasure of the Lusitanian identity from the Portuguese settlers. In 1835, all the religious orders: the Jesuits (who were expelled in 1759), Augustinians, Franciscans and Dominicans working in Portugal and India (including Bengal) were suppressed, and the Portuguese religious missionaries of Bengal, including the Augustinians, had to either leave India or get married and quit the religious profession (Malekandathil, 2009: 24, n. 44; Malekandathil & Dias, 2008: xii). The absence of Portuguese missionaries in Bengal and the increasing use of the English language and cultural practices by the English Jesuits and, later, the Belgian Jesuits resulted in the anglicizing of this community, which, in turn, intensified ethnic mutation and made them a manoeuvrable social base for the English in the long run.

The foregoing discussion shows the changing images that evolved out of the Portuguese and Indo-Portuguese activities in the northern zones of the Bay of Bengal. The multiple engagements that the

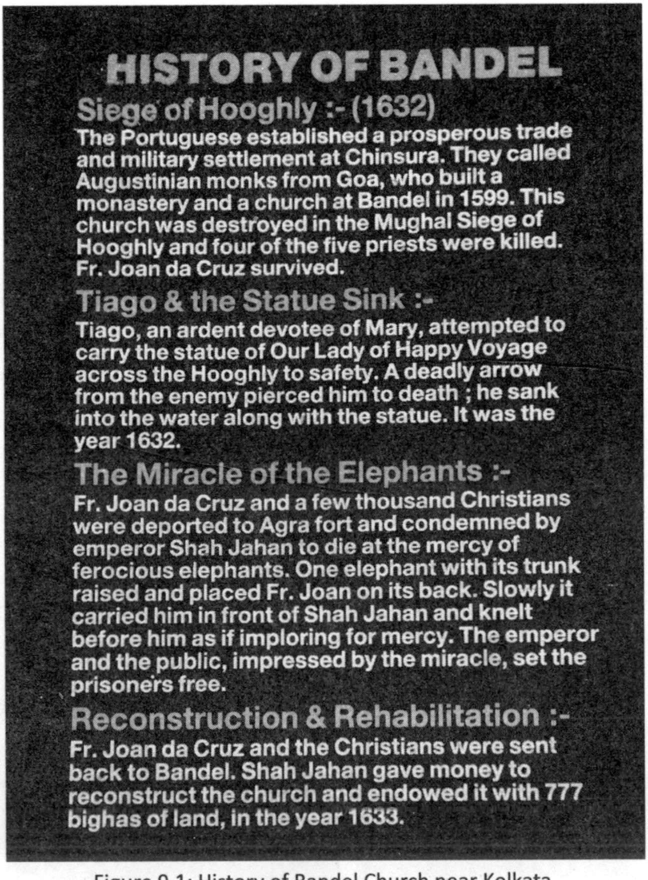

HISTORY OF BANDEL

Siege of Hooghly :- (1632)

The Portuguese established a prosperous trade and military settlement at Chinsura. They called Augustinian monks from Goa, who built a monastery and a church at Bandel in 1599. This church was destroyed in the Mughal Siege of Hooghly and four of the five priests were killed. Fr. Joan da Cruz survived.

Tiago & the Statue Sink :-

Tiago, an ardent devotee of Mary, attempted to carry the statue of Our Lady of Happy Voyage across the Hooghly to safety. A deadly arrow from the enemy pierced him to death ; he sank into the water along with the statue. It was the year 1632.

The Miracle of the Elephants :-

Fr. Joan da Cruz and a few thousand Christians were deported to Agra fort and condemned by emperor Shah Jahan to die at the mercy of ferocious elephants. One elephant with its trunk raised and placed Fr. Joan on its back. Slowly it carried him in front of Shah Jahan and knelt before him as if imploring for mercy. The emperor and the public, impressed by the miracle, set the prisoners free.

Reconstruction & Rehabilitation :-

Fr. Joan da Cruz and the Christians were sent back to Bandel. Shah Jahan gave money to reconstruct the church and endowed it with 777 bighas of land, in the year 1633.

Figure 9.1: History of Bandel Church near Kolkata.

Portuguese had in the various eco-zones of the northern Bay of Bengal as traders, fighters, adventurers and pirates were, in no way part of the official scheme of actions of the Portuguese crown. These were all private initiatives, carried out by individuals or groups in the periphery of the Portuguese empire, where there existed little control of the power centre in Goa. Hence, the task of taming them and integrating them into the Portuguese mainstream agenda fell upon various religious orders, particularly the Augustinians. Though some of these programmes backfired, by the eighteenth century, most of the settlements were already on the path of the mainstream economic

Figure 9.2: Façade of the Church at Bandel.

Figure 9.3: Lady of the Happy Voyage at Bandel.

Figure 9.4: Replica of Our Lady.

Figure 9.5: Renovated church at Bandel.

Figure 9.6: Boats on the river near Bandel.

activities of the land, causing larger entrepreneurs like the big agency houses of the Farias and the Barretos to evolve out of them. This new breed of the Indo-Portuguese entrepreneurs of Bengal linked it with China, Mozambique, Brazil and Lisbon, pumping bullion into the region, besides introducing new crops and plants from across the world. With the localization of English power in Bengal, the identity of these Indo-Portuguese settlers was mutated and made to merge with the identity of the Anglo-Indians. By keeping the Portuguese missionaries out of Bengal, the linkages of the Luso-Indians with the Portuguese culture and language and their memories were made to diminish. The social engineering, which began with the intermarriages and the absorption of Indo-Portuguese settlers as a fighting militia and as commercial collaborators for the English, reached a hectic phase when they became anglicized in their customs and practices through social gatherings and ecclesiastical spaces. And the result was the constant reformulation and redefinition of the evolving fluvial segment of the Luso-Indian community until they merged into Anglo-Indians, thereby suiting the colonial agenda of the English.

NOTES

1. Usually pilots to the Ganga were obtained from Balasore in Orissa. (Hartmann, 1994: 254, 257). The distance from Balasore till Calcutta was 320 miles (ibid.: 257). Balasore had several thousand Portuguese settlers with their own parish church once (*Nossa Senhora do Rosario*—Our Lady of Rosary). Later, many of them left Balasore for other places because of poverty (Rego, 1955, vol. XI: 191).
2. Pipli or Piply (Pipilipatam) in the kingdom of Cuttack had about three hundred Christians with a considerable number of Portuguese settlers and a church of their own. The Dutch had a factory at Pipli. But the Portuguese priest Fr. Francisco da Piedade sought the help of the ruler of the principality to expel the Dutch in 1622. The English founded their factory in 1636 on the ruins of Portuguese factory (Rego, 1955, vol. XI: 191).
3. Angelim (whose present name is Hijili) was another centre of Portuguese concentration on the border between Orissa and Bengal, where they had a church titled *Nossa Senhora do Rosario* (Rego, 1955, vol. XI: 191).
4. Tamboly (Tamluk?) had had a relatively significant Portuguese presence with a church (*Nossa Senhora da Esperança*—Church of our Lady of Hope). The Augustinian document of 1817 says that Tamboly was located in Orissa (Rego, 1955, vol. XI: 192).
5. Banja, located in Bengal had a considerable number of rich Portuguese settlers and a church titled *Nossa Senhora da Saude* (Our Lady of Health). But later when the commerce dwindled with the entry of the Dutch, many left the place (Rego, 1955, vol. XI: 192).
6. An unidentified place in Bengal, where there was a small number of Portuguese settlers and a church titled *Nossa Senhora da Saude*. By the eighteenth century this settlement had disappeared (Rego, 1955: 192).
7. Cajosy seems to have been the coastal town of Khajuri. This place had some Portuguese settlers with a church. After the Mughal conquest of Bengal, the Christians of this place served the Mughal and Muslim masters and later both the church and the settlement disappeared (Rego, 1955, vol. XI: 192).
8. Jassor (Jessore) is located at a distance of two days' journey from Hugli and it principally was a settlement of Portuguese soldiers (Rego, 1955, vol. XI: 192).
9. This was located near Hugli and the settlers were relatively very poor and could not sustain their church and eventually the number of Christians dwindled (Rego, 1955, vol. XI: 192).

10. Chinchura (Chinsura or Chunchura) is located on the banks of river Hugli and was almost 4 miles away from the Portuguese settlement of Hugli and was a settlement of the Dutch from 1656 till 1825. It is located 45 km away from Calcutta. In 1740 a Catholic church was erected in the name of *Menino Jesus* (Child Jesus) for the Catholics who were in the service of the Dutch (Rego, 1955, vol. XI: 193, 764, 769).
11. Barnagor (Baranagar) was a place where the Dutch had their gardens and recreation houses. The Augustinians took the Portuguese Catholic settlers of this place under their spiritual protection (Rego, 1955, vol. XI: 193).
12. Chandernagore (Chandannagar) was a French settlement since 1690. However, the Portuguese Augustinians erected a church here (ibid: 193). It is located thirty kilometers north of Calcutta (Rego, 1955, vol. XI: 193).
13. As early as 1690, a church (*Nossa Senhora do Rosario*—Our Lady of Rosary) was erected at Calcutta to cater to the spiritual needs of the Portuguese settlers and Catholics. Eventually Calcutta became the core area of concentration for the descendants of the Portuguese and by the mid-eighteenth century, there were about 20,000 Catholics in the vicinity of Calcutta, out of whom the majority were descendants of the Portuguese. The new church of *Nossa Senhora das Dores* was erected with the increase in Catholic population in 1810 (Rego, 1955, vol. XI: 193, 337, 558, 559, 587, 595, 644, 697-9, 710, 718, 730-4, 738, 758, 764, 776, 783, 789, 799, 818).
14. Bottocana (Bottokhanna) was located in the vicinity of Calcutta and the church was founded in 1810 by Madame Izabel Gracia (Rego, 1955, vol. XI: 194, 337, 798, 799, 803, 805, 830).
15. Dacca, which had become the power centre by this time, had a considerable number of Portuguese settlers. The Augustinians started catering to the spiritual needs of the Portuguese settlers from 1612. There were two churches in Dacca (the old church of *Nossa Senhora da Assumpção* and the new church of *Nossa Senhora das Dores* built in 1813 (Rego, 1955, vol. XI: 195, 337, 438, 519, 766, 816).
16. Norikul (Noricul) was located about 28 miles south of Dacca. The Church of Norikul was erected by Nicolão de Paiva who was baptized by the Augustinians in the seventeenth century. He was highly respected and venerated by many including the Muslims. For building the churches of Hugli and Norikul he spent about Rs. 20,000 in the second half of the seventeenth century. Later by 1720 this settlement

became relatively poor and could not maintain a resident priest (Rego, 1955: 194; 1958: 25-6).

17. In 1681, there were 2,000 Catholics in Chandipur, of whom 30 were Portuguese (Rego, 1955: 195).
18. Seripur (Sripur) located in the south of Dacca was the capital of Chand Rai and Kedar Rai. It had a significant Portuguese presence with a church; however, they disappeared by 1681 (Rego, 1955, vol. XI: 195).
19. Tasgão (Tezgaon) is located almost 2 km away from Dacca and at a distance of ten days' journey from Calcutta. It had a church titled *Nossa Senhora do Rosario.* Many Christians were there (Rego, 1955, vol XI: 195).
20. Cambalim also had a considerable number of Christian and Portuguese settlers with a church; however they disappeared after 1681 (Rego, 1955, vol. XI: 196).
21. Balva had a considerable number of Christians with a church of a late origin (Rego, 1955, vol. XI: 196).
22. This was an English settlement and the Catholic church was built in 1771 (Rego, 1955, vol. XI: 196).
23. Ossompur (Hossumpur or Usumdupur) had a church and a Christian settlement till 1766 (Rego, 1955, vol. XI: 196).
24. Cassimbazar was an English settlement. However this had a lot of noble Catholic Christians as settlers (Rego, 1955, vol. XI: 196).
25. Sirampur, or Serampur was a Danish settlement. It had a considerable Catholic population with a church called *Nossa Senhora da Madre de Deos* (Rego, 1955, vol. XI: 197, 728, 745, 792, 805, 841).
26. Ossunabar (Ashwinipur?) in the province of Zaninagor had a sizeable Catholic population with a church (Rego, 1955, vol. XI: 197).
27. The Portuguese soldiers, merchants and adventurers had settled down in Chatigão (Chittagong) in the 1530s. Initially the Jesuits (1599) and later the Augustinians (since 1621) began to spiritually tame the settlers of this port-town through different mechanisms. There were two churches in Chittagong. (Rego, 1955, vol. XI: 200-201, 334, 505, 545, 554, 567, 766, 802; Hartmann, 1994: 200).
28. Rego, 1955, vol. XI: 200.
29. Both Concão and Jamalcão were located in the city of Chittagong (Rego, 1955: 200; Rego, 1958: 23-6).
30. Dianga is in the vicinity of Chittagong. It is located at the mouth of the river Karwafuli, which connects it with Chittagong (Rego, 1955: 200).

31. Angaracale, with Portuguese settlers and a church, was located in the vicinity of Chittagong. Earlier it was situated in the kingdom of Arakan (Rego, 1955: 200).
32. F.S. Downs says that Rangamati was located in Goalpara on the banks of the river Brahmaputra, about 45 km west of Gauhati (Rego, 1955, vol. XI: 200; Downs, 1978: 88-99).
33. Pedro Tavares is referred to as the captain-general of the foreigners residing in 'Porto Pequeno'.
34. As early as 1566, Padre Melchior Nunes Barreto S.J, writes that many Portuguese Christians were living in Bengal in utter poverty.
35. The *Ain-i-Akbari* says that Chittagong, at that point of time, was the resort of the Christians.
36. The Augustinians used to claim that Bengal did not belong to the diocese of Mylapore or any other dioceses but to their religious order.
37. *Relação das Plantas & Dezcripções de Todas as Fortalezas, Cidades e Povoações que os Poruguezes tem no Estado da India,* Lisboa, MCMXXXVI: 38-9.
38. The viceroy Conde de Linhares sent in 1633 an envoy along with Fr. Luis do Espirito Santo for establishing peace.
39. The Portuguese settlements of Balassore (with 1,000 Christians), Pipli (300 Christians), Tamluk, Banja (with three churches for 8,000-9,000 commercially active Christian residents) Hijli, Khajuri, Jessore (400 Christians), Chinsura (Dutch settlement), Baranagar (Dutch settlement), Chandernagar (French settlement), Calcutta and Syedabad (in the suburb of Murshidabad) formed the major commercial or quasi-commercial centres that existed around Hugli-Bandel.

REFERENCES

Abu-l Fazal, Allami, 2006, *The Ain-i- Akbari*, tr. H. Blochmann, vol. II, New Delhi: Low Price Publications.

Anthony, Philomena Sequeira, 2004, *The Goa-Bahia Intra-Colonial Relations, 1675-1825*, Tellicherry: Institute for Research in Social Sciences and Humanities.

Bernier, François, 1989, *Travels in the Mogul Empire, AD 1656-1668*, ed. Vincent A. Smith, New Delhi: Low Price Publications.

Biblioteca Nacional de Lisboa (BNL), *Fundo Geral,* 1980, 'Livro das Despezas de hum porcento', fols. 7-25

Boxer, Charles R., 1969, *The Portuguese Sea-borne Empire,* London: Hutchinson & Co.

Campos, Joachim Joseph A., 1998, *History of the Portuguese in Bengal*, New Delhi: Asian Educational Services.

Collis, Maurice, 1995, *The Land of the Great Image, Being Experiences of Friar Manrique in Arakan*, New Delhi: Asian Educational Services.

Correia, Gaspar, 1921, *Lendas da India*, tom. II, Lisbon: Academia das Ciencias de Lisboa.

Costa, João Paulo e, 2005, 'The Padroado and the Catholic Mission in Asia during the 17th Century', *Rivalry and Conflict: European Traders and Asian Trading Networks in the 16th and 17th Centuries*, ed. Ernst van Veen and Leonard Blusse, Leiden: CNWS Publications: 71-88.

Cunha, João Manuel Teles e, 2006, 'Economia e Finanças', in Maria de Jesus dos Martires Lopes (ed.), *O Imperio Oriental, 1660-1820*, vol. I, Lisbon: Editorial Estampa: 162-338.

de Souza, Teotonio R., 1991, 'Rogerio de Faria: an Indo-Portuguese Trader with China Links', Paper presented at the Sixth International Seminar on *Indo-Portuguese History*, Macao, 21-6 October.

Dominic, 1972, 'The Latin Missions under the Jurisdiction of Propaganda (1637-1838)', Hormice C. Perumalil, and Edward Rene Hambye (eds.), *Christianity in India*, Alleppey: Prakasham Publications.

Downs, F.S., 1978, 'Rangamati: A Christian Community in North-East India during the Seventeenth and Eighteenth Century', *Indian Church History Review*, XII: 88-99.

Eaton, Richard, 1994, *The Rise of Islam and the Bengal Frontier*, New Delhi: Oxford University Press.

Foster, William (ed.), 1995, *The Voyage of Thomas Best to the East Indies, 1612-14*, New Delhi: Asian Educational Services.

Hambye, Edward Rene, 1997, *History of Christianity in India*, vol. III, Bangalore: The Church History Association of India.

Hartmann, Arnulf, OSA (ed.), 1994, 'Historia das Missões dos Padres Agostinianos na India nos Principios do 18 seculo, escrita pelo P.Fr. Jorge da Presentação Missionario', *Analecta Augustiniana*, vol. LVII: 193-341.

Josson, H., 1921, *La Mission du Bengale Occidental ou Archidiocese de Calcutta: Province belge de la Comapgnie de Jesus*, vol. I, Bruges: Imprimerie Sainte-Catherine.

Khan, Maksud Ahmad, 2004, 'Sufis and their Contribution in the Process of Urbanization', in Neeru Misra (ed.), *Sufis and Sufism*, New Delhi: Manohar: 93-128.

Lapa, Roberto do Amaral, 1989, 'Dimensões do Commercio Colonial entre o Brazil e o Oriente', *Studia*, vol. 49: 394-6.

Long, James, 1869, *Selections from Unpublished Records of Government 1748-1767*, vol. I, Calcutta: Office of the Superintendent of Government Printing.

Maclagan, Edward, 1972, *The Jesuits and the Great Moghul*, London: Octagon Books.

Malekandathil, Pius, 2001, *Portuguese Cochin and the Maritime Trade of India*, A Volume in the South Asian Study Series of Heidelberg University, Germany, New Delhi: Manohar.

———, 2003, *Jornada of Dom Alexis de Menezes: A Portuguese Account of the sixteenth Century Malabar*, Kochi: LRC Publishers.

———, 2009, 'City in Space and Metaphor: A Study on the Port-City of Goa, 1510-1700', *Studies in History*, 25, 1: 13-38.

———, 2010, *Maritime India: Trade, Religion and Polity in the Indian Ocean*, New Delhi: Primus Books.

Malekandathil, Pius and Remy Dias (eds.), 2008, *Goa in the Twentieth Century: History and Culture*, Panaji: Institute Menezes Braganza.

Manucci, Niccolao, 2005, *Mogul India or Storia do Mogor*, vol. II, New Delhi: Low Price Publications.

Misra, Neeru (ed.), 2004, *Sufis and Sufism*, New Delhi: Manohar.

Mitra, Debendra, 1978, *Cotton Weavers of Bengal*, Calcutta: Firma KLM.

Moraes, George M., 1972, 'The Catholic Church under the Portuguese Patronage in the 18th and 20th Centuries', in H.C. Perumalil and E.R. Hambye (eds.), *Christianity in India*, Alleppey: Prakasam Publications.

Pallippurathukkunnel, Thomas, 1982, *A Double Regime in the Malabar Church*, Alwaye: Pontifical Institute.

Pinto, Celsa, 2000, 'Luso-Brazilian Commerce and the Eastern Littoral of India, 1780-1821', Paper presented at the 10th International seminar on Indo-Portuguese History, Salvador, December.

———, 2003, *Situating Indo-Portuguese Trade History: A Commercial Resurgence, 1770-1830*, Tellicherry: Institute for Research in Social Sciences and Humanities.

Ptak, Roderich, 1987, 'China, Portugal under der Maldiven-Handel vom frühen 15. bis zum frühen 16.Jahrhundert: Einige Bemerkungen zur Wirtschaftsgeschichte Südasiens', in Roderich Ptak (ed.), *Portuguese Asia: Aspects in History and Economic History (Sixteenth and Seventeenth Centuries)*, Wiesbaden: Steiner-Verlag.

Rego, Antonio da Silva (ed.), 1955, *Documentação para a Historia das Missões do Padroado Portugues do Oriente*, vol. XI, Lisbon: Agencia Geral do Ultramar.

——— (ed.), 1958, *Documentação para a Historia das Missões do Padroad Portugues do Oriente*, vol. XII, Lisbon: Agencia Geral do Ultramar.

———, 1956, *Le Patronage Portugais de l'Orient,un aperçu historique,* Lisbon: Agencia Geral do Ultramar: 150-67.

Russell-Wood, Anthony John R., 2001, 'A Brazilian Commercial Presence Beyond the Cape of Good Hope, 16th-19th Centuries', in Pius Malekandathil and Jamal Mohammed (eds.), *The Portuguese, Indian Ocean and European Bridgehead: Festschrift in Honour of Prof. K.S. Mathew*, Fundação Oriente: Institute for Research in Social Sciences and Humanities of MESHAR: 191-211.

Sa, Isabel dos Guimaraes, 2007, 'Ecclesiastical Structures and Religious Action', *Portuguese Oceanic Expansion, 1400-1800,* ed. Francisco Bethencourt and Diogo Ramada Curto, Cambridge: Cambridge University Press: 255-80.

Sanceau, Elaine, 1978, *Colecção de São Lourenço,* vol. III, Lisboa: Centro de Estudos Históricos Ultramarinos.

Thekkedath, Joseph, 1988, *History of Christianity in India,* vol. II, Bangalore: Church History Association of India.

Wicki, Josef, 1960, *Documenta Indica (1563-1566),* vol. VI, Rome: Institutum Historicum Societatis Jesu.

———, 1970, *Documenta Indica (1577-1580),* vol. XI, Rome: Institutum Historicum Societatis Jesu.

Winius, George, 1983, 'The Shadow-Empire of Goa in the Bay of Bengal', *Itinerario*, vol. VII, no. 2: 83-101.

CHAPTER 10

Voyages of 'Discovery': Mapping the Bay of Bengal

HIMANSHU PRABHA RAY

In recent writings, scholars have emphasized global interconnections that stimulated new knowledge and learning in the eighteenth and nineteenth century. Trade created channels of communication and, along with commodities, scholars, religious leaders and others also travelled, as did ideas, new forms of knowledge and technology transfer, both within littoral societies and across the Ocean. Traders themselves were often agents who negotiated within several cultural domains and whose mediations gave rise to new intellectual material and technical practices.

> In addition to translators, interpreters, money changers, bankers and moneylenders, the regional trade network was predicated upon specific maritime knowledge and skills. Pilots, navigators and theorists of navigation helped guide ships around maritime Asia and East Africa, thus forming yet another intermediary profession. (Raj, 2009: 107)

Kapil Raj argues that a new development in the second millennium CE was the emergence of cross-cultural mediation as a specialized activity in its own right and one that was autonomous from trading communities. One of the intermediary types suggested by him that is of interest to this paper is that of the knowledge broker. Knowledge mediation, Raj argues, gained increasing status throughout the eighteenth century, especially as a result of sustained European presence in the Indian Ocean region and its eventual colonization. The new knowledge that he discusses is generally linked to trade activities such as botany, geography, cartography, navigation, astronomy, ethnography, accounting, law and so on (Raj, 2009: 110-11; Pearson, 2010: 32-47).

The new knowledge of interest to this paper is that of archaeology and oceanography. Both these emerging eighteenth-century disciplines were unconnected with the requirements of trade, though they were closely linked to colonial expansion and imperial needs to control the documentation and study of the past through material culture, as well as mastery of the ocean through the study of currents and tides. In the context of archaeology, Colin Mackenzie (1753-1821), a Scotsman, stands out. He was the Surveyor-General of India and compiled an immense collection of manuscripts and drawings mainly in south India, but also in north and east India, Sri Lanka, and Java. Thus, with Mackenzie, the canvas broadened beyond South Asia to include island Southeast Asia.

The widened canvas of oceanic expansion in the eighteenth and nineteenth century was also crucial to the study of oceanography, as evident through the travels of James Rennell (1742-1830). Rennell is best known for his *Map of Hindoostan* (Rennell, 1783), and his survey of Bengal, Bihar and Orissa. Scholars have increasingly argued for the major contributions of astronomer-pundits from Benares and the sepoy, Ghulam Muhammad, in the making of this map: 'Without their mediation, it is hard to imagine Rennell gaining access to any of the knowledge circuits so crucial to the compilation of his innovative map' (Raj, 2009: 133-4). Here, I move beyond the making of the *Map* to Rennell's navigational understanding as he surveyed the east coast of India and the overall contributions he made to render shipping safer for British ships. In both these cases, I would maintain that the new forms of knowledge that emerged were radically different from those of the preceding periods. The selection of elements for mapping and their measurement helped establish a new image of the land that facilitated governance. The expanding British presence in the Indian Ocean region linked it to the Atlantic and the Mediterranean in the late eighteenth-early nineteenth century. It was these newly-established networks that facilitated James Rennell's maritime travels and exposed him to a different set of oceanographic challenges.

The discussion is divided into two sections: in the first part, I examine the conceptualization of maritime space in early Buddhist texts and inscriptions from the subcontinent; and, in the second, I introduce the theme of disjunction in maritime networks across the Indian Ocean in the nineteenth century. This second section underscores a redefinition of the maritime landscape in the nineteenth century through the creation of coastal enclaves and the transformation in the nature of watercraft employed. This had far-reaching implications for interconnectedness across the Bay of Bengal and colonial cultural hegemony in the region.

A remarkable feature of the early teachings of the Buddha was their trans-locality and the endorsement of the way of life of the wandering teacher among the monks. The propagation of these teachings transcended political, social and geographical boundaries, and created a bond of common adherence to a shared ethos and ritual. This is evident from the Buddhist textual tradition that was marked by fluidity and universal appeal embedded in religious travel. This proposition also counters the oft-made claim that world religions such as Buddhism, Hinduism, Islam and Christianity cannot be seen as expressions of interconnectedness since they remained centred in specific regions. This static state of affairs of the Asian religions is contrasted with the global consciousness of the ancient Greeks and the global awareness of the elite of the Roman Empire who attempted to write histories of the world (Hopper, 2007: 16-18). Buddhism and Hinduism, it is remarked, were rooted in Asia prior to 1500; after that period, they spread slowly or through imperial systems. For example, Thomas R. Metcalf argues that India itself became a nexus of imperial power that made British conquest, control, and governance across a wide arc of territory stretching from Africa to eastern Asia possible (Metcalf, 2007: 1-2).

In a paper in 2009, Robert Buswell explored the Indian ascetic traditions of itinerant wanderers and suggested that the travel impulse became an integral part of Buddhism's self-identity. He proposed that the motivation to travel was, by no means, restricted to the terrestrial world but was deeply ingrained in the Buddhist cosmology, as evident from the massive anthologies of spiritual journeys (Buswell, 2009: 1055-75).

The *Gaṇḍavyūha*, part of the *Avataṁsakasūtra*, is an important text for the study of trans-locality in early Buddhism. It dates back, in all probability, to the early centuries of the Common Era and describes the attainment of enlightenment through pilgrimage—the primary aim of the writing being to stress that constraints placed by fixed systems need to be overcome to attain full consciousness. Prince Sudhana is inspired to travel by the Bodhisattva Manjusri and advised to visit fifty-three 'spiritual friends' in order to learn *bodhicaryā* or 'the Bodhisattva practice' (Cleary, 1993: 47). These enlightened people, according to the text, could belong to all walks of life and to all regions because 'the wisdom and virtues of Buddha are in all people, but people are unaware of it because of their preoccupations' (Cleary, 1993: 47). Historicity is of little account in this Buddhist text as the discourse is presented by trans-historical, symbolic beings, representing various aspects of universal enlightenment.

The somewhat slender narrative provided by the text of the *Gaṇḍavyūha* has been profusely sculpted on the eighth-century Buddhist monument at Borobudur in central Java (Figure 10.1), though there are a number of variations between the sculpted panels and the textual data, and there is 'no clear correlation between the iconography and location of the narrative scenes and the corresponding passages in the text' (Fontein, 1967: 125).

Figure 10.1: General view of the stupa at Borobudur in central Java, courtesy Indian Institute for Indian Studies, Gurgaon.

Travel to Buddhist imaginaries no doubt helped break down the temporal and spatial barriers between the universal *dhamma* and the local practices followed by lineages of Buddhist teachers. The representation of the *Gaṇḍavyūha* narrative at Borobudur was matched by data from a variety of sources, as discussed in the next section.

The Maritime Networks: Continuities

A cluster of fifth-century inscriptions of unequivocal Buddhist affiliation was found in Kedah on the west coast of the Malay peninsula. Three of these inscriptions are made of local stone and bear similar illustrations of Buddhist stupas. Texts very similar to these inscriptions have been found on the island of Borneo and on the coast of Brunei (Christie, 1995: 256). The most interesting of these inscriptions in Sanskrit is that of Buddhagupta, which refers to the setting up of the stone by the mariner Buddhagupta, resident of Raktamrttika, identified with Rajbadidanga in Bengal, on the successful completion of his voyage (Chhabra, 1965: 23-4) (Figures 10.2 and 10.3).

Another network that needs to be taken into account was that with China. As recorded in the written history of the Han (*Qian Hanshu*) under the reign of Emperor Wudi (140-87 BCE), the emperor sent a mission to the kingdom of Huangzhi, which contemporary writers generally agree was located on the shores of the Indian Ocean,

Figure 10.2: Inscription of Buddhagupta now in the Indian Museum, Kolkata.

Figure 10.3: Side view of the inscription.

very likely in India (Wheatley, 1961: 8-13). More often quoted are records left by Chinese pilgrims who travelled to India and visited Buddhist sites. The pilgrim, Faxian, arrived overland in India in CE 399 and returned by sea to China in CE 413-14 from Sri Lanka, heading towards the north-west tip of Sumatra. The ship was wrecked on the way and perhaps landed in the Andamans. The next phase took Faxian to the north-west of Borneo where he arrived in 414 after ninety days at sea. The pilgrim remained in Borneo for five months and then left for China in mid-414, heading towards Canton.

The second Chinese pilgrim to visit India in the seventh century was Xuanzang, though he travelled by the overland route. While his writings are of not much relevance to maritime archaeology, they formed the basis of the archaeological exploration and survey conducted by Alexander Cunningham (1814-93), the first Director-General of the Archaeological Survey of India, who brought Buddhism to the forefront and established its study as a separate branch in the second quarter of the nineteenth century. A point that Cunningham did not take into account was the audience of Xuanzang's writings.

Recent research has shown that the Chinese pilgrim's narrative of his pilgrimage to India was written specifically for the eyes of the Chinese emperor, Taizong, of the Tang dynasty (618-907) and, hence, Xuanzang highlighted aspects that would satisfy the curiosity of the emperor and also indicate his personal contacts and knowledge of foreign political leaders. Peiyi Wu argues that Xuanzang's narrative includes 'almost everything except his pilgrimage' (Wu, 1992: 67). Nevertheless, Xuanzang's writings seem to have had the desired effect at the royal court and official Chinese sources record the arrival of an embassy from the ruler of Kanauj in central India in CE 641 and crediting Xuanzang with initiating contacts between the Chinese empire and King Harsha of Kanauj (Sen, 2001: 6).

In addition to the land routes into the subcontinent, there is ample evidence for the travel of Chinese pilgrims along sea routes across the Bay of Bengal. The most interesting information on the circumnavigation of the Malay peninsula is contained in Yijing's accounts of the voyage of the Chinese pilgrims who travelled to

India and returned during the second half of the seventh century CE. Yijing provides an account of his journey from Canton in October-November with the north-east monsoon and his arrival in Palembang on Sumatra a month later. He stayed there for six months in CE 671 and then went to Jambi near Palembang sometime around May. He stayed there for another two months and then re-embarked in order to make use of the winds of the south-west monsoon and reach Kedah (Jiecha) on the west coast of the Malay Peninsula. He did not leave this region for India until the beginning of the following year when the north-east monsoon was well established. Yijing reached the Nicobar islands in ten days and arrived at Tamralipti in Bengal fifteen days later. This was clearly the most direct route to the holy places of historic Buddhism (Jacq-Hergoualc'h, 2002: 53-4).

Twelve years later, Yijing returned by the same route, travelling on the winds of the north-east monsoon to reach Kedah, but this trip required two months while the outward journey had taken only twenty-five days. Sailing against the winds was a well-tried technique but it took much longer than sailing with the winds. One of the voyages recounted by Yijing lasted only the time of one monsoon—the pilgrim, Wujing left China 'in the period of the east winds', i.e. in October-November and arrived in Srivijaya at the end of one month. After stopping at Jambi, he took another month reaching Jiecha and left for Negapatam on the Tamil coast from there with the same winds before they began to wane towards the end of March. As late as the seventeenth century, the ships of the French diplomatic missions to Siam still had the same concern: they must not miss the 'season' as it took seven months on an average to sail from Brest and reach the estuary of the Chao Phraya (Jacq-Hergoualc'h, 2002: 55).

Pilgrimage continued to be a prime motive for travellers from China and, in CE 1021 the monk, Yunshu, worshipped at the site of Bodh Gaya. In addition to the accounts of Chinese monks, five stone tablets with tenth and eleventh-century Chinese inscriptions were found at Bodhgaya, and two of the names that have been identified include those of Chi-I and Ho-yun, the former in the company of some other priests (Beal, 1881: 552-72). It is significant that Chinese visitors to Bodhgaya included not just monks but also members of the naval fleets sent by the third emperor of the Ming dynasty, Yong-le (1403-25) to more than twenty coastal centres in Southeast Asia, as well as to Bengal, the Malabar coast and Aden, popularly known as the voyages of Zheng He. Accounts of these voyages are available in the *Mingshi* (*History of the Ming Dynasty*), which is considered the most elaborate and complete history of the Ming dynasty (Ray, 1993: 7). It is based on the *Ming Shi-lu*, each of the *shi-lu* comprising an account of one emperor's reign compiled after that emperor's death on the basis of a number of sources created during the reign (Wade, 2005). What is relevant for this paper is the description of visits undertaken to Bengal, *Zhao-na-pu-er* or Jaunpur in 1412 located to the west of Bengal, and to Dilli or Delhi. The accounts also mention that Hou Xian, the lesser eunuch, stopped at *Jin-gang bao zuo*, the Vajrasana at Bodhgaya on his way to or from Jaunpur and offered gifts to the elders there (Ray, 1993: 78).

It is evident that while trade provided an important motive for sea-travel, it was by no means the only reason for travel by sea and needs to be studied within a wider perspective of seafaring activity and maritime networks. Second, the role of religions, such as those of Buddhism, Hinduism or Islam in motivating and supporting seafaring activity needs to be recognized and accepted. Finally, for an appreciation of cultural interchanges across the Bay of Bengal, it is crucial to highlight the diverse channels of communication, which also included oral transmission by priests and pilgrims, traders, wandering minstrels and entertainers. It is only then that a holistic understanding of cultural interaction across the maritime world will emerge.

At this stage we need to shift the focus and to move to the second objective of this paper, i.e. to what extent did these networks change with the entry of the Europeans, especially in the eighteenth and nineteenth century with the East India Company's colonization in the Bay of Bengal. How did the East India Company establish control in its maritime empire?

Discontinuities, Control and Territorial Expansion

In 1890, 63 per cent of the world's combined ship tonnage sailed under the British flag. By late in the eighteenth century this industrializing country had major centres in Mumbai, Kolkata, Chennai,

Penang and beyond the edge of the ocean in Sydney. Over the next fifty years a series of vital ports were taken or created: Colombo in 1796, Cape Town in 1806, Singapore in 1819, Aden in 1839, and beyond the ocean, Hong Kong in 1852 (Pearson, 2003: 191).

Michael Pearson goes on to suggest that once the British economy had made the transition from merchant capital to industrial capital, there was a need to control not just the coastal centres but the entire productive process and, hence, territorial control and expansion made the vision of a maritime empire a reality. Another development that contributed to the making of the maritime empire was the change to the steamship, especially in the period from 1850 to 1945. Steam navigation altered the power relations dramatically in the Indian Ocean by pushing local participation to the periphery. Mechanization of water vessels also resulted in new developments, such as the emergence of ports and dockyards where larger ships could be serviced and commodities loaded. It also enlarged the area of operations by drawing both Australia and the Atlantic into its field of operations. New skills were required, not just for manning ships, but more as navigational aids (Pearson, 2003: 194-200).

It is no coincidence that interest in the material heritage of Southeast Asia corresponds with British control, starting with the occupation of Penang in the Straits of Malacca by Captain Francis Light in 1786. By 1815, Ceylon became a Crown colony but the English were soon ousted from Indonesia. Though the Dutch were able to establish control over Java, they had to undertake a hard and bitter campaign for dominance over the northern Sumatran region of Aceh and the island of Bali. There are several similarities between the British experience in India and the emergence of the Dutch as a territorial power in Java, although Dutch control over the Indonesian archipelago was a slower process and was only completed by the early twentieth century. In 1819, Sir Thomas Stamford Raffles (1781-1826), the erstwhile Malay translator to the East India Company, established the free port of Singapore (Benjamin, 2007: 370). However, the Anglo-Dutch Treaty of 1824 limited the British sphere of influence to the 'Straits Settlements' of Malacca, Penang and Singapore.

Up to the end of the eighteenth century, Burma had not been the target of European expansion but this changed with the Treaty of Yandabo in 1826 that gave the East India Company control over Arakan and Tenasserim in lower Burma. The Indian subcontinent came under the British Raj in 1858 after the unsuccessful Revolt of 1857 and, thereafter, 'British Burma' came into existence, after the defeat of the Burmese king in the Third Burma War (1885-7). Thus by the late nineteenth century, the British were able to establish their control over large parts of South Asia and keep the French commercial influence at bay. How did these shifts in the balance of power impact connections across the Bay of Bengal? I will discuss this issue with reference to two colonial officials: one was Colin Mackenzie; and the other James Rennell.

Colin Mackenzie (1754–1821): Creating the Material Record

Many of those involved in archaeological research, especially in the early years, played a dual role, being both military personnel and colonial administrators who were also engaged in archaeological work. A good example of this is the career of Colin Mackenzie. In 1783, Mackenzie secured a commission in the East India Company's Madras Army and carried out two surveys in what is now Andhra Pradesh: one of Guntur and the other of the roads from Nellore to Ongole. In 1792, he was appointed Engineer and Surveyor to the Subsidiary Force in the service of the Nizam of Hyderabad 'for the purpose of acquiring some information of the geography of these countries' (Howes, 2010: 2).

Mackenzie accumulated massive collections over a thirty-eight-year period from 1783 at the age of twenty-nine, when he arrived in India, until his death in 1821. In 1822, his widow sold his collections that were made largely in south India to the East India Company, and these were then catalogued by Horace Hayman Wilson. Over 1,700 of Mackenzie's drawings are in the British Library alone. He came to India as a military engineer, and two of his largest surveys were the Survey of the Nizam of Hyderabad's Dominions (1792-8) and the Mysore Survey (1799-1810), which were meant to define territories controlled by the Indian rulers. Thus, one aspect of Mackenzie's work was an official topographical survey and compilation of detailed maps, and he was supplied with a staff for this. At the same time, he was involved in the collection of historical, literary and cultural material for which he built his own team of specially-trained helpers and brahmana assistants.

During the Mysore survey (1799-1810), Mackenzie gathered a large number of drawings, plans and histories relating to the temples of the Deccan. In 1795, he was sent to Sri Lanka to assist in the military campaign to Colombo and, in 1811, was ordered to participate in the Java campaign. These campaigns expanded the scope of Mackenzie's operations. In 1813, he returned to Calcutta and was appointed Surveyor-General of India.

Although, unlike his better-known contemporaries, Mackenzie left no published monument to his own scholarly endeavours during the British interregnum in Java, his European and Javanese language manuscript collections are invaluable. Not only do they provide documentation of Java's political and economic organization during the colonial period, but they also reflect their author's broader purpose of acquiring 'materials for a complete view of the geography, statistics, and history ancient and modern of Java, and the Dutch dependencies in the Eastern islands.' In 1812, Mackenzie visited the temple complex of Prambanan in central Java, surveyed the area and sketched the ruins. His notes and drawings were published in the seventh volume of the *Transactions of the Batavian Society*. In addition, Mackenzie travelled extensively in Java, collecting manuscripts from a diverse range of sources:

> Some were saved from the wreck of the Sultan's library at the storm of the Craten [Kraton] of Djocjacarta, by permission of the prize agents and the concurrence indeed of all the military present—others were purchased and collected on the tour through that island: some were presented by Dutch colonists and regents, and others are transcripts by Javanese writers employed by Colonel Mackenzie to copy them from the originals in the hands of the regents, and with their permission. (Weatherbee, 1978: 65)

The Mackenzie collection is especially valuable for insights into the literary and historical traditions of the Yogyakarta court and formed the basis of Thomas Stamford Raffles's (1781-1826), The *History of Java* published in 1817. In the context of Java, the name of Raffles stands out, first as a Malay translator to the Company and later, in 1811, as the Lieutenant-Governor of Java, who was soon promoted as the Governor of Bencoolen (now Sumatra) where he continued his work until 1824 when Java was ceded to the Dutch. Raffles' *The History of Java* remained the standard work for an understanding of the island's past until the end of the century.

Like many others, Raffles, too, saw 'foreign traders' as the most important factor in the progress of a people. The Dutch, by their trade monopolies which restricted foreign trade, had 'interfered with, checked [and] changed in its character' the natural development of the Javanese (Raffles, 1817: 192). Raffles believed that the English were the best rulers of Java because by freeing up trade, they would allow the Javanese to return to their 'natural' course of development and also retain their ancient glory—a theme that he returns to in his second volume, as he painstakingly documented the ancient temples of Java. Thus, a running theme in many of the writings of this period was the benign and civilizing nature of English trade, though the large collections of manuscripts, inscriptions and sculptures being made at this time also undoubtedly initiated writings on the political history of South Asia.

Philip Wagoner suggests that Mackenzie recognized the historical importance of inscriptions and the native assistants that accompanied the surveying team were accordingly instructed to collect any inscriptions that they could find. What made the task easier was the fact that the Niyogi brahmanas employed by Mackenzie had traditionally worked in the courts of the local rulers, such as the twelfth-thirteenth-century Kakatiyas in Andhra, for collection of revenue information. In the eighteenth century, the Niyogis were spread across the Deccan and, like Mackenzie, 'accepted the proposition that the production of knowledge meant the generation of "statistical" information for the use of the state, whether colonial or pre-colonial, and both accepted that such knowledge was most effectively produced through the modality of field-survey' (Wagoner, 2003: 799).

By 1807, the members of Mackenzie's survey team had collected texts of more than 1,100 inscriptions and had translated and analysed enough of them for Mackenzie to write 'An Introductory

Memoir on the Use and Advantage of Inscriptions and Sculptured Monuments in illustrating Hindu History' (unpublished manuscript, British Library, OIOC Mackenzie collection vol. 18, recensions A & B). This manuscript remained unpublished though Mackenzie did correspond and share this information with members of the Asiatic Society based in Calcutta. One of them, Henry Colebrooke, published many of the epigraphs provided by Mackenzie in *Asiatick Researches*. In addition, Narrain Row Brahmin who worked for Mackenzie from 1803 to 1818 published a historiographic work, the *Śrīśaila Devālaya Kaiphiyatu,* in Telugu in 1810.

> Without them, we would have only the shakiest knowledge of chronology, historical geography, the actual boundaries of regions and territories, the changing nature of language use, and most forms of political, social, and economic life as they were actually lived. (Wagoner, 2003: 786)

The issue that Wagoner leaves unanswered is that of the framework adopted by colonial officials and within which these inscriptions were used to establish a past for the Indian subcontinent, though he does accept that the use of inscriptions for the writing of history was a British construct, which had not been undertaken in the pre-colonial period. The inscriptions were essentially records of land donations and recorded in detail the markers that identified a piece of land that was to be given. Did Mackenzie take recourse to data provided by the inscriptions to complete his survey or were the inscriptions merely of antiquarian interest? The 'objective' nature of the survey is an issue that was questioned by Peter Robb in a 1998 paper, which Wagoner does not take into account.

According to Robb, Mackenzie's contribution lies in the official acceptance of the survey as a means of governance. Mackenzie was the first 'to regard the survey as a means of providing an historical, economic and social understanding of India', rather than as a device merely to rule.

> It is true that Europeans made significant changes in the perceptions of India—in this instance in the understanding of place. The selection of elements for mapping and their measurement helped establish a new image of the land. (Robb, 1998: 183)

It is evident that the survey was not merely the description of a place; instead, it was intended to demarcate and delimit it. This was especially critical when establishing borders. Were boundaries to be fixed based on established practice, matters of convenience, or purely objective principles? How were boundary disputes to be resolved by the surveyors, or were both sides to be presented to a higher body?

John Warren, an assistant of Mackenzie, highlighted several ambiguities in land ownership, such as the fragmentation of holdings, with one unit having multiple owners; the partition of land formerly held jointly; unconnected villages sharing a common identity; and the proliferation of places with the same name. Thus, the complexity involved in naming and combining territorial units was apparent.

> Clearly previous rulers and peoples had varied notions of geographical location and political space, as reflected in political and military structures, land-grants, sacred geography, myths of origin, attachments to villages and so on. (Robb, 1998: 203)

How were these ambiguities rationalized in the colonial period? What were the new principles adopted by Mackenzie and his team in 'defining' space? These are key issues that need to be considered when deciding the extent to which new forms of knowledge transformed not only the study of the past but also created new social relations. No doubt, many of Mackenzie's informants or pundits, as they were termed, were scholars in their own right. Thus, Pundit Sri Nivasia may be described as the first Indian antiquarian who wrote a description of the ruins of Rajgir, identified as the first capital of Magadha and located in the present district of Nalanda, in *The Calcutta Annual Register for the year 1822*.

Mackenzie published little but shared the information from his surveys and other collections with his contemporaries, and many of them relied on his data for their studies on south India, such as Mark Wilks (1760-1831) who published his two-volume work *Historical Sketches of South India* using some of the documents collected by Mackenzie. Mackenzie's work overlapped with that of Francis Buchanan (1762-1829), who was a surgeon, surveyor and natural historian. In addition to his work in Mysore, Buchanan took part in surveys of Assam (1793-4), Nepal (1802-3) and the

Bengal Presidency (1807-14) (Howes, 2010: 58-60). In the absence of analytical studies by Mackenzie based on data generated by him, how does one assess his contribution? In his own words, Mackenzie summed up his inputs as follows:

> The discovery of Jain religion and philosophy and its distinction from that of the Boudh; nature and uses of inscriptions on stone and copper throwing light on the subject of Hindu tenures; design and nature of monumental stones called Veeracul and Maastie cul; sepulchral tumuli, mounds and barrows of the early times. (Wilson, 1828: xi)

We do know that one of Mackenzie's colleagues, James Lillyman Caldwell (1770-1863) excavated a prehistoric burial near Coimbatore around this time, and sent drawings and detailed descriptions of the antiquities to him. Megalithic monuments were conspicuous features of the landscape of India extending from Kashmir in the north to Tamil Nadu in the south, and it was these that first drew the attention of archaeologists and historians, such as Caldwell and Babington of the Bombay Civil Service, who excavated at Paddiangaddy in the Cannanore district of Kerala in 1819. These megaliths resembled the standing structures at Stonehenge, Avebury and Carnac in England, and were often described in European terms by colonial officers in the later period, though Mackenzie still used local terms for them.

Mackenzie was perhaps the first European to recognize Jainism as a distinct religious system. He labelled the stupa at Amaravati as belonging to the Jains after a visit to the site in 1798 and published an 'Account of the Jains' in *Asiatick Researches* (Mackenzie, 1809: 244-78). During his several visits to Mysore, he had visited Sravana-Belgola and other Jain monuments still under worship in Karnataka and had learnt much from the local pundits. It was not until 1821, i.e. just before his death, that he suggested for the first time that the sculptures from Amaravati were Buddhist rather than Jain (Mackenzie, 1823: 464-78).

James Fergusson (1808-86), a late contemporary of Mackenzie, also from Scotland, was critical of the latter's work. He came to India to work for the family firm of Fairlie, Fergusson & Co. of Calcutta. His interest soon shifted from merchandising to architecture, and for about six years from 1836 to 1841, he travelled to various parts of India, studying and documenting Indian architecture. After returning to London in 1845, his sketches were lithographed and published in a book entitled *Illustrations of the Rock Cut Temples of India*, which consisted of 18 plates.

In his book, *Tree and Serpent Worship*, Fergusson remarked on the lack of details on Amaravati in Mackenzie's notes (1868: 149-50). He speculated that many of the slabs of the Buddhist monument, which Mackenzie first saw in 1797 were, most likely, *in situ*, but since Mackenzie left no record of their precise location, it is difficult to use them for analysis. Fergusson continued that it was due to this carelessness and the fact that Mackenzie published very little on this site that Amaravati remained neglected in scholarly discussion. This was in spite of the 80 detailed drawings of sculptures made by his draughtsmen Henry Hamilton, John Newman, J. Mustie and R. Burke and the careful plans available of the countryside surrounding Amaravati. Fergusson's remarks provide insights into the academic discourse that emerged in the nineteenth century that was based on the production of new forms of knowledge, such as surveys of monuments and drawings of sculptures recorded by Mackenzie and his associates.

In 1876, Fergusson published his *History of Indian and Eastern Architecture* and used the writings of John Crawfurd (1820) in it. Born in 1783, Crawfurd was a doctor, colonial administrator, diplomat, political candidate and orientalist scholar. He served the British East India Company in northern India, Penang, Java and Singapore, and as a diplomat in Burma and Siam. In Crawfurd's three-volume study, *History of the Indian Archipelago,* he defined the Indian archipelago as comprising of island Southeast Asia. Fergusson argued that Burma and Cambodia received their religions through missionaries from India.

> The one country to which they overflowed was Java and there they colonised to such an extent as for nearly 1000 years to obliterate the native arts and civilization and supplant it by their own. What is still more singular is that certain of the traditions assert that it was not from the nearest shores of India that these emigrants departed but from the western coast. It is possible to suggest that the colonists were not Indians, but nations from the north-west—the inhabitants of Gandhara and Kamboja. (Fergusson, 1876: 414-15)

Thus, it is evident that, British political interests in Burma, Indonesia and other regions of Southeast Asia had already in the nineteenth century resulted in the concept of 'Further India', as John Marshall termed Southeast Asia in 1902. Academic discourse included discussions on topics such as that of language, architecture and religious structures of Southeast Asia, in addition to the more direct Archaeological Survey of India (ASI) intervention in conservation policies in Burma. This emphasis on conservation and a change in the status of the ASI in 1895 resulted in the division of the organization into five Circles, with Burma, which the British had annexed in 1852, being provided for separately 'by the continuance of the existing Imperial grant to the local government of Rupees ten thousand a year'. How did Mackenzie's career in South and Southeast Asia compare with that of another surveyor, viz., James Rennell?

James Rennell (1742-1830):
Mapping the Present and the Past

Mapping the past is an essential tool for understanding, in a schematic manner, where and when things happened. Is it possible to expect accuracy as regards the locations and borders of states/cities/regions in the ancient past and their continued existence into the present? These questions are important as we discuss the contribution of James Rennell. Born in Devonshire (close to Chudleigh in England), James Rennell, lost his father at a young age. He was looked after by the Vicar of Chudleigh, the Reverend Gilbert Burrington, in whose house he found a supportive family. The only formal schooling that he had was at the local grammar school but he showed a keen interest in making maps from a young age. At the age of fourteen, he obtained his first naval appointment as a sea-captain's servant in January 1756 at a time when England was going to war with France. In 1758, Rennell made his first plan of St. Cast Bay on the north coast of France where he saw action and the decimation of a large flank of Grenadiers. In 1760, he secured a place as a midshipman on the frigate *America* and sailed for Madras. After reaching Madras, he transferred to another ship and took part in the five-month naval blockade of Pondicherry by the British fleet, comprising sixteen ships.

During the rainy season the majority of the ships went to Ceylon, and there Rennell made a survey of the harbour of Trincomali. It was no doubt also at this time that he first investigated the chain of sandbanks, known as Adam's Bridge, separating Ceylon from the south-eastern extremity of the Coromandel coast, across which he declared that a navigable passage could be maintained by dredging the strait of Ramisseram. It was pointed out in a biographical sketch of Rennell issued in 1842 by Baron de Walkenaer, the secretary of the French Academy, that, though no notice was taken at the time of the suggestions put forward by so young and unknown an officer, the idea was revived some sixty years later. (Rodd, 1930: 291)

After six years of meritorious service and having made charts not only of the Tamil coast, but also of the Nicobar Islands, Malacca and north-west Borneo, Rennell left the navy in 1763. In the following year he had procured a commission as Surveyor-General of the East India Company's dominions in Bengal.

While in the navy, Rennell had lost no opportunity to survey the places at which the ships anchored, and had acquired the reputation of an enthusiastic and diligent surveyor. As an employee of the East India Company, he found a strong supporter in Robert Clive, Governor of Bengal and prepared maps of Bengal, Bihar, Orissa and of the Mughal Empire as far as Delhi, as well as charts of the river Ganga. The actual fieldwork for the survey took seven years. These maps were then sent back to England and formed the basis for Robert Orme's (1728-1801) study titled *History of the Military Transactions of the British Nation in Indostan from 1745*, which highlighted the military achievements of the English in India and was published in 1763 in three volumes. Thus, one aspect of Rennell's work was the delineation of the Company's territories in India in order to publicize, in England, the gains that were made.

Rennell's career may be divided into two periods: the first part was spent as a sailor and surveyor in the navy. It was in this role that he was able to draw the coastline of India with an accuracy that had not been managed before. In this he received the unflinching support of his friend Alexander Dalrymple (1737-1808), the Hydrographer to the East India Company. In 1795, Dalrymple became the first Hydrographer to the Admiralty, a post that he held until his death in

1808. He had made a large collection of maps and charts of the east coast of India and regions further to the east. Other surveyors were also active at this time. Captain Michael Topping (1747-96) made a chart of the Bay of Bengal in 1788; in 1790, he was employed to make a survey of the Godavari River and, in 1792, he was involved in taking observations for determining the course of the currents in the Bay of Bengal. On his suggestion, the Madras Survey School was established for training Indians on 17 May 1794. Topping died of fever at Masulipatam in 1796, where there is a monument to his memory with a Latin inscription (Markham, 1895: 88).

On his long return voyage from India in 1777 round the Cape of Good Hope, Rennell mapped 'the banks and currents at Lagullas'. It was published as the 'Chart of the Bank and the Current of Cape Lagullas' in 1778. His biographer, Clement Markham, considers this 'the very first contribution to the science of oceanography' and rightly calls Rennell 'the father of oceanography' (Markham, 1895: 212). Rennell undoubtedly benefitted from several improvements in the science of navigation from the 1760s. Perhaps the most significant was the system of finding the longitude at sea by means of a chronometer.

Though the use of stars and certain constellations for finding one's way across the desert or the waters dates to a very early period, astronomical navigation did not appear until the fifteenth century.

> It is, however, customary to regard as astronomical only the type of navigation that is based on observations to obtain the horizontal co-ordinates of the sun or of a star. This allowed the pilot to select more confidently the direction to be taken for his voyage, once he had determined more closely the position of his ship. (Cortesão, 1971: 222)

By this method, it was easier to keep the ship on the same parallel and to travel in an east–west direction. Navigators also found that it was simpler to take observations from the sun and the pole star and to travel along the latitude. Finding the longitude was harder and more problematic. In 1714, an Act of Parliament was passed in Britain, offering rewards from 10,000 to 20,000 pounds for the discovery of a method for finding the longitude at sea (Markham, 1895: 149). After the invention of the chronometer, the knowledge of ocean currents expanded rapidly and Rennell was the first to collect materials for understanding ocean currents in the Atlantic and Indian Oceans.

After his return to England in 1778, Rennell spent his time in study and research. In 1779, he published the *Bengal Atlas* comprising several large-scale maps of Bengal based on his fieldwork. In 1781 he was elected a fellow of the Royal Society. He then started work on the *Memoir of a Map of Hindoostan*, a purely geographical work dedicated to the service of the country. The Frontispiece to the Map shows Britannia receiving in her protection the sacred books of the Hindoos presented to her by the pundits or learned brahmanas (Figure 10.4).

Figure 10.4: Frontispiece to James Rennell's *Memoir of a Map of Hindoostan*.

Rennell starts by defining the boundaries of Hindoostan, which the Europeans have traditionally regarded as lying between the rivers Indus and the Ganga with the mountains of Tibet to the north, thereby leaving out the Deccan and south India which were not considered a part of it.

The provinces of Hindoostan proper have seldom continued under one head during a period of twenty successive years, from the earliest history down to the reign of Acbar [*sic*] in the sixteenth century (Rennell, 1783: 2).

Thus for the map of Hindoostan, Rennell continued to follow the divisions into *subahs* (districts) established by Akbar but, for the Deccan and the south, he used information made available by several English officials. When discussing the course of the Ganga, Rennell made a long digression to discuss the location of the site of Palibothra mentioned by Pliny, who places it 425 miles below the conflux of the Ganga and the Yamuna, and states that 'the city meant by Pliny stood on the site of Patna' (Rennell, 1783: 40).

Another region that interested Rennell was the Punjab, the region that was traversed by the three great conquerors of India: Alexander, Timur and Nadir Shah. This engagement with the history of Alexander, thus, appears in a major way in Rennell's writings. To define this surveyor's multi-pronged strategies as he projected the Company's advances and territorial aggrandizements on a map as merely 'the will to knowledge' and as a continuation of the Ptolemaic legacy (Trautman, 2009: 172) would be to simplify the complex creation of the hegemony of 'colonial knowledge' of mapping the past on to the present.

It was during the second phase of his career after his return to London that Rennell devoted his time to reading the geographical literature of the Greek and medieval writers as part of his ambitious study of the geography of West Asia from the Mediterranean to India. The first part of this work was devoted to the geography of Herodotus. (Rodd, 1930: 296)

On the subject of Asia, Herodotus has said a great deal. . . . The Asia of Herodotus was in his own idea even *less* than Europe. . . . Beyond India, Herodotus confesses that he knew nothing. . . . And hence it must also be inferred that the Persians of those days had no commercial intercourse with either China or Cathai, as in latter times; otherwise, either Herodotus, Alexander, or the Seleucidae would at least have heard of China and Eratosthenes would have noticed it. (Rennell, 1800: 164-8)

Alexander admitted that there was no land beyond the eastern borders of India, though Herodotus had extended a vast desert beyond it. Rennell thus argues that the expedition of Alexander had the effect of falsifying the geography of Asia (Rennell, 1800: 172). Not only was there confusion about lands beyond India but there was also no clear notion of the Erythraean Sea. Herodotus described it as the entire sea between India, Persia and Arabia, though he pointedly distinguished it from the Arabian Gulf. Arrian, on the other hand, drew his data from the voyage of Nearchus and called the Persian Gulf the Erythraean Sea.

> The source of these errors was the difficulty of adjusting the meridians of different places, previous to the discovery of the polarity of the magnet; and of the improved and facile mode of taking observations of longitude.
>
> (Rennell, 1800: 188).

In 1793, Rennell presented a paper to the Royal Society titled 'Observations of a current which often prevails to the westward of Sicily, endangering the safety of ships that approach the English Channel'. Until then this information was not known to navigators, often resulting in the loss of ships. As a service rendered to navigation, the current was named after him. His charts of the winds and currents of the Atlantic, the trade winds and the monsoons was however, published after his death by his daughter Jane.

Thus, Rennell's reputation rests not only on his work in India but on his contribution to the science of oceanography. As a sailor he had studied by personal observation the currents of the Atlantic, the trade-winds, the monsoons, and their influence on the drift in the ocean, and he assembled over a number of years, all the information he could gather from the experience and the log-books of his naval friends. This was clearly made possible by the wide-ranging coastal enclaves of the British across the Indian Ocean and the Atlantic in the nineteenth century.

In the final analysis, how does one explain the enormous explosion of knowledge about archaeology and the study of the past in South and Southeast Asia, as well as in the understanding of ocean currents and tides in the nineteenth century? Was there an ideological foundation to the search for this new knowledge? In order to answer these questions, it is important to understand European consciousness that underwrote the themes of colonial empire and expansion.

Proponents of the Company's military expansion in the 1760s tended to see landed settlements as necessary adjuncts of an essentially maritime empire, creating self-financing settlements with an extra provision against future danger. As the Company's publicists stressed, with the new income from territorial revenues in India, the Company no longer needed to export bullion to pay for its 'investment' in Indian textiles after 1757; rather it would pay for its cotton from local revenue surpluses of silver rupees. 'Nor would the Indian territories require a drain of manpower from Britain, unlike the American colonies; silver rupees would pay for Indian troops to police the Company's domains' (Travers, 2007: 52). It was this search for a maritime empire in Asia that radically transformed the landscape of the Indian Ocean from the Bay of Bengal to the South China Sea.

REFERENCES

Archaeological Survey of India: Annual Report 1902-03.

Babington, J., 1823, 'Description of the Pandoo Coolies in Malabar', *Transactions of the Literary Society of Bombay*, 3: 224-330.

Beal, Samuel, 1881, 'Two Chinese Buddhist Inscriptions found at Buddha Gaya', *Journal of the Royal Asiatic Society*, New Series, 13, 4: 552-72.

Benjamin, Thomas (ed.), 2007, *Encyclopedia of Western Colonialism since 1450*, Farmington Hills: Thomson-Gale.

Brown, Stewart J. (ed.), 1997, *William Robertson and the Expansion of Empire*, Cambridge: Cambridge University Press.

Buswell Jr., Robert E., 2009, 'Korean Buddhist Journeys to Lands Worldly and Otherworldly', *Journal of Asian Studies*, 68, 4: 1055-75.

Carnall, Geoffrey, 1997, 'Robertson and Contemporary Images of India', in Stewart J. Brown (ed.), *William Robertson and the Expansion of Empire*, Cambridge: Cambridge University Press: 210-30.

Chhabra, Bahadur Chand, 1965, *Expansion of the Indo-Aryan Culture during Pallava Rule*, Delhi: Munshiram Manoharlal.

Christie, Jan Wisseman, 1995, 'State Formation in Early Maritime Southeast Asia: A Consideration of the Theories and the Data', *Bijdragen tot de Taal-, Land- en Volkenkunde*, 151, 2: 235-88.

Cleary, Thomas, 1993, *The flower ornament Scripture*, Boston and London: Shambhala.

Cortesão, Armando, 1971, *History of Portuguese Cartography*, Lisboa: Junta de Investigações do Ultramar.

Crawfurd, John, 1820, *History of the Indian Archipelago*, Edinburgh: Archibald Constable and Company.

Fergusson, James, 1845, *Illustrations of the Rock Cut Temples of India*, London: J. Weale.

———, 1868, *Tree and Serpent Worship*, London: Allen.

———, 1876, *History of Indian and Eastern Architecture*, London: Murray.

Fontein, Jan, 1967, *The Pilgrimage of Sudhana: A Study of Gandavyūha Illustrations in China, Japan and Java*, The Hague: Mouton.

Hopper, Paul, 2007, *Understanding Cultural Globalization*, Cambridge: Polity Press.

Howes, Jennifer, 2010, *Illustrating India: The Early Colonial Investigations of Colin Mackenzie (1784-1821)*, Oxford: Oxford University Press.

Jacq-Hergoualc'h, Michel, 2002, *The Malay Peninsula: Crossroads of the Maritime Silk Road (100 BC-1300 AD)*, Leiden: Brill.

Mackenzie, Colin, 1809, 'Account of the Jains', *Asiatick Researches*, vol. 9: 244-78.

Mackenzie, Colin, 1823, 'Ruins of Amravutty, Depauldina and Durnacotta', *Asiatic Journal*, 15: 464-78.

Markham, Clements R., 1895, *Major James Rennell*, London-Paris-Melbourne: Cassell and Company.

Metcalf, Thomas R., 2007, *Imperial Connections: India in the Indian Ocean Arena, 1860-1920*, Berkeley and Los Angeles: California University Press.

Orme, Robert, 1763, *History of the Military Transactions of the British Nation in Indostan from 1745*, London: J. Norse.

Pearson, Michael N., 2003, *The Indian Ocean*, London: Routledge.

———, 2010, 'Connecting the Littorals: Cultural Brokers in the Early Modern Indian Ocean', in Pamila Gupta, Isabel Hofmeyr and Michael Pearson (eds.), *Eyes Across the Water: Navigating the Indian Ocean*, Pretoria: Unisa Press: 32-47.

Raffles, T. Stamford, 1817, *History of Java*, London: Black, Parbury and Allen.

Raj, Kapil, 2009, 'Mapping Knowledge Go-betweens in Calcutta, 1770-1820', in Simon Schaffer, Lissa Roberts, Kapil Raj and James Delbourgo (eds.), *The Brokered World: Go-Betweens and Global*

Intelligence, 1770-1820, Sagamore Beach: Watson Publishing International: 105-50.

Ray, Haraprasad, 1993, *Trade and Diplomacy in India-China Relations: A Study of Bengal during the Fifteenth Century*, New Delhi: Radiant Publishers.

Rennell, James, 1783, *Memoir of a Map of Hindoostan or the Mogul's Empire*, London: Printed by M. Brown for the author.

———, 1800 'The Geographical System of Herodotus Examined and Explained', Bulmer (published 1800 and 1830).

Rodd, Rennell, 1930, 'Major James Rennell', *The Geographical Journal*, 75, 4, April: 289-99.

Robb, Peter, 1998, 'Completing "Our Stock of Geography", or an Object "Still More Sublime": Colin Mackenzie's Survey of Mysore, 1799-1810', *Journal of the Royal Asiatic Society*, Third Series, vol. 8, no. 2, July: 181-206.

Sen, Tansen, 2001, 'In Search of Longevity and Good Karma', *Journal of World History*, vol. 12, no. 1: 1-28.

Trautmann, Thomas R., 2009, *The Clash of Chronologies: Ancient India in the Modern World*, New Delhi: Yoda Press.

Travers, Robert, 2007, *Ideology and Empire in Eighteenth Century India: The British in Bengal*, Cambridge: Cambridge University Press.

Wade, Geoff (tr.), 2005, 'Southeast Asia in the Ming Shi-lu, An Open Access Resource', Asia Research Institute and the Singapore E-Press, National University of Singapore, Singapore.

Wagoner, Phillip B., 2003, 'Precolonial Intellectuals and the Production of Colonial Knowledge', *Comparative Studies in Society and History*, vol. 45, no. 4, October: 783-814.

Weatherbee, Donald E., 1978, 'Raffles' Sources for Traditional Javanese Historiography and the Mackenzie Collections', *Indonesia*, 26: 63-93.

Wheatley, Paul, 1973 (1st pub. 1961), *The Golden Khersonese*, Westport: Greenwood Press.

Wilson, Horace Hayman, 1828, *Mackenzie Collection: A Descriptive Catalogue of the Oriental Manuscripts*, Calcutta: Asiatic Press.

Wu, Peiyi, 1992, 'An Ambivalent Pilgrim to T'ai Shan in the Seventeenth Century', in Susan Naquin and Chun-fang Yü (eds.), *Pilgrims and Sacred Sites in China*, Berkeley: University of California Press: 65-88.

CHAPTER 11

Indian Trade Textiles as a Thai Legacy

PRAPASSORN POSRITHONG

Textiles have played an important role in concepts of power and kingship throughout Asia. Indian textiles traded across the Bay of Bengal have had a formative influence on local societies as prestige items and have often taken on significant ritual roles (Barnes, 2005: 150). Though a local weaving tradition has existed for nearly 4,000 years in the Indonesian archipelago, Indian textiles are, nonetheless, considered special and continued to be imported. These imports included the double-*ikat* silk *patola* and the block-printed cotton textiles, which were traded to the region because of their status and then provided the motivation for the development of local design (Bühler 1959: 4-4611). Inscriptions from Java dated from the late ninth to the thirteenth century contain lists of gifts presented at ceremonies connected with *sīmā* (religious benefice) tax transfers and these often included imported Indian textiles. From the eleventh century onwards, the textiles bestowed privileges associated with status, which 'included the right to wear certain restricted patterns of cloth, to use certain types of cloth in a range of colours in ritual contexts, the right to build certain elaborate types of village shrine, to use certain furnishings, ceremonial dress and cosmetics in ritual contexts, and to eat certain types of restricted food' (Christie, 1999: 225).

India has a long and distinguished history of textiles with a vast repository of ancient motifs, techniques and ideas. She is unique among textile-producing countries for her rich variety of weaves and colours, which were influenced by several factors. Geography and climate were as influential as religions, traditions and historical factors. Textile imagery in India has distinctive characteristics that combine Indian craftsmanship with foreign influences so completely that they appear to be Indian. Their techniques are intricate requiring not only talent but infinite patience and employment of several arts. Indian textiles have a lasting legacy of motifs that have appeared and reappeared over the centuries to echo their cultural and historical context as well as its popularity.

The Portuguese, Tomé Pires, who was based at Malacca on the Malay peninsula from 1512 to 1515 wrote of the import of fine textiles from different parts of the Indian subcontinent into Thailand, especially to the kingdom of Ayutthaya (1350-1767). These included muslins, not only from the Coromandel coast, but also from Bengal, and carpets and brocades from Cambay (Pires, 1944: 108). This early report suggests the availability of Indian textiles in the Southeast Asian archipelago and the high esteem accorded to them. They were uploaded at centres in western India like Cambay, Broach and Calicut to trade with the Far East for spices. Ships returned from Malacca and Sumatra laden with spices via Calicut, and travelled across the Arabian Sea to Oman in the Persian Gulf. Gujarat in western India and regions adjacent to it have provided the oldest continuous history of textile manufacture and are particularly renowned for their arts of block-printing and dyeing (Gittinger, 1982: 137-74). The evidence of textile remains at Al-Fustat in Egypt give ample proof that block-printing of both mordant and resist dyeing was a long-established textile art in western India by the fifteenth century. From about CE 1600 to 1800 India became the greatest exporter of textile fabrics the world had hitherto known, particularly the technique of mordant dyeing, which gives intense colours that do not fade, has been used by Indian textile workers since the second millennium BCE. Until at least the eighteenth century, India was able to produce more technically advanced textiles than anywhere else in the world.

The network of the Indian textile trade extended over the entire region of South and Southeast Asia in the sixteenth and seventeenth centuries. Every region had its particular costume preference, seasonal and ritual needs, and aesthetic sense. The silk patola from Gujarat were more popular and considered as ancestral legacy in Indonesia. Brocade was in greater demand in the Malay peninsula, while the

Thais preferred printed and painted cotton pieces. Initially, Indian trade textiles were bartered for spices in Southeast Asia. Later, they were re-exported to Japan and China in exchange for ceramics and lacquerware.

Ayutthaya Kingdom (1350-1767) and Maritime Trade

Indian textiles were first recorded in Thai history during the Ayutthaya kingdom, a major trade centre in Southeast Asia from the early sixteenth century. In traditional Thai historiography, Ayutthaya is seen as a successor to the Sukhothai kingdom (1238-1438), though it also inherited much from Angkor, the centre of Khmer rule from the ninth to fifteenth centuries (Kasetsiri, 1976). Chris Baker has suggested that the kingdom of Ayutthaya emerged as a maritime power in the fourteenth century, focused on becoming a dominant force in the trading world of the Gulf of Siam and the Malay peninsula in the post-Srivijayan era. He says:

> Unlike most of the island-based coastal states which emerged in the same era, Ayutthaya was backed by a large hinterland. Driven by the commercial logic of controlling the trade routes and supply sources on which its commercial prominence depended, Ayutthaya set out to *become* a territorial power'. (Baker, 2003: 62)

The maritime relations of Ayutthaya were invested in the ministry popularly known as the Pra Klang in Thai. The Department of Royal Warehouses functioned under this ministry and provided a link between domestic trade-related administration and the maritime affairs managed by the ministry.

> This department tapped the internal movements of the domestic products within the kingdom to secure supplies for the international markets. Governors and other officials in various parts of the kingdom were required to gather exportable local products and transport them to the royal warehouses in the capital, thus providing these goods to the state under the system of taxation-in-kind. Imported cargoes arriving on the king's vessels were likewise deposited in these storage facilities. The royal warehouses were thus "treasuries" in a broad sense, filled not solely with money but with the most valuable trade goods. (Breazeale, 1999: 6)

Indian textiles were highly rated and formalized into royal monopolies on particular export goods. They were reserved for the use of the royalty and courtiers, and distributed to the latter according to their rank in the Thai social order. The French envoy Nicolas Gervaise (Gervaise, 1989: 91-2), describes the dressing style of the Thai in 1688. Men's dress consisted of two pieces of silk or cotton with an approximate size of 240 × 90 cm. One was used for covering their shoulders like a scarf and the other used as *panung* or lower garment. The *panung* worn by the courtiers was fuller and richer than that of the others, usually being made of cloth of silver or gold, or of the beautiful painted Indian cloth that is commonly called *chitte* (chintz) from Masulipatam.

These trade textiles were also used as royal gifts for visiting dignitaries and for the granting of favour in recognition of service to the king. These Siamese cloths were gifted to the French when Louise XIV received ambassadors from Ayutthaya. Their dresses of native printed or painted cloth decorated with stripes and squares impressed the French. According to François Henri Turpin, silk was less popular than cotton as there was no silk production in Siam and the dull-coloured local cotton fabric could not compete with the vibrant colour of imported Indian cottons (Turpin, 1997). However, the demand for silk textiles from India is evident in an official letter of the English East India Company in Ayutthaya to the office in Surat, dated 2 December 1662, commissioning of *patola* for the king: 'The king of Siam expects those *puttelaes* to be made according to those patterns Mr. Bladwell carried to Surat; if not to be procured, those patterns are to be returned' (Indian Office Records, 1915-21, 2). *Puttelaes* is an Old Dutch word for *patola* or the silk double *ikat* that was mainly produced in the Paithan district in the north of Gujarat.

The first involvement of Ayutthaya in the Indian textile trade documented in VOC (Dutch East India Company) records dates from 1628 and mentions that King Song Tham (1611-28) sent a trade ship from Tenasserim to Masulipatam. Later, during the 1680s King Narai (1656-88) also established factories in India in an attempt to compete more favourably for Indian goods (Smith, 1977: 91). The demand for Indian textiles in Ayutthaya was not just for local consumption. They were also re-exported to neighbouring countries like Japan and China (Figures 11.1 and 11.2). Dutch records of different years are in agreement that about 15,000 pieces of various Indian cloths was the limit of the Siamese market. The overall expansion of trade during the reign of King Narai was apparently more the result of the increased re-export trade of Chinese and Japanese wares than of increased consumption by the Siamese.

After the kingdom of Ayutthaya ended due to war with Burma (Myanmar) in 1767, the Thais finally regained power and established a new political centre on the banks of the Chao Phraya River first at Thon Buri and later at Bangkok in 1782. Ayutthaya was considered an ideal city, physically and spiritually, for these new centres. So the Bangkok royal court built palaces and temples in the Ayutthaya style and continued the traditions practised by the Ayutthaya royal court including the prohibition of the use of Indian textiles outside the royal court. The early Bangkok revised code of CE 1805 known as

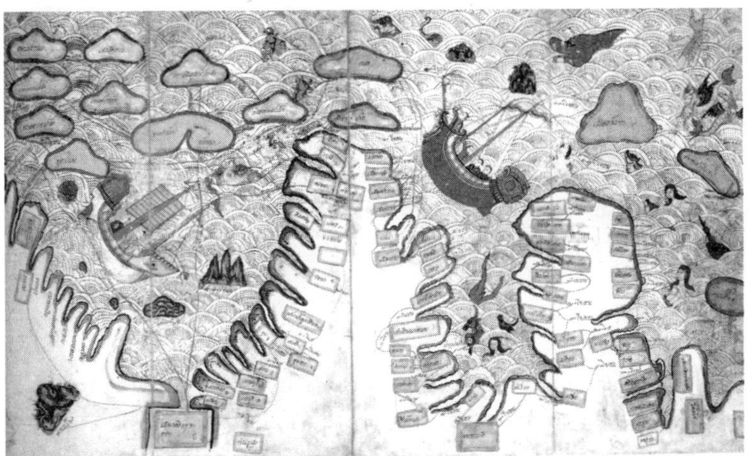

Figure 11.1: Map in a Buddhist textbook called Tripoom made in CE 1776, showing coastlines in Asia with the names of seaports and distances in Thai. This part depicts seaports along the coast of the southern Thai peninsula and around the Indian subcontinent where Thai vessels might have visited or traded. Bengal, Pulicat, and Masulipatam on the Coromandel coast, as well as Surat and Gujarat in western India were mentioned in European records of the seventeenth and eighteenth centuries as major ports where Indian textiles were exported for Ayutthaya.

Figure 11.2: Wooden cabinet with golden decoration of Ayutthaya art of *c.* seventeenth century showing Muslim and European merchants on its doors indicating two prominent groups of traders in Siam at the time.

the Law of Three Seals, states that this prohibition was neglected due to the uncertain situation after the war with Burma. Hence, the law was reissued and indicated particular types and designs of textiles that were reserved for high-ranking officials and was not be used without the permission by the king.

European Presence in the South China Sea

After the Portuguese capture of Melaka in 1511, Duarte Barbosa collated information from sea captains and envoys who were sent out to explore the region. He reported that the Ayutthaya ruler controlled ports on both sides of the peninsula—especially Tenasserim, Mergui, Kedah and Selangor—to which ships from Arabia and Bengal brought copper, quicksilver, vermilion, cloth, silk, saffron, coral and opium (Baker, 2003: 48). Ayutthaya had a thriving commerce in 'forest products', principally sappanwood, eaglewood, benzoin, gumlac, deer-hide, elephant teeth, and rhinoceros horns.

Ayutthaya also sold provisions such as rice and dried fish to other Southeast Asian states. The range of minerals found in the kingdom was limited, but tin from Phuket and Nakhon Si Thammarat was much sought after by both Asian and European traders.

Historical accounts of the Dutch East India Company mention that there was well-established trade between India and Ayutthaya long before the arrival of European traders. Muslim merchants sailed from various ports on the Coromandel Coast, Bengal and Gujarat in western India, as well as from further west to Tenasserim in lower Myanmar, where they unloaded their goods and carried them overland across the peninsula and then up to Ayutthaya. The goods from India were heavily dominated by cloth, the most important product imported into Ayutthaya. European records state that Muslim merchants from India and Persia were their competitors in the Indian textile trade with Ayutthaya. This was especially so when some of them were appointed court officials and governors of port cities, which gave them power to support Muslim traders in the textile business in the kingdom of Ayutthaya.

After the arrival of European traders in Ayutthaya in the early seventeenth century, the Indian textiles trade, which was previously in the hands of Muslim merchants, was shared with European agents. However, the Europeans faced stiff competition from Indian merchants who had lower investment cost in textiles and were even willing to sell Indian textiles at a loss in order to buy elephants which they could then sell in India at a higher profit. Turpin (1997) records in 1771 that elephants sent from Ayutthaya to Mergui and Tenasserim had been bartered for textiles brought by merchants from Coromandel, Bengal, Surat and Persia. These elephants provided the Siamese access to all kinds of textiles from every region in the east, which showed the real prosperity of the kingdom. Interestingly, the role of the Indian Muslim merchant in the Indian textile trade continued in Thailand for more than a century after Ayutthaya was destroyed in 1767, as discussed in a later section.

John Crawfurd, who led an embassy from the governor-general of India, reported on his visit to the royal court of Siam in 1823. He noted the foreign products which the Siamese took in exchange from India:

The cotton piece goods of India, especially the chintzes of Surat and the Coromandel Coast, appear from time immemorial to have been articles of considerable demand. About the capital (Bangkok) especially a very large proportion is clothed with these articles. I have been informed that the annual quantity either imported direct by European vessels, brought by junks from Batavia and the Straits of Malacca, or across the peninsula, does not fall short of five hundred bales. (Crawfurd, 1915: 115)

He also mentions that:

The trade with British India is conducted principally from Surat and Bombay, and occasionally from Bengal. During the long war with France, when every other branch of this trade ceased, the Surat ships, generally from two to three annually, continued to frequent the port of Bangkok. The supercargoes of these vessels have generally been Parsees or Mohamedans [Muslim]. They have commonly imported gold and silver, silk tissues, and printed cloth, the manufacture of Western India. (Crawfurd, 1915: 119)

The Asian trend of Indian textiles finally flowed to Europe and undermined the wool and silk industries there. Therefore, the French banned Indian fabrics in 1686 and began to create imitations of their own just as the British tried a decade later. The British forbade the import of Indian chintz by passing an ineffectual loophole-riddled law in 1701 that allowed its re-export from England to foreign ports. In 1721, a subsequent law banning the use of Indian pattern-printed cloths for clothing and household furnishing within Britain had little effect on its popularity.

However, the invention of copper plate printing in 1775, the roller-printing machine in 1783 and the legislation on restrictive export policies established in the latter part of the eighteenth century by the British Raj in India changed the textile industry forever. Indian textile makers experienced a reversal in trade. Mills in Manchester processed and printed Indian cotton into finished goods for Indian use. Though their designs were directly derived from Indian sources and intended for an Indian market, they frequently reflected the English conventional taste of flora and wall-paper designs. India, master dyer to the world for millennia, was to see its traditional craft virtually vanish in less than a century.

The Nineteenth Century and Sartorial Transformations

As mentioned earlier, the traditional dress of the Siamese from the Ayutthaya to the early Bangkok periods was an untailored long piece of cloth about 3.5 yards long, worn as the lower garment called *panung*. It was called *chong kraben* when worn by passing it round the waist, between the thighs, and inserting the ends of the cloth behind in the Indian *dhoti* style. This style was for both men and women. Sometimes men simply wore the cloth around the hip like a *sarong*. Women could wear it with a pleated fold in front called *na nang* with a separate breast-cloth called *sabai*. This cloth was made of cotton, linen or silk, and was embroidered or decorated according to the taste and wealth of the wearer. Two types of cloth were used as the uniform of royal court officials known as *sompak* which probably derived from the Khmer word meaning lower garment. One was *pa poom* or the Cambodian weft-*ikat* silk and another was the Indian painted or printed cotton called *pa lai*. Before European fashion was accepted by the Siamese royal court in the mid-nineteenth century, the Siamese did not care much for any upper garment due to the hot weather. In order to be more respectable, King Mongkut (r. 1851-68) ordered courtiers to wear a shirt in his presence. Early photographic evidence from the mid-nineteenth century shows that Indian brocade was also tailored as a shirt for Thai dignitaries and courtiers (Figure 11.3).

Figure 11.3: Picture taken during King Chulalongkorn's reign showing Indian brocade tailored as a shirt for a Thai dignitary and courtier.

European fashion became more popular during King Chulalongkorn's reign (crowned as Rama V, 1853-1910). He was well prepared to cope with the undeniable European power surrounding Siam before he came to the throne. The king made state visits to European colonies in Asia, i.e. Batavia (Jakarta) in Indonesia, Singapore and India, and later made royal visits to Europe twice (Sartraproong, 2008). When Prince Damrong (1862-1943), King Chulalongkorn's younger brother, visited India in 1891, he was scheduled to see the manufacturing of *pa lai* in British India, since the fabric was exported to Thailand and was worth millions of rupees each year. He described his visit as follows:

> There is nothing that looks like a factory. Only women and youngsters work at their houses. They use white cloth imported from England, cut it in desirable sizes and wash to remove starch. Then the cloth is placed on the floor and stamped on entirely with a wooden block. Other blocks dipped in different colours are then stamped to complete the designs. They are all by the handmade process done within the household. Textile agents only provide them white cloth and come back to collect their orders. (Damrong Rajanuphap and Naritsarānuwattiwong, 1962: 91)

These visits broadened the king's view on how he could build modern Siam, including improving the government uniforms. After his visit to India in 1872 he introduced a long-sleeved shirt known as *ratcha pataen* or *raj pattern,* meaning shirt designed by the king to wear along with the plain long silk called *pa muang*. This new uniform and other new European-style uniforms designed during this reign led to the decline of uniforms using Indian textiles that had been the norm in the Thai royal court for centuries. However Indian textiles or their imitations continue to be in use for royal ceremonies on occasions such as coronation, royal funeral and Buddhist ceremonies till today.

These Indian trade textiles used by the Thai royalty and courtiers of Bangkok period are now kept and exhibited at the National Museum in Bangkok and other branches in the regions. Many temple museums particularly those located in the central plain of Thailand also possess Indian trade textiles in their collections, which are mostly used as manuscript-wrappers. *Pa lai* or colourful printed and painted cottons of various types and qualities are prominent among these collections. Some of them have designs of Indian classical styles, Persian designs or European motifs that reflect the extent of international commerce at its height in the seventeenth and eighteenth centuries. However, there are great numbers of intricate mordant-painted cottons, specifically made for the Thai market known as *pa lai yang* meaning a textile made as a Thai sample (Figures 11.4-11.9).

The *pa lai yang* show distinct motifs and ornamentations created by Thai artists and reflecting the Thai taste of the time. These motifs are geometric forms with figurative images of gods, deities or winged figures in different gestures related to the Thai belief. These are *narai song krut* or Vishnu riding on Garuda, *thepanom* or deity in the gesture of respect with palms joined, deity in a dancing gesture, *prom si na* or four-faced Brahma, and *kirttimukha* or mythical protector, etc. (see Figure 11.5). There are also Persian geometric motifs adapted to Thai taste like the *rachawat* or stepped square, *pracham yam* or four-petalled diamond shape, *kan yang* or trellis and *kanok* or flame-like leaf motifs. They are mainly freely drawn motifs similar to the *kalamkari* produced in the Coromandel coast. Old photographs show that the bold motif *pa lai yang* was mostly worn by the kings and high-ranking courtiers, while the court ladies preferred smaller floral motifs. These textile motifs and designs were identical to other elements in Thai arts such as the architectural and ceramic arts.

The restriction on using Indian textiles by the common people was lifted after European fashion became more popular in the Thai royal court. Indian textiles then became available to and fashionable with the common people from early nineteenth century. Trade with India, however, continued. An official letter written in 1884 by Chao Phraya Paskornwongse, the director of the custom house headquarters in Bangkok, to King Chulalongkorn states that there were two Muslim Indian traders who did *pa lai* business. One is *Sita* shop that sold fine quality *pa lai*, and another was Nakhoda Abdultyeb Esmailji who owned a big shop and sold lower quality of *pa lai*, which were mostly sent to the countryside markets.

Figure 11.4: Indian *pa lai* comprise a centrefield dominated by geometric, vegetal or figurative repeat-patterns, narrow longitudinal borders, and elaborate end borders. The richness of the structure, motifs and quality of the fabrics signify the status of the wearers.

Figure 11.5: *Pa lai yang* with a distinctive typical Thai design of Vishnu riding Garuda from the Coromandel coast (cotton, painted mordant-and resist-dyed, and painted) Bangkok National Museum.

Figure 11.6: *Pa lai yang* with a distinctive typical Thai design of a four-faced Brahma from the Coromandel coast.

Figure 11. 7: *Pa lai yang* with small repeat patterns of flowers (Coromandel coast, cotton, painted mordant- and resist-dyed, and painted) Bangkok National Museum.

Figure 11.8: Indian embroidery used as a sash for a lady of the royal court, from the collection of the Grand Palace in Bangkok.

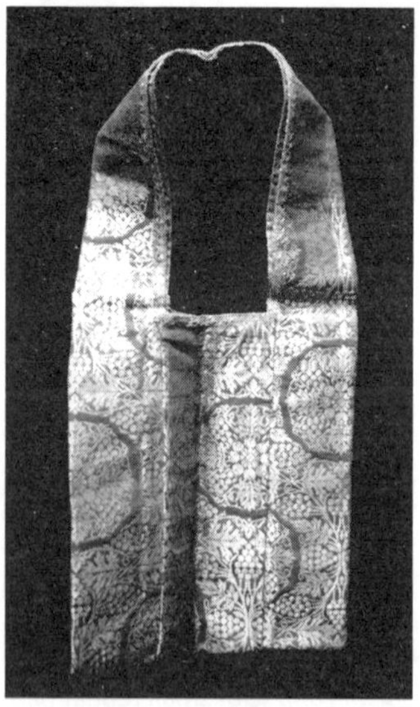

Figure 11.9: Buddhist monk's shoulder-bag made of Indian brocade, Matchimawas Temple Museum, Songkhla.

Indian Textile Traders in Bangkok

Nakhoda Abdultyeb Esmailji was the founder of the Maskati Company, the most famous Indian textiles agent in Bangkok. The Maskati Company owned a textile factory in the Astodia area of Ahmedabad, and textile shops in Ahmedabad and Bangkok, as well as in Phnom Penh in Cambodia. The process of making *pa lai* started when the grey cloth was sent from a company in Bombay to Ahmedabad. There, the cloth was washed and bleached before being printed by the factory workers who were mostly Muslim. The printed cloths were then allowed to dry on the sand basin of the river which was believed to facilitate the absorbtion of colours very well. After starching, the finished products were then sent back to Bombay for export to Bangkok. During the peak time of the Company in the early twentieth century about 600 workers had worked with Maskati in the *pa lai* business. Maskati and other Indian textile agencies in Bangkok, namely Malbari, Vasi and Baghwall, got their design guidelines from their Siamese counterparts and, accordingly, commissioned the making of blocks in Pethapur near Ahmedabad. The blocks were then sent for printing to Ahmedabad. Sample books of these designs are still kept by Maneklal T. Gujjar, a block-maker whose family had been commissioning textiles for the Maskati Company since the founding of the company in the mid-nineteenth century. These printed cottons, for the Thai market were known to the Gujarati producers as *saudagiri*, meaning trade textiles, till today.

The *saudagiri* motifs were floral and geometric though the geometric grid always governed the pattern. The basic floral form was conceived as bound in by a square, a rectangle, a circle, a triangle, a rhombus or a combination of some of these forms. The cloth was first dyed in any one colour and block-printed in three other colours. These three colours were printed with three different blocks which corresponded respectively to the line block, the block for the inner filling, and the one for the background. There were blocks for the body of the fabric, and different ones for the borders.

Maskati and other textile agents, mostly Gujarati, first came to seek their fortune in Bangkok as British citizens (Figure 11.10).

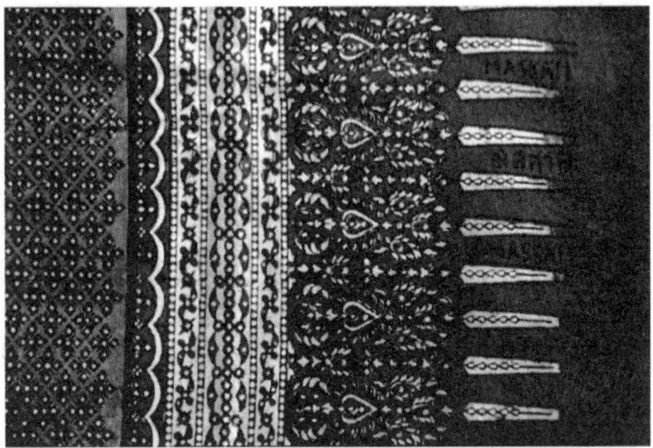

Figure 11.10: Maskati *pa lai* with trade mark in Thai and English block-printed mordant-dyed, resist-dyed specimen belonging to Chawangwan family, Bangkok.

After the Treaty of Friendship and Commerce between the kingdom of Siam and the British empire known as the Bowring Treaty dated 18 April 1855, was signed, Indian merchants were allowed to trade and own land in Thailand as local citizens. They bought land to build a mosque in 1910 and lived in the area known to the Thai as the Indian Market on the west bank of the Chao Phraya River. Later when their business expanded, they moved across the River to the Rajawongse area adjacent to the China Town area of Bangkok. Apart from textiles there were many other kinds of businesses owned by Indians in this area during the late nineteenth to the early twentieth centuries.

Apart from specific classical designs made to order for the Thai royal court and specific design of *saudagiri*, there were also a number of Indian painted and printed cottons of different designs and quality (Figure 11.11).

They were made of different materials, both fine and crude cotton, with the size about 1 × 3.2 yard. These textiles were significant evidence of Thai economic growth during the late nineteenth to the early twentieth centuries. Their import quantity was measured against the rice export quantity as they were used as barter for rice. The rice-buyers, mostly Chinese, exchanged these Indian textiles for rice in many areas of the central plain of Thailand where rice

Figure 11.11: Foreign design *pa lai* in the custody of the temple museum in the Ratchaburi province, central Thailand *c.* late nineteenth-early twentieth century.

growing was expanding. The imported textiles had been gradually replacing the local textile production of the farmer communities in the areas and finally caused the decline of local textile production. The trade report in Bangkok mentioned that 68,361 *culies* worth 549,380 baht of Indian painted and printed cotton were imported to Thailand in 1887 (Bangkokpasittikan, 1889: 19). This increased to 102,587 *culies* worth 671,460 bahts in 1888. This means that in 1888 alone more than 2 million pieces of Indian *pa lai* were imported into Bangkok. These textiles were sold in the market in *culie,* 20 pieces. The Thai preferred to buy the whole *culie* and give this to their family members or friends on special occasions like the Thai New Year and for merit-making.

The Indian textile business struggled during Second World War and began to decline after the war due to many reasons. One of the causes was beginning of the Thai design-printed cotton called *pa lai thai,* which was started in 1932 by a Chinese named Ak Seng. He was good at dyeing and had knowledge of industrial chemistry. Ak Seng had first experimented with textile printing with a brass block which was successful. He was then supported by the German dye agent of the Windsor Company in Bangkok and set-up a small factory on Surawongse Road to make printed cotton using brass blocks. The dyes used were of naphthols and indanthrenes, which were the best synthetic dyes available after First World War. The result was superior with good quality, bright colours, and distinctive Thai designs. After two years of success, the factory began to use a screen-printing machine to replace hand-printed block printing, which was more time-consuming and not suitable to the market demand of the time. The factory next got support from the Holland Siam Company, which provided Holland white cloth for production in return for being the agent of *pa lai thai* under the brand *ramasur-mekhala* (Rakwitthayasart, 1984: 102).

In 1939, another factory named Praneet Industries was founded to produce *pa lai thai* (Figure 11.12).

In the beginning, the factory produced four-coloured hand-printed cottons under the brand Sawitri. When the market demand increased, it started using screen-printing by setting up printing machines of its own. In 1941, Second World War affected Thailand, which led to an economic crisis and the shortage of materials for the machine-production of textiles. The factory returned to hand-printed production, which helped the business to survive while the first factory founded by Ak Seng was badly affected by the war and finally sold its business to Praneet Industries.

After the war, the Thai government under Field Marshall Plaek Piboonsongkram (1941-4; 1949-57) announced the Nationalism

Figure 11.12: *Pa lai thai* or Thai design-printed cotton of Praneet Industries whose business started in 1939 and replaced imported Indian trade textiles from Second World War.

regime which led to the fashion change from the traditional lower garment of *panung chong kraben* to the *pa tung* or tubular skirt. Therefore, Praneet Industries, which expanded its business during the crisis, lowered their production cost by changing to the *pa tung*, to suit the market demand. European cotton fabric, which had been used for printing since the business started, was replaced by cheap Japanese white cotton. The company also produced two-coloured printed cotton under the brand *viranaree*. The good quality printed cottons with low price sold well during the war time. After Second World War, the factory went back to good quality printed cottons again. An artist named Plang Maneerat was hired as a designer and his designs have been used as a prototype of the *pa lai thai* till today.

Khomapastr, meaning white cloth, is another hand-printed cotton inspired by the Indian *pa lai* founded in 1948 by His Royal Highness Prince Bavoradej and his wife, Her Serene Highness Princess Pajongrachit Kritakara in Hua Hin of the Prachuabkirikhan province. The Prince was interested in fabric dyeing, and gained experience in printing techniques and dye chemicals while he was in exile in Saigon, Vietnam, between 1933 and 1948. After Second World War, the Prince returned to Thailand and set-up residence in Hua Hin, a seaside resort with fresh air and warm sunshine where he built a small textile-printing factory with the initial aim to preserve classical Thai designs and create jobs for local people. Originally, the *Khomapastr* had its own handlooms to weave the thick cotton, which would later be hand-printed with classical Thai designs. Later, the handloom cotton was unable to meet the high market demand. The factory then started buying cotton from the Ratchaburi province instead. Today, thick, and fine cotton, cotton blend and voile are purchased from factories in Bangkok. The early Thai designs printed on the *khomapastr* fabric have been copied from the classical Thai motifs preserved on Indian textiles for Thai market in the collection of the National Museum in Bangkok. These are exclusive gold-printed classical Thai designs called *pa kiao*, formerly used for outer garments by the Thai royalty, which is much-admired for its beautiful and exotic hand-printed Thai classical designs. In past few years, the gold-printed *pa kiao* of *khomapastr* were used to represent Thai textiles in the Miss World beauty contests.

Indian trade textiles, just like other objects of Indian cultural inspiration in Thailand, have long roots in Thai history. This is supported by actual evidence and the stories of various groups of people. It is not just as imported items but also the fusion of art between Thai designers and Indian producers that led to their uniqueness. Moreover they are a Thai cultural legacy that will inspire Thais to learn, to invent, and to expand their imagination in the present and future generations.

REFERENCES

Archambault, Michele, 1989, 'Block printed Fabrics of Gujarat for Export to Siam: An Encounter with Mr. Maneklal T. Gajjar', *Journal of Siam Society*, 77 (2): 71-3.

Baker, Chris, 2003, 'Ayutthaya Rising: From Land or Sea?', *Journal of Southeast Asian Studies*, 34 (1): 41-62.

Bangkokpasittikan Co. Ltd, 1889, *Patitinbat lae Chotmaihet*, I: 19.

Barnes, Ruth (ed.), 2005, *Textiles in Indian Ocean Societies*, London and New York: Routledge Curzon.

Breazeale, Kennon (ed.), 1999, *From Japan to Arabia: Ayutthaya's Maritime Relations with Asia*, Bangkok: Foundation for the Promotion of Textbooks.

Bühler, Alfred, 1959, 'Patola Influences in Southeast Asia', *Journal of Indian Textile History*, IV: 4-46.

Chongkol, Chira, 1982, 'Textiles and Costume in Thailand', *Art of Asia*, 12 (6): 124-31.

Christie, Jan Wisseman, 1999, 'Asian Sea Trade between the Tenth and Thirteenth Centuries and its Impact on the States of Java and Bali', in Himanshu Prabha Ray (ed.), *Archaeology of Seafaring: The Indian Ocean in the Ancient Period*, ICHR Monograph I, New Delhi: Pragati Publications: 221-70.

Crawfurd, John, 1915, *The Crawfurd Papers: A Collection of Official Records Relating to the Mission of Dr. John Crawfurd sent to Siam by the Government of India in the year 1821*, England: Gregg International.

Damrong Rajanubhab, 1962, 'Prince and Prince Naritsarānuwattiwong', *San Somdet* [Royal letters], Bangkok: Kurusapa Printing Press.

Fine Arts Department, 1993, *Heritage of Thai Culture*, Bangkok: Rungsilp Printing.

Gajjar, Maneklal T., Interview by author, Pethapur, Gujarat, India, 19 April 1995.

Gervaise, Nicolas, 1998, *The Natural and Political History of the Kingdom of Siam*, Bangkok: White Lotus.

Gittinger, Mattiebelle, 1982, *Master Dyers to the World*, Washington: The Textile Museum.

Kasetsiri, Charnvit, 1976, *The Rise of Ayudhya: A History of Siam in the Fourteenth and Fifteenth Centuries*, Kuala Lumpur: Oxford University Press.

la Loubere, Simon de., rpt. 1986, *A New Historical Relation of the Kingdom of Siam* (1688), translation of Du royaume de Siam, Paris, 1691, Singapore: Oxford University Press.

Loftus, A.J., 2011, *A New Year's Paper of the Development of the Kingdom of Siam* 1890 (with a Map), Historical Print Editions: British Library.

Maskati, Rasheed, Interview by author. Bangkok, Thailand, 25 December 2001.

Posrithong, Prapassorn, 2007, 'Muslim Indian and Textiles Trade in Thai History', *Aksornsart Journal*, 36 (1): 173-88.

Rakwitthayasart, Mana, 1984, *Brief History of Thai Printed textiles (Crematio Volume for Praneet Rukwitthayasart)*, Bangkok: Graphic Art.

Paskornwongse, Chao Phraya, 1884, *Taxation on Indian Textiles*, Bangkok: Custom Office (Bangkok National Archive's document).

Pires, Tomé, 1944, *The Suma Oriental of Tomé Pires (1512-1515)*, tr. A. Contesão, 2 vols., London: Hakluyt Society.

Sartraproong, Kannikar, 2008, *A True Hero*, Institute of Asian Studies, Bangkok: Chulalongkorn University.

Smith, George Vinal, 1977, *The Dutch in Seventeen Century Thailand.* (Special Report No. 16), Northern Illinois University: Center for Southeast Asian Studies.

Thanapradit, Sawet, Interview by author, Bangkok, Thailand, 28 April 1993.

Turpin, François Henri, 1997, *A History of the Kingdom of Siam and of the Revolutions that have caused the Overthrow of the Empire up to 1770*; tr. Basil Osborne Cartwright, Bangkok: American Presby Mission Press.

Turpin, M., 1808-14, 'The Political and Natural History of the Kingdom of Siam', in *A General Collection of the Best and Most Interesting Voyages and Travels in all Parts of the World.* 17 vols. Tr. from the French and ed. John Pinkerton, London. (Turpin's account is in vol. 9.)

Index